IMAGE COMICS PRESENTS

GEMINI

THE COMPLETE SERIES

CREATED BY JAY FAERBER & JON SOMMARIVA

STORY BY
JAY FAERBER

ART BY
JON SOMMARIVA

COLOR BY
FCO PLASCENCIA

LETTERS BY
RUS WOOTON

BOOK DESIGN BY
VINCENT KUKUA

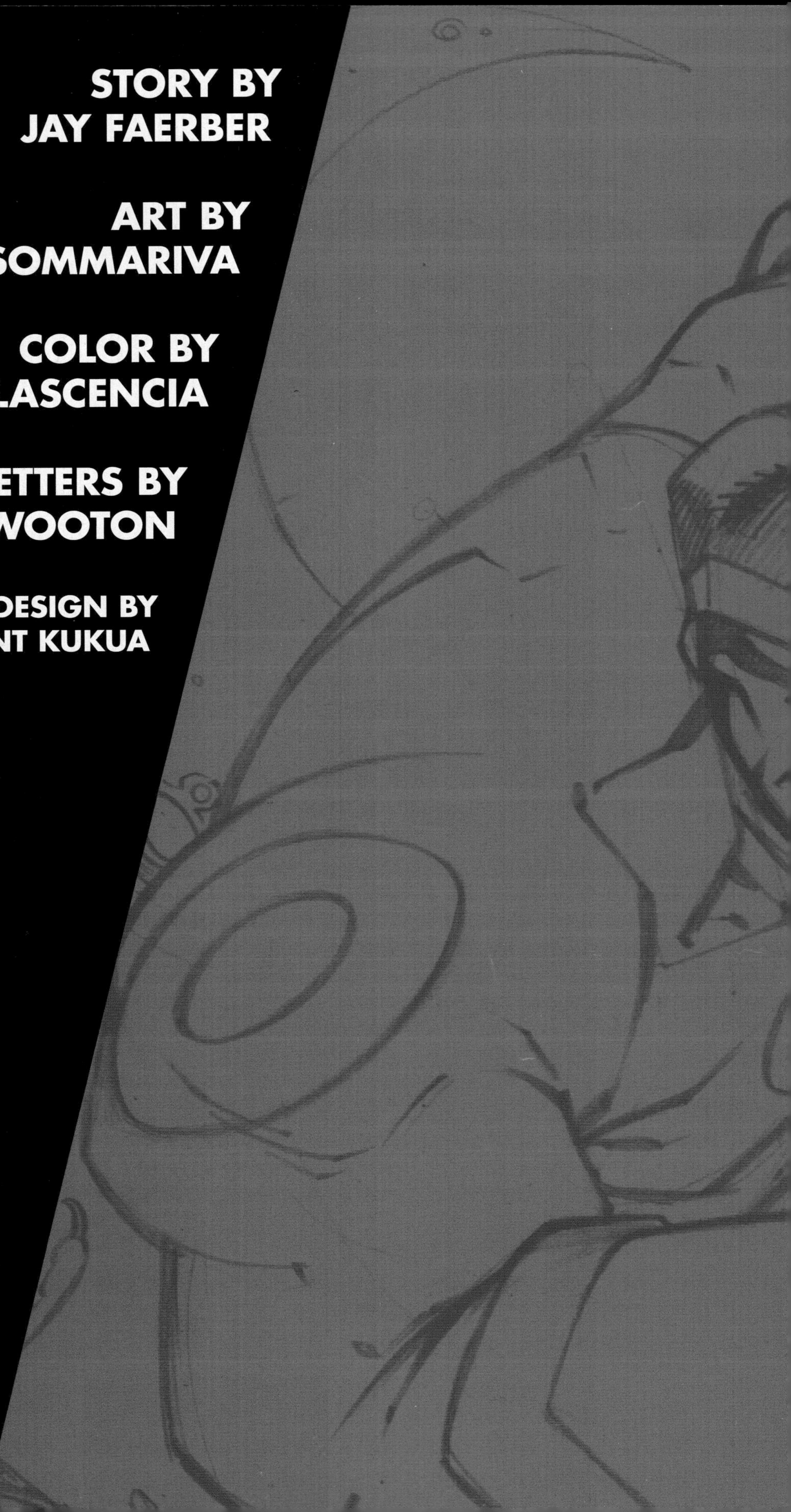

FOR IMAGE COMICS, INC.

Robert Kirkman - Chief Operating Officer
Erik Larsen - Chief Financial Officer
Todd McFarlane - President
Marc Silvestri - Chief Executive Officer
Jim Valentino - Vice-President

Eric Stephenson - Publisher
Corey Murphy - Director of Sales
Jeff Boison - Director of Publishing Planning & Book Trade Sales
Jeremy Sullivan - Director of Digital Sales
Kat Salazar - Director of PR & Marketing
Branwyn Bigglestone - Controller
Drew Gill - Art Director
Jonathan Chan - Production Manager
Meredith Wallace - Print Manager
Briah Skelly - Publicist
Sasha Head - Sales & Marketing Production Designer
Randy Okamura - Digital Production Designer
David Brothers - Branding Manager
Olivia Ngai - Content Manager
Addison Duke - Production Artist
Vincent Kukua - Production Artist
Tricia Ramos - Production Artist
Jeff Stang - Direct Market Sales Representative
Emilio Bautista - Digital Sales Associate
Leanna Caunter - Accounting Assistant
Chloe Ramos-Peterson - Library Market Sales Representative
IMAGECOMICS.COM

CHAPTER ONE

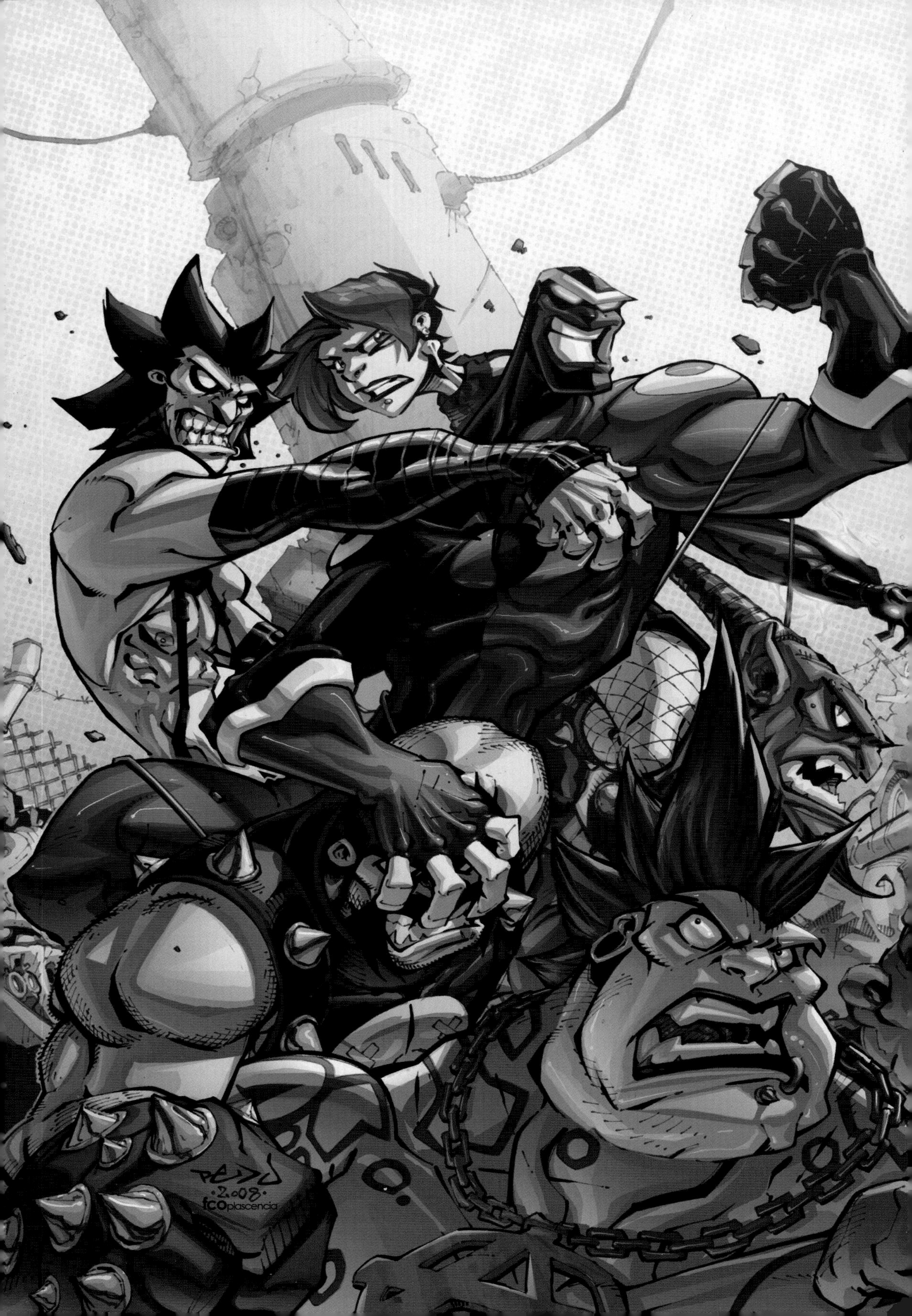
2008
fcoplascencia

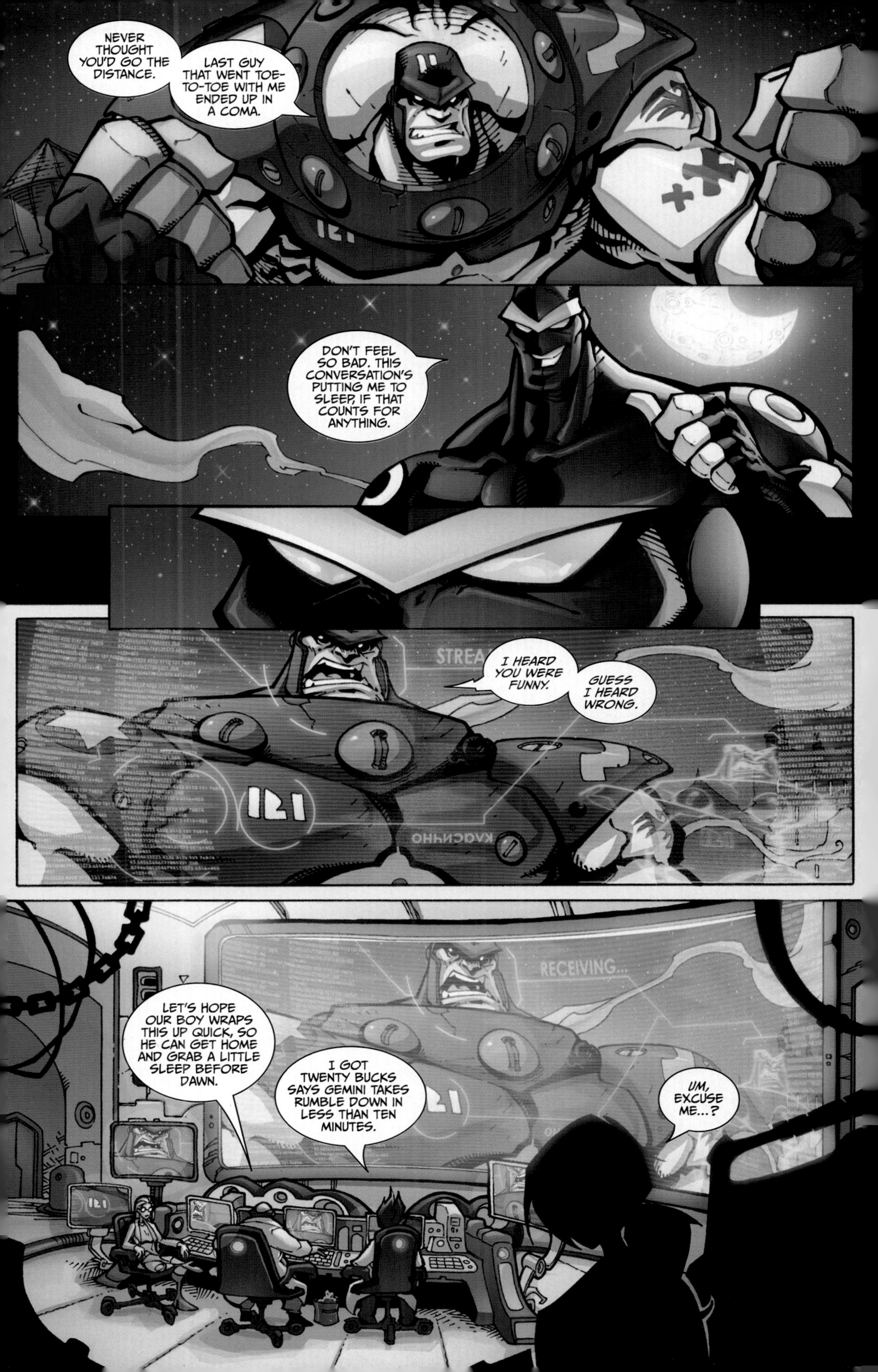
NEVER THOUGHT YOU'D GO THE DISTANCE.
LAST GUY THAT WENT TOE-TO-TOE WITH ME ENDED UP IN A COMA.
DON'T FEEL SO BAD. THIS CONVERSATION'S PUTTING ME TO SLEEP, IF THAT COUNTS FOR ANYTHING.
STREA
I HEARD YOU WERE FUNNY.
GUESS I HEARD WRONG.
RECEIVING...
LET'S HOPE OUR BOY WRAPS THIS UP QUICK, SO HE CAN GET HOME AND GRAB A LITTLE SLEEP BEFORE DAWN.
I GOT TWENTY BUCKS SAYS GEMINI TAKES RUMBLE DOWN IN LESS THAN TEN MINUTES.
UM, EXCUSE ME...?

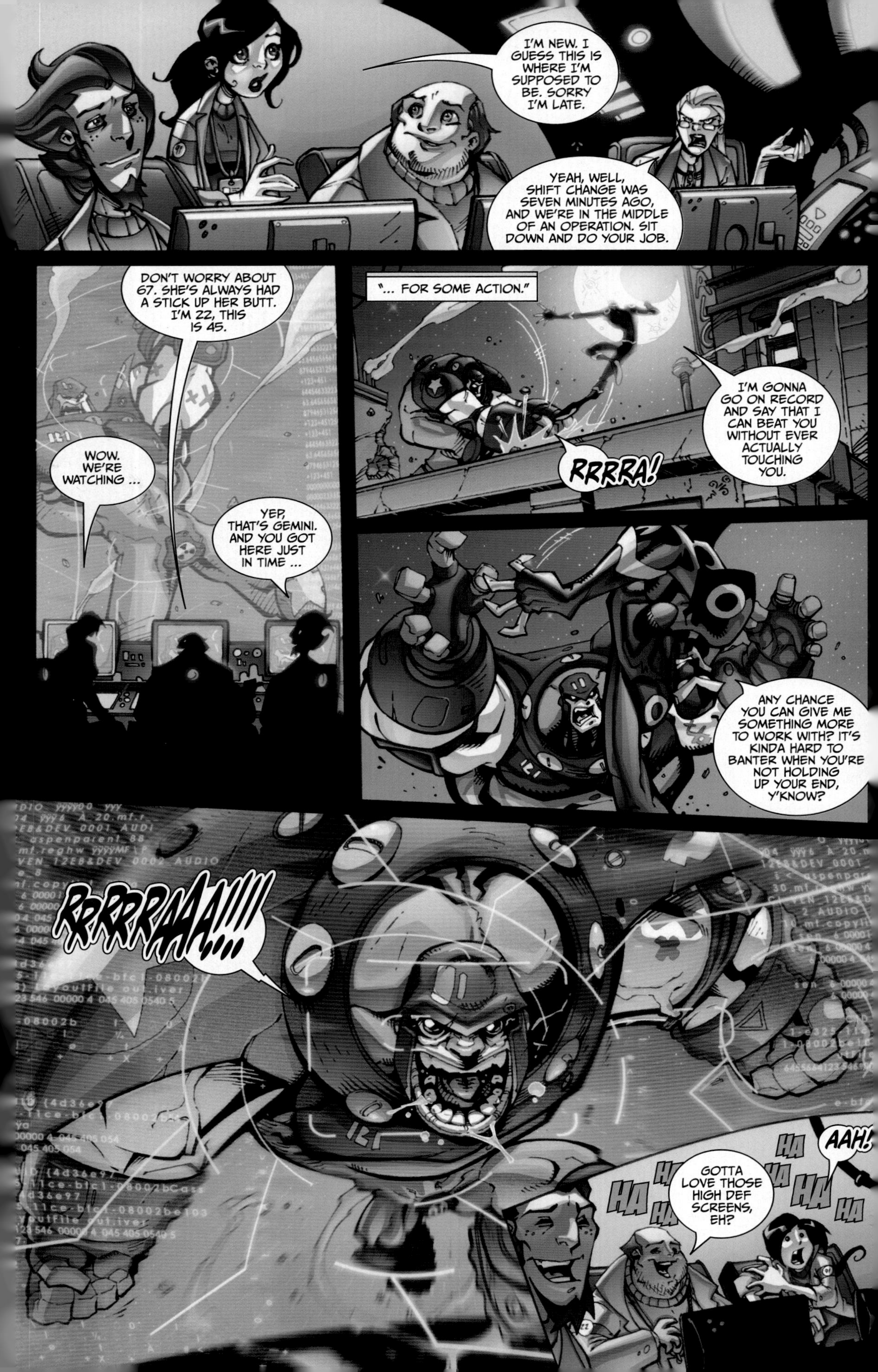
I'M NEW. I GUESS THIS IS WHERE I'M SUPPOSED TO BE. SORRY I'M LATE.
YEAH, WELL, SHIFT CHANGE WAS SEVEN MINUTES AGO, AND WE'RE IN THE MIDDLE OF AN OPERATION. SIT DOWN AND DO YOUR JOB.
DON'T WORRY ABOUT 67. SHE'S ALWAYS HAD A STICK UP HER BUTT. I'M 22, THIS IS 45.
WOW. WE'RE WATCHING ...
YEP, THAT'S GEMINI. AND YOU GOT HERE JUST IN TIME ...
"... FOR SOME ACTION."
I'M GONNA GO ON RECORD AND SAY THAT I CAN BEAT YOU WITHOUT EVER ACTUALLY TOUCHING YOU.
RRRRA!
ANY CHANCE YOU CAN GIVE ME SOMETHING MORE TO WORK WITH? IT'S KINDA HARD TO BANTER WHEN YOU'RE NOT HOLDING UP YOUR END, Y'KNOW?
RRRRRAAAA!!!!
GOTTA LOVE THOSE HIGH DEF SCREENS, EH?
HA HA HA HA HA HA HA HA
AAH!

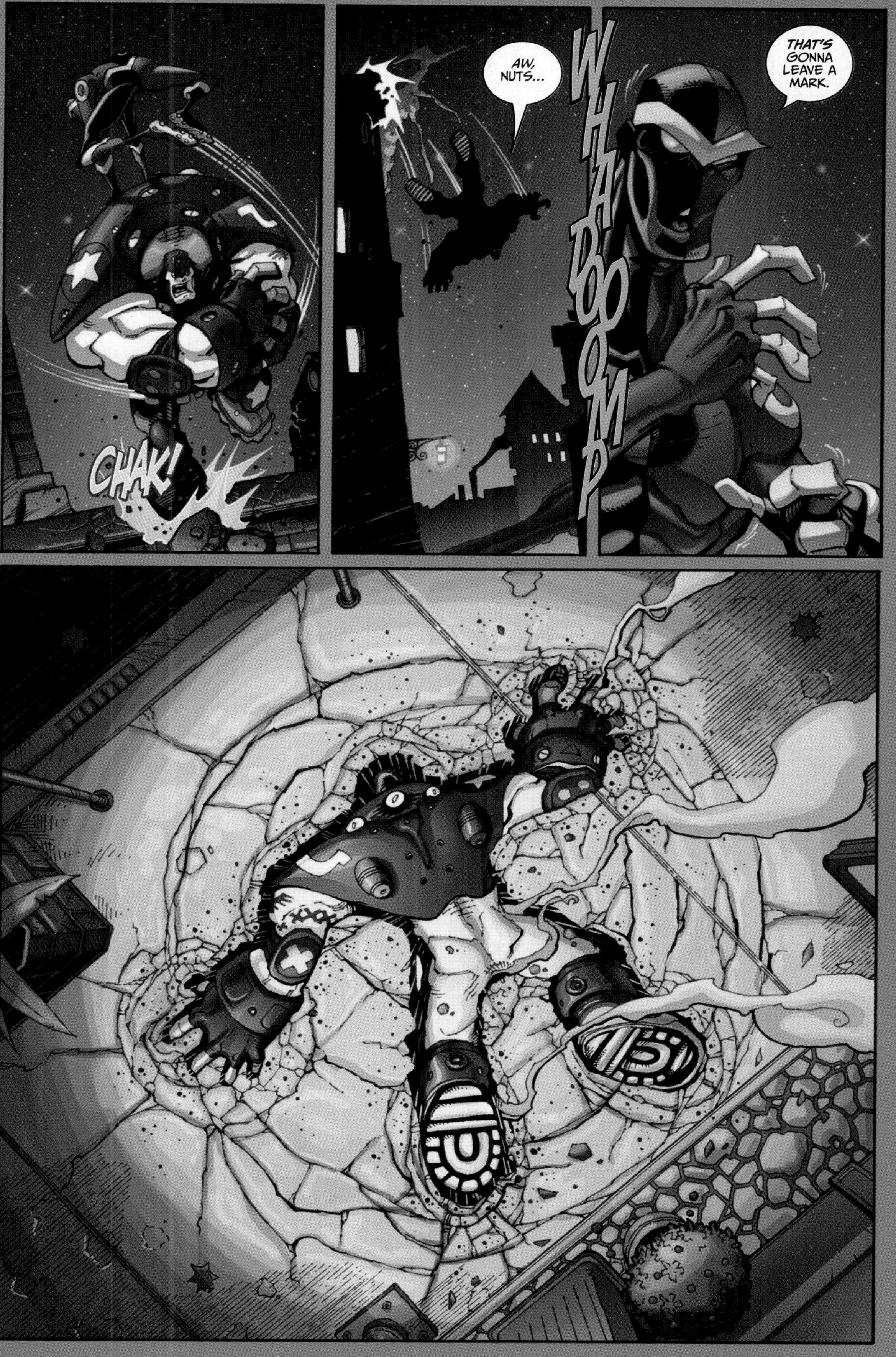
CHAK!
AW, NUTS...
WHADOOOMP
THAT'S GONNA LEAVE A MARK.

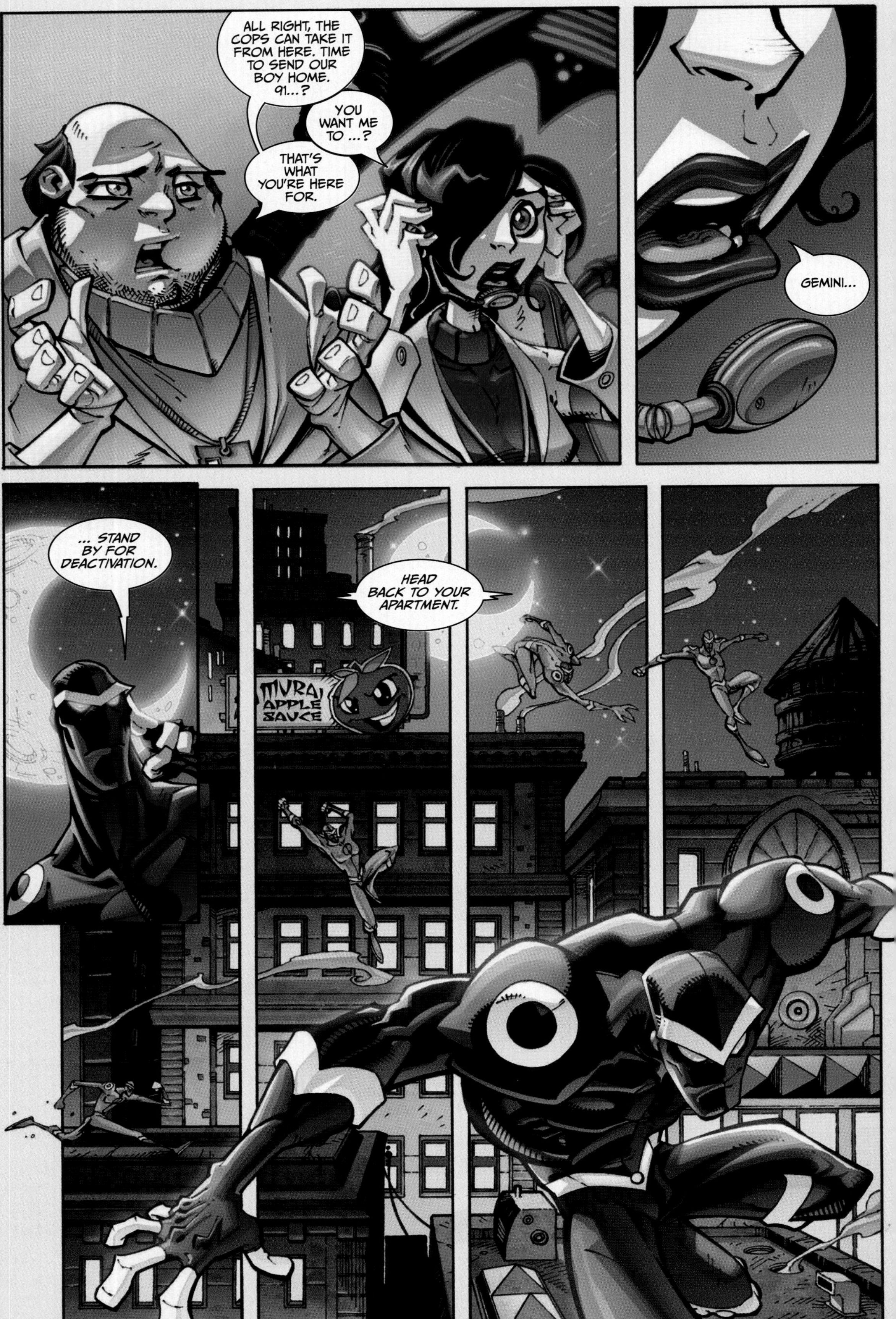
ALL RIGHT, THE COPS CAN TAKE IT FROM HERE. TIME TO SEND OUR BOY HOME. 91...?
YOU WANT ME TO ...?
THAT'S WHAT YOU'RE HERE FOR.
GEMINI...
... STAND BY FOR DEACTIVATION.
MURAI APPLE SAUCE
HEAD BACK TO YOUR APARTMENT.

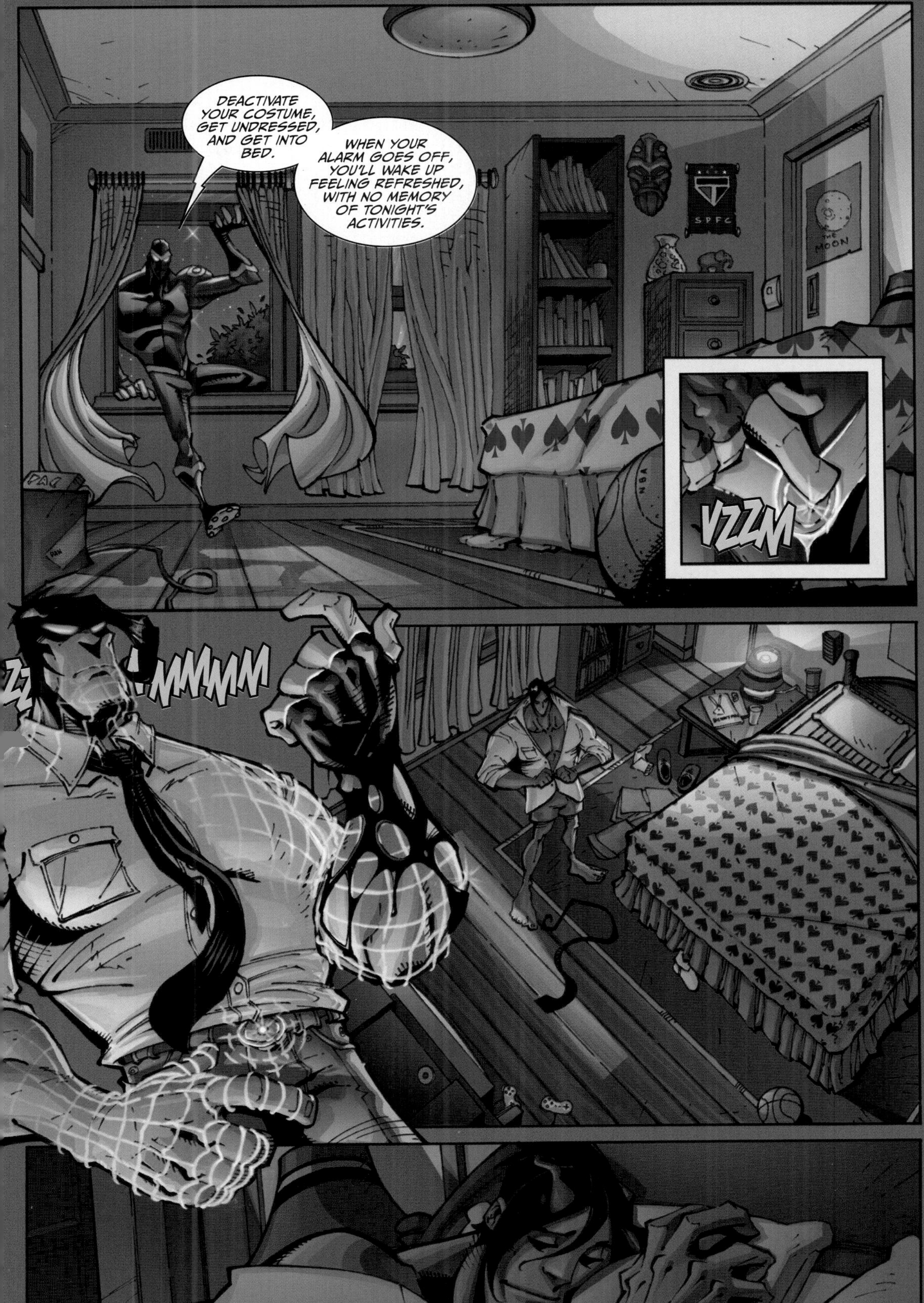
DEACTIVATE YOUR COSTUME, GET UNDRESSED, AND GET INTO BED.
WHEN YOUR ALARM GOES OFF, YOU'LL WAKE UP FEELING REFRESHED, WITH NO MEMORY OF TONIGHT'S ACTIVITIES.
VZZM
ZZMMMMM

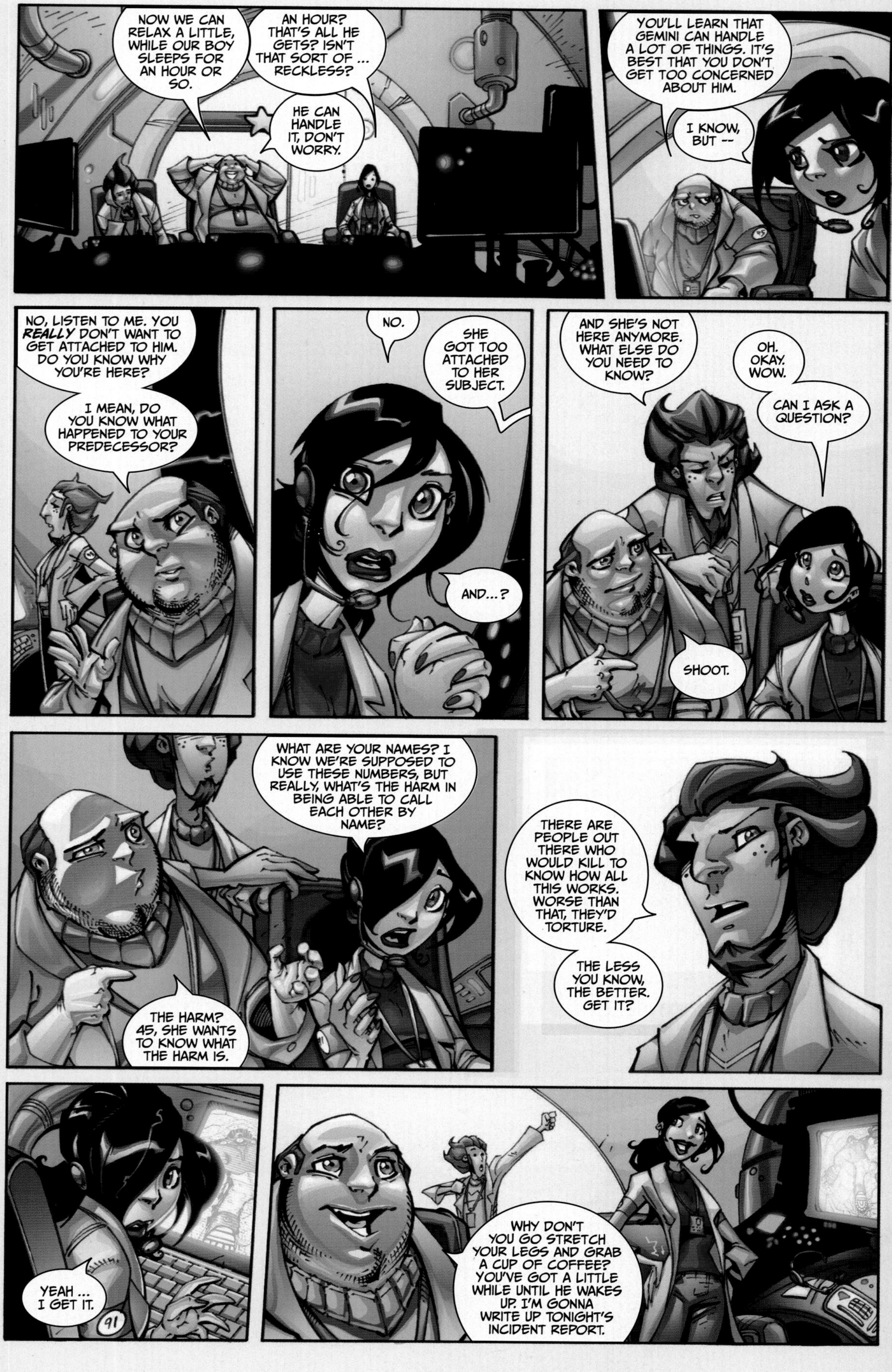
NOW WE CAN RELAX A LITTLE, WHILE OUR BOY SLEEPS FOR AN HOUR OR SO.
AN HOUR? THAT'S ALL HE GETS? ISN'T THAT SORT OF ... RECKLESS?
HE CAN HANDLE IT, DON'T WORRY.
YOU'LL LEARN THAT GEMINI CAN HANDLE A LOT OF THINGS. IT'S BEST THAT YOU DON'T GET TOO CONCERNED ABOUT HIM.
I KNOW, BUT --
NO, LISTEN TO ME. YOU *REALLY* DON'T WANT TO GET ATTACHED TO HIM. DO YOU KNOW WHY YOU'RE HERE?
I MEAN, DO YOU KNOW WHAT HAPPENED TO YOUR PREDECESSOR?
NO.
SHE GOT TOO ATTACHED TO HER SUBJECT.
AND...?
AND SHE'S NOT HERE ANYMORE. WHAT ELSE DO YOU NEED TO KNOW?
OH. OKAY. WOW.
CAN I ASK A QUESTION?
SHOOT.
WHAT ARE YOUR NAMES? I KNOW WE'RE SUPPOSED TO USE THESE NUMBERS, BUT REALLY, WHAT'S THE HARM IN BEING ABLE TO CALL EACH OTHER BY NAME?
THE HARM? 45, SHE WANTS TO KNOW WHAT THE HARM IS.
THERE ARE PEOPLE OUT THERE WHO WOULD KILL TO KNOW HOW ALL THIS WORKS. WORSE THAN THAT, THEY'D TORTURE.
THE LESS YOU KNOW, THE BETTER. GET IT?
YEAH ... I GET IT.
91
WHY DON'T YOU GO STRETCH YOUR LEGS AND GRAB A CUP OF COFFEE? YOU'VE GOT A LITTLE WHILE UNTIL HE WAKES UP. I'M GONNA WRITE UP TONIGHT'S INCIDENT REPORT.

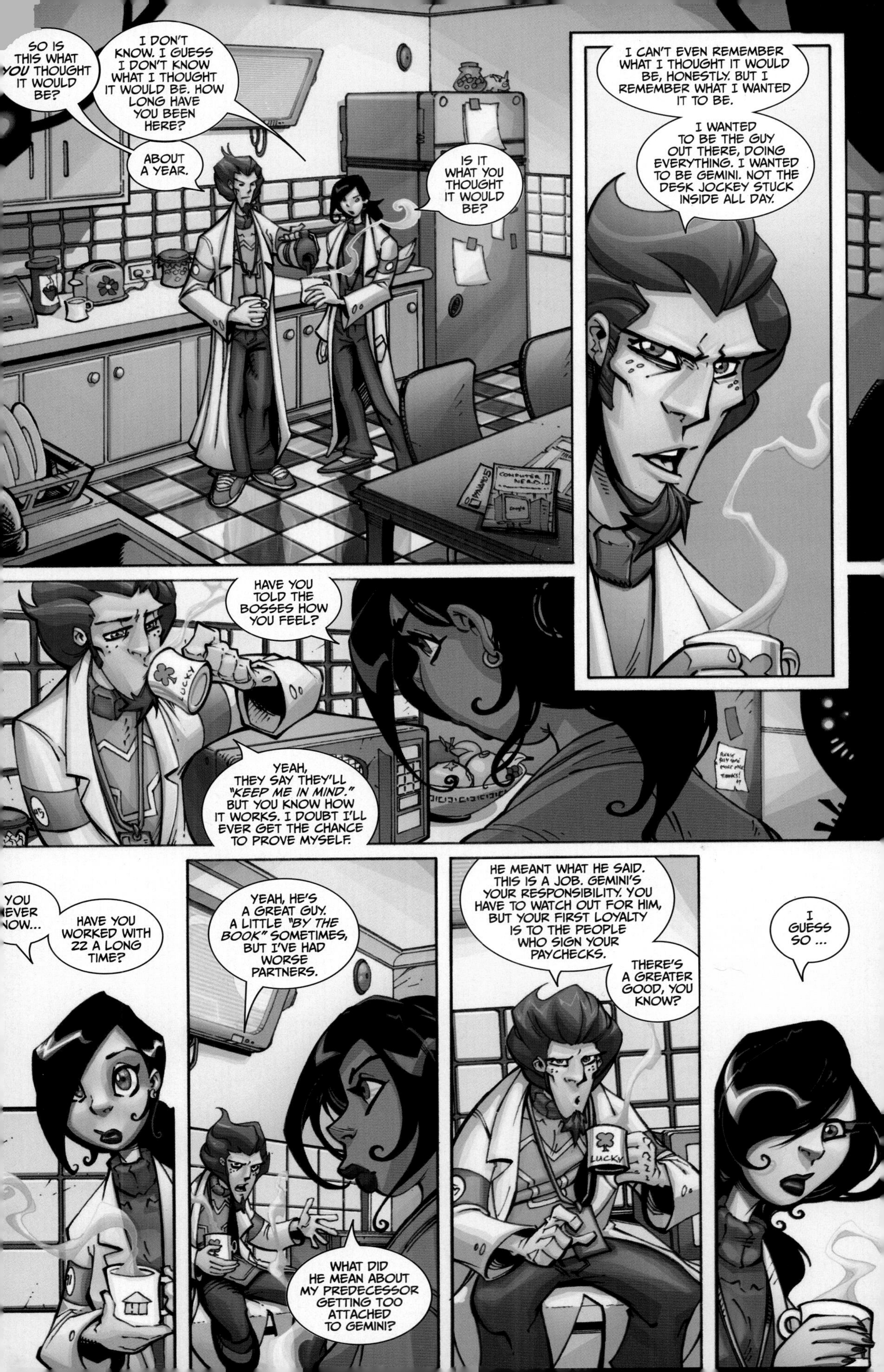
SO IS THIS WHAT *YOU* THOUGHT IT WOULD BE?
I DON'T KNOW. I GUESS I DON'T KNOW WHAT I THOUGHT IT WOULD BE. HOW LONG HAVE YOU BEEN HERE?
ABOUT A YEAR.
IS IT WHAT YOU THOUGHT IT WOULD BE?
I CAN'T EVEN REMEMBER WHAT I THOUGHT IT WOULD BE, HONESTLY. BUT I REMEMBER WHAT I WANTED IT TO BE.
I WANTED TO BE THE GUY OUT THERE, DOING EVERYTHING. I WANTED TO BE GEMINI. NOT THE DESK JOCKEY STUCK INSIDE ALL DAY.
HAVE YOU TOLD THE BOSSES HOW YOU FEEL?
YEAH, THEY SAY THEY'LL *"KEEP ME IN MIND."* BUT YOU KNOW HOW IT WORKS. I DOUBT I'LL EVER GET THE CHANCE TO PROVE MYSELF.
YOU EVER NOW...
HAVE YOU WORKED WITH 22 A LONG TIME?
YEAH, HE'S A GREAT GUY. A LITTLE *"BY THE BOOK"* SOMETIMES, BUT I'VE HAD WORSE PARTNERS.
WHAT DID HE MEAN ABOUT MY PREDECESSOR GETTING TOO ATTACHED TO GEMINI?
HE MEANT WHAT HE SAID. THIS IS A JOB. GEMINI'S YOUR RESPONSIBILITY. YOU HAVE TO WATCH OUT FOR HIM, BUT YOUR FIRST LOYALTY IS TO THE PEOPLE WHO SIGN YOUR PAYCHECKS.
THERE'S A GREATER GOOD, YOU KNOW?
I GUESS SO ...
LUCKY
LUCKY

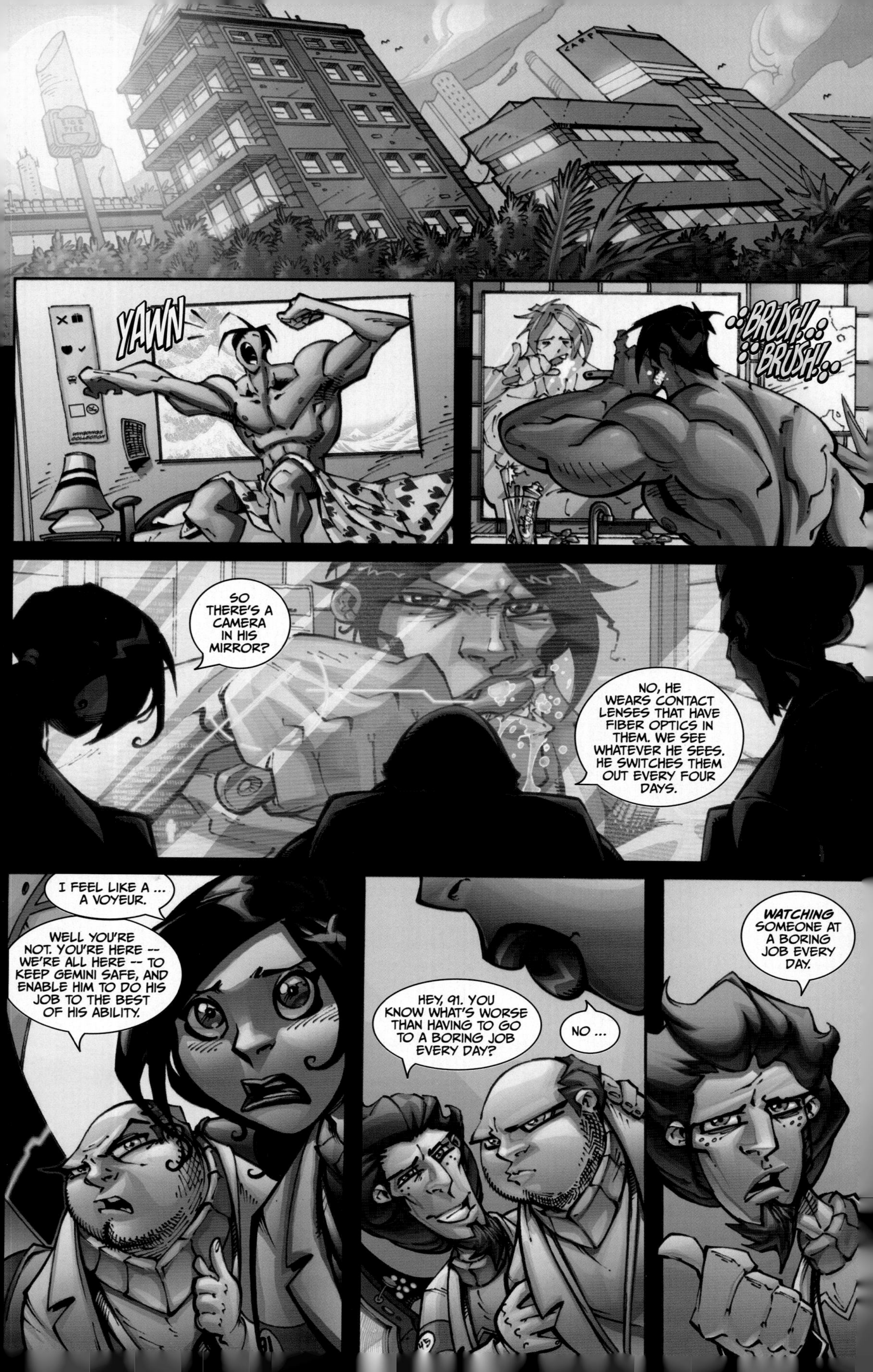
YAWN
BRUSH! BRUSH!
SO THERE'S A CAMERA IN HIS MIRROR?
NO, HE WEARS CONTACT LENSES THAT HAVE FIBER OPTICS IN THEM. WE SEE WHATEVER HE SEES. HE SWITCHES THEM OUT EVERY FOUR DAYS.
I FEEL LIKE A ... A VOYEUR.
WELL YOU'RE NOT. YOU'RE HERE -- WE'RE ALL HERE -- TO KEEP GEMINI SAFE, AND ENABLE HIM TO DO HIS JOB TO THE BEST OF HIS ABILITY.
HEY, 91. YOU KNOW WHAT'S WORSE THAN HAVING TO GO TO A BORING JOB EVERY DAY?
NO ...
WATCHING SOMEONE AT A BORING JOB EVERY DAY.

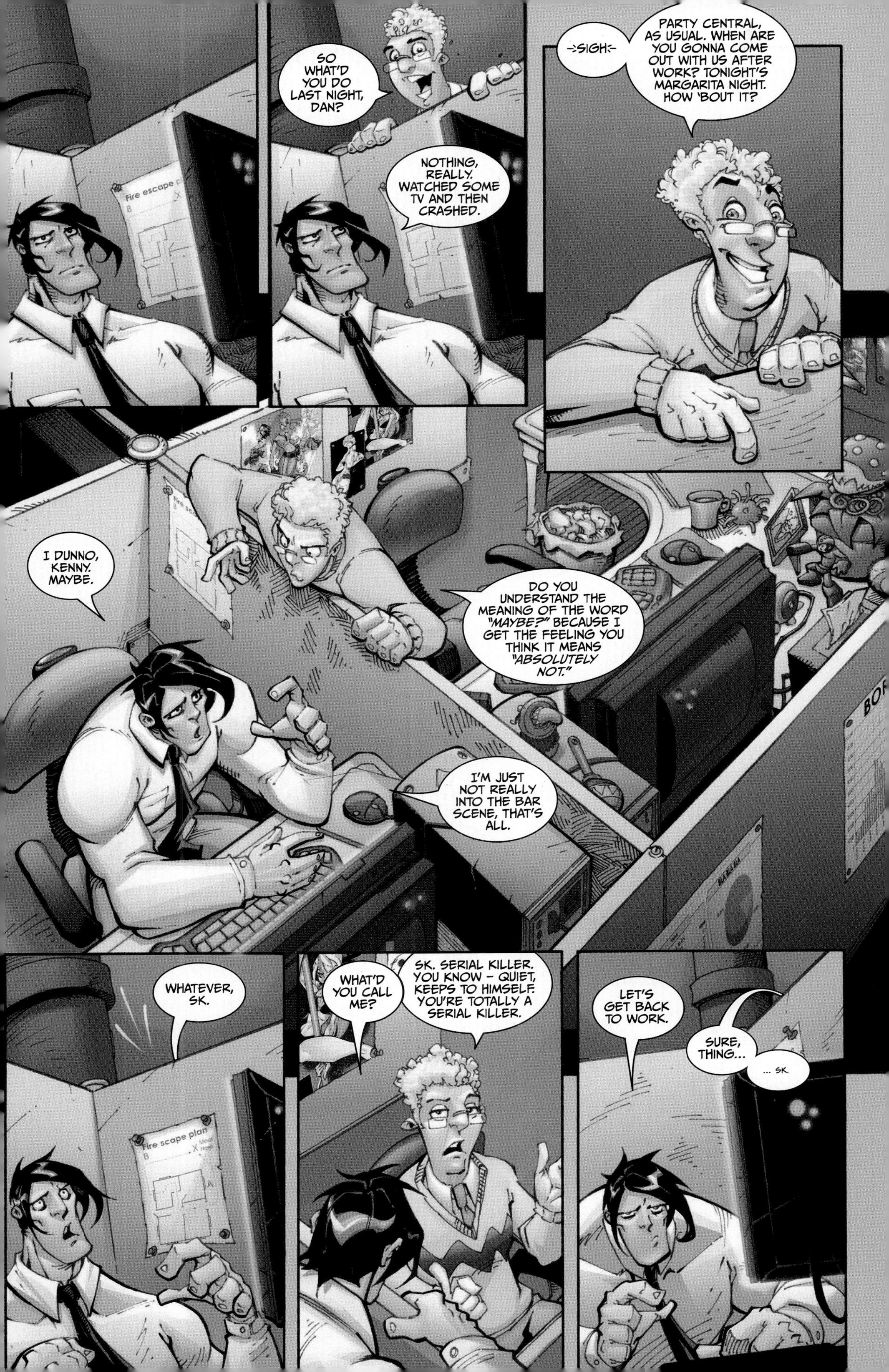

Fire escape p
SO WHAT'D YOU DO LAST NIGHT, DAN?
NOTHING, REALLY. WATCHED SOME TV AND THEN CRASHED.
-SIGH-
PARTY CENTRAL, AS USUAL. WHEN ARE YOU GONNA COME OUT WITH US AFTER WORK? TONIGHT'S MARGARITA NIGHT. HOW 'BOUT IT?
I DUNNO, KENNY. MAYBE.
DO YOU UNDERSTAND THE MEANING OF THE WORD "MAYBE?" BECAUSE I GET THE FEELING YOU THINK IT MEANS "ABSOLUTELY NOT."
I'M JUST NOT REALLY INTO THE BAR SCENE, THAT'S ALL.
WHATEVER, SK.
Fire scape plan
Meet Here
WHAT'D YOU CALL ME?
SK. SERIAL KILLER. YOU KNOW - QUIET, KEEPS TO HIMSELF. YOU'RE TOTALLY A SERIAL KILLER.
LET'S GET BACK TO WORK.
SURE, THING...
... SK.

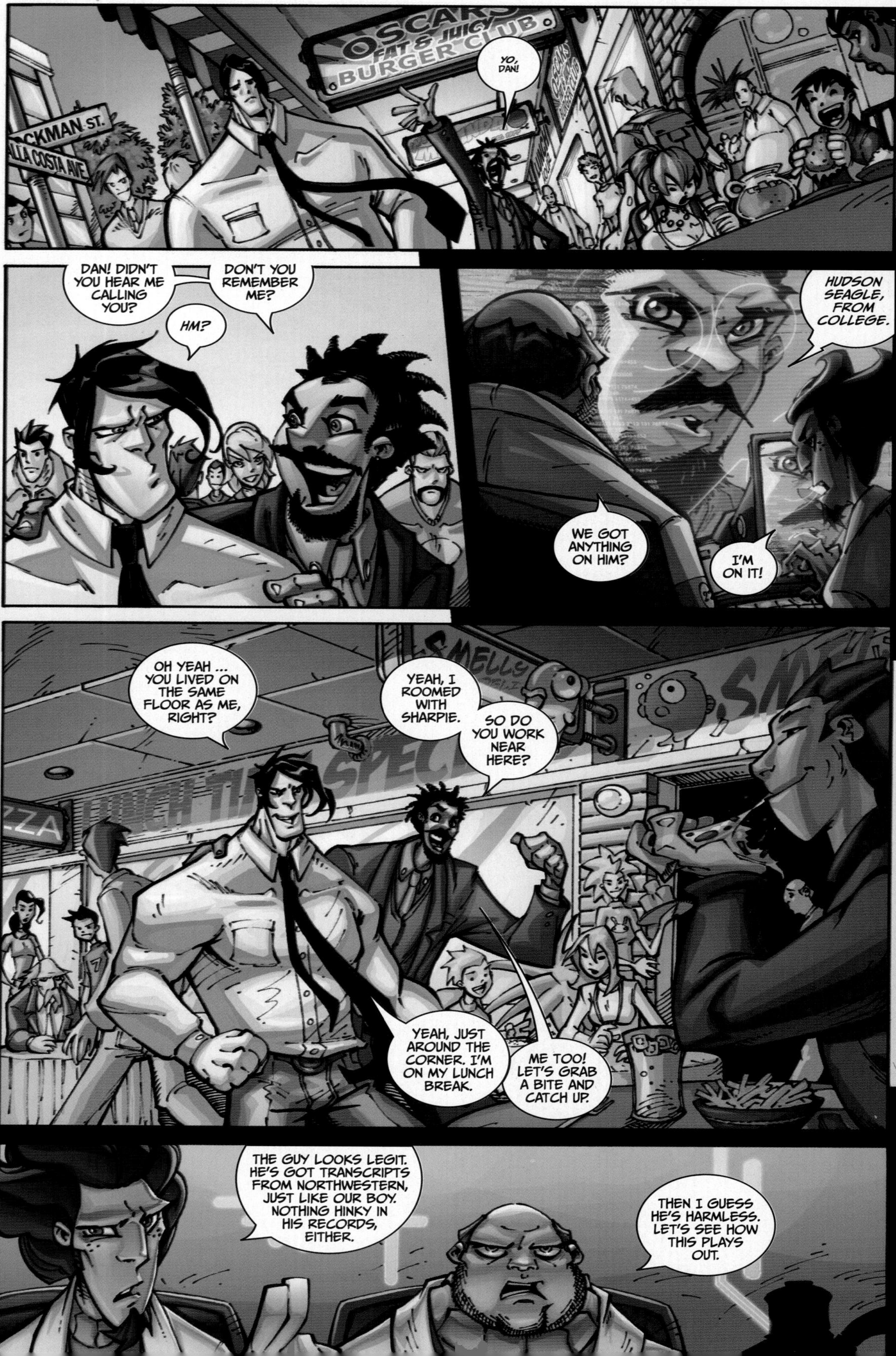
OSCAR'S FAT & JUICY BURGER CLUB
ACKMAN ST.
ALLA COSTA AVE
YO, DAN!
DAN! DIDN'T YOU HEAR ME CALLING YOU?
DON'T YOU REMEMBER ME?
HM?
HUDSON SEAGLE, FROM COLLEGE.
WE GOT ANYTHING ON HIM?
I'M ON IT!
OH YEAH ... YOU LIVED ON THE SAME FLOOR AS ME, RIGHT?
YEAH, I ROOMED WITH SHARPIE.
SO DO YOU WORK NEAR HERE?
YEAH, JUST AROUND THE CORNER. I'M ON MY LUNCH BREAK.
ME TOO! LET'S GRAB A BITE AND CATCH UP.
THE GUY LOOKS LEGIT. HE'S GOT TRANSCRIPTS FROM NORTHWESTERN, JUST LIKE OUR BOY. NOTHING HINKY IN HIS RECORDS, EITHER.
THEN I GUESS HE'S HARMLESS. LET'S SEE HOW THIS PLAYS OUT.

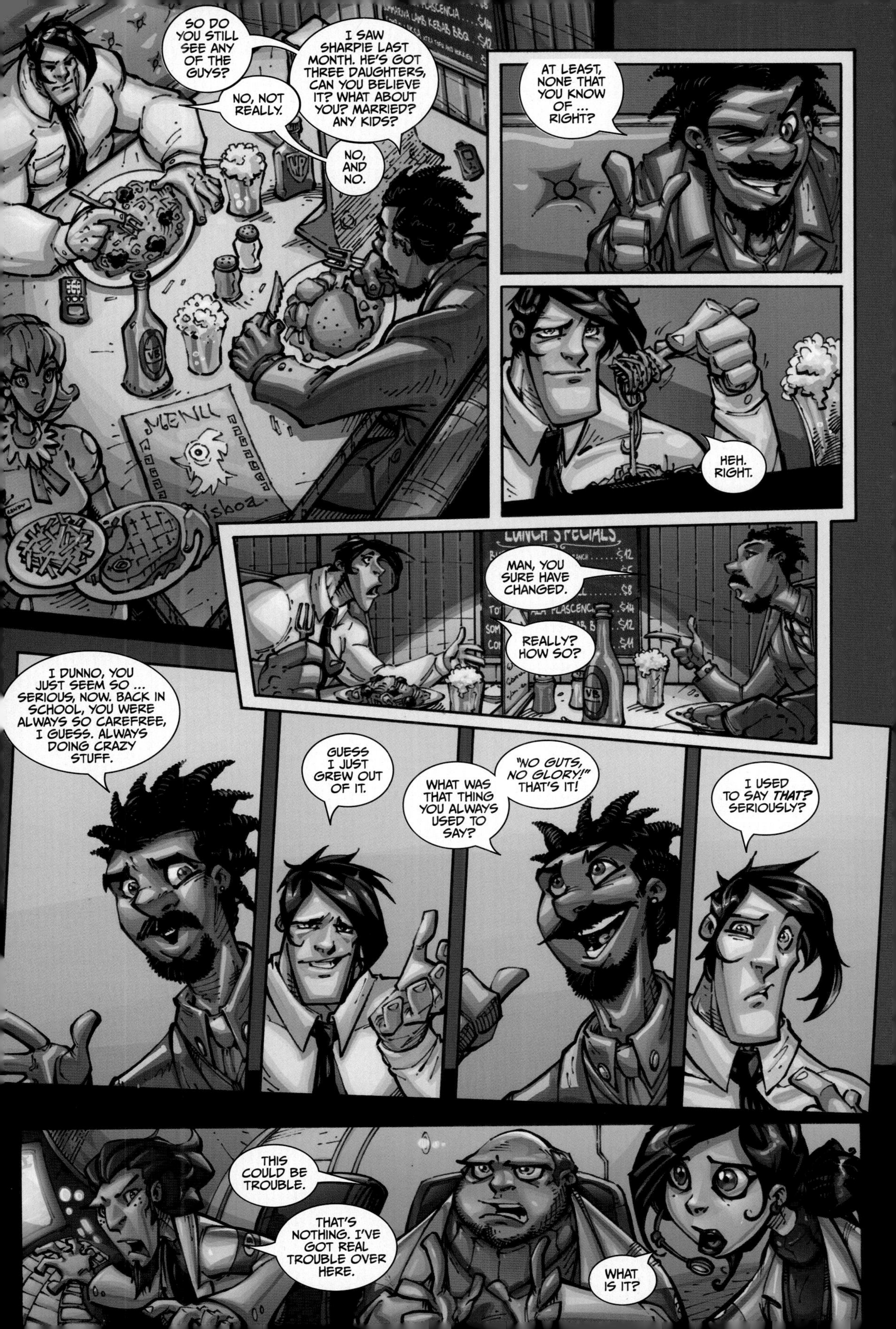
SO DO YOU STILL SEE ANY OF THE GUYS?
I SAW SHARPIE LAST MONTH. HE'S GOT THREE DAUGHTERS, CAN YOU BELIEVE IT? WHAT ABOUT YOU? MARRIED? ANY KIDS?
NO, NOT REALLY.
NO, AND NO.
AT LEAST, NONE THAT YOU KNOW OF ... RIGHT?
HEH. RIGHT.
LUNCH SPECIALS
MAN, YOU SURE HAVE CHANGED.
REALLY? HOW SO?
I DUNNO, YOU JUST SEEM SO ... SERIOUS, NOW. BACK IN SCHOOL, YOU WERE ALWAYS SO CAREFREE, I GUESS. ALWAYS DOING CRAZY STUFF.
GUESS I JUST GREW OUT OF IT.
WHAT WAS THAT THING YOU ALWAYS USED TO SAY?
"NO GUTS, NO GLORY!" THAT'S IT!
I USED TO SAY *THAT?* SERIOUSLY?
THIS COULD BE TROUBLE.
THAT'S NOTHING. I'VE GOT REAL TROUBLE OVER HERE.
WHAT IS IT?

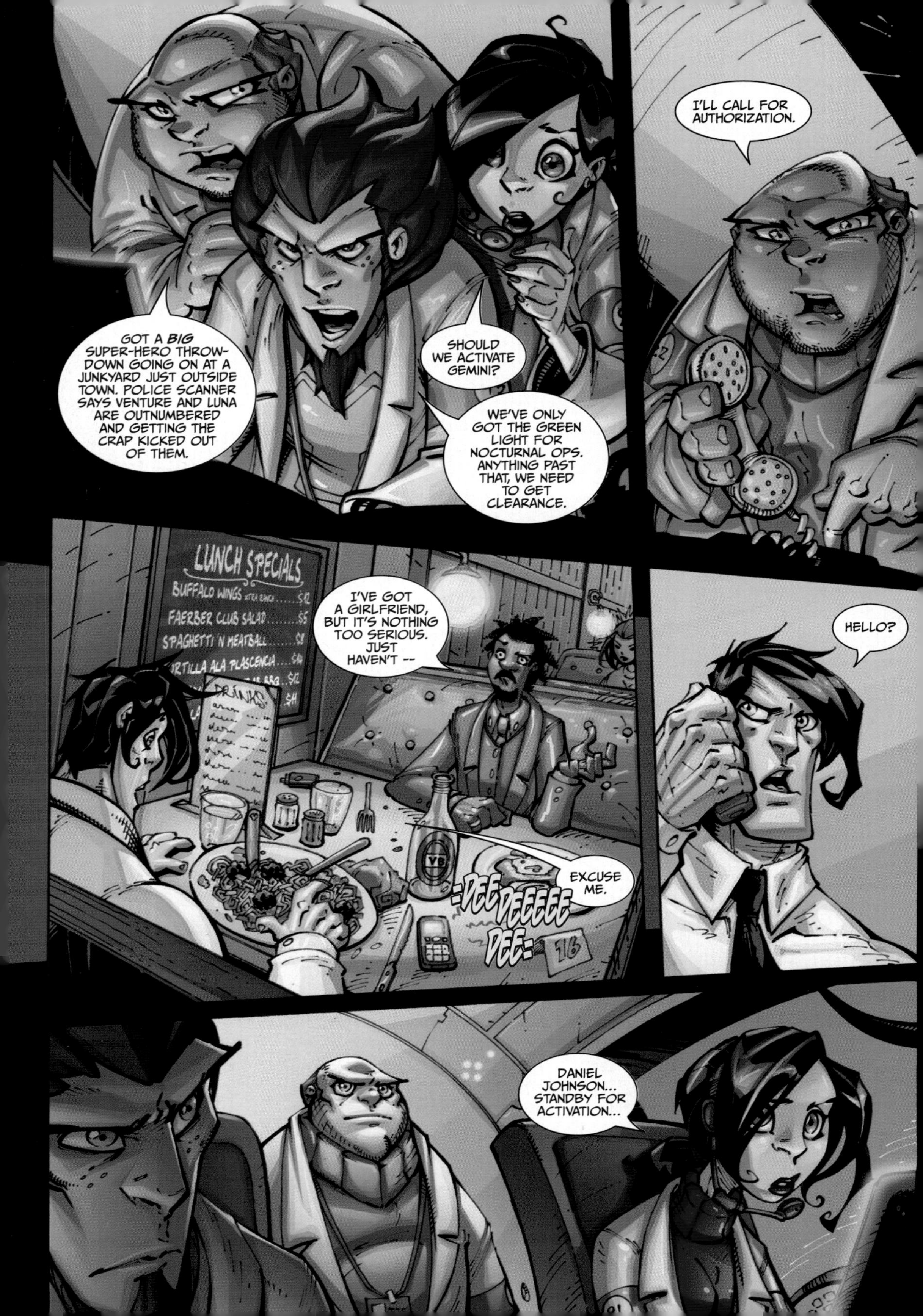
GOT A *BIG* SUPER-HERO THROW-DOWN GOING ON AT A JUNKYARD JUST OUTSIDE TOWN. POLICE SCANNER SAYS VENTURE AND LUNA ARE OUTNUMBERED AND GETTING THE CRAP KICKED OUT OF THEM.
SHOULD WE ACTIVATE GEMINI?
WE'VE ONLY GOT THE GREEN LIGHT FOR NOCTURNAL OPS. ANYTHING PAST THAT, WE NEED TO GET CLEARANCE.
I'LL CALL FOR AUTHORIZATION.
LUNCH SPECIALS
BUFFALO WINGS
FAERBER CLUB SALAD
SPAGHETTI 'N MEATBALL
DRINKS
I'VE GOT A GIRLFRIEND, BUT IT'S NOTHING TOO SERIOUS. JUST HAVEN'T --
EXCUSE ME.
DEE DEEEEEE DEE
16
HELLO?
DANIEL JOHNSON... STANDBY FOR ACTIVATION...

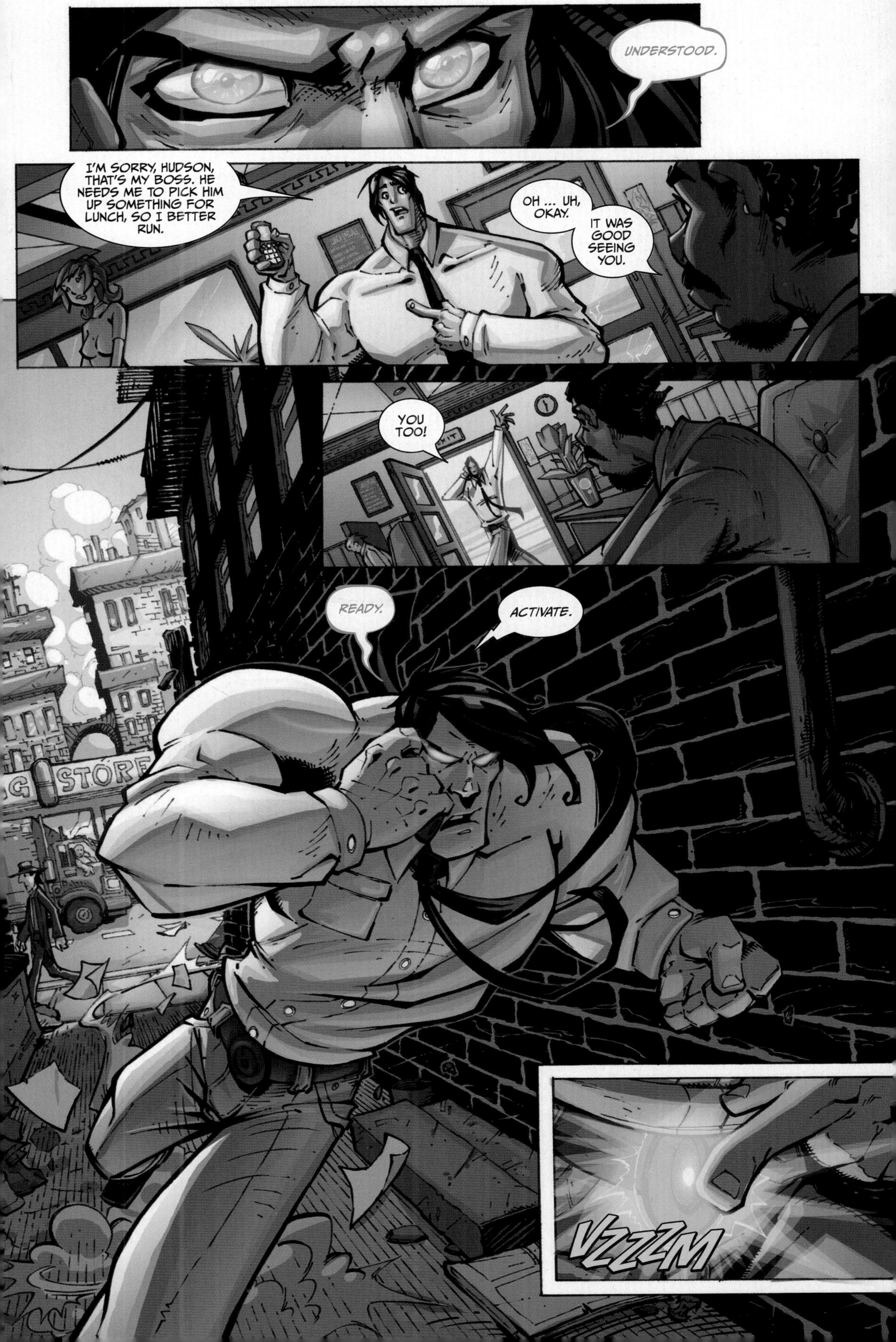
UNDERSTOOD.
I'M SORRY, HUDSON, THAT'S MY BOSS. HE NEEDS ME TO PICK HIM UP SOMETHING FOR LUNCH, SO I BETTER RUN.
OH ... UH, OKAY.
IT WAS GOOD SEEING YOU.
YOU TOO!
READY.
ACTIVATE.
VZZZM

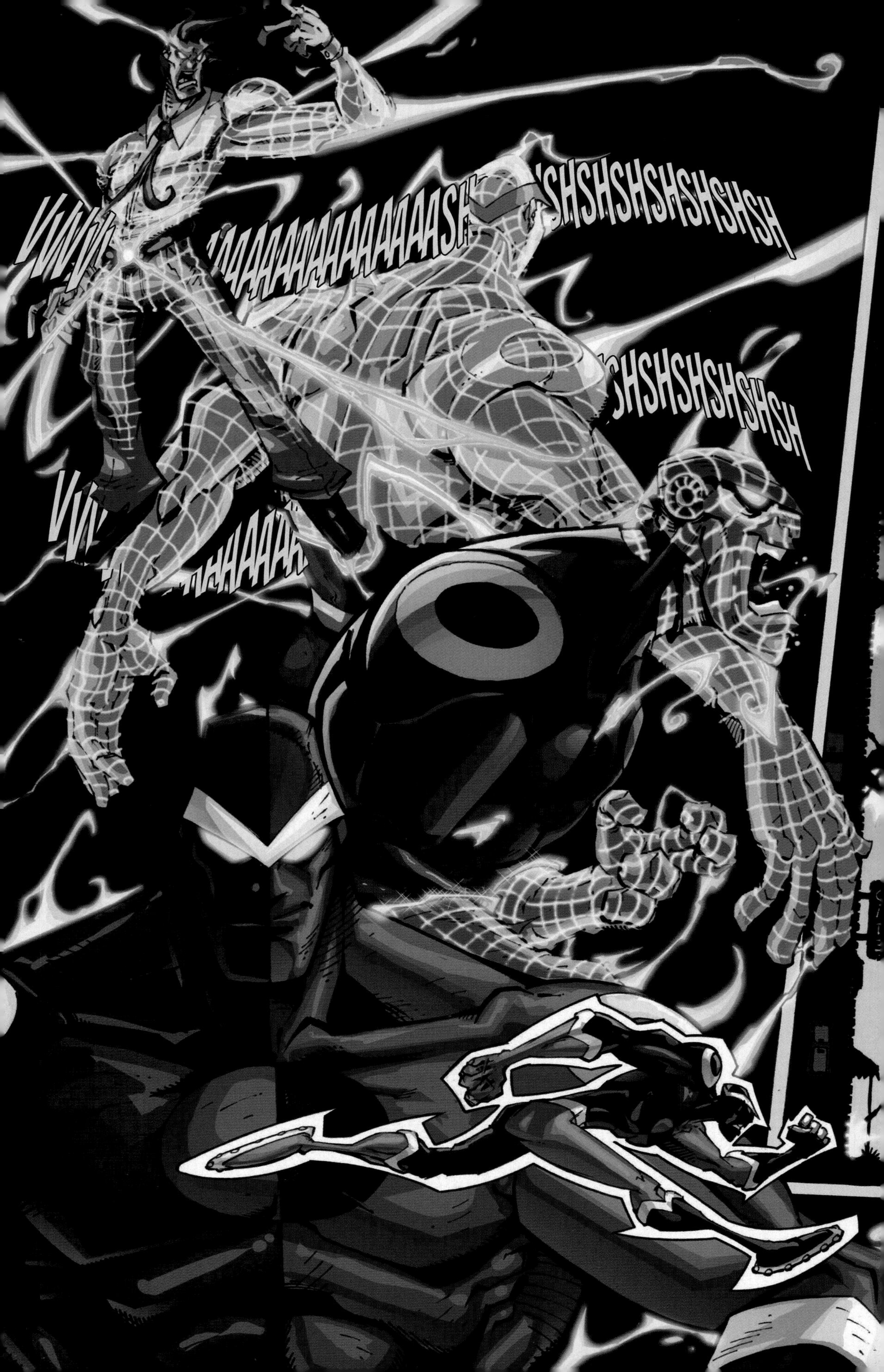

AAAAAAAAAAAAASH
SHSHSHSHSHSHSH
SHSHSHSHSHSH

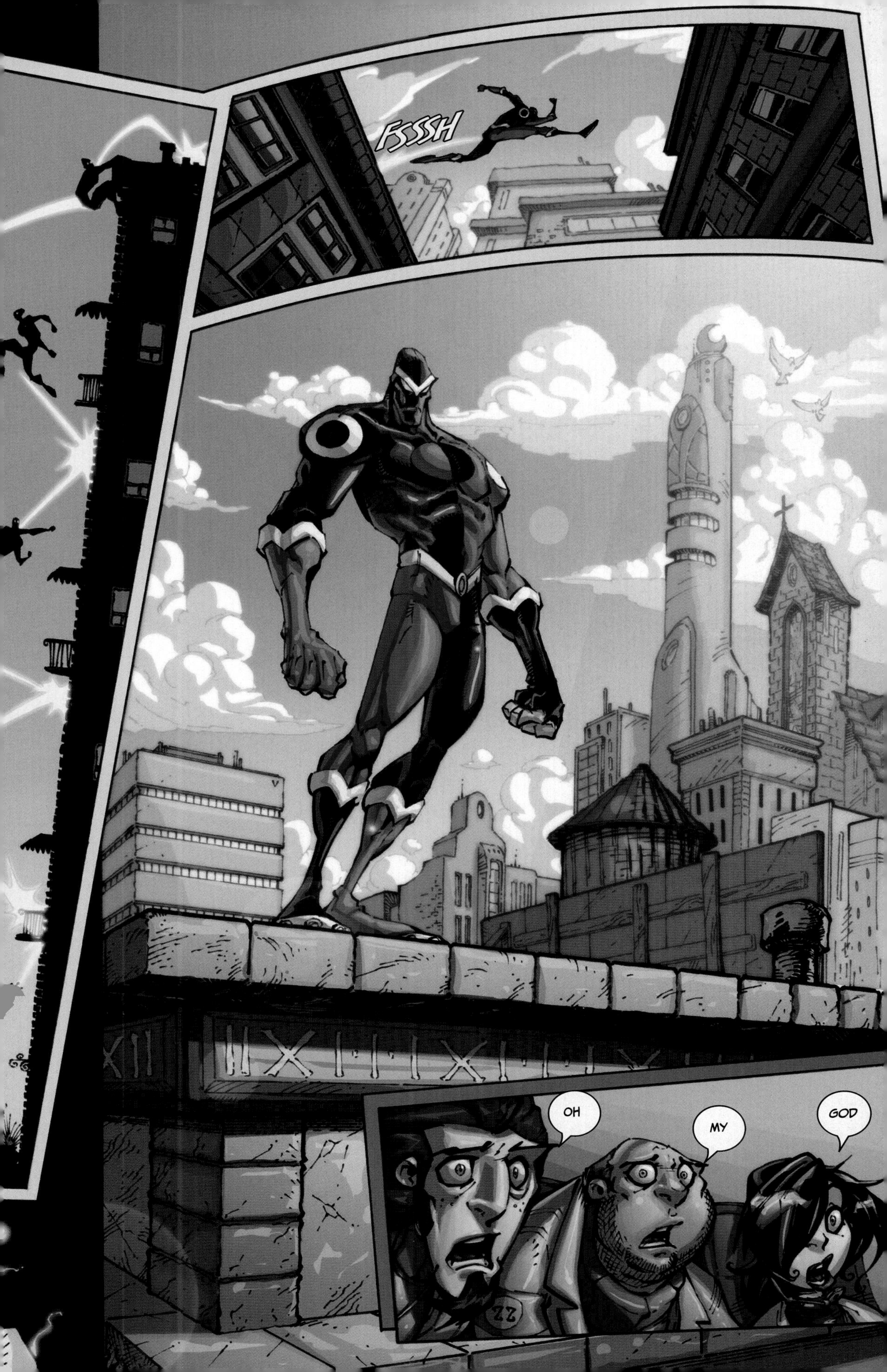
FSSSH
OH
MY
GOD

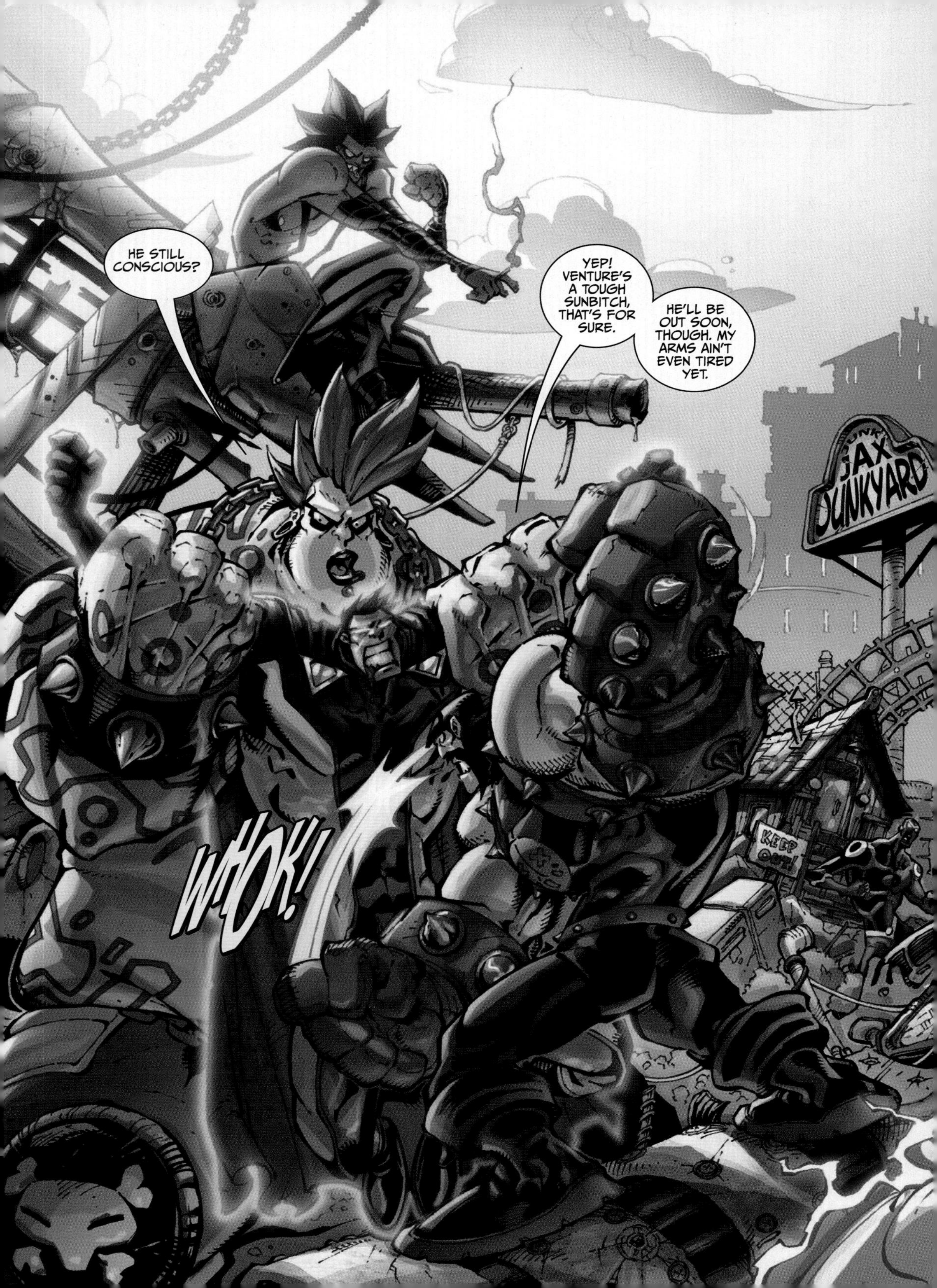
HE STILL CONSCIOUS?
YEP! VENTURE'S A TOUGH SUNBITCH, THAT'S FOR SURE.
HE'LL BE OUT SOON, THOUGH. MY ARMS AIN'T EVEN TIRED YET.
JAX JUNKYARD
KEEP OUT!
WHOK!

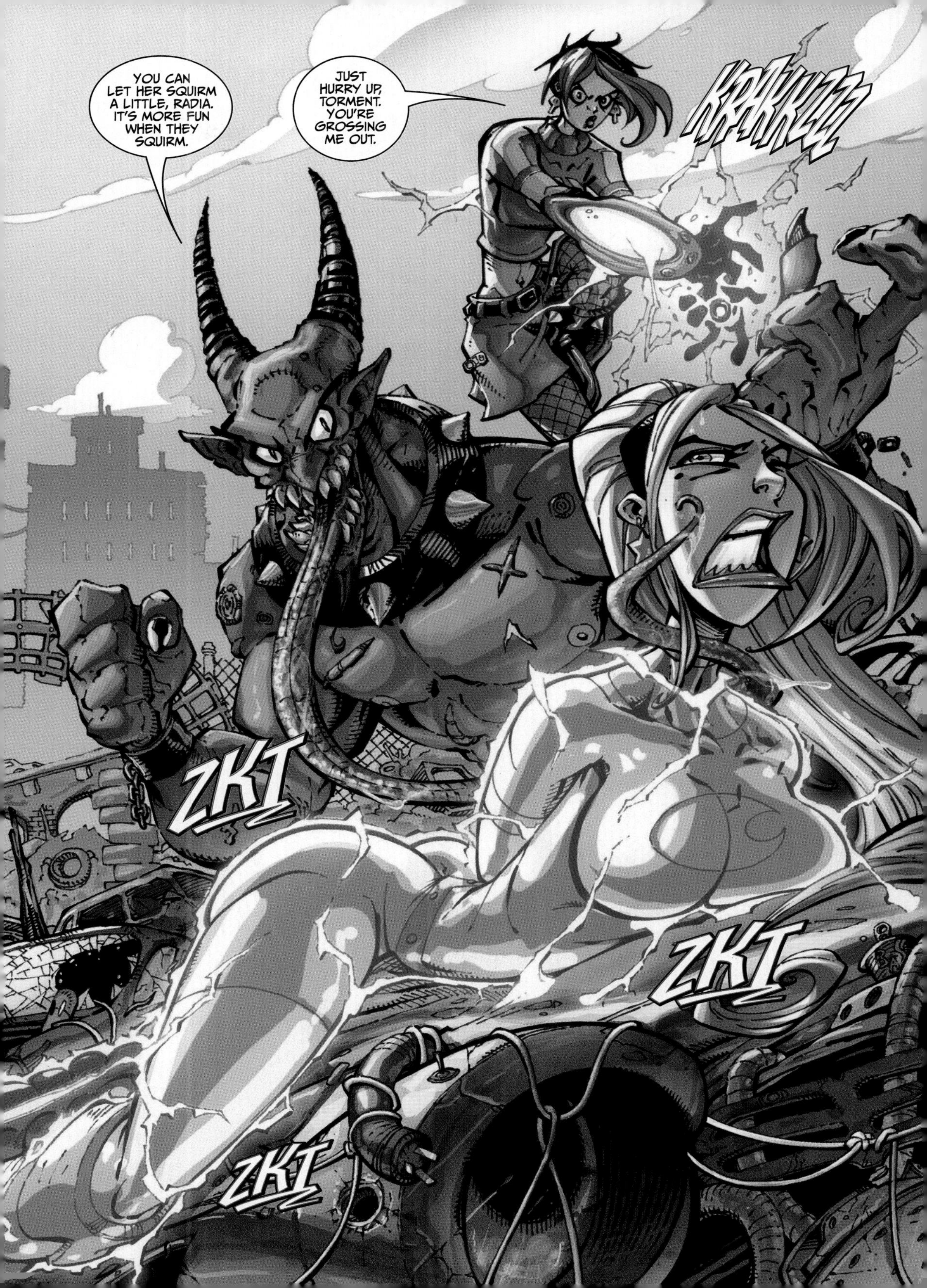
YOU CAN LET HER SQUIRM A LITTLE, RADIA. IT'S MORE FUN WHEN THEY SQUIRM.
JUST HURRY UP, TORMENT. YOU'RE GROSSING ME OUT.
KRAKKLZZ
ZKT
ZKT
ZKT

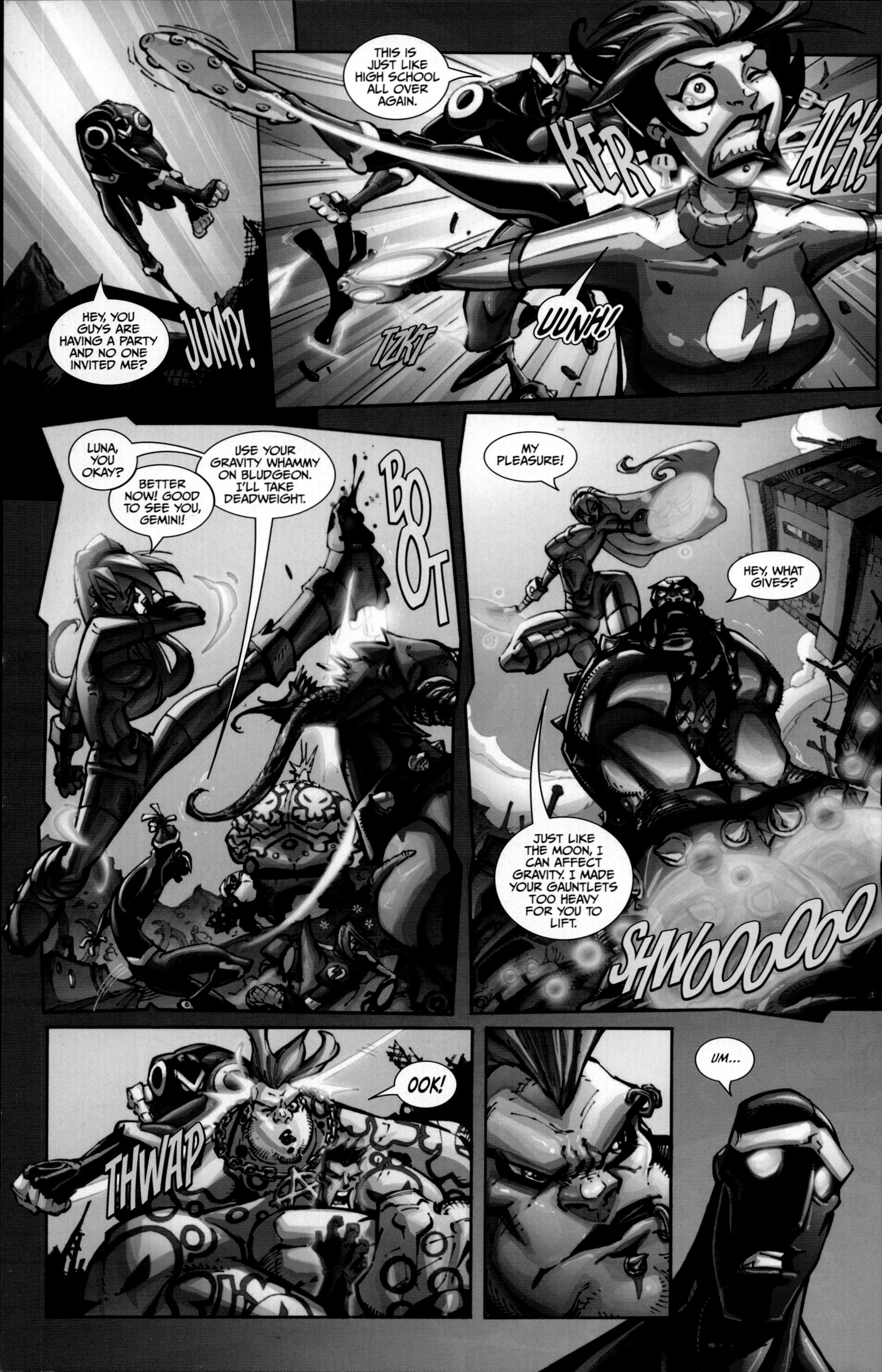

HEY, YOU GUYS ARE HAVING A PARTY AND NO ONE INVITED ME?
JUMP!
THIS IS JUST LIKE HIGH SCHOOL ALL OVER AGAIN.
KER-
ACK!
UUNH!
TZKT
LUNA, YOU OKAY?
BETTER NOW! GOOD TO SEE YOU, GEMINI!
USE YOUR GRAVITY WHAMMY ON BLUDGEON. I'LL TAKE DEADWEIGHT.
BOOT
MY PLEASURE!
HEY, WHAT GIVES?
JUST LIKE THE MOON, I CAN AFFECT GRAVITY. I MADE YOUR GAUNTLETS TOO HEAVY FOR YOU TO LIFT.
SHWOOOOOO
OOK!
THWAP
UM...

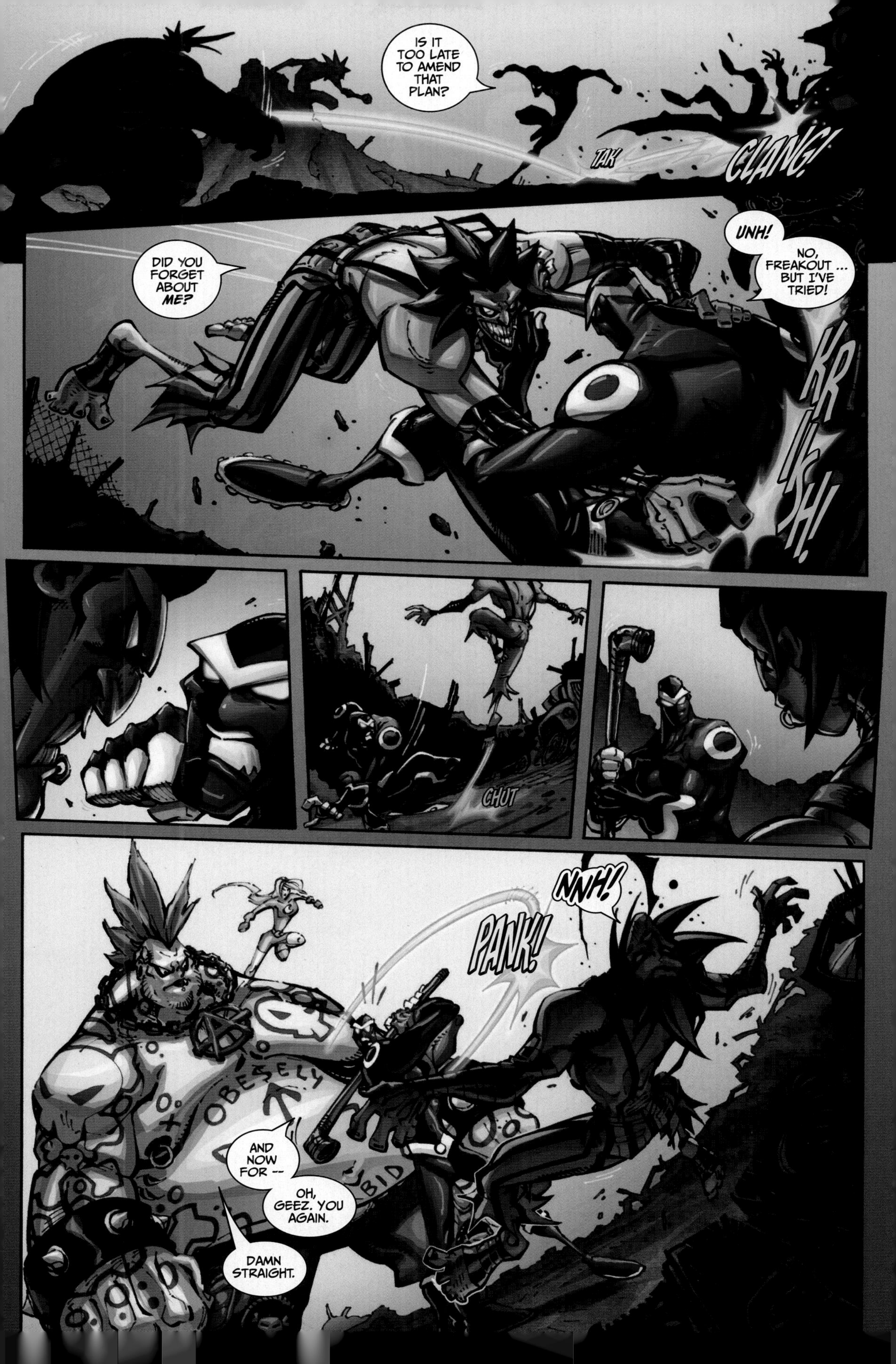
IS IT TOO LATE TO AMEND THAT PLAN?
TAK
CLANG!
DID YOU FORGET ABOUT *ME?*
UNH!
NO, FREAKOUT ... BUT I'VE TRIED!
KRIKSH!
CHUT
NNH!
PANK!
AND NOW FOR --
OH, GEEZ. YOU AGAIN.
DAMN STRAIGHT.

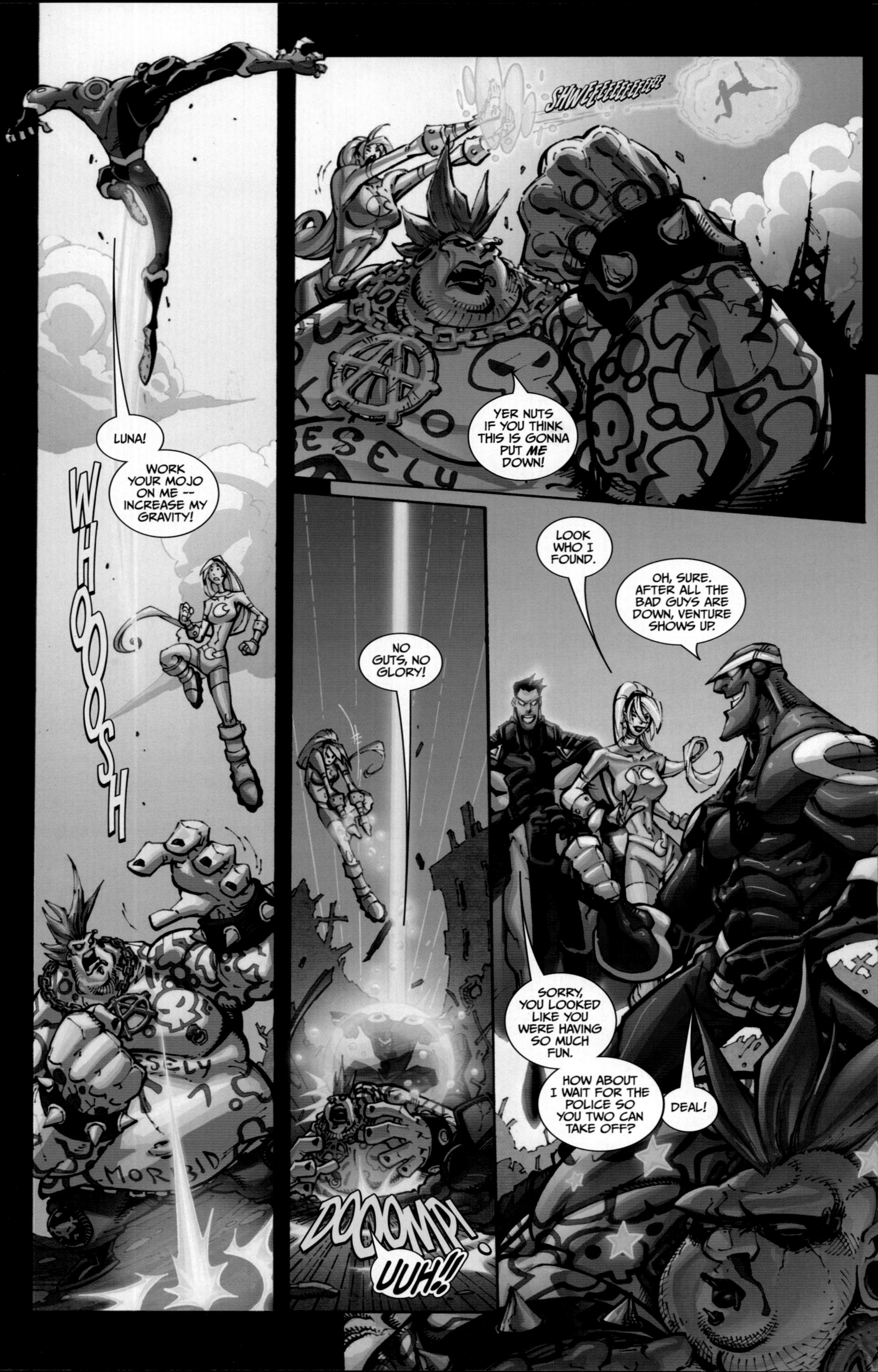
LUNA!
WORK YOUR MOJO ON ME -- INCREASE MY GRAVITY!
WHOOOOSH
SHWEEEEEEEEEEEE
YER NUTS IF YOU THINK THIS IS GONNA PUT *ME* DOWN!
NO GUTS, NO GLORY!
DOOOMP!
UUH!!
LOOK WHO I FOUND.
OH, SURE. AFTER ALL THE BAD GUYS ARE DOWN, VENTURE SHOWS UP.
SORRY, YOU LOOKED LIKE YOU WERE HAVING SO MUCH FUN.
HOW ABOUT I WAIT FOR THE POLICE SO YOU TWO CAN TAKE OFF?
DEAL!

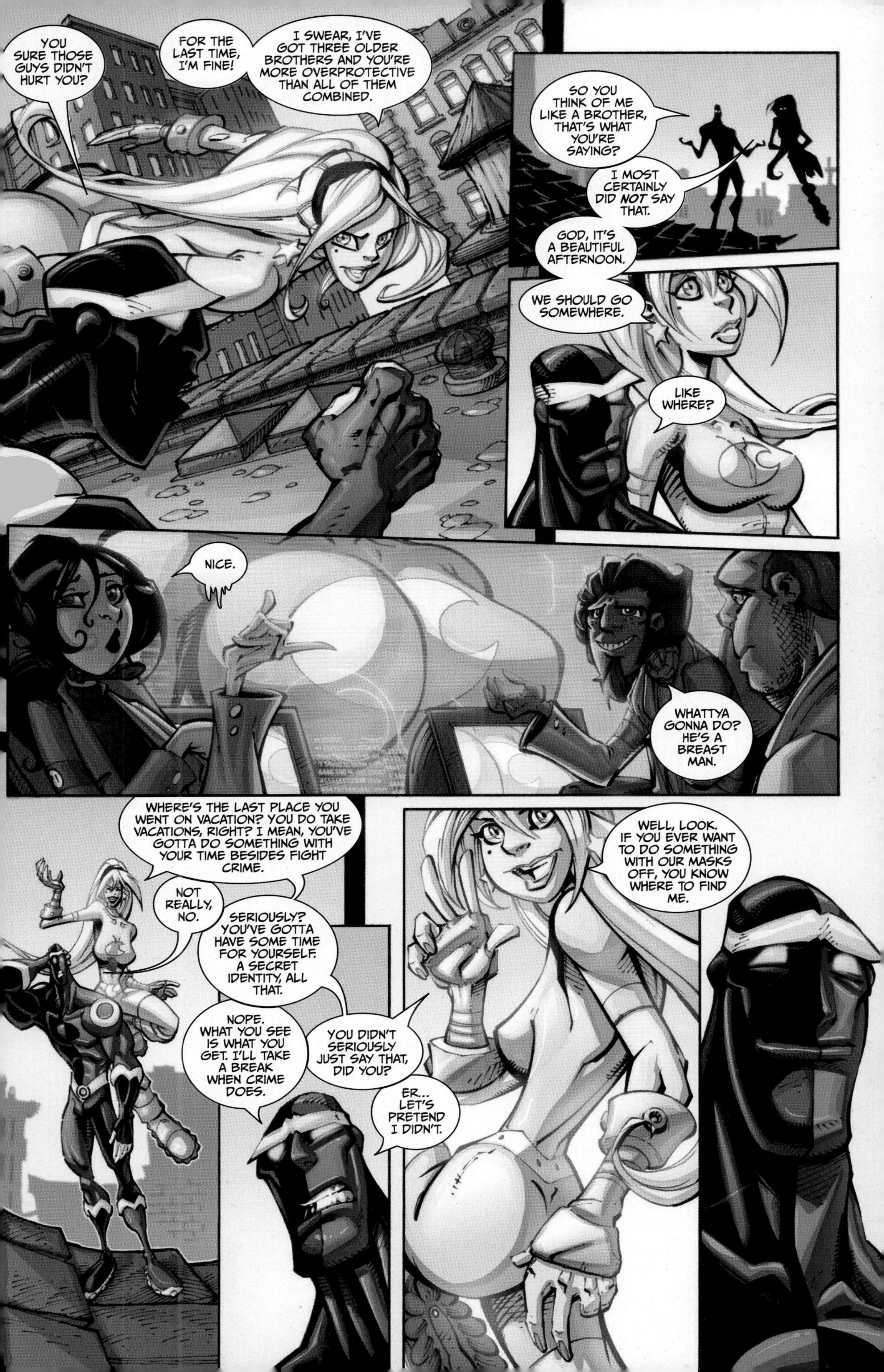

YOU SURE THOSE GUYS DIDN'T HURT YOU?
FOR THE LAST TIME, I'M FINE!
I SWEAR, I'VE GOT THREE OLDER BROTHERS AND YOU'RE MORE OVERPROTECTIVE THAN ALL OF THEM COMBINED.
SO YOU THINK OF ME LIKE A BROTHER, THAT'S WHAT YOU'RE SAYING?
I MOST CERTAINLY DID *NOT* SAY THAT.
GOD, IT'S A BEAUTIFUL AFTERNOON.
WE SHOULD GO SOMEWHERE.
LIKE WHERE?
NICE.
WHATTYA GONNA DO? HE'S A BREAST MAN.
WHERE'S THE LAST PLACE YOU WENT ON VACATION? YOU DO TAKE VACATIONS, RIGHT? I MEAN, YOU'VE GOTTA DO SOMETHING WITH YOUR TIME BESIDES FIGHT CRIME.
NOT REALLY, NO.
SERIOUSLY? YOU'VE GOTTA HAVE SOME TIME FOR YOURSELF. A SECRET IDENTITY, ALL THAT.
NOPE. WHAT YOU SEE IS WHAT YOU GET. I'LL TAKE A BREAK WHEN CRIME DOES.
YOU DIDN'T SERIOUSLY JUST SAY THAT, DID YOU?
ER... LET'S PRETEND I DIDN'T.
WELL, LOOK. IF YOU EVER WANT TO DO SOMETHING WITH OUR MASKS OFF, YOU KNOW WHERE TO FIND ME.

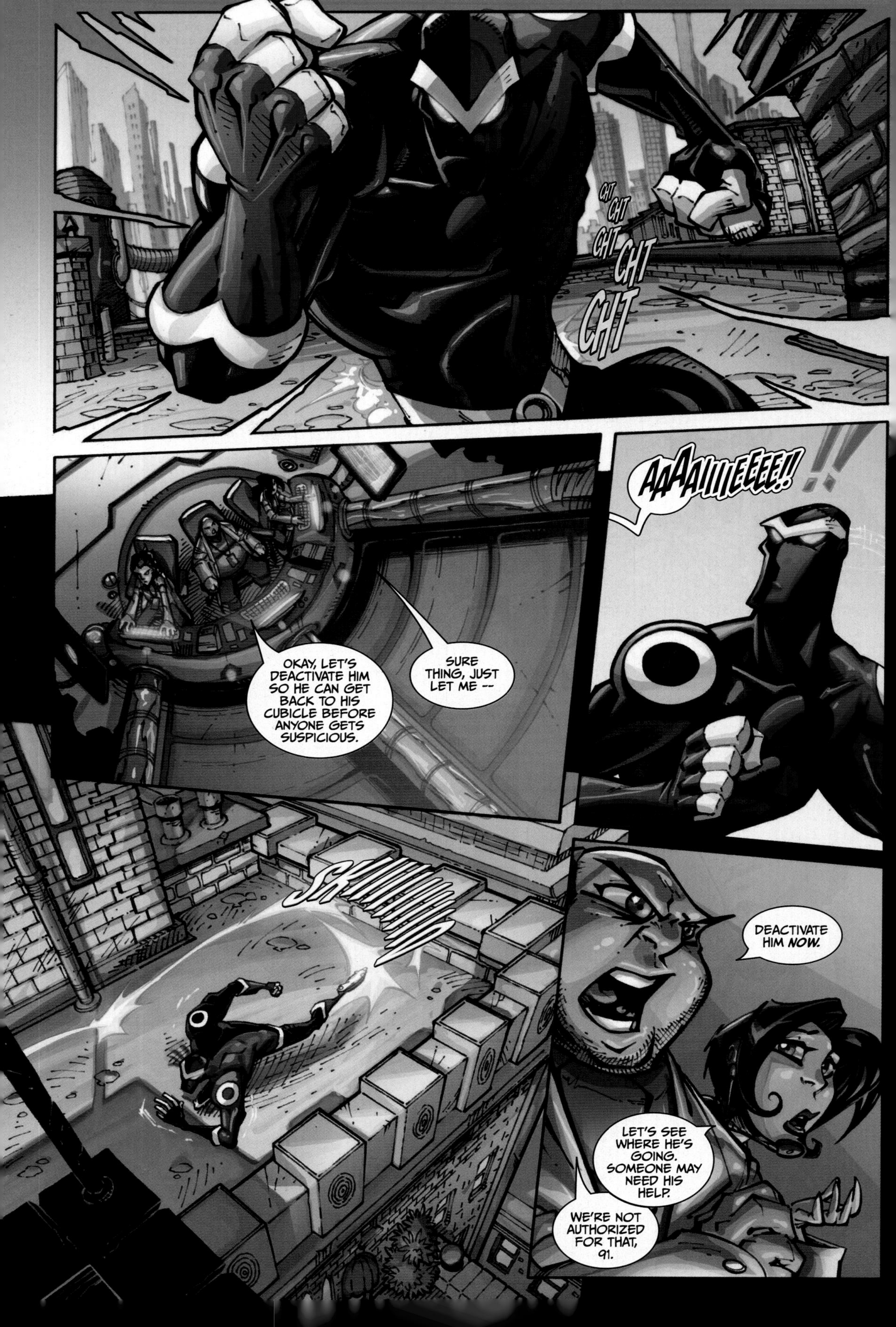
CHT CHT CHT CHT CHT
OKAY, LET'S DEACTIVATE HIM SO HE CAN GET BACK TO HIS CUBICLE BEFORE ANYONE GETS SUSPICIOUS.
SURE THING, JUST LET ME --
AAAAIIIIEEEE!! !!
SKIIIIIII
DEACTIVATE HIM NOW.
WE'RE NOT AUTHORIZED FOR THAT, 91.
LET'S SEE WHERE HE'S GOING. SOMEONE MAY NEED HIS HELP.

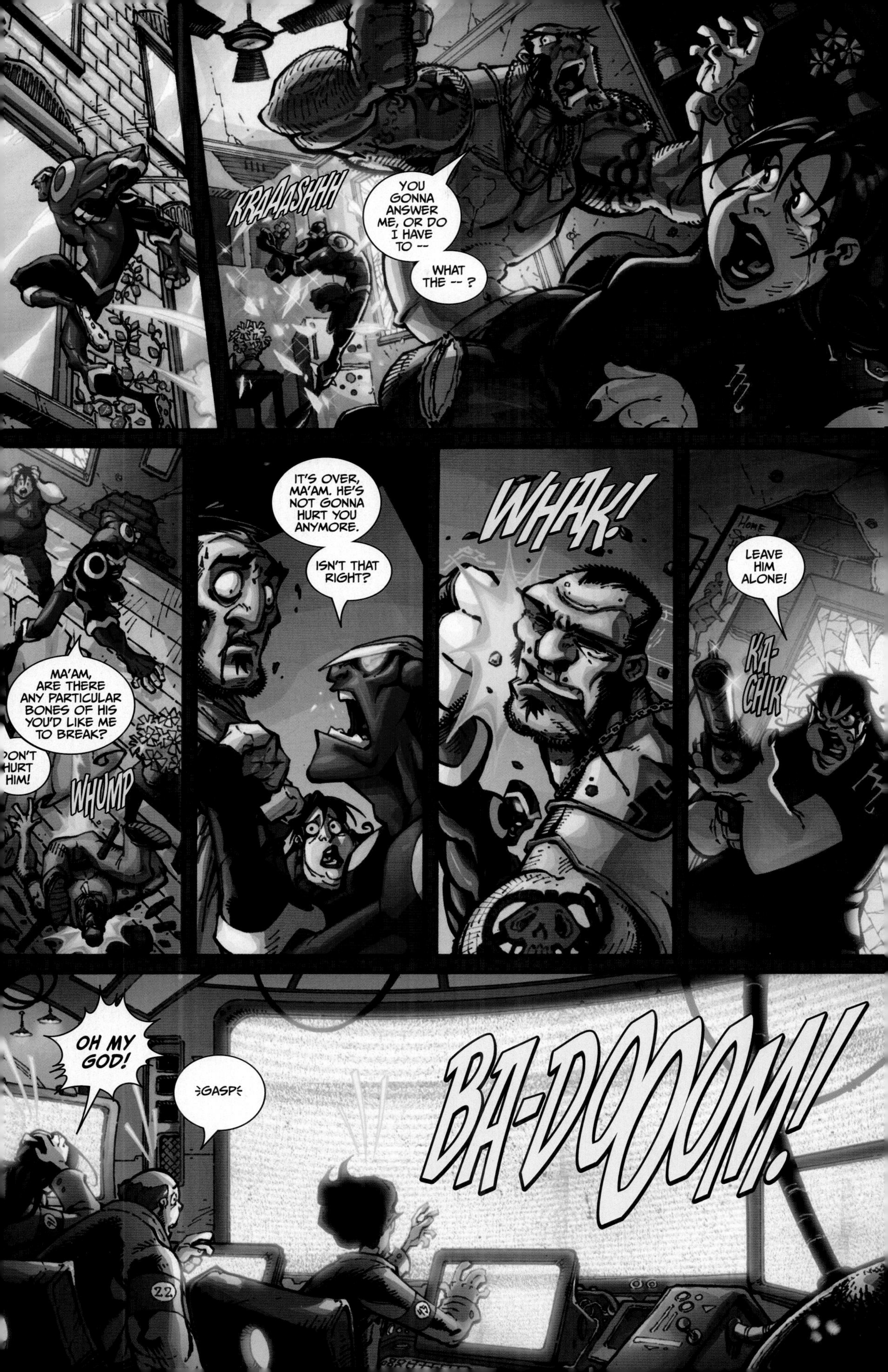
KRAAASHHH
YOU GONNA ANSWER ME, OR DO I HAVE TO --
WHAT THE -- ?
MA'AM, ARE THERE ANY PARTICULAR BONES OF HIS YOU'D LIKE ME TO BREAK?
DON'T HURT HIM!
WHUMP
IT'S OVER, MA'AM. HE'S NOT GONNA HURT YOU ANYMORE.
ISN'T THAT RIGHT?
WHAK!
LEAVE HIM ALONE!
KA-CHIK
OH MY GOD!
GASP
BA-DOOOM!

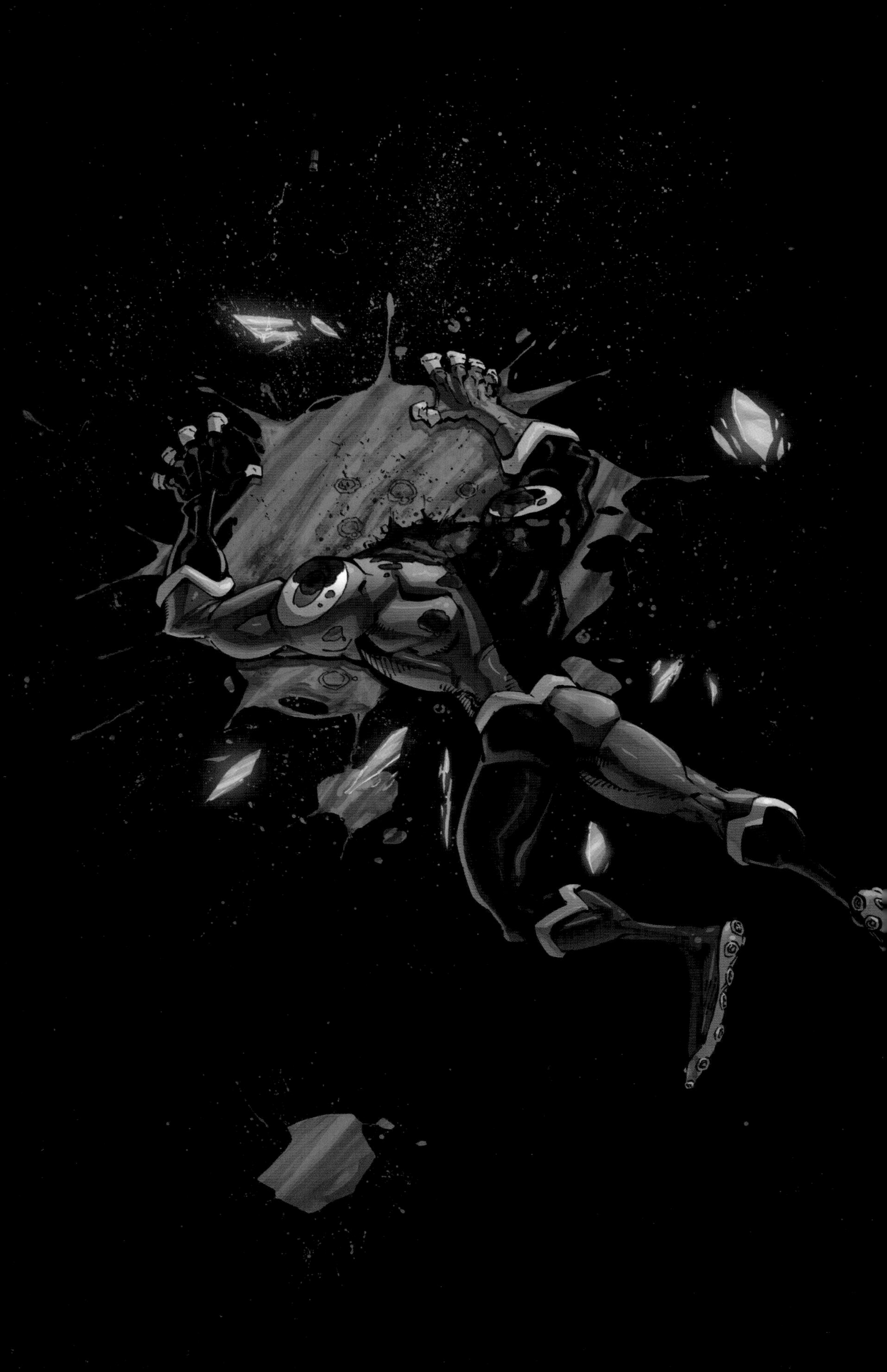

CHAPTER TWO

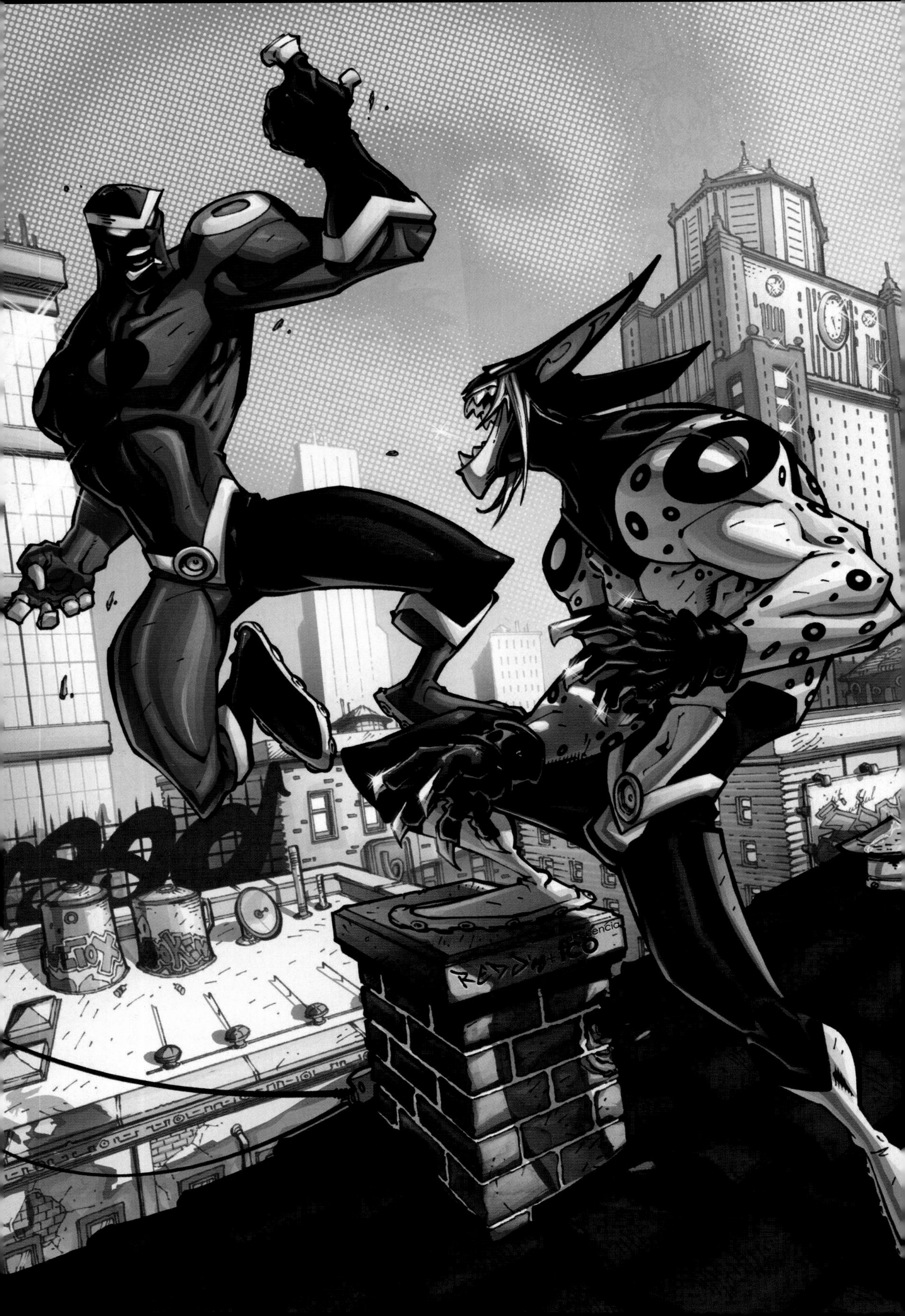

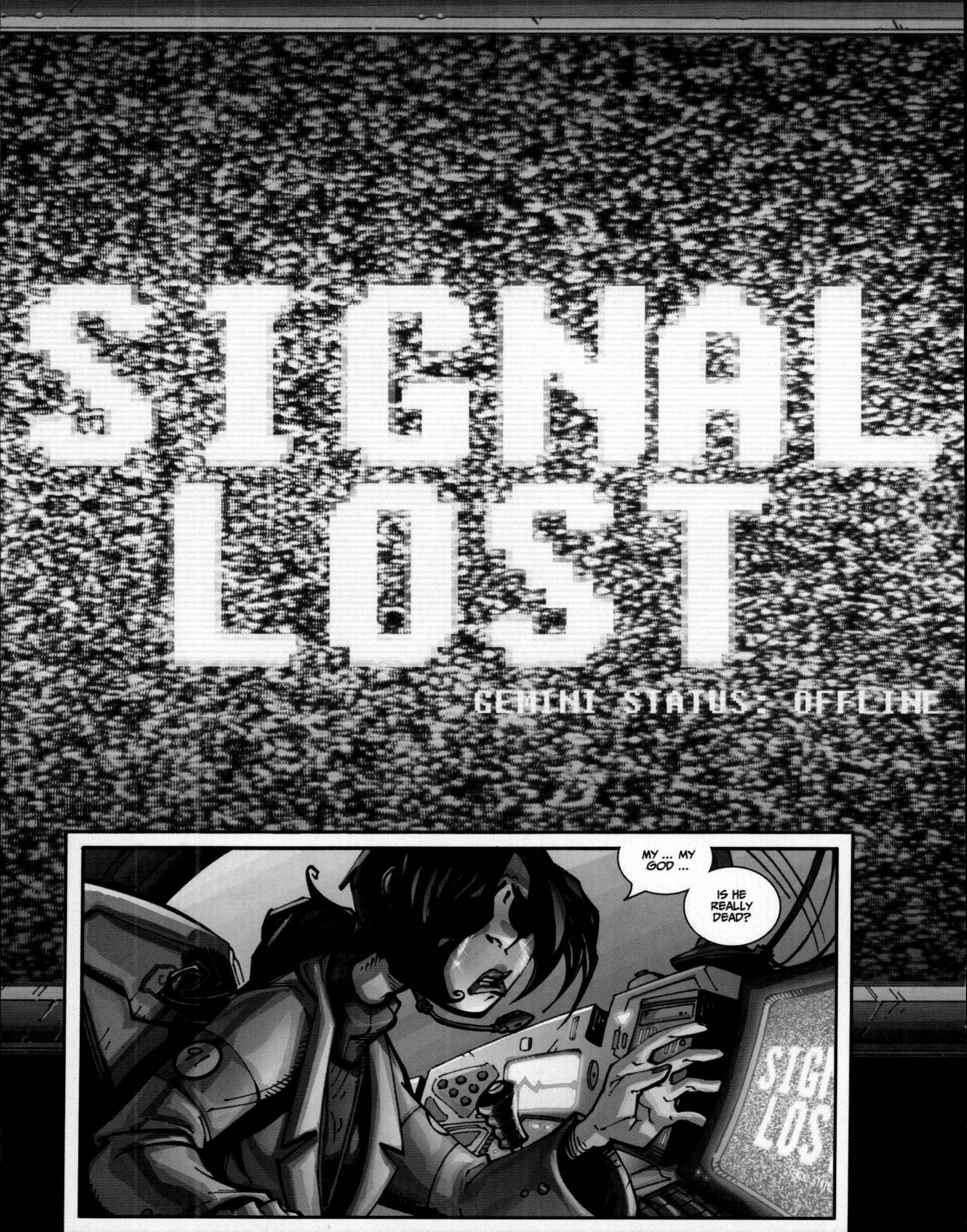
SIGNAL LOST
GEMINI STATUS: OFFLINE
MY ... MY GOD ...
IS HE REALLY DEAD?
SIGN LOS

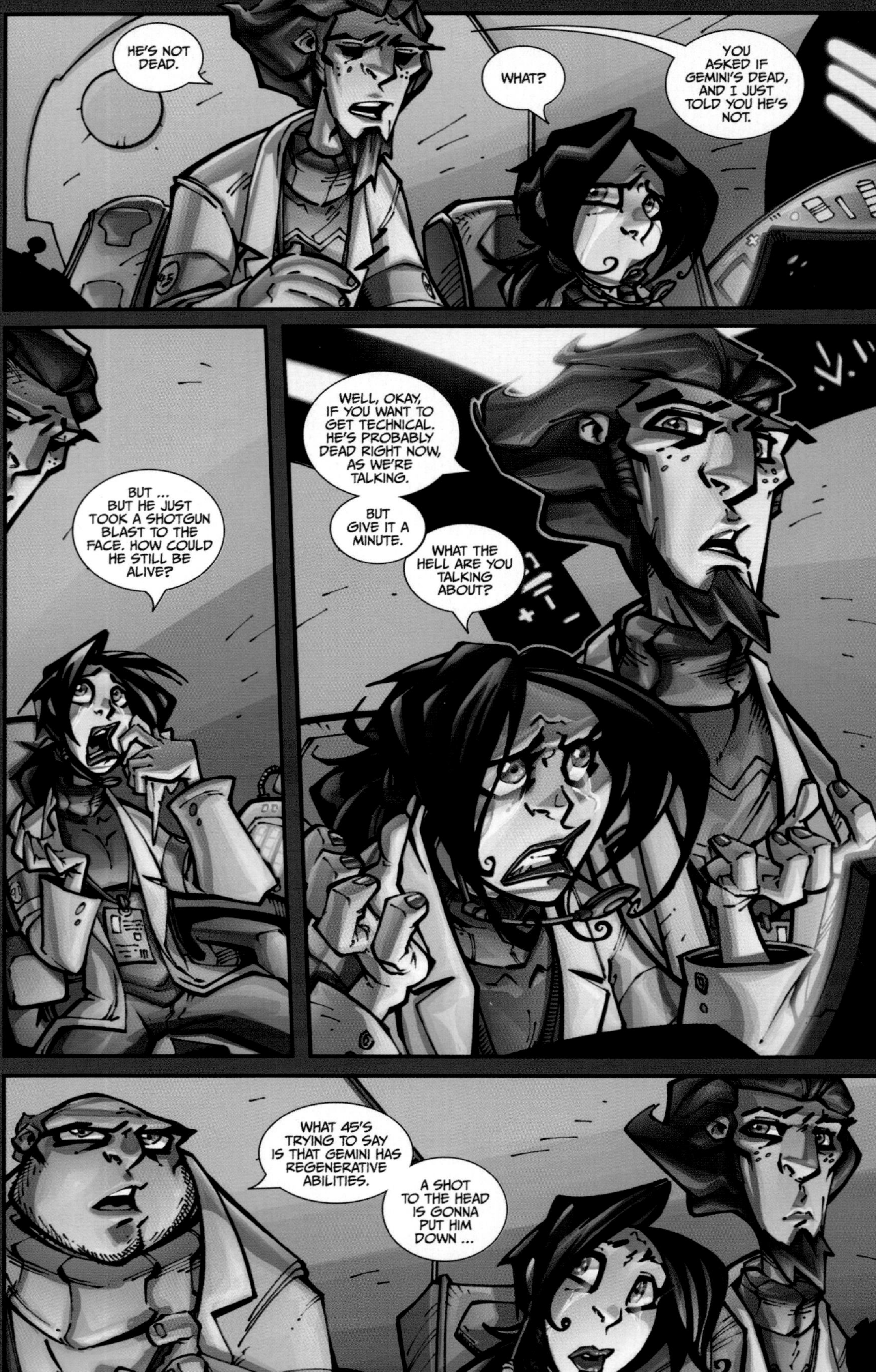
HE'S NOT DEAD.
WHAT?
YOU ASKED IF GEMINI'S DEAD, AND I JUST TOLD YOU HE'S NOT.
BUT ... BUT HE JUST TOOK A SHOTGUN BLAST TO THE FACE. HOW COULD HE STILL BE ALIVE?
WELL, OKAY, IF YOU WANT TO GET TECHNICAL. HE'S PROBABLY DEAD RIGHT NOW, AS WE'RE TALKING.
BUT GIVE IT A MINUTE.
WHAT THE HELL ARE YOU TALKING ABOUT?
WHAT 45'S TRYING TO SAY IS THAT GEMINI HAS REGENERATIVE ABILITIES.
A SHOT TO THE HEAD IS GONNA PUT HIM DOWN ...

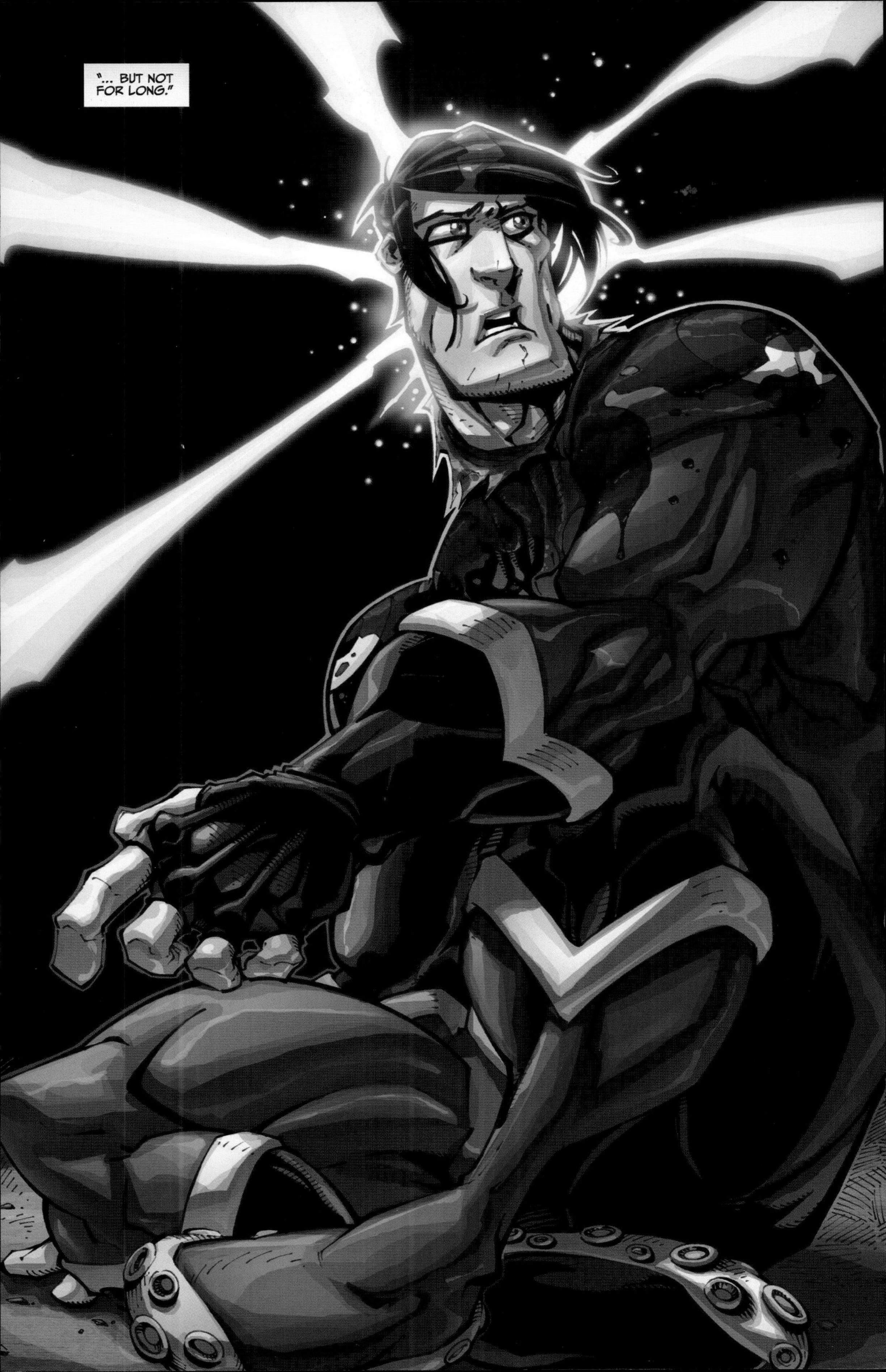
"... BUT NOT FOR LONG."

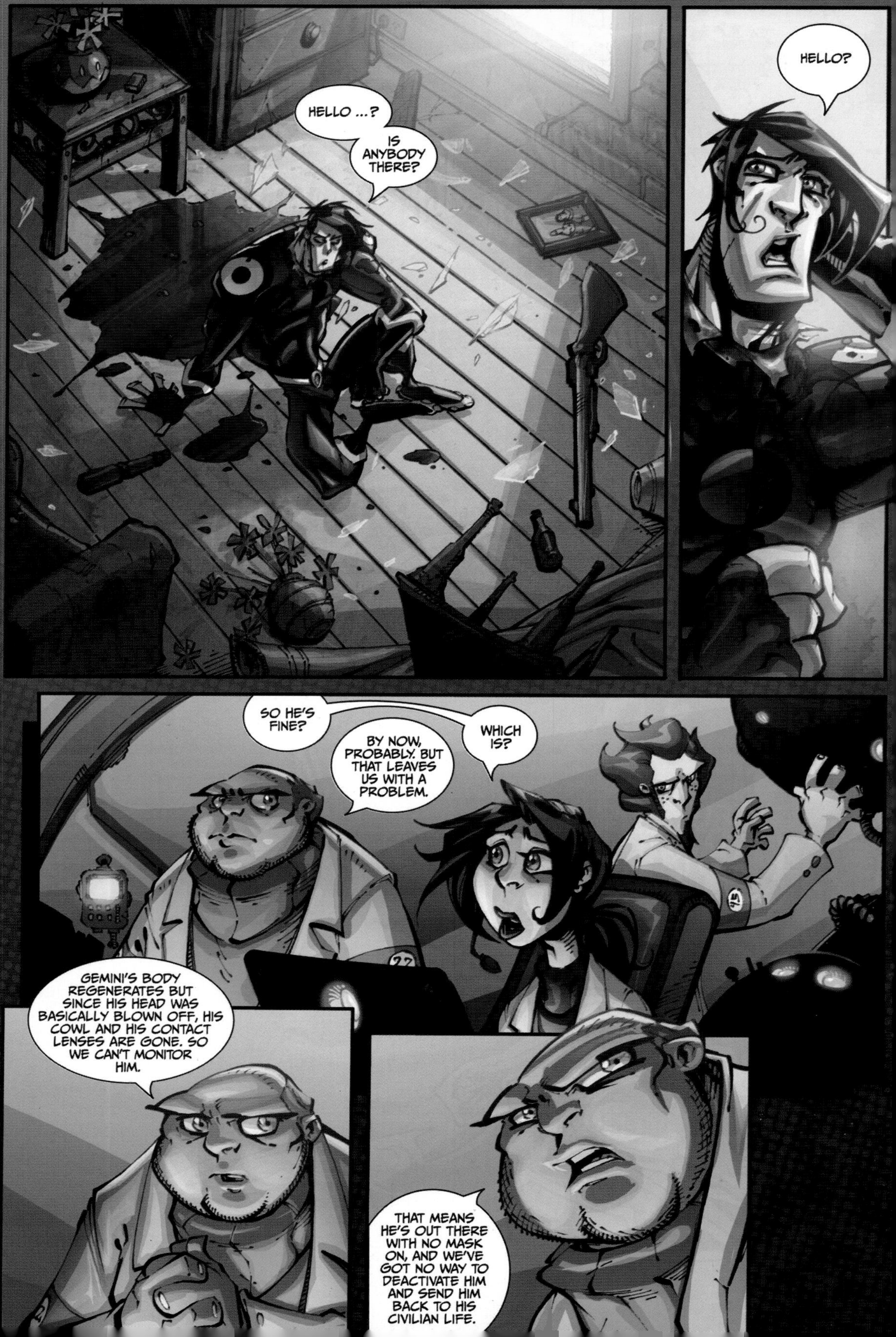
HELLO ...?
IS ANYBODY THERE?
HELLO?
SO HE'S FINE?
BY NOW, PROBABLY. BUT THAT LEAVES US WITH A PROBLEM.
WHICH IS?
GEMINI'S BODY REGENERATES BUT SINCE HIS HEAD WAS BASICALLY BLOWN OFF, HIS COWL AND HIS CONTACT LENSES ARE GONE. SO WE CAN'T MONITOR HIM.
THAT MEANS HE'S OUT THERE WITH NO MASK ON, AND WE'VE GOT NO WAY TO DEACTIVATE HIM AND SEND HIM BACK TO HIS CIVILIAN LIFE.

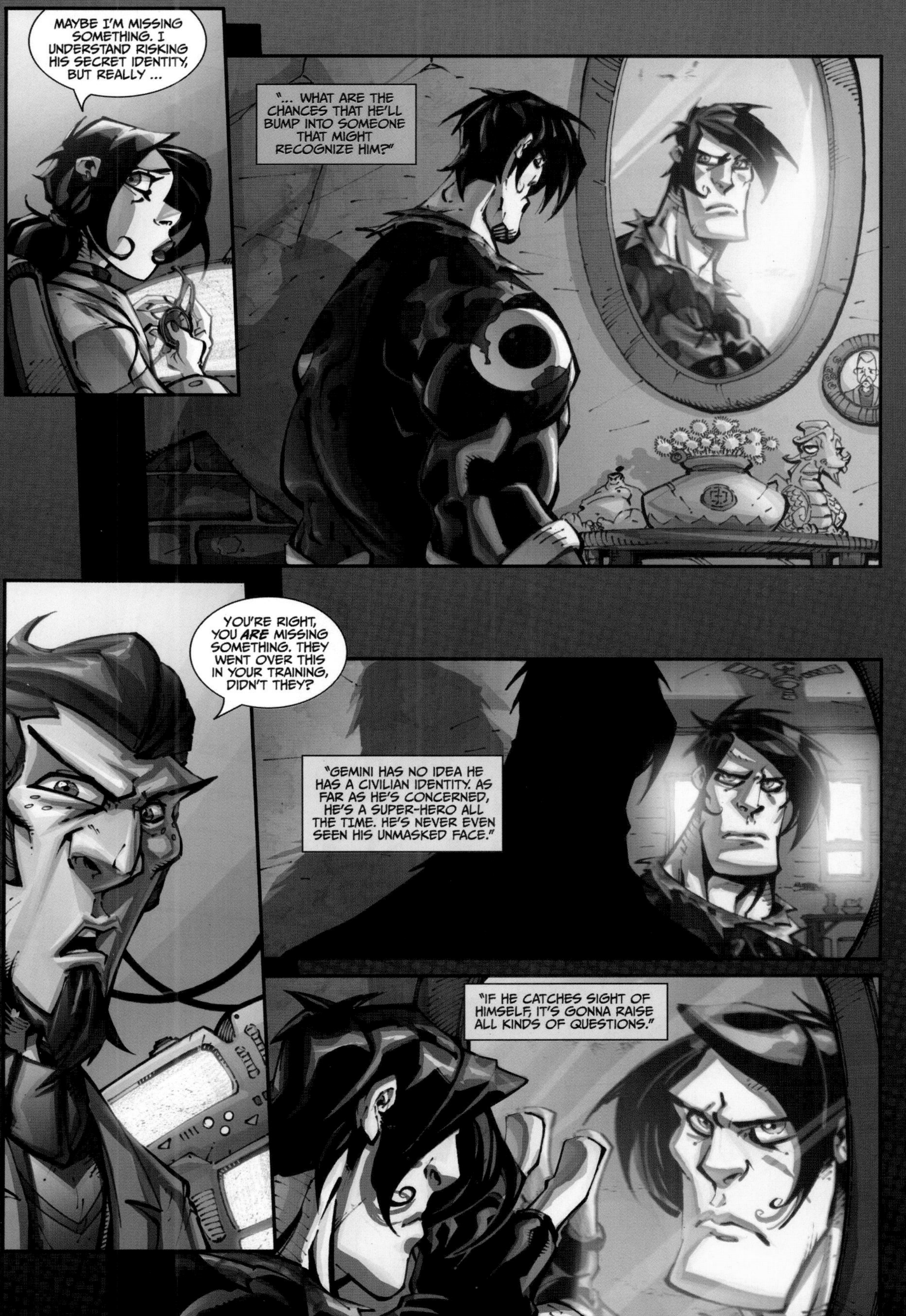
MAYBE I'M MISSING SOMETHING. I UNDERSTAND RISKING HIS SECRET IDENTITY, BUT REALLY ...
"... WHAT ARE THE CHANCES THAT HE'LL BUMP INTO SOMEONE THAT MIGHT RECOGNIZE HIM?"
YOU'RE RIGHT, YOU *ARE* MISSING SOMETHING. THEY WENT OVER THIS IN YOUR TRAINING, DIDN'T THEY?
"GEMINI HAS NO IDEA HE HAS A CIVILIAN IDENTITY. AS FAR AS HE'S CONCERNED, HE'S A SUPER-HERO ALL THE TIME. HE'S NEVER EVEN SEEN HIS UNMASKED FACE."
"IF HE CATCHES SIGHT OF HIMSELF, IT'S GONNA RAISE ALL KINDS OF QUESTIONS."

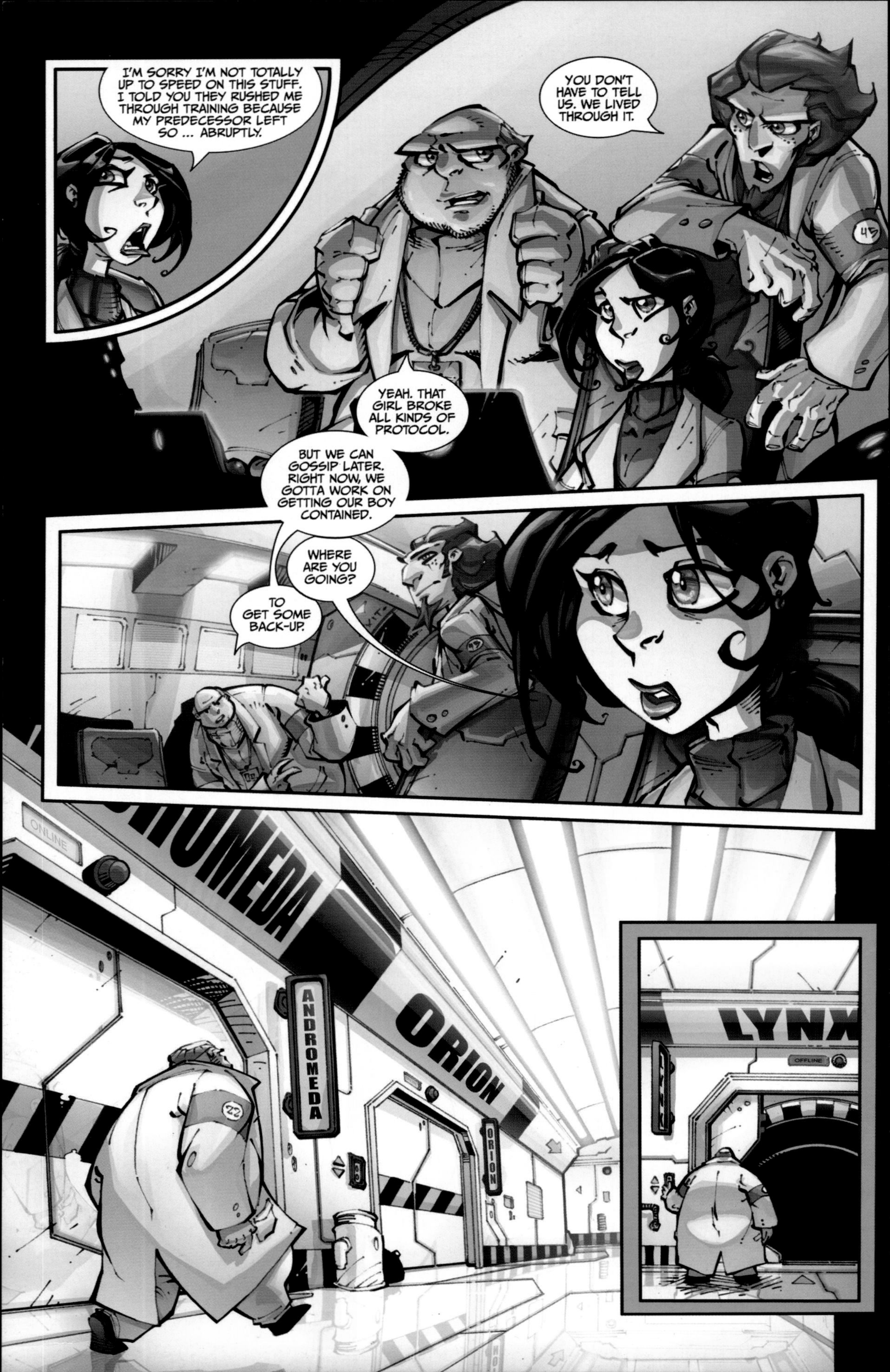
I'M SORRY I'M NOT TOTALLY UP TO SPEED ON THIS STUFF. I TOLD YOU THEY RUSHED ME THROUGH TRAINING BECAUSE MY PREDECESSOR LEFT SO ... ABRUPTLY.
YOU DON'T HAVE TO TELL US. WE LIVED THROUGH IT.
45
YEAH. THAT GIRL BROKE ALL KINDS OF PROTOCOL.
BUT WE CAN GOSSIP LATER. RIGHT NOW, WE GOTTA WORK ON GETTING OUR BOY CONTAINED.
WHERE ARE YOU GOING?
TO GET SOME BACK-UP.
ONLINE
ANDROMEDA
ORION
LYNX
OFFLINE

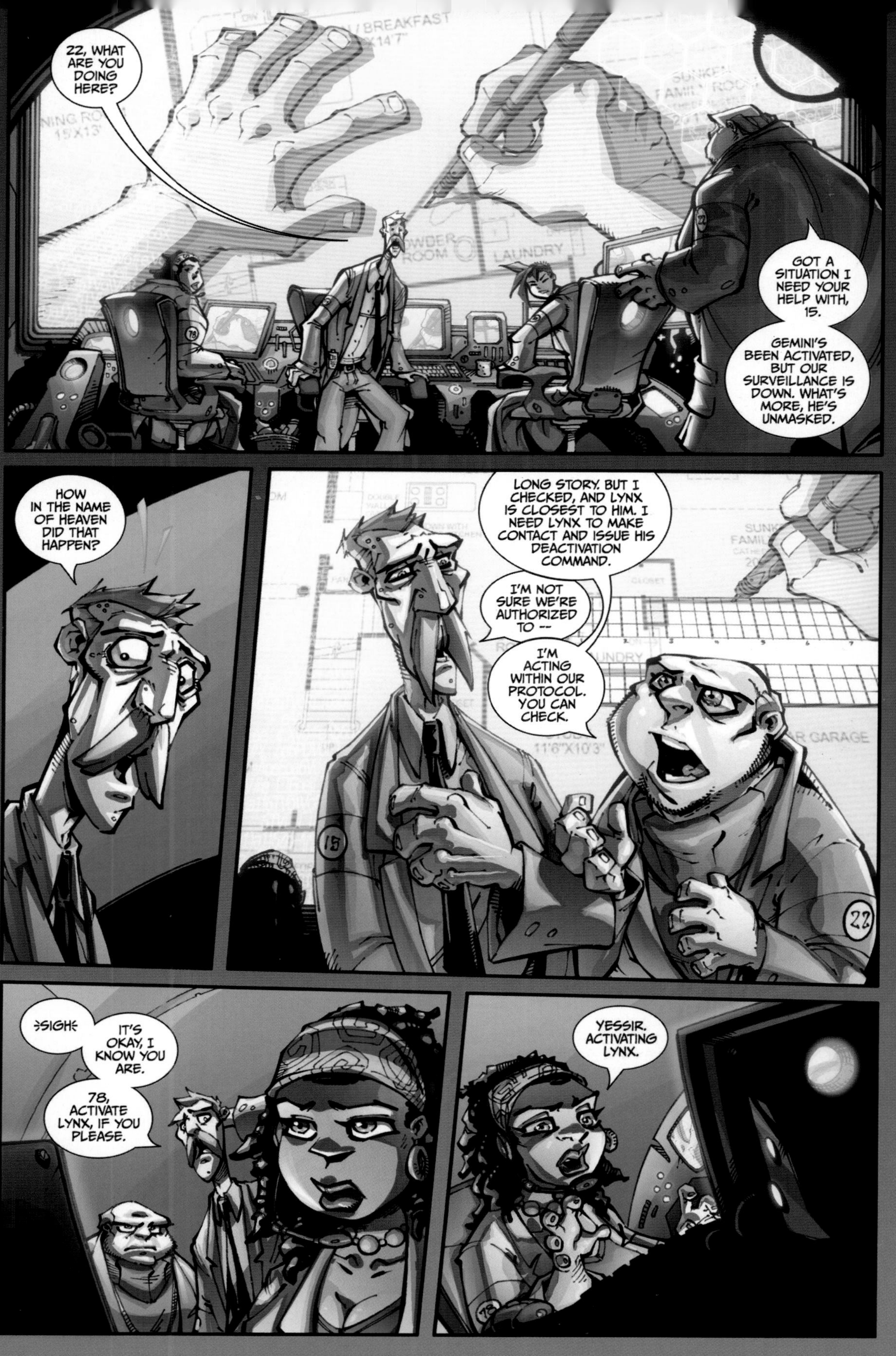
22, WHAT ARE YOU DOING HERE?
GOT A SITUATION I NEED YOUR HELP WITH, 15.
GEMINI'S BEEN ACTIVATED, BUT OUR SURVEILLANCE IS DOWN. WHAT'S MORE, HE'S UNMASKED.
HOW IN THE NAME OF HEAVEN DID THAT HAPPEN?
LONG STORY. BUT I CHECKED, AND LYNX IS CLOSEST TO HIM. I NEED LYNX TO MAKE CONTACT AND ISSUE HIS DEACTIVATION COMMAND.
I'M NOT SURE WE'RE AUTHORIZED TO --
I'M ACTING WITHIN OUR PROTOCOL. YOU CAN CHECK.
SIGH
IT'S OKAY, I KNOW YOU ARE.
78, ACTIVATE LYNX, IF YOU PLEASE.
YESSIR. ACTIVATING LYNX.

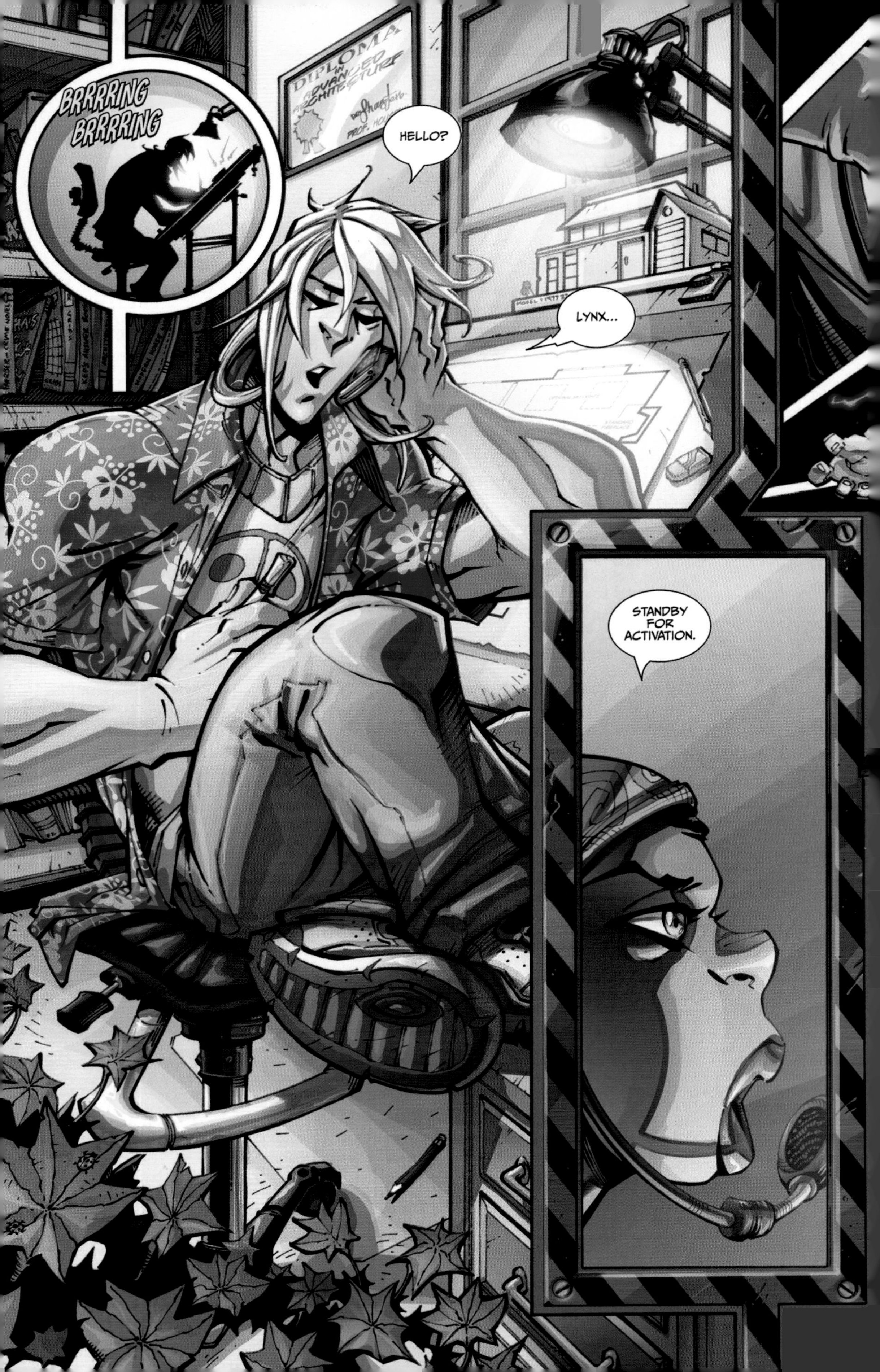
BRRRRING
BRRRRING
DIPLOMA IN ADVANCED ARCHITECTURE
HELLO?
LYNX...
STANDBY FOR ACTIVATION.

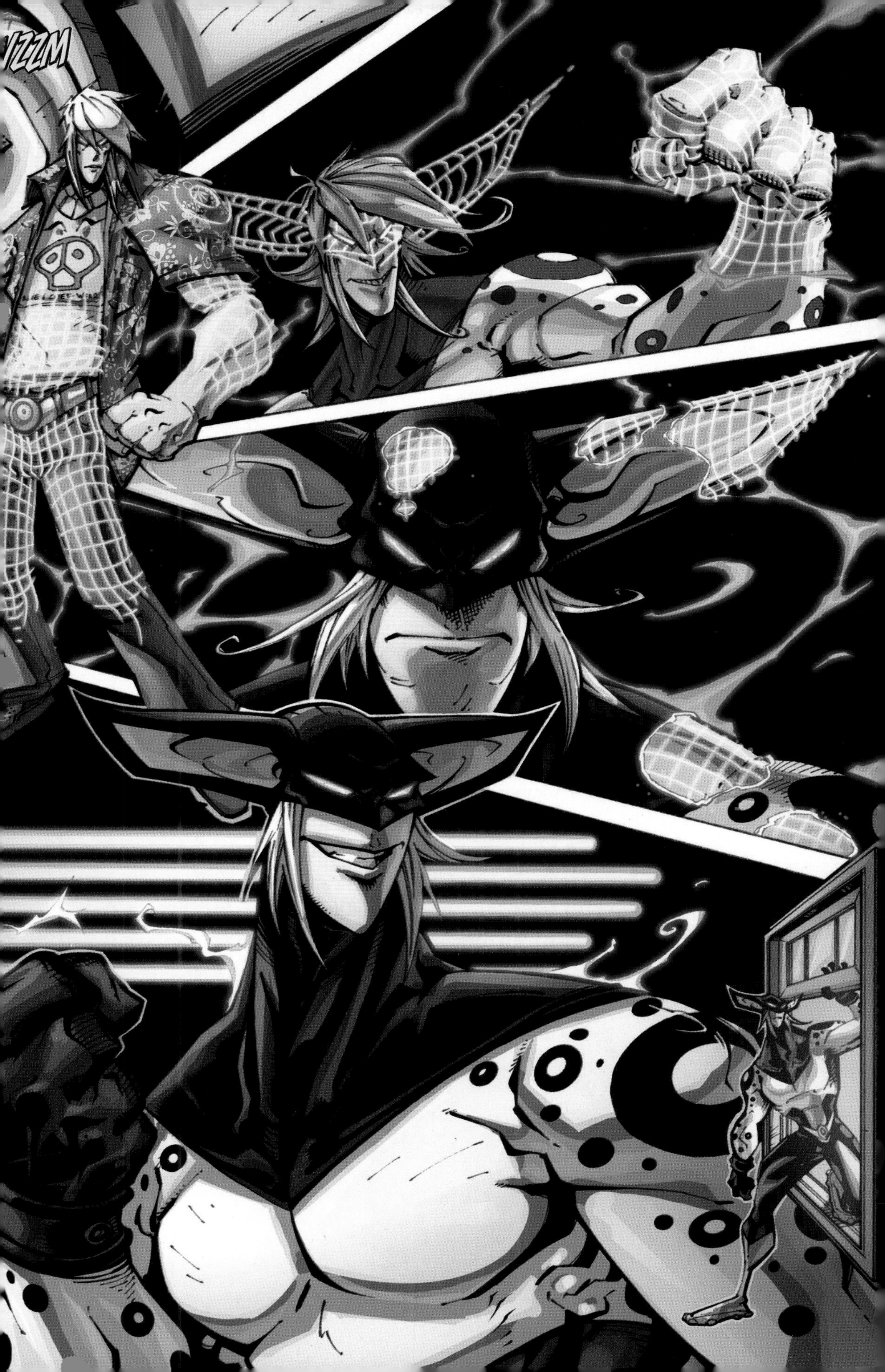
IZZM

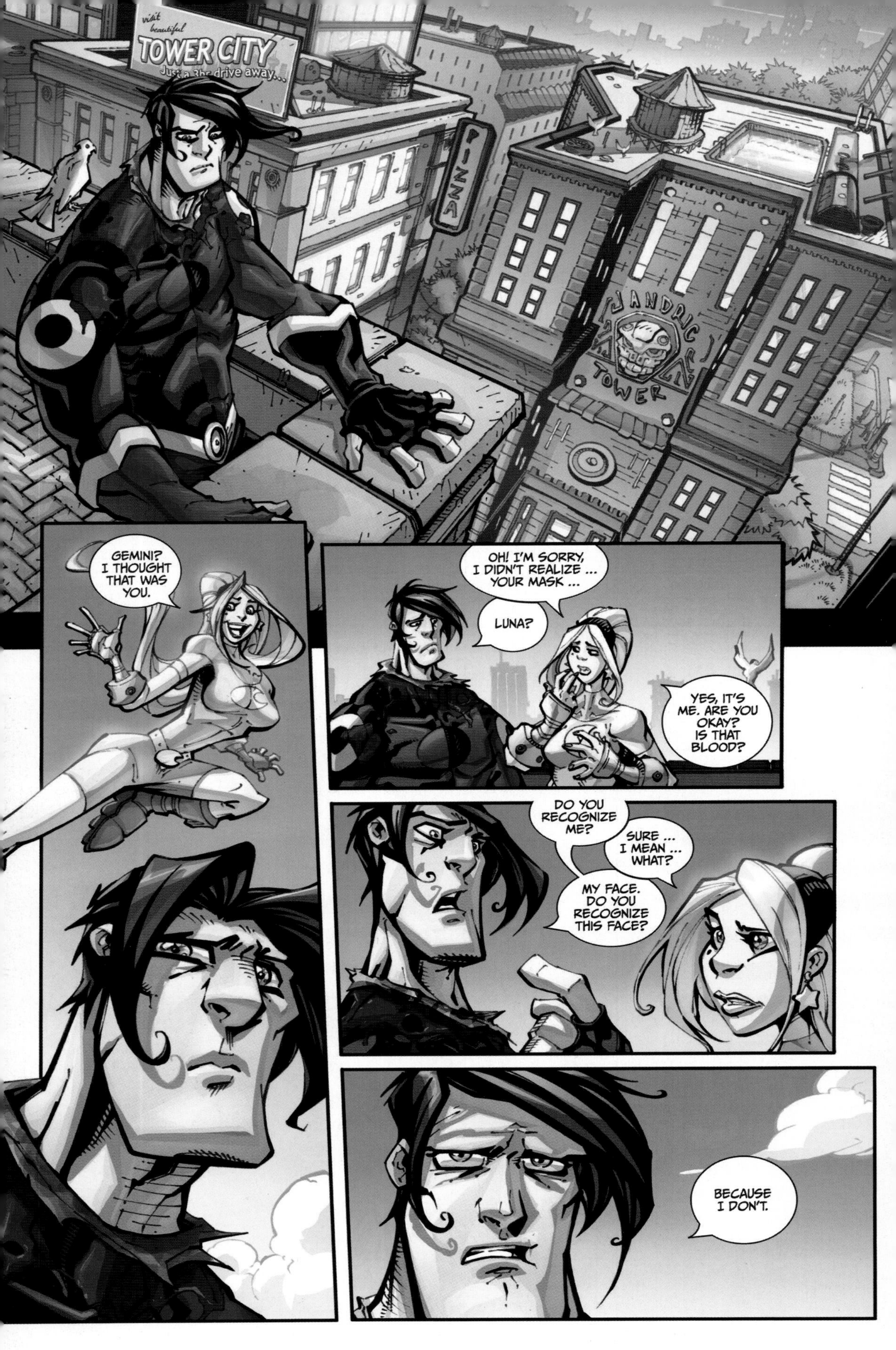
visit beautiful
TOWER CITY
Just a 3hr drive away...
PIZZA
JANDRIC TOWER
GEMINI? I THOUGHT THAT WAS YOU.
OH! I'M SORRY, I DIDN'T REALIZE ... YOUR MASK ...
LUNA?
YES, IT'S ME. ARE YOU OKAY? IS THAT BLOOD?
DO YOU RECOGNIZE ME?
SURE ... I MEAN ... WHAT?
MY FACE. DO YOU RECOGNIZE THIS FACE?
BECAUSE I DON'T.

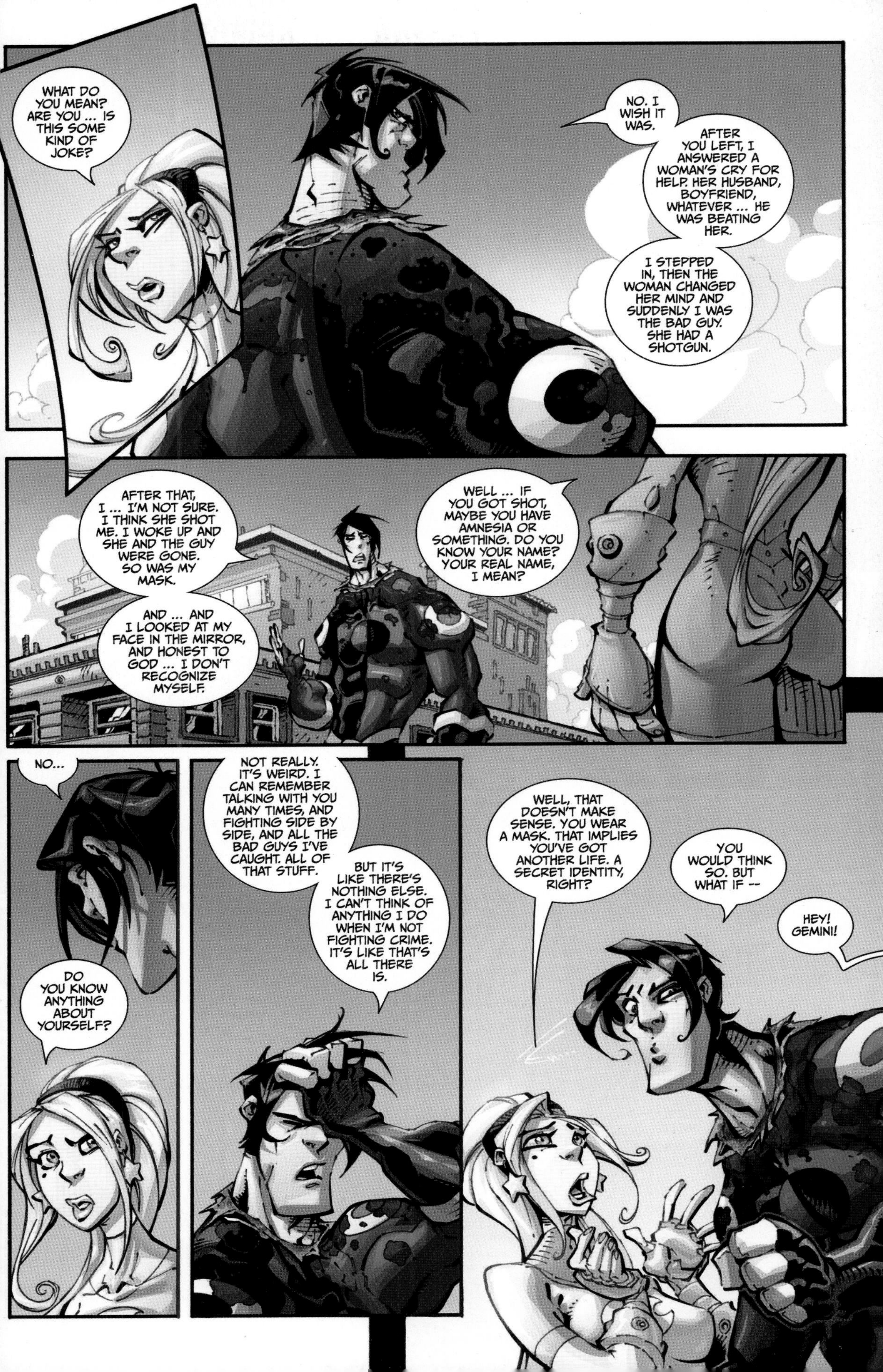
WHAT DO YOU MEAN? ARE YOU ... IS THIS SOME KIND OF JOKE?
NO. I WISH IT WAS.
AFTER YOU LEFT, I ANSWERED A WOMAN'S CRY FOR HELP. HER HUSBAND, BOYFRIEND, WHATEVER ... HE WAS BEATING HER.
I STEPPED IN, THEN THE WOMAN CHANGED HER MIND AND SUDDENLY I WAS THE BAD GUY. SHE HAD A SHOTGUN.
AFTER THAT, I ... I'M NOT SURE. I THINK SHE SHOT ME. I WOKE UP AND SHE AND THE GUY WERE GONE. SO WAS MY MASK.
AND ... AND I LOOKED AT MY FACE IN THE MIRROR, AND HONEST TO GOD ... I DON'T RECOGNIZE MYSELF.
WELL ... IF YOU GOT SHOT, MAYBE YOU HAVE AMNESIA OR SOMETHING. DO YOU KNOW YOUR NAME? YOUR REAL NAME, I MEAN?
NO...
DO YOU KNOW ANYTHING ABOUT YOURSELF?
NOT REALLY. IT'S WEIRD. I CAN REMEMBER TALKING WITH YOU MANY TIMES, AND FIGHTING SIDE BY SIDE, AND ALL THE BAD GUYS I'VE CAUGHT. ALL OF THAT STUFF.
BUT IT'S LIKE THERE'S NOTHING ELSE. I CAN'T THINK OF ANYTHING I DO WHEN I'M NOT FIGHTING CRIME. IT'S LIKE THAT'S ALL THERE IS.
WELL, THAT DOESN'T MAKE SENSE. YOU WEAR A MASK. THAT IMPLIES YOU'VE GOT ANOTHER LIFE. A SECRET IDENTITY, RIGHT?
YOU WOULD THINK SO. BUT WHAT IF --
HEY! GEMINI!

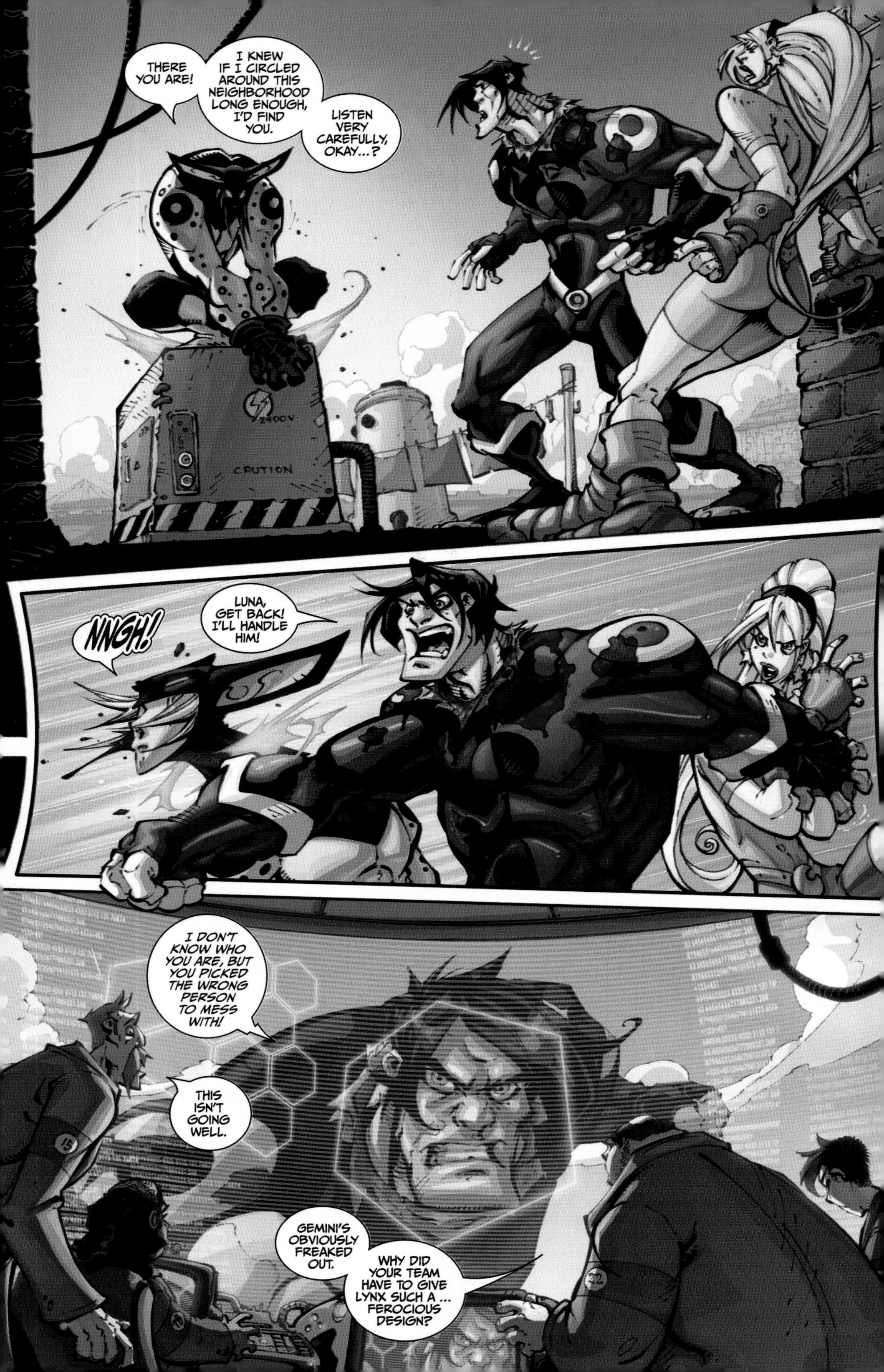
THERE YOU ARE!
I KNEW IF I CIRCLED AROUND THIS NEIGHBORHOOD LONG ENOUGH, I'D FIND YOU.
LISTEN VERY CAREFULLY, OKAY...?
2400V
CAUTION
NNGH!
LUNA, GET BACK! I'LL HANDLE HIM!
I DON'T KNOW WHO YOU ARE, BUT YOU PICKED THE WRONG PERSON TO MESS WITH!
THIS ISN'T GOING WELL.
GEMINI'S OBVIOUSLY FREAKED OUT.
WHY DID YOUR TEAM HAVE TO GIVE LYNX SUCH A ... FEROCIOUS DESIGN?

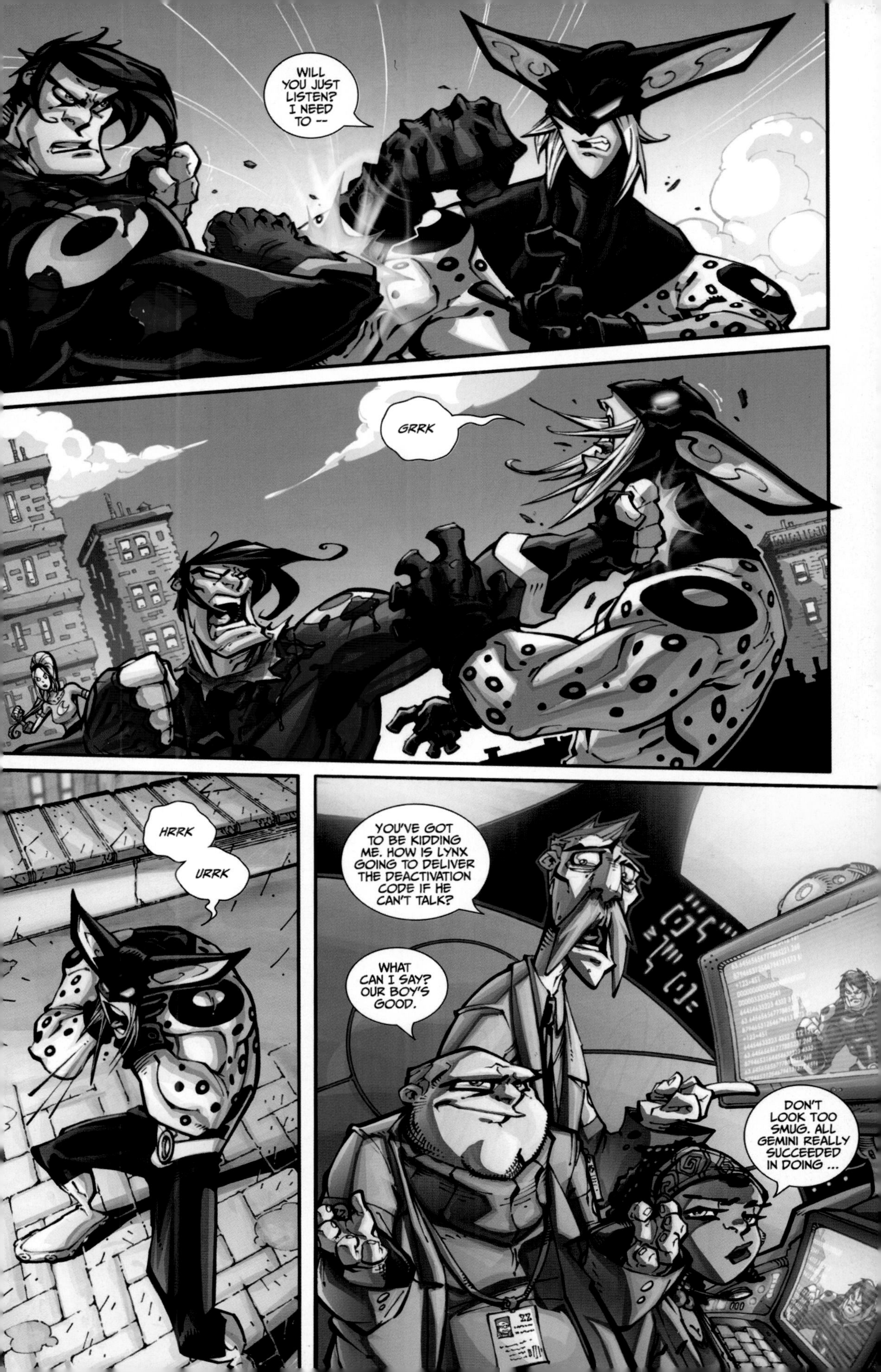
WILL YOU JUST LISTEN? I NEED TO --
GRRK
HRRK
URRK
YOU'VE GOT TO BE KIDDING ME. HOW IS LYNX GOING TO DELIVER THE DEACTIVATION CODE IF HE CAN'T TALK?
WHAT CAN I SAY? OUR BOY'S GOOD.
DON'T LOOK TOO SMUG. ALL GEMINI REALLY SUCCEEDED IN DOING ...

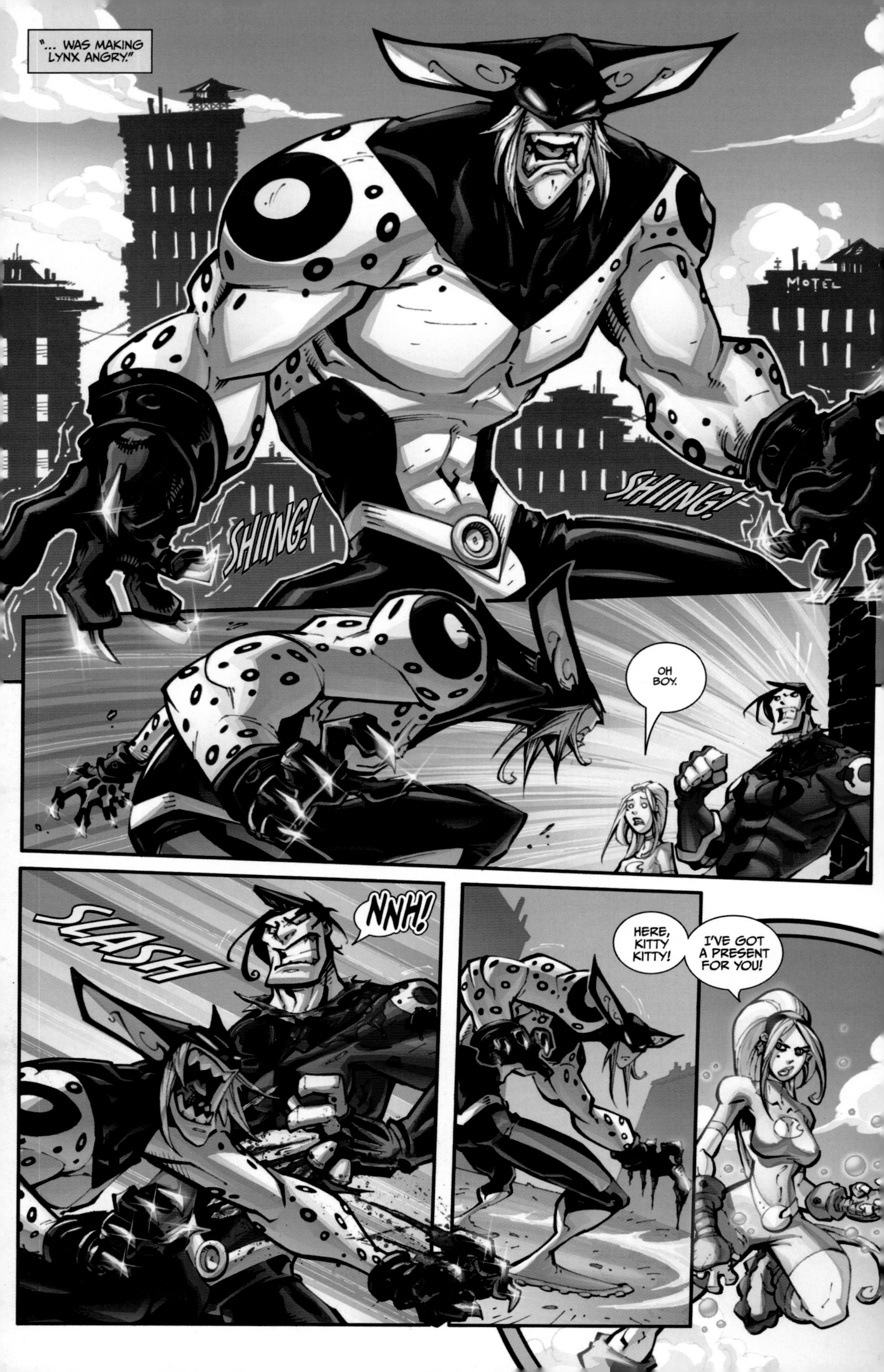
"... WAS MAKING LYNX ANGRY."
MOTEL
SHIING!
SHIING!
OH BOY.
SLASH
NNH!
HERE, KITTY KITTY!
I'VE GOT A PRESENT FOR YOU!

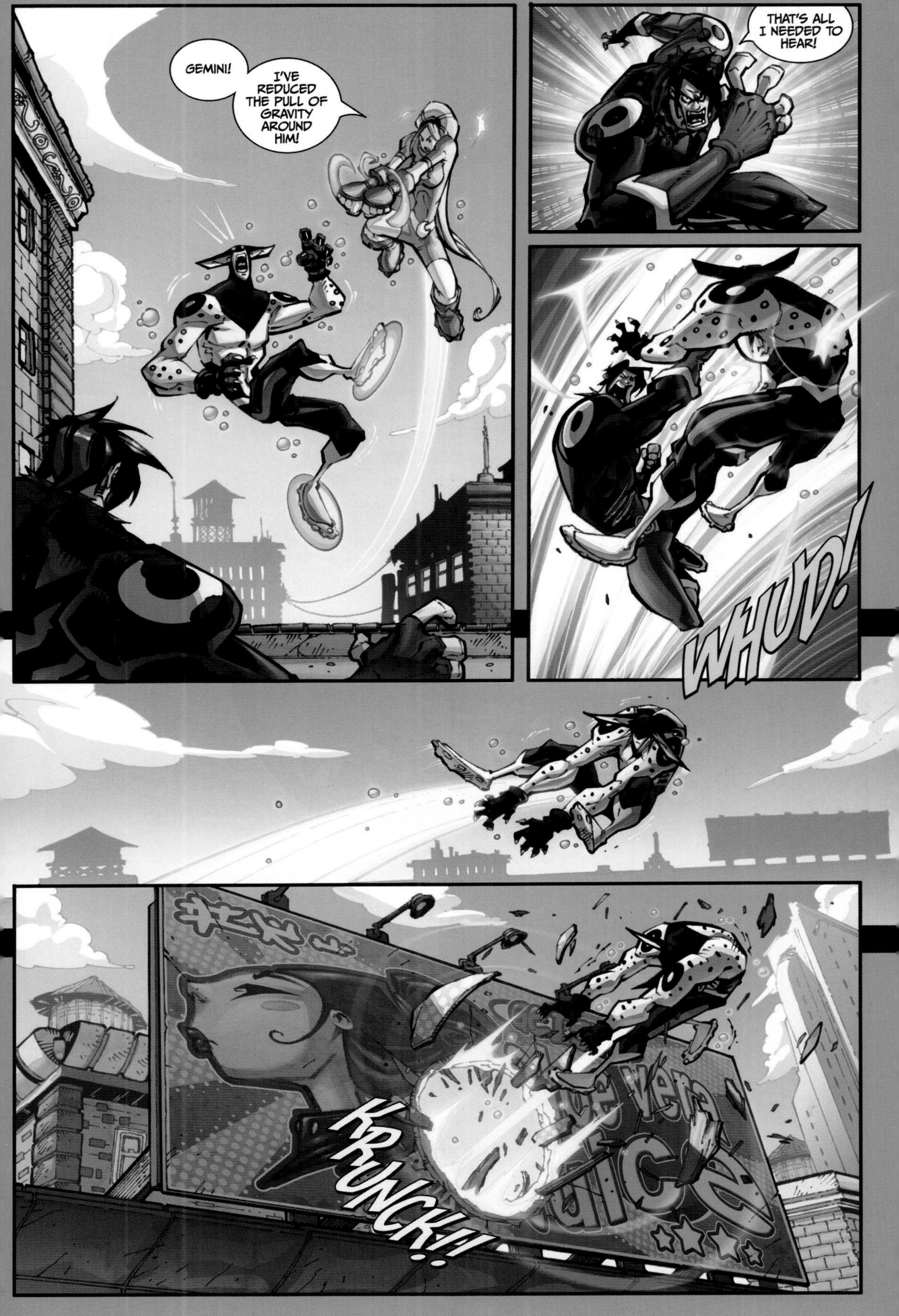

GEMINI!
I'VE REDUCED THE PULL OF GRAVITY AROUND HIM!
THAT'S ALL I NEEDED TO HEAR!
WHUD!
KRUNCH!!

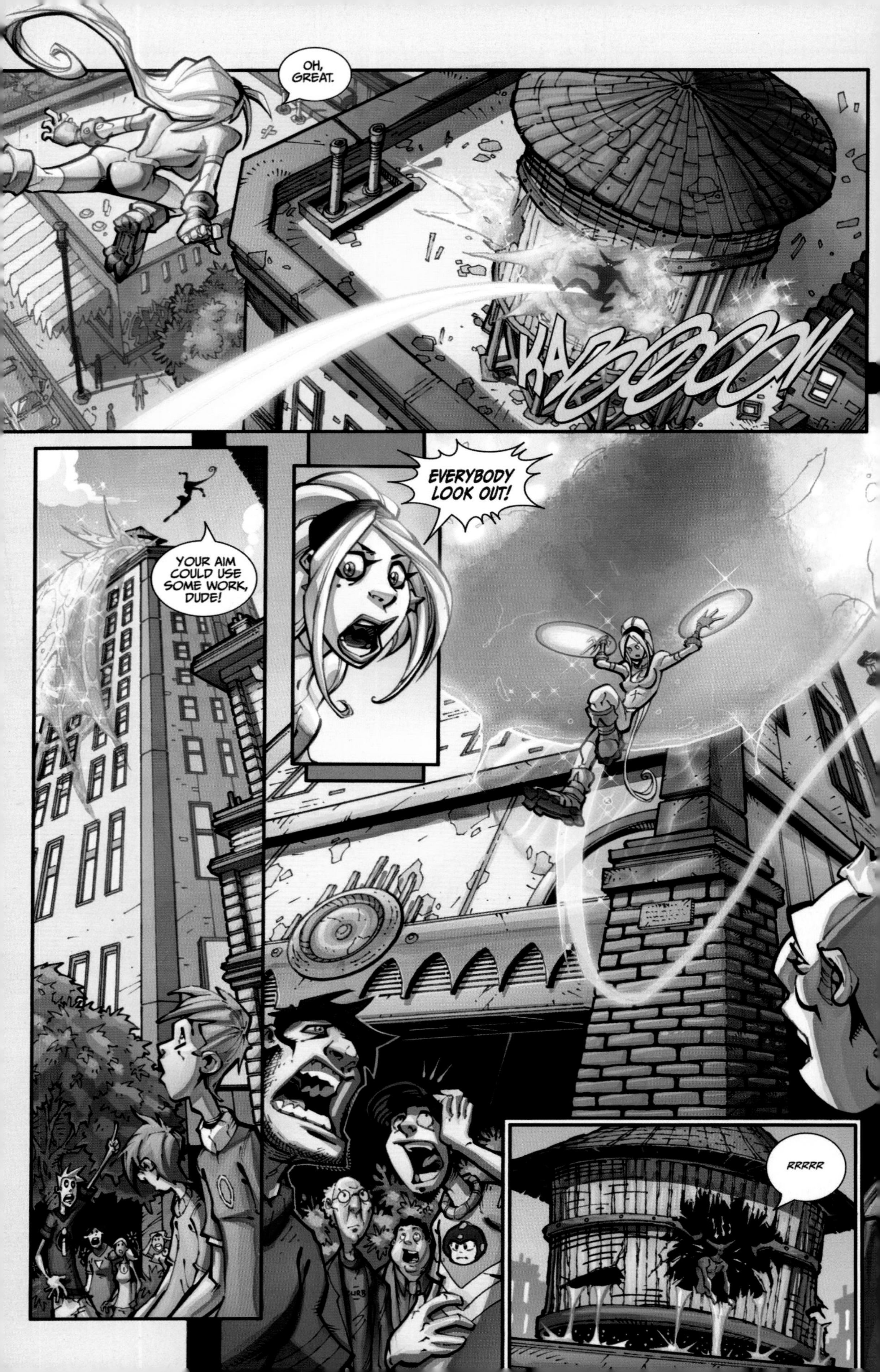
OH, GREAT.
KA-BOOOOM!
YOUR AIM COULD USE SOME WORK, DUDE!
EVERYBODY LOOK OUT!
RRRRR

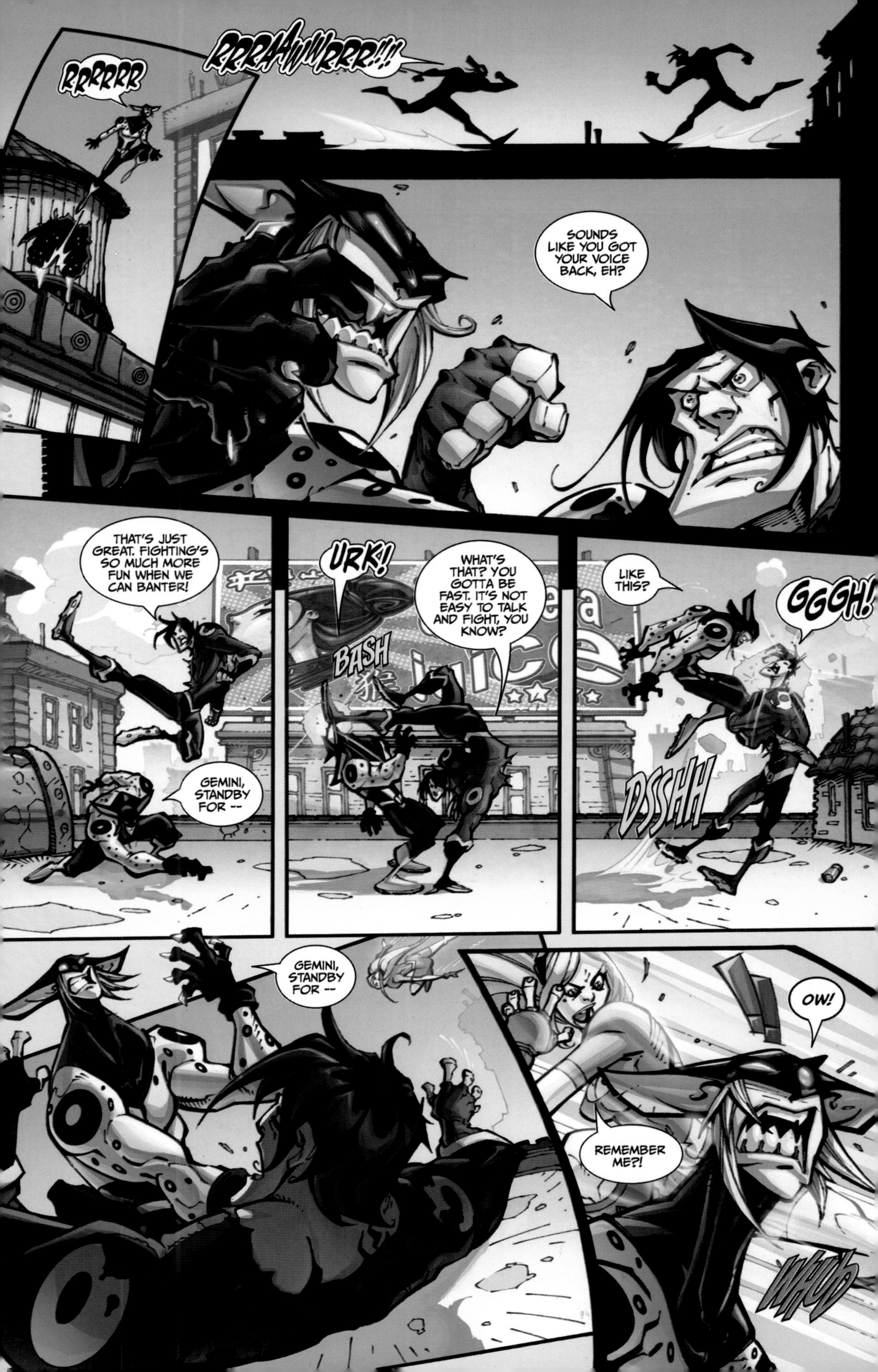
RRRRRR
RRRRAAWWRRRR!!!
SOUNDS LIKE YOU GOT YOUR VOICE BACK, EH?
THAT'S JUST GREAT. FIGHTING'S SO MUCH MORE FUN WHEN WE CAN BANTER!
GEMINI, STANDBY FOR --
URK!
BASH
WHAT'S THAT? YOU GOTTA BE FAST. IT'S NOT EASY TO TALK AND FIGHT, YOU KNOW?
LIKE THIS?
GGGH!
DSSHH
GEMINI, STANDBY FOR --
OW!
REMEMBER ME?!

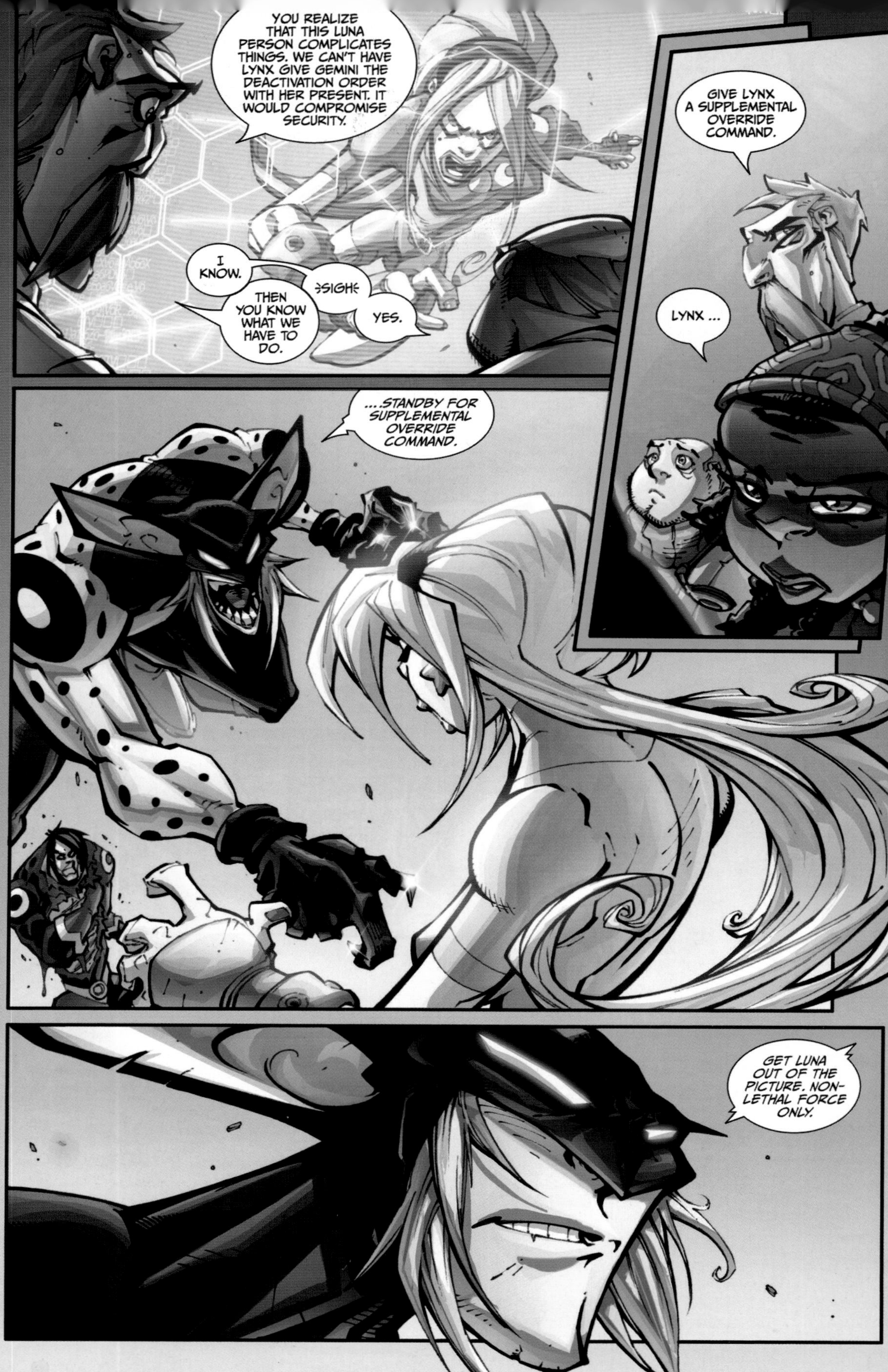
YOU REALIZE THAT THIS LUNA PERSON COMPLICATES THINGS. WE CAN'T HAVE LYNX GIVE GEMINI THE DEACTIVATION ORDER WITH HER PRESENT. IT WOULD COMPROMISE SECURITY.
I KNOW.
SIGH
THEN YOU KNOW WHAT WE HAVE TO DO.
YES.
GIVE LYNX A SUPPLEMENTAL OVERRIDE COMMAND.
LYNX ...
...STANDBY FOR SUPPLEMENTAL OVERRIDE COMMAND.
GET LUNA OUT OF THE PICTURE. NON-LETHAL FORCE ONLY.

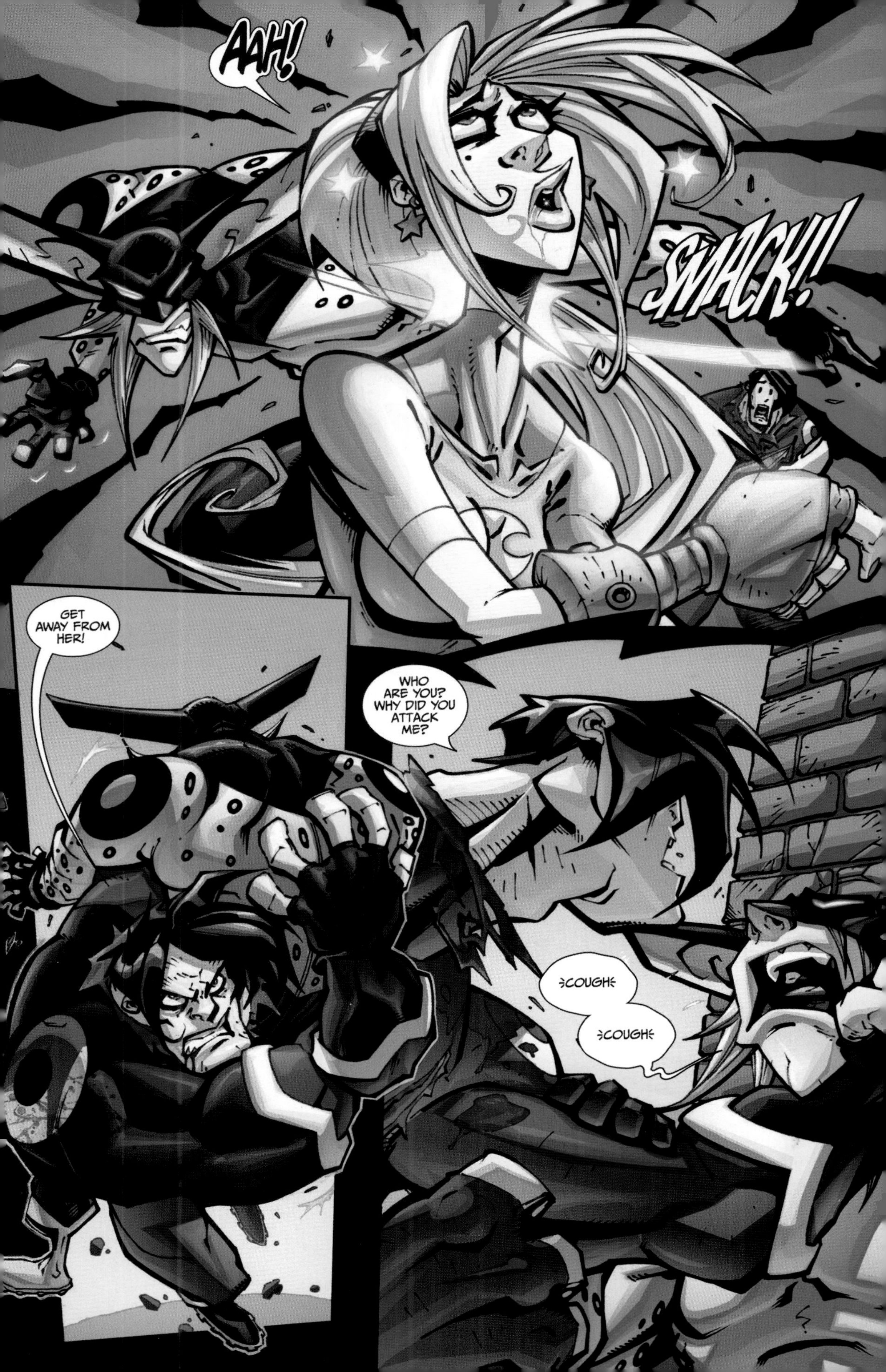
AAH!
SMACK!!
GET AWAY FROM HER!
WHO ARE YOU? WHY DID YOU ATTACK ME?
COUGH
COUGH

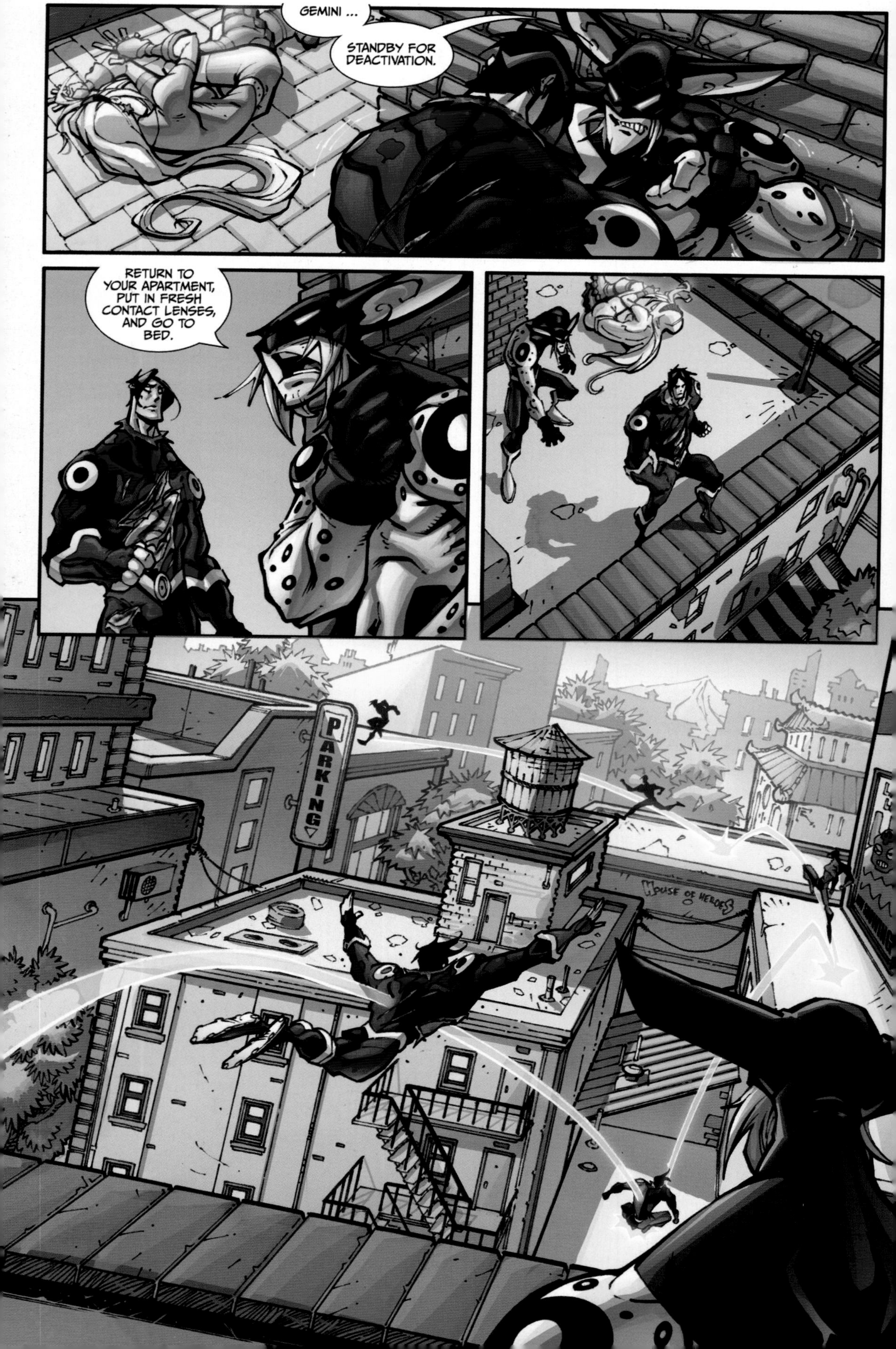
GEMINI ...
STANDBY FOR DEACTIVATION.
RETURN TO YOUR APARTMENT, PUT IN FRESH CONTACT LENSES, AND GO TO BED.
PARKING
HOUSE OF HEROES

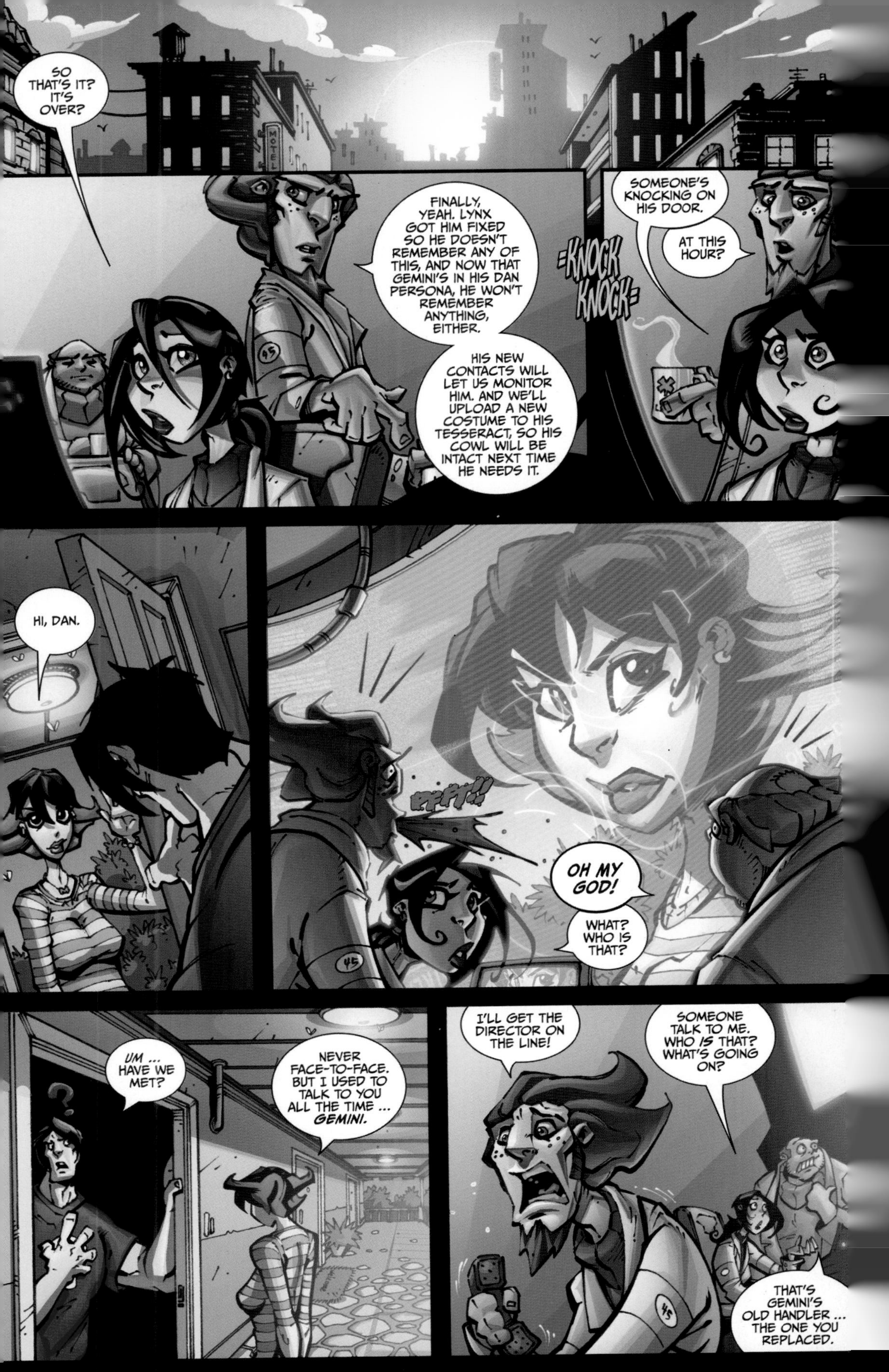
SO THAT'S IT? IT'S OVER?
FINALLY, YEAH. LYNX GOT HIM FIXED SO HE DOESN'T REMEMBER ANY OF THIS, AND NOW THAT GEMINI'S IN HIS DAN PERSONA, HE WON'T REMEMBER ANYTHING, EITHER.
HIS NEW CONTACTS WILL LET US MONITOR HIM. AND WE'LL UPLOAD A NEW COSTUME TO HIS TESSERACT, SO HIS COWL WILL BE INTACT NEXT TIME HE NEEDS IT.
KNOCK KNOCK
SOMEONE'S KNOCKING ON HIS DOOR.
AT THIS HOUR?
HI, DAN.
PFFT!!
OH MY GOD!
WHAT? WHO IS THAT?
UM ... HAVE WE MET?
NEVER FACE-TO-FACE. BUT I USED TO TALK TO YOU ALL THE TIME ... *GEMINI.*
I'LL GET THE DIRECTOR ON THE LINE!
SOMEONE TALK TO ME. WHO *IS* THAT? WHAT'S GOING ON?
THAT'S GEMINI'S OLD HANDLER ... THE ONE YOU REPLACED.

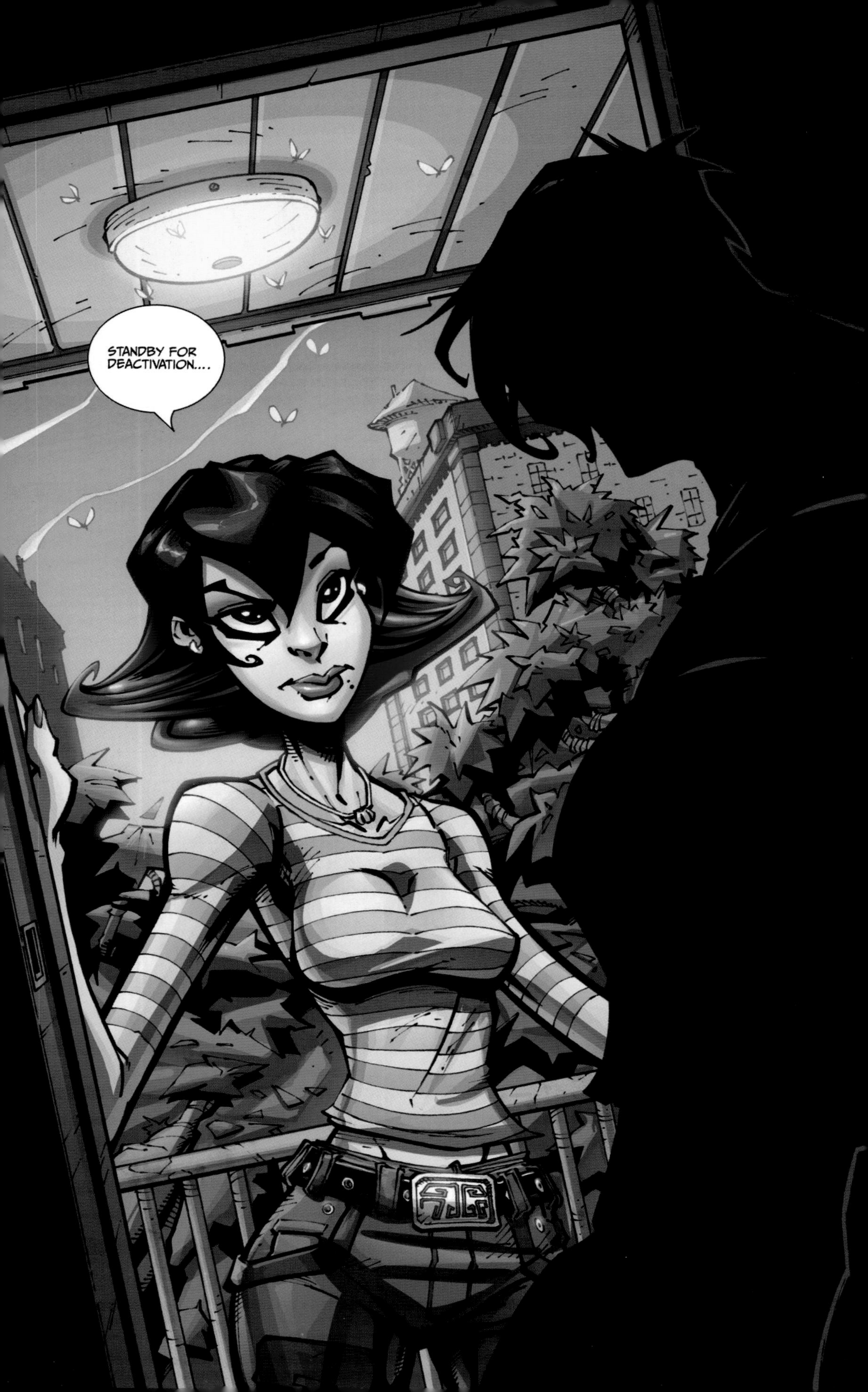
STANDBY FOR DEACTIVATION....

CHAPTER THREE

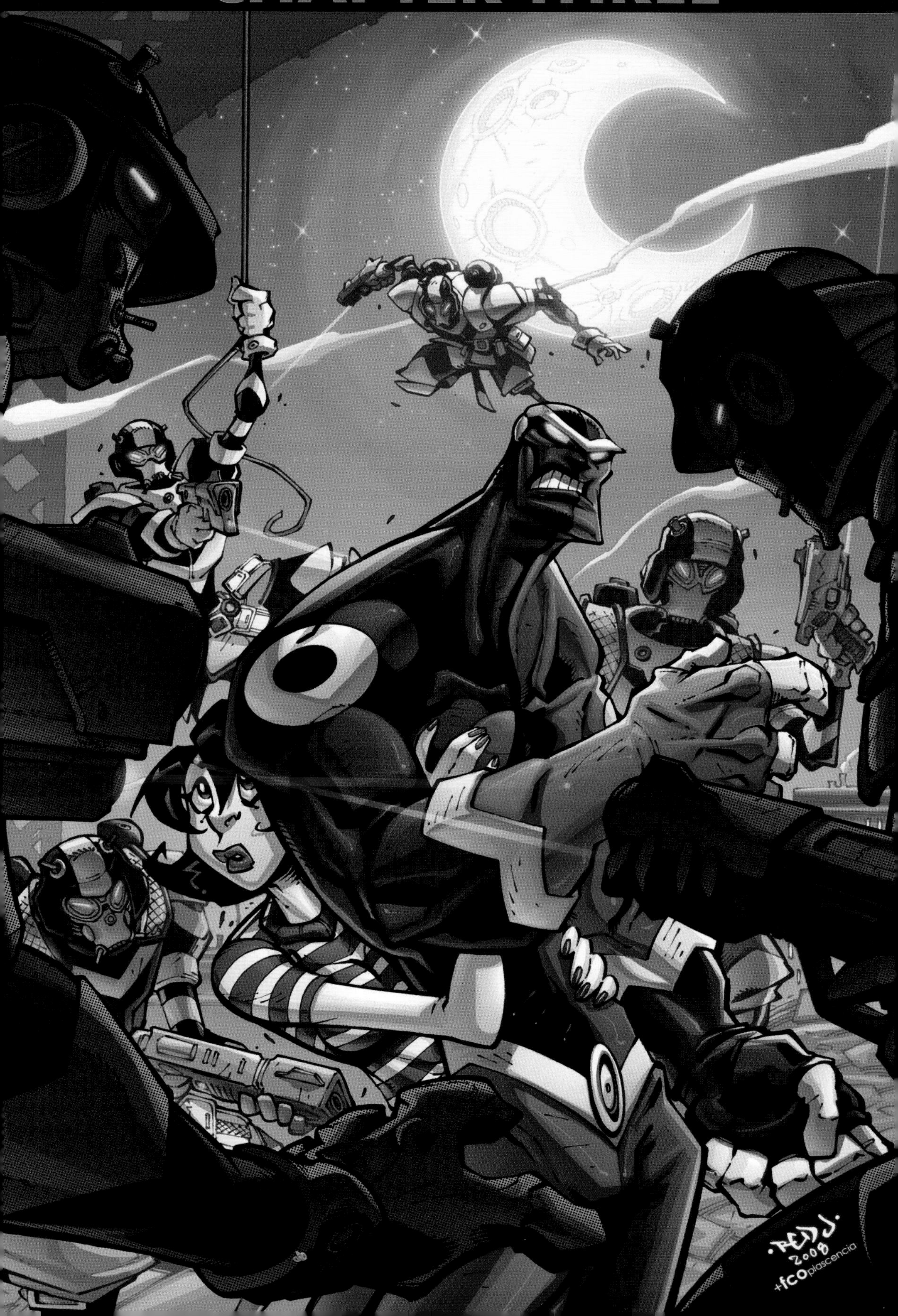

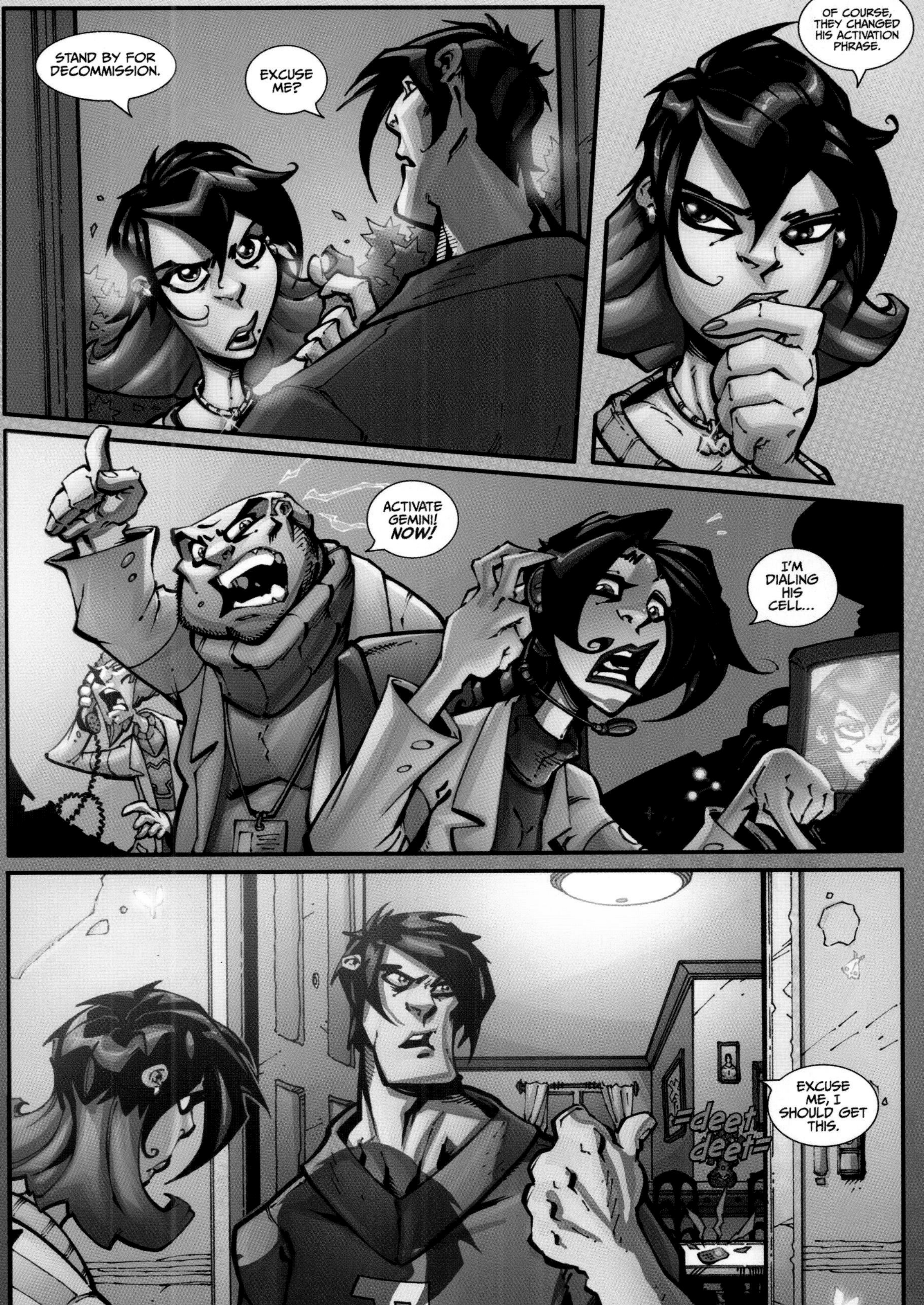
STAND BY FOR DECOMMISSION.
EXCUSE ME?
OF COURSE, THEY CHANGED HIS ACTIVATION PHRASE.
ACTIVATE GEMINI! NOW!
I'M DIALING HIS CELL...
EXCUSE ME, I SHOULD GET THIS.
=deet deet=

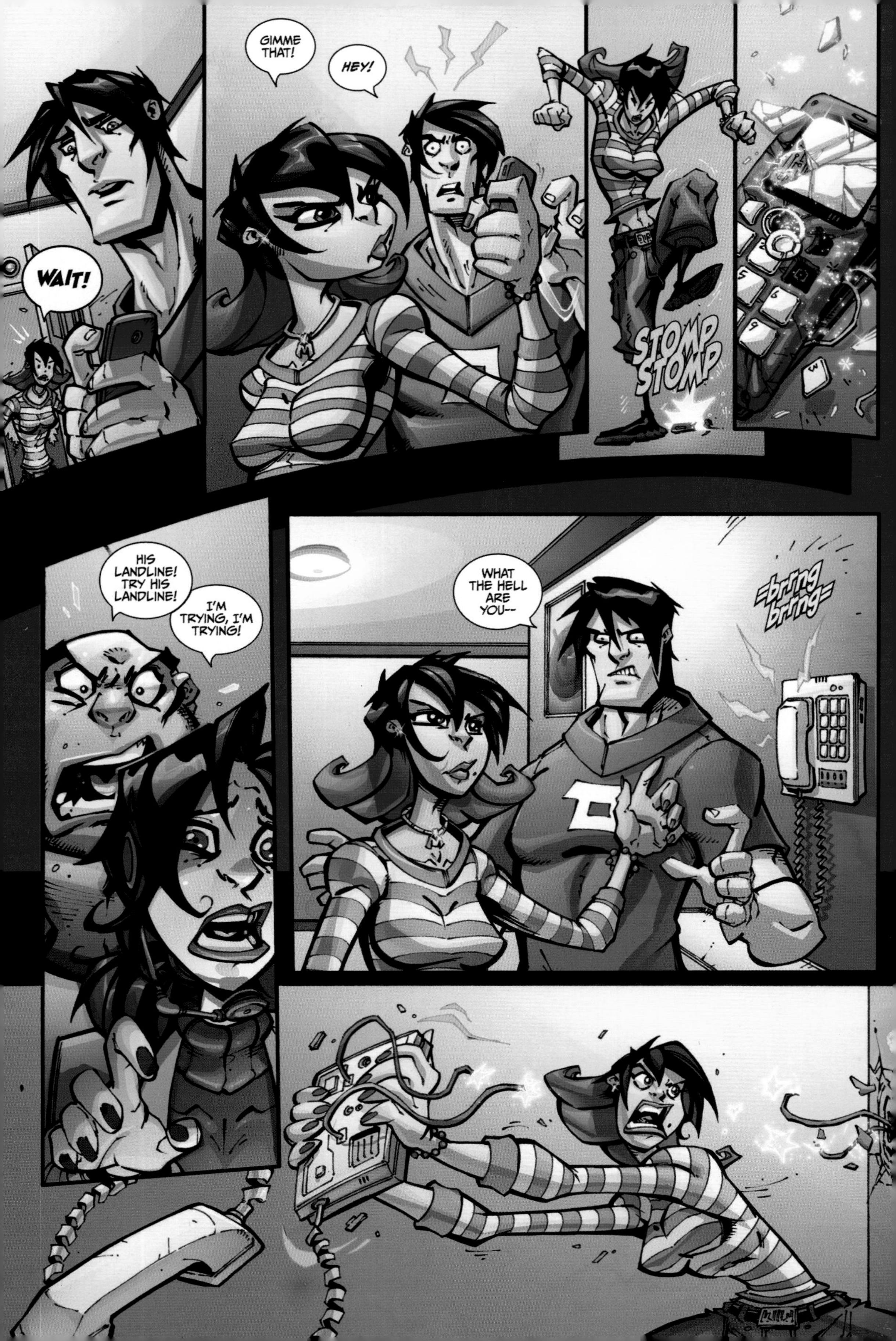
WAIT!
GIMME THAT!
HEY!
STOMP STOMP
HIS LANDLINE! TRY HIS LANDLINE!
I'M TRYING, I'M TRYING!
WHAT THE HELL ARE YOU--
=brring brring=

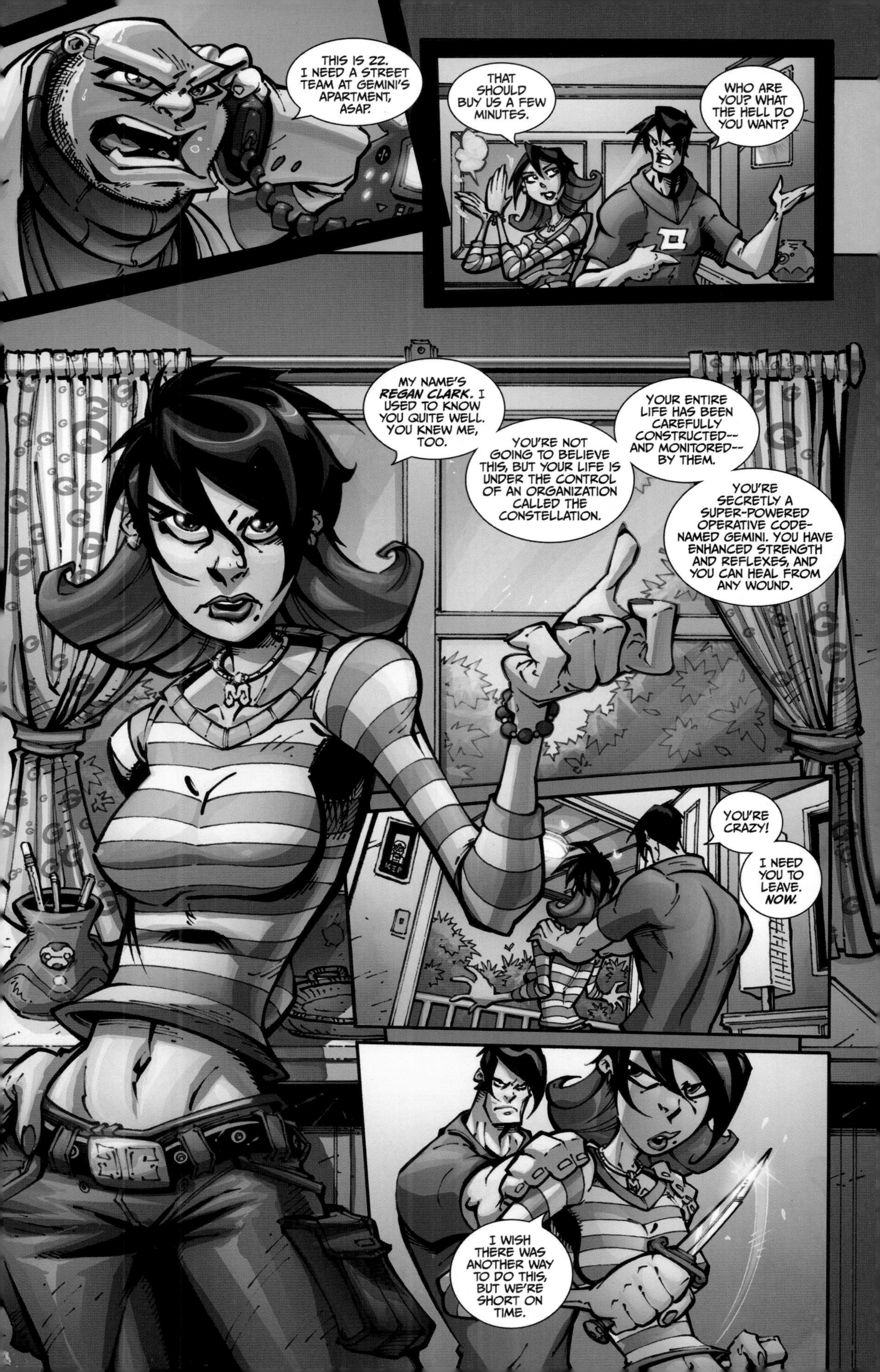

THIS IS 22. I NEED A STREET TEAM AT GEMINI'S APARTMENT, ASAP.
THAT SHOULD BUY US A FEW MINUTES.
WHO ARE YOU? WHAT THE HELL DO YOU WANT?
MY NAME'S *REGAN CLARK*. I USED TO KNOW YOU QUITE WELL. YOU KNEW ME, TOO.
YOU'RE NOT GOING TO BELIEVE THIS, BUT YOUR LIFE IS UNDER THE CONTROL OF AN ORGANIZATION CALLED THE CONSTELLATION.
YOUR ENTIRE LIFE HAS BEEN CAREFULLY CONSTRUCTED-- AND MONITORED-- BY THEM.
YOU'RE SECRETLY A SUPER-POWERED OPERATIVE CODE-NAMED GEMINI. YOU HAVE ENHANCED STRENGTH AND REFLEXES, AND YOU CAN HEAL FROM ANY WOUND.
YOU'RE CRAZY!
I NEED YOU TO LEAVE. *NOW.*
I WISH THERE WAS ANOTHER WAY TO DO THIS, BUT WE'RE SHORT ON TIME.

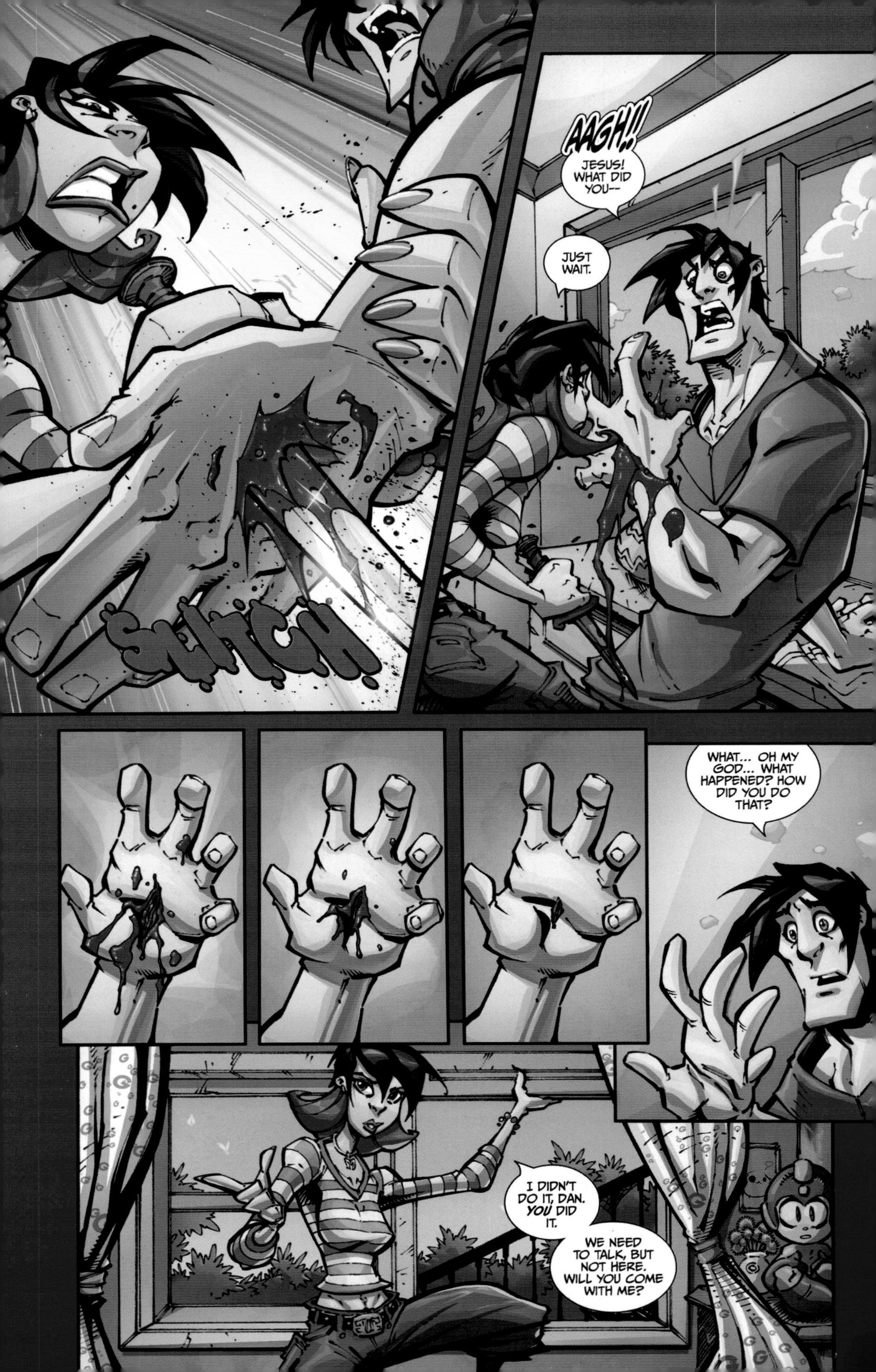
SHLICH
AAGH!!
JESUS! WHAT DID YOU--
JUST WAIT.
WHAT... OH MY GOD... WHAT HAPPENED? HOW DID YOU DO THAT?
I DIDN'T DO IT, DAN. *YOU* DID IT.
WE NEED TO TALK, BUT NOT HERE. WILL YOU COME WITH ME?

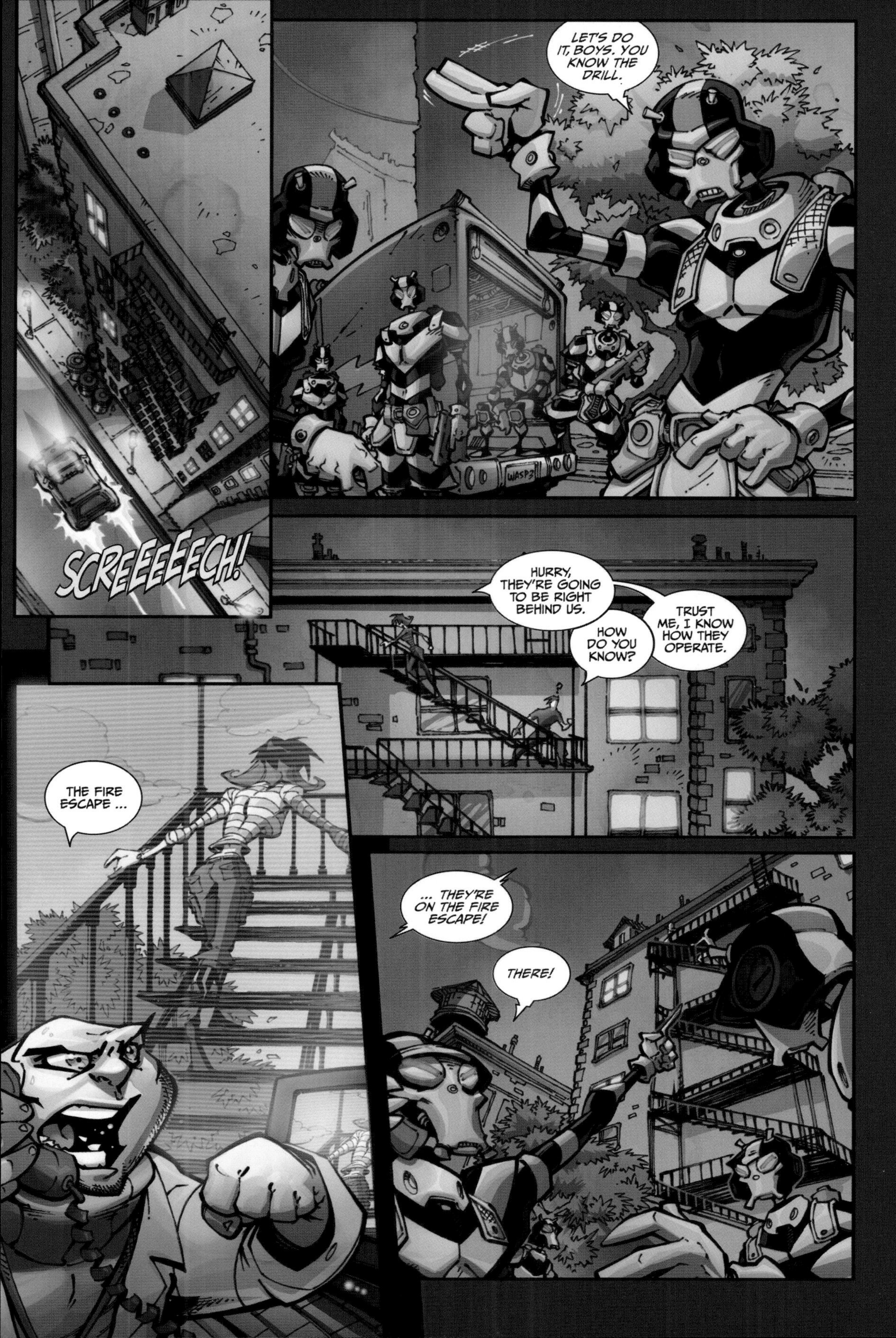
SCREEEEEECH!
LET'S DO IT, BOYS. YOU KNOW THE DRILL.
WASP3
HURRY, THEY'RE GOING TO BE RIGHT BEHIND US.
HOW DO YOU KNOW?
TRUST ME, I KNOW HOW THEY OPERATE.
THE FIRE ESCAPE ...
... THEY'RE ON THE FIRE ESCAPE!
THERE!

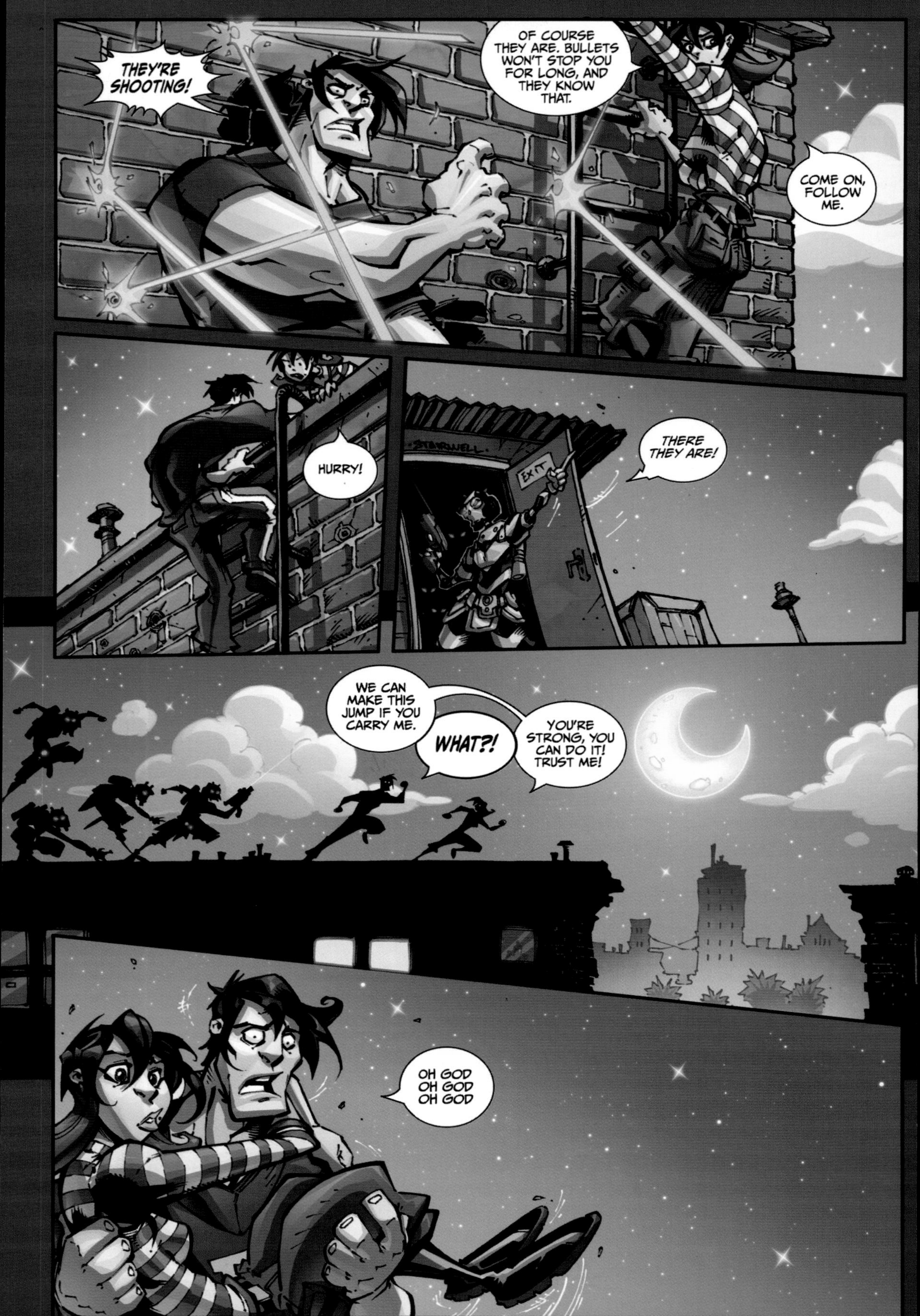
THEY'RE SHOOTING!
OF COURSE THEY ARE. BULLETS WON'T STOP YOU FOR LONG, AND THEY KNOW THAT.
COME ON, FOLLOW ME.
HURRY!
STAIRWELL
EXIT
THERE THEY ARE!
WE CAN MAKE THIS JUMP IF YOU CARRY ME.
WHAT?!
YOU'RE STRONG, YOU CAN DO IT! TRUST ME!
OH GOD OH GOD OH GOD

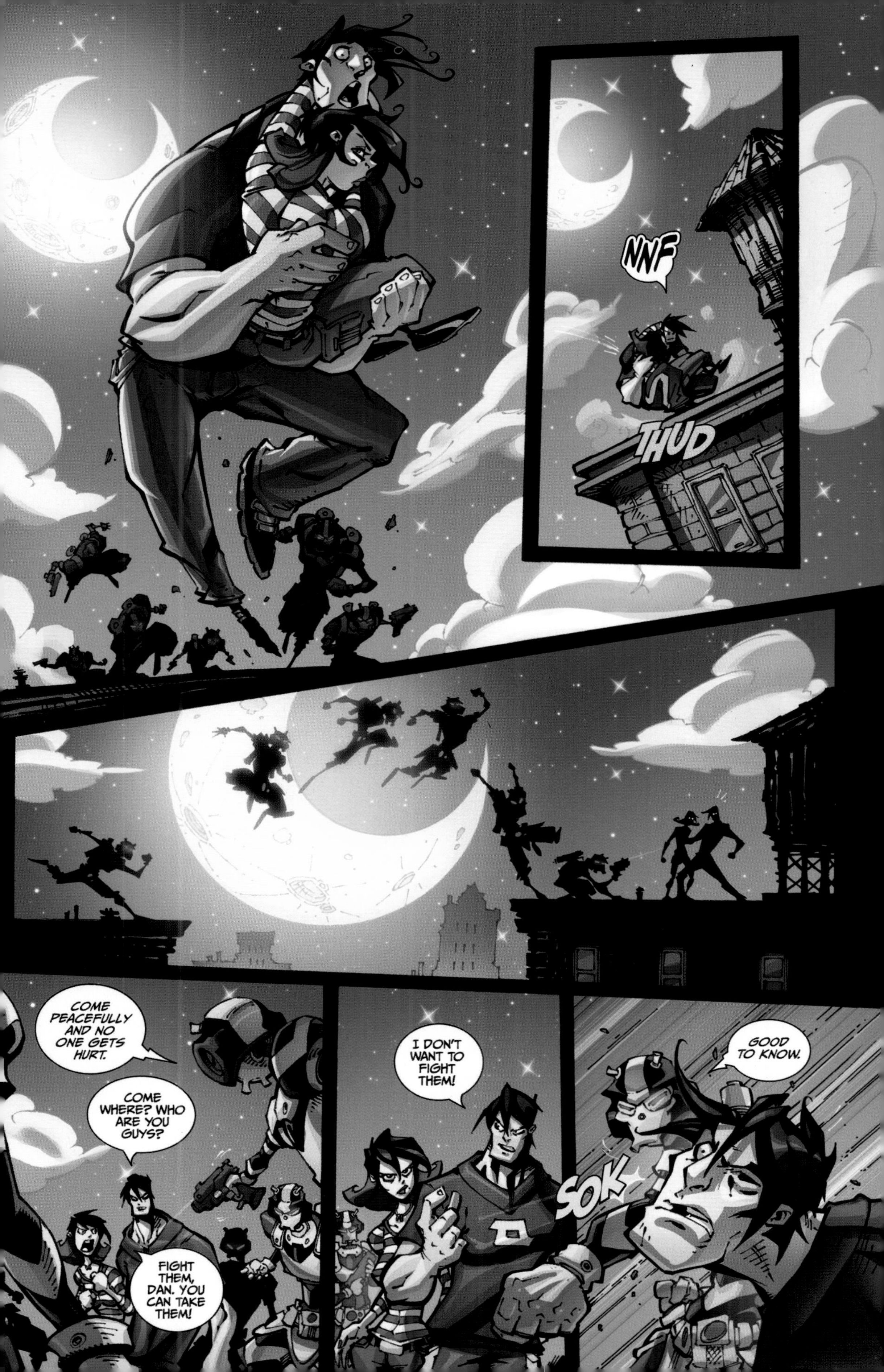
NNF
THUD
COME PEACEFULLY AND NO ONE GETS HURT.
COME WHERE? WHO ARE YOU GUYS?
FIGHT THEM, DAN. YOU CAN TAKE THEM!
I DON'T WANT TO FIGHT THEM!
GOOD TO KNOW.
SOK

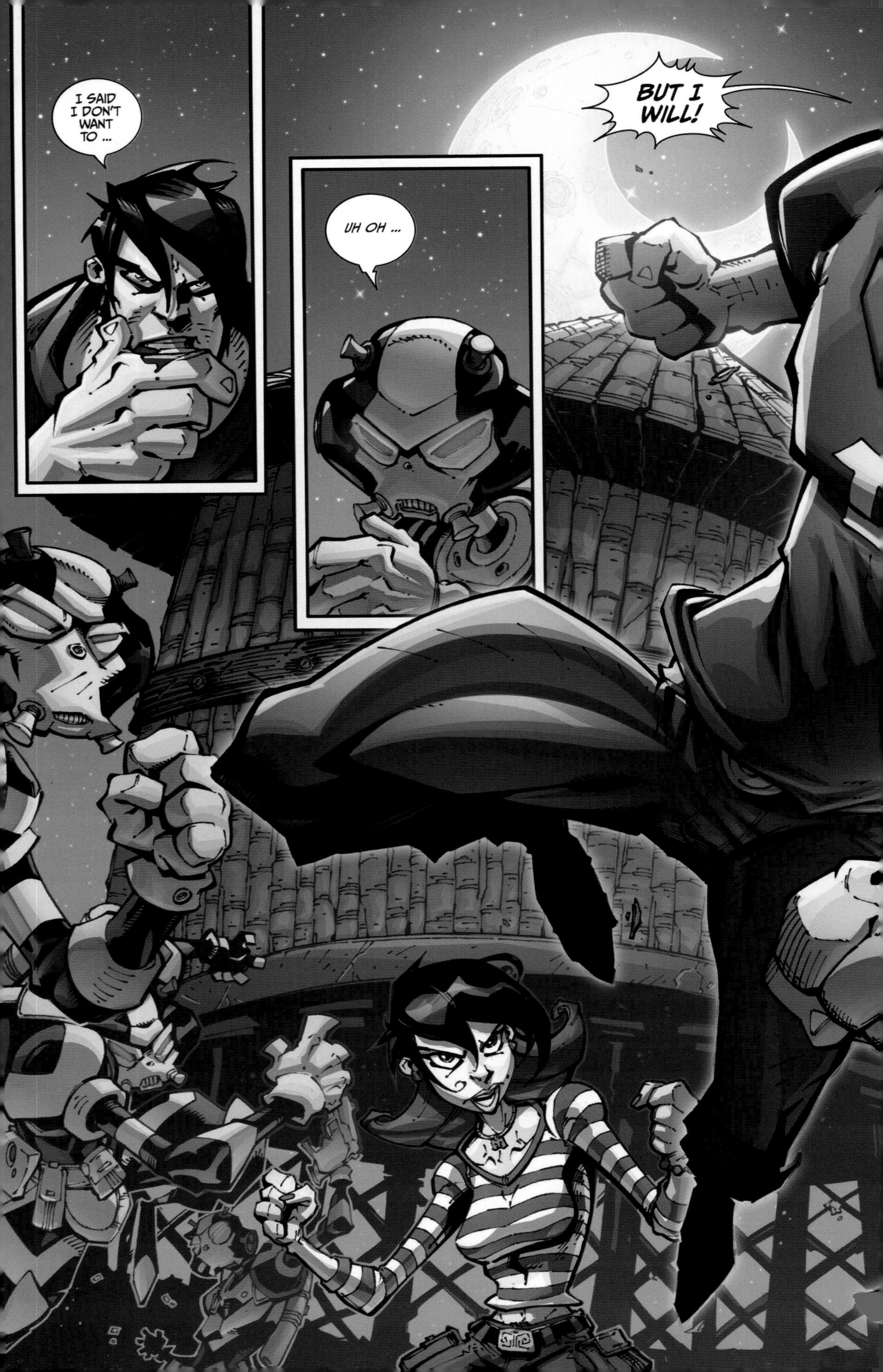
I SAID I DON'T WANT TO ...
UH OH ...
BUT I WILL!

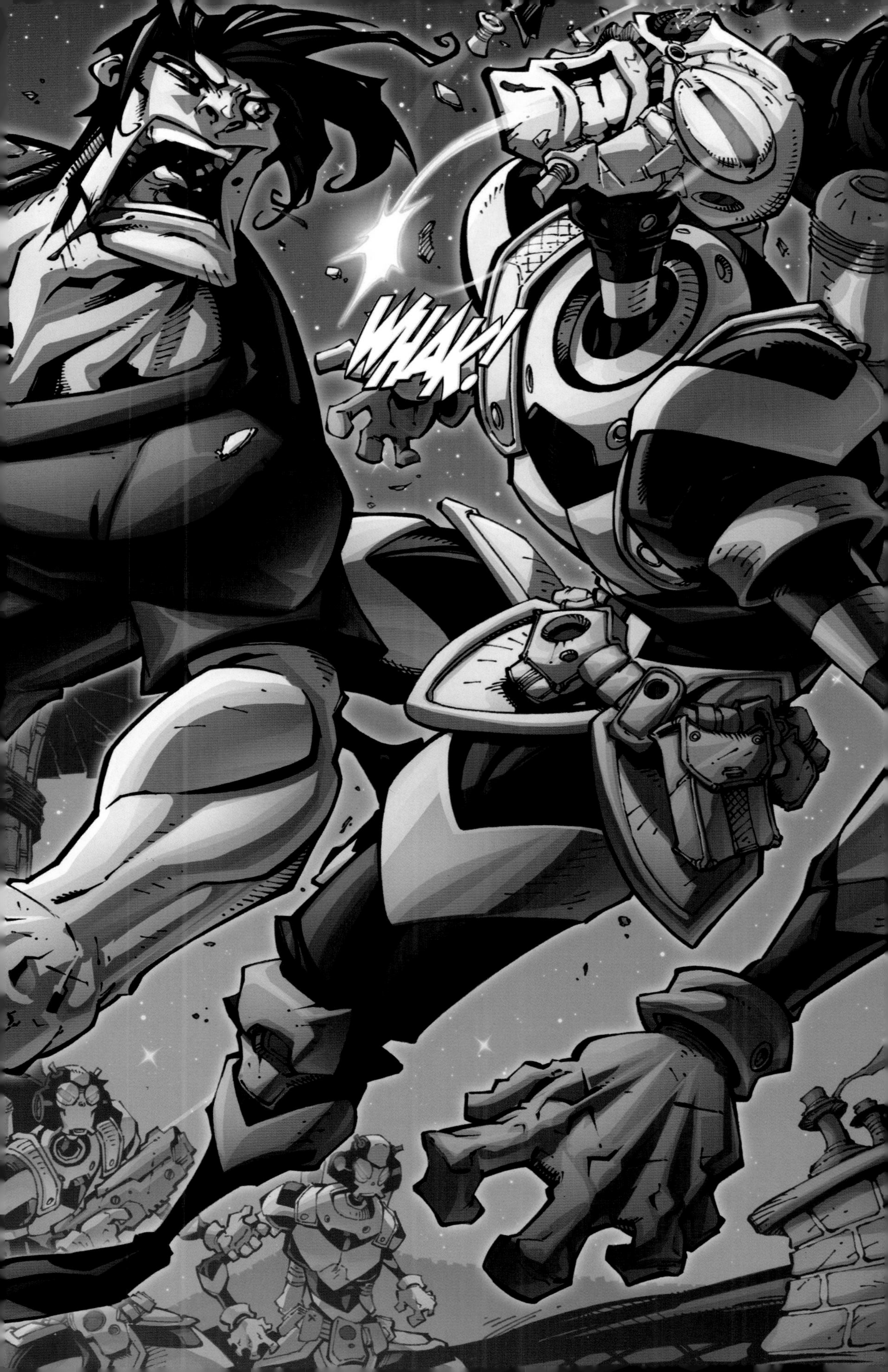
WHAK!

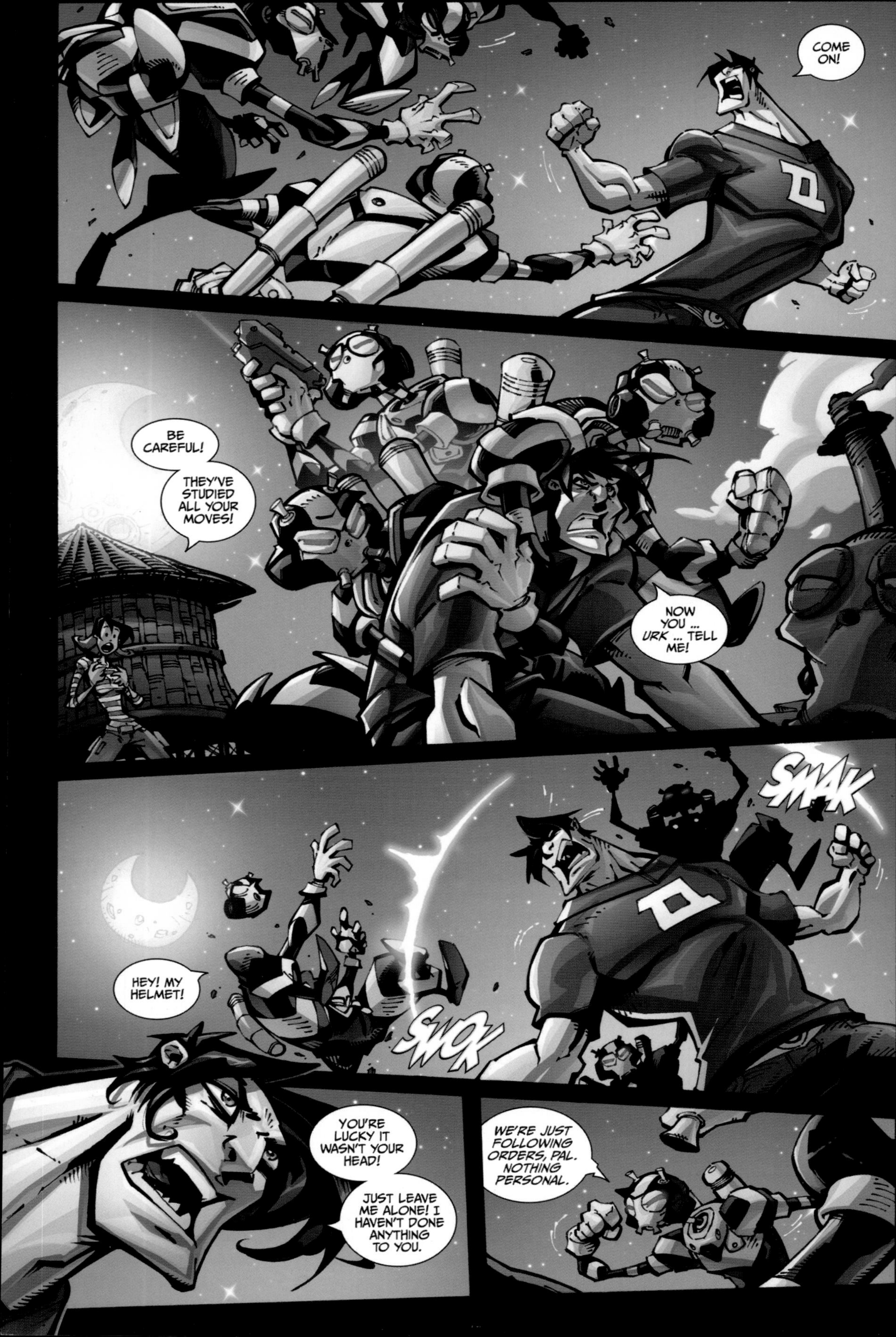
COME ON!
BE CAREFUL!
THEY'VE STUDIED ALL YOUR MOVES!
NOW YOU ... URK ... TELL ME!
SMAK
HEY! MY HELMET!
SWOK
YOU'RE LUCKY IT WASN'T YOUR HEAD!
JUST LEAVE ME ALONE! I HAVEN'T DONE ANYTHING TO YOU.
WE'RE JUST FOLLOWING ORDERS, PAL. NOTHING PERSONAL.

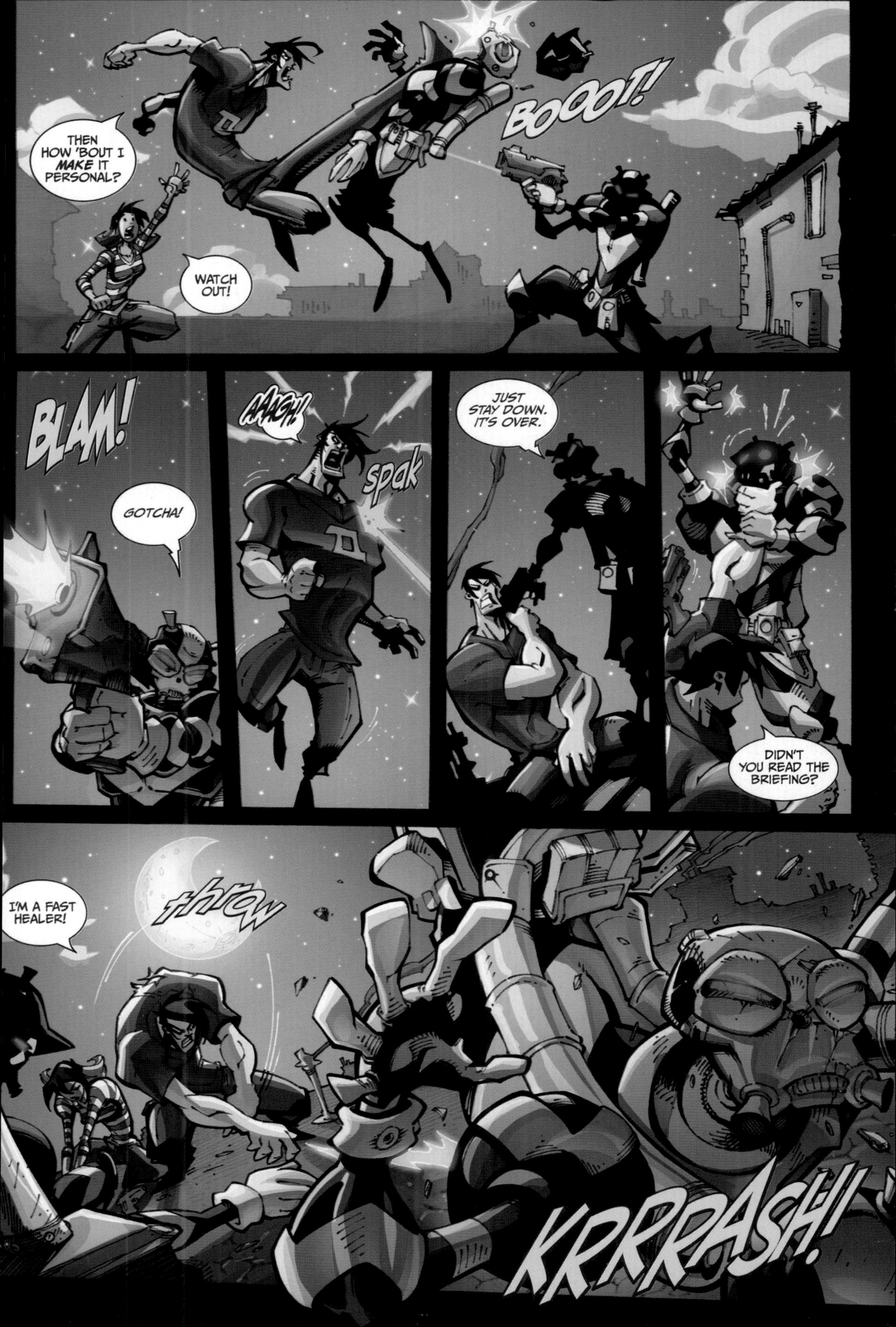
THEN HOW 'BOUT I MAKE IT PERSONAL?
BOOOOT!
WATCH OUT!
BLAM!
GOTCHA!
AAAGH!
spak
JUST STAY DOWN. IT'S OVER.
DIDN'T YOU READ THE BRIEFING?
I'M A FAST HEALER!
throw
KRRRASH!

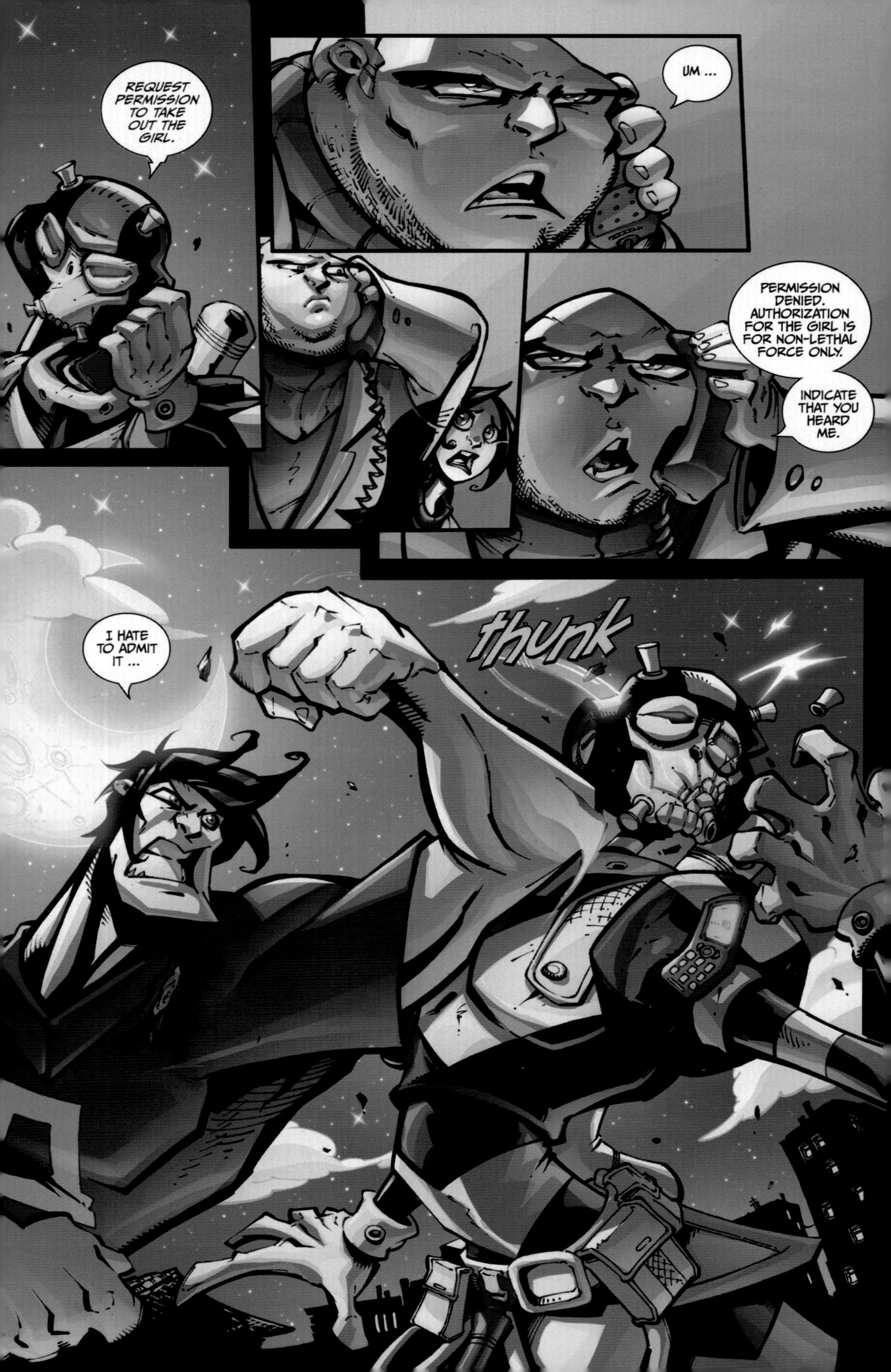
REQUEST PERMISSION TO TAKE OUT THE GIRL.
UM ...
PERMISSION DENIED. AUTHORIZATION FOR THE GIRL IS FOR NON-LETHAL FORCE ONLY.
INDICATE THAT YOU HEARD ME.
I HATE TO ADMIT IT ...
thunk

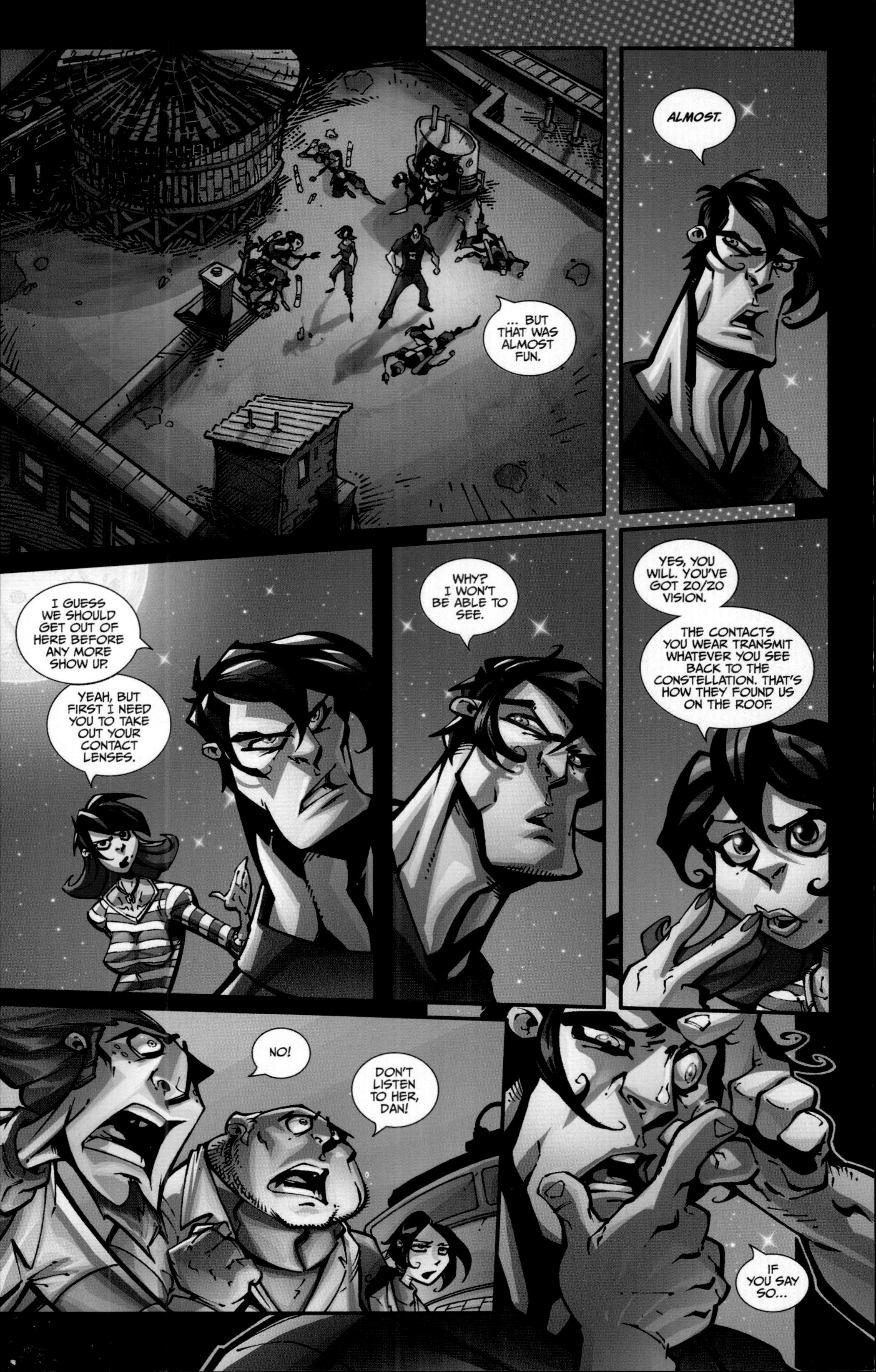
... BUT THAT WAS ALMOST FUN.
ALMOST.
I GUESS WE SHOULD GET OUT OF HERE BEFORE ANY MORE SHOW UP.
YEAH, BUT FIRST I NEED YOU TO TAKE OUT YOUR CONTACT LENSES.
WHY? I WON'T BE ABLE TO SEE.
YES, YOU WILL. YOU'VE GOT 20/20 VISION.
THE CONTACTS YOU WEAR TRANSMIT WHATEVER YOU SEE BACK TO THE CONSTELLATION. THAT'S HOW THEY FOUND US ON THE ROOF.
NO!
DON'T LISTEN TO HER, DAN!
IF YOU SAY SO...

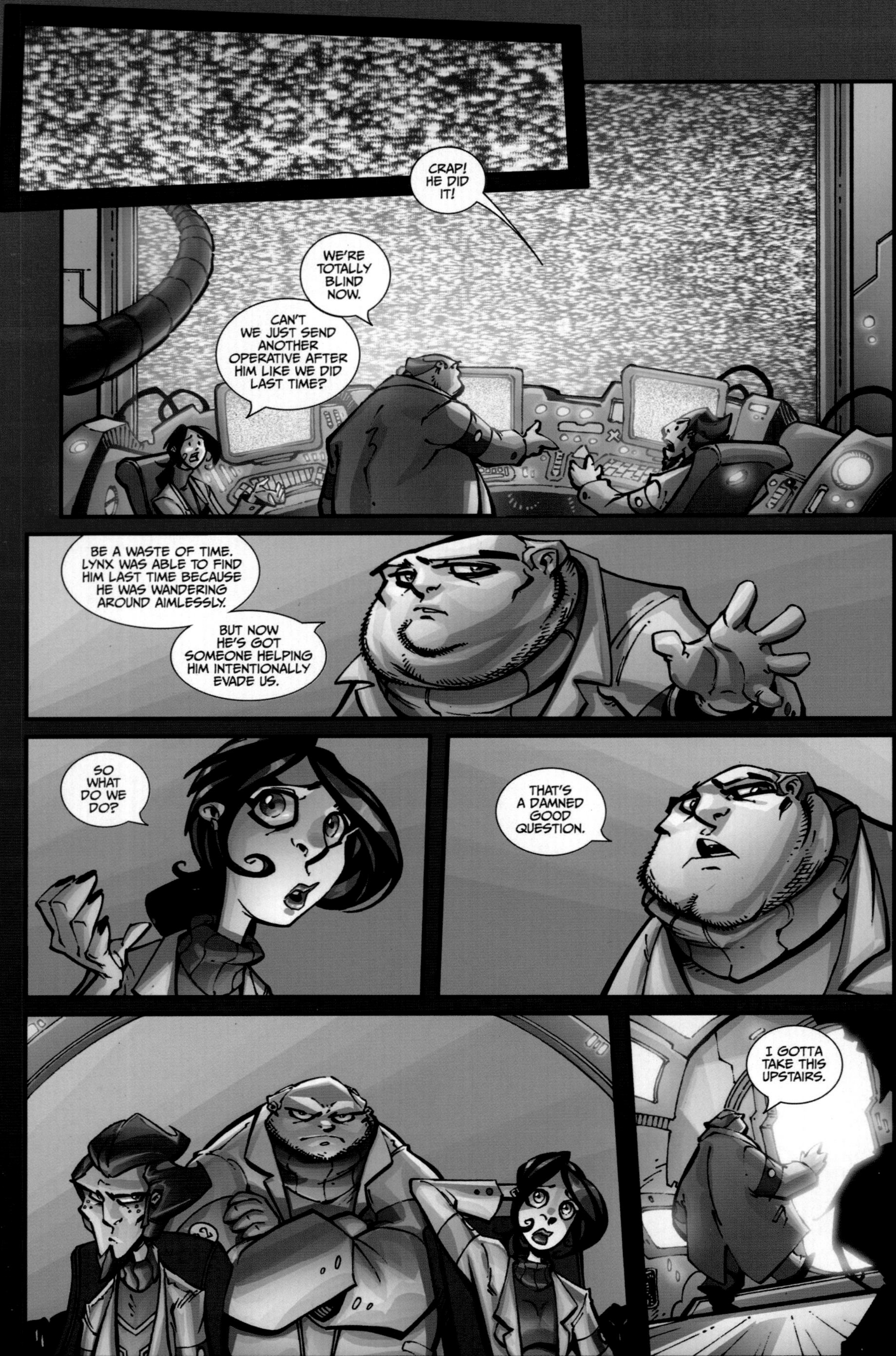
CRAP! HE DID IT!
WE'RE TOTALLY BLIND NOW.
CAN'T WE JUST SEND ANOTHER OPERATIVE AFTER HIM LIKE WE DID LAST TIME?
BE A WASTE OF TIME. LYNX WAS ABLE TO FIND HIM LAST TIME BECAUSE HE WAS WANDERING AROUND AIMLESSLY.
BUT NOW HE'S GOT SOMEONE HELPING HIM INTENTIONALLY EVADE US.
SO WHAT DO WE DO?
THAT'S A DAMNED GOOD QUESTION.
I GOTTA TAKE THIS UPSTAIRS.

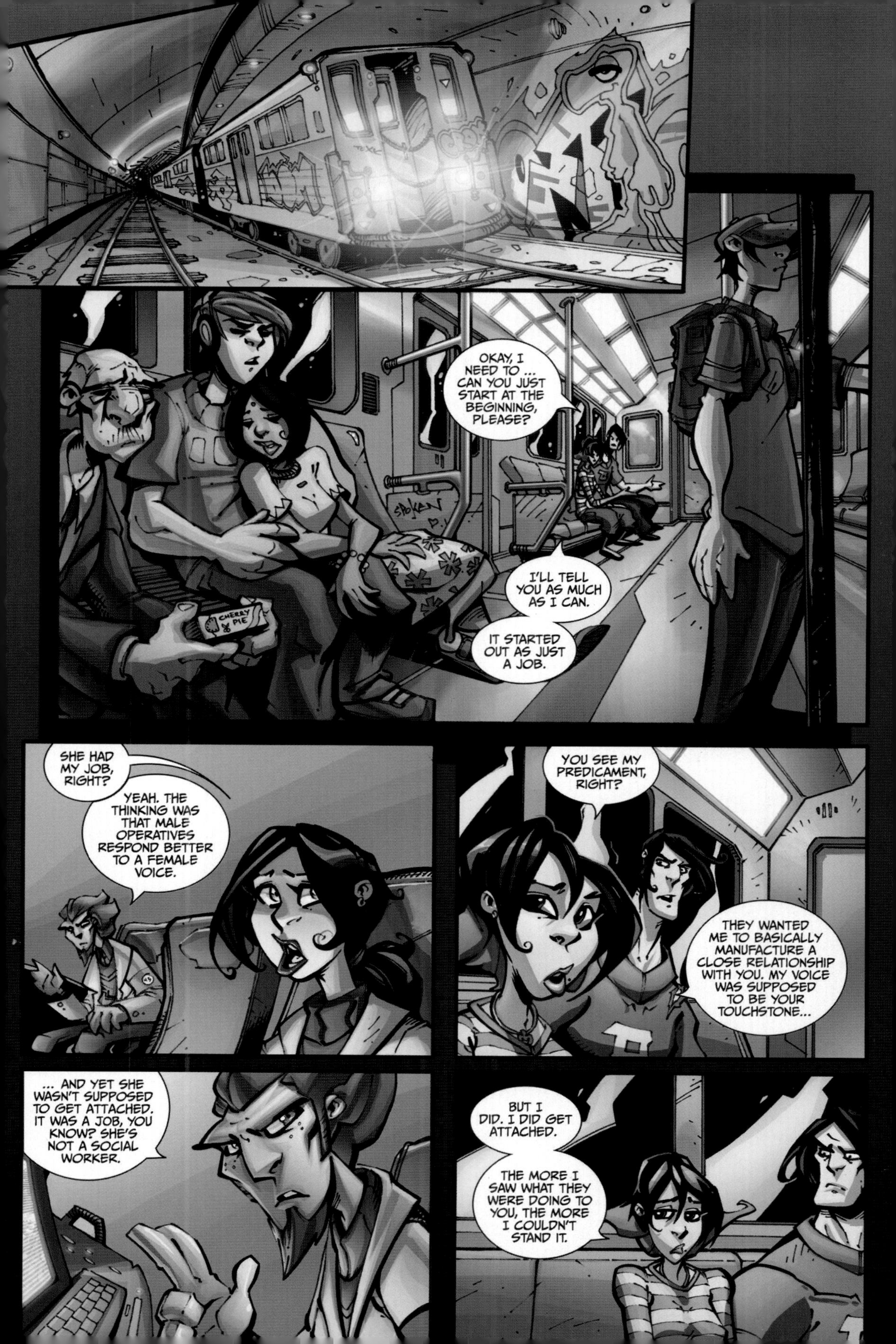
SPOKEN
CHERRY PIE
OKAY, I NEED TO ... CAN YOU JUST START AT THE BEGINNING, PLEASE?
I'LL TELL YOU AS MUCH AS I CAN.
IT STARTED OUT AS JUST A JOB.
SHE HAD MY JOB, RIGHT?
YEAH. THE THINKING WAS THAT MALE OPERATIVES RESPOND BETTER TO A FEMALE VOICE.
YOU SEE MY PREDICAMENT, RIGHT?
THEY WANTED ME TO BASICALLY MANUFACTURE A CLOSE RELATIONSHIP WITH YOU. MY VOICE WAS SUPPOSED TO BE YOUR TOUCHSTONE...
... AND YET SHE WASN'T SUPPOSED TO GET ATTACHED. IT WAS A JOB, YOU KNOW? SHE'S NOT A SOCIAL WORKER.
BUT I DID. I DID GET ATTACHED.
THE MORE I SAW WHAT THEY WERE DOING TO YOU, THE MORE I COULDN'T STAND IT.

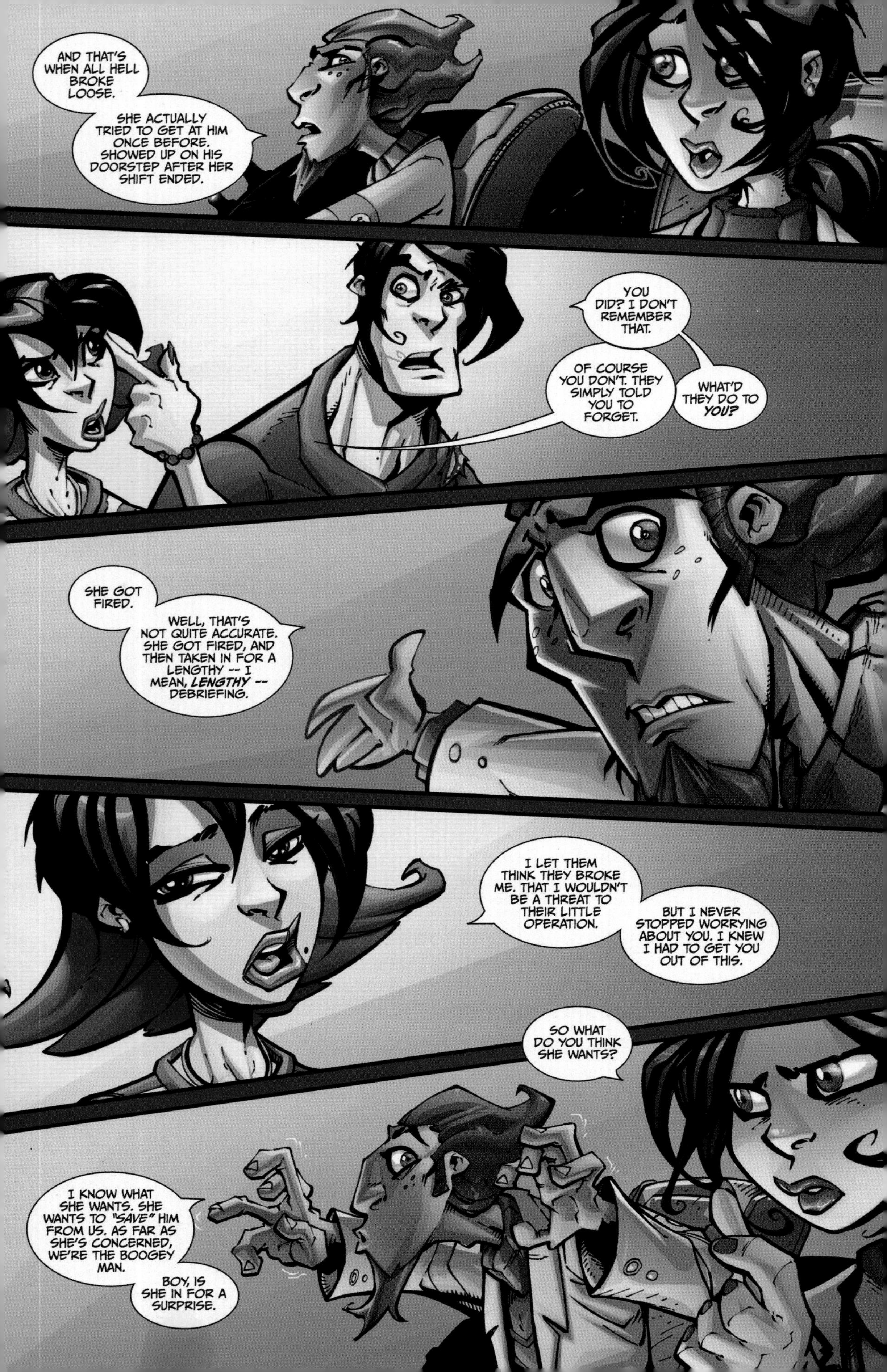
AND THAT'S WHEN ALL HELL BROKE LOOSE.
SHE ACTUALLY TRIED TO GET AT HIM ONCE BEFORE. SHOWED UP ON HIS DOORSTEP AFTER HER SHIFT ENDED.
YOU DID? I DON'T REMEMBER THAT.
OF COURSE YOU DON'T. THEY SIMPLY TOLD YOU TO FORGET.
WHAT'D THEY DO TO *YOU?*
SHE GOT FIRED.
WELL, THAT'S NOT QUITE ACCURATE. SHE GOT FIRED, AND THEN TAKEN IN FOR A LENGTHY -- I MEAN, *LENGTHY* -- DEBRIEFING.
I LET THEM THINK THEY BROKE ME. THAT I WOULDN'T BE A THREAT TO THEIR LITTLE OPERATION.
BUT I NEVER STOPPED WORRYING ABOUT YOU. I KNEW I HAD TO GET YOU OUT OF THIS.
SO WHAT DO YOU THINK SHE WANTS?
I KNOW WHAT SHE WANTS. SHE WANTS TO *"SAVE"* HIM FROM US. AS FAR AS SHE'S CONCERNED, WE'RE THE BOOGEY MAN.
BOY, IS SHE IN FOR A SURPRISE.

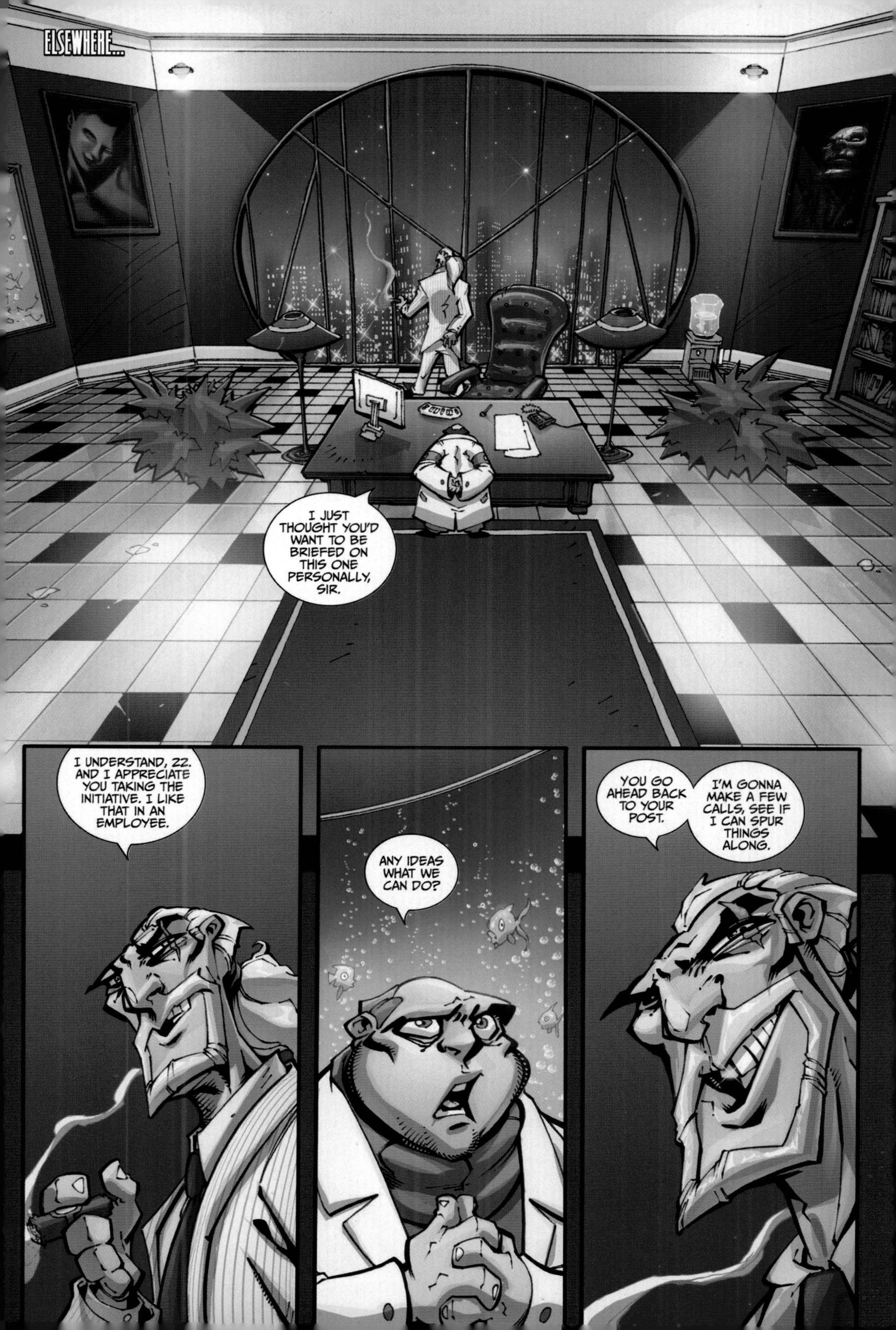
ELSEWHERE...
I JUST THOUGHT YOU'D WANT TO BE BRIEFED ON THIS ONE PERSONALLY, SIR.
I UNDERSTAND, 22. AND I APPRECIATE YOU TAKING THE INITIATIVE. I LIKE THAT IN AN EMPLOYEE.
ANY IDEAS WHAT WE CAN DO?
YOU GO AHEAD BACK TO YOUR POST.
I'M GONNA MAKE A FEW CALLS, SEE IF I CAN SPUR THINGS ALONG.

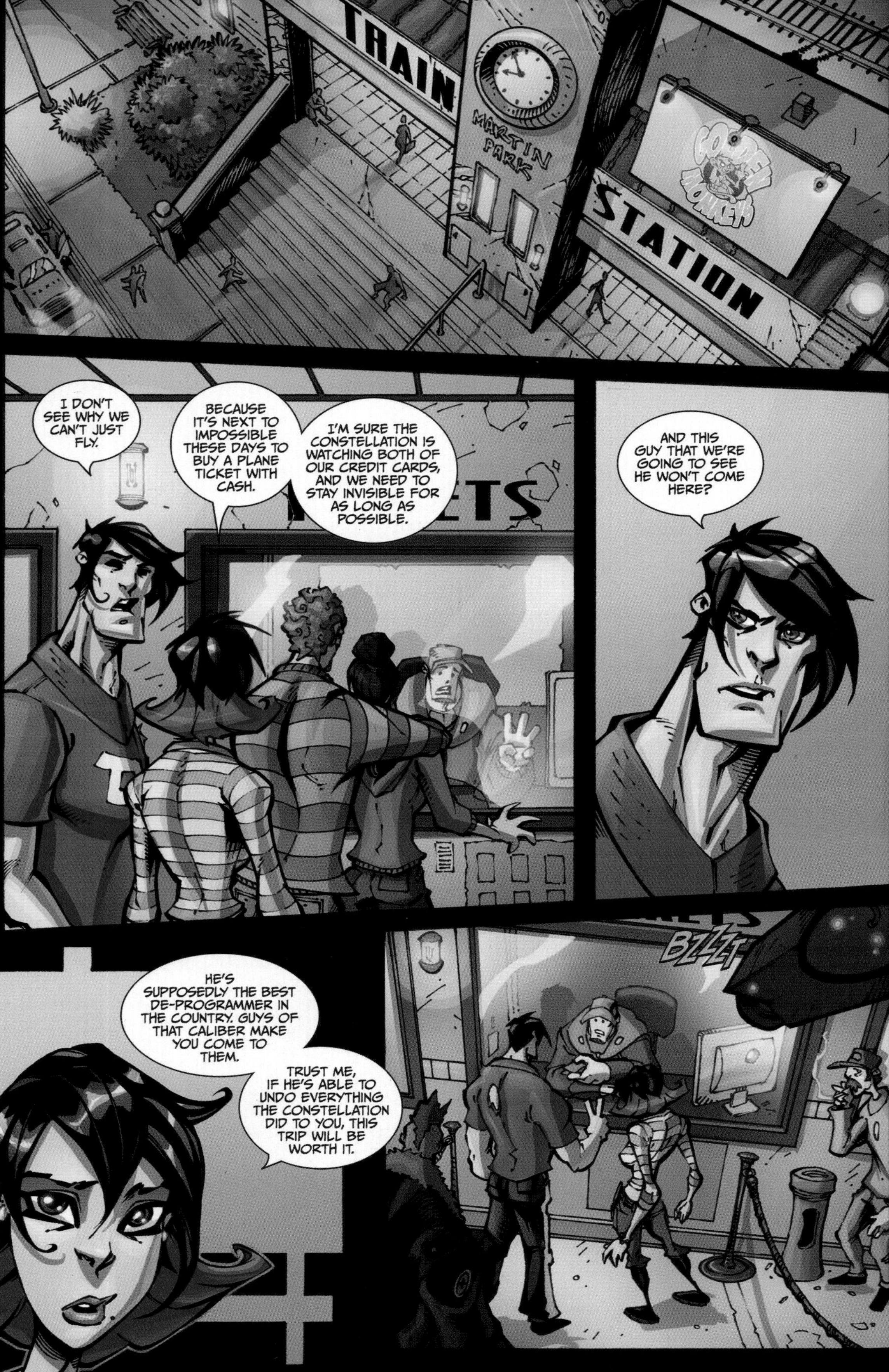
TRAIN
MARTIN PARK
GOLDEN MONKEYS
STATION
I DON'T SEE WHY WE CAN'T JUST FLY.
BECAUSE IT'S NEXT TO IMPOSSIBLE THESE DAYS TO BUY A PLANE TICKET WITH CASH.
I'M SURE THE CONSTELLATION IS WATCHING BOTH OF OUR CREDIT CARDS, AND WE NEED TO STAY INVISIBLE FOR AS LONG AS POSSIBLE.
AND THIS GUY THAT WE'RE GOING TO SEE HE WON'T COME HERE?
HE'S SUPPOSEDLY THE BEST DE-PROGRAMMER IN THE COUNTRY. GUYS OF THAT CALIBER MAKE YOU COME TO THEM.
TRUST ME, IF HE'S ABLE TO UNDO EVERYTHING THE CONSTELLATION DID TO YOU, THIS TRIP WILL BE WORTH IT.
BZZZT

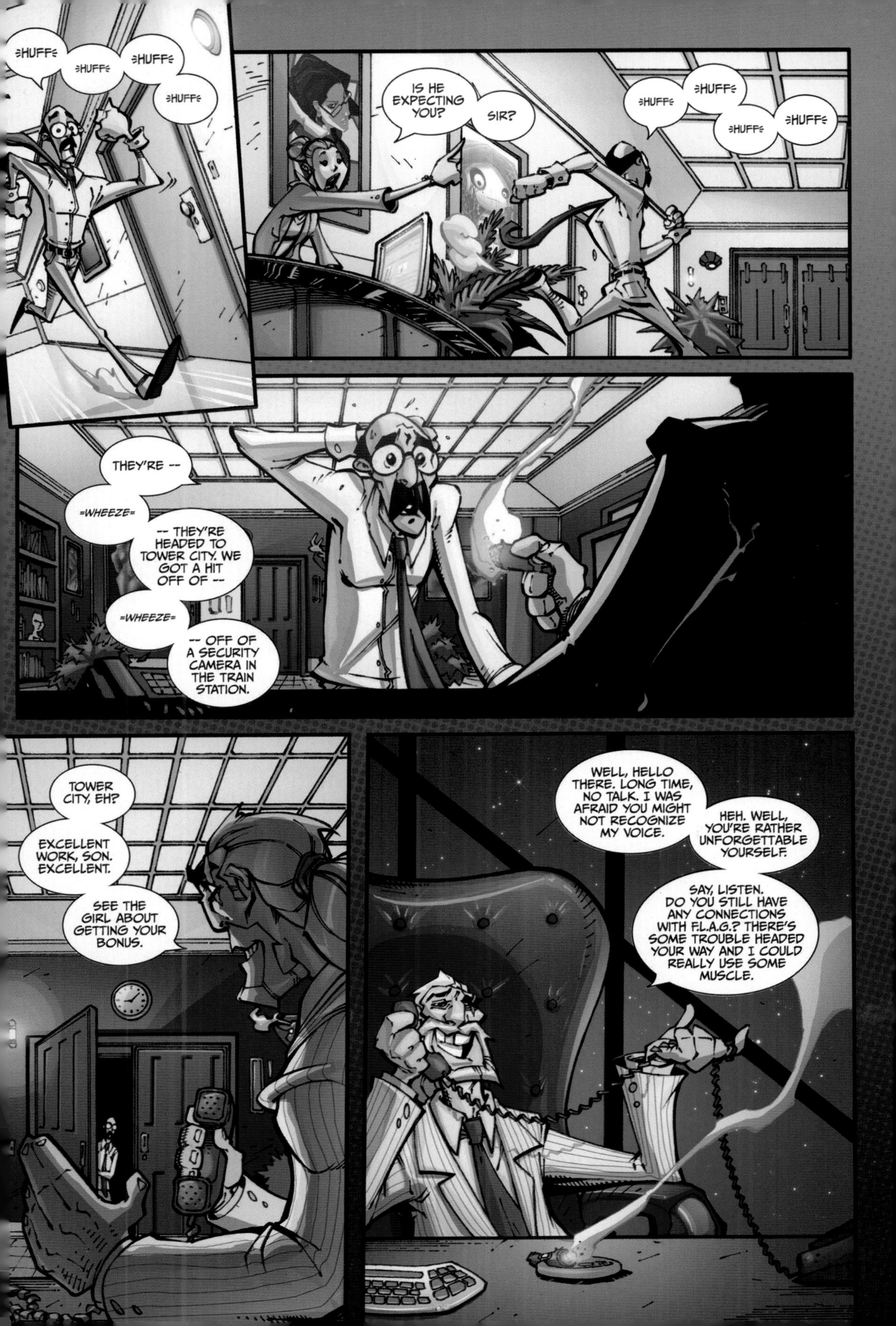
=HUFF=
=HUFF=
=HUFF=
=HUFF=
IS HE EXPECTING YOU?
SIR?
=HUFF=
=HUFF=
=HUFF=
=HUFF=
THEY'RE --
=WHEEZE=
-- THEY'RE HEADED TO TOWER CITY. WE GOT A HIT OFF OF --
=WHEEZE=
-- OFF OF A SECURITY CAMERA IN THE TRAIN STATION.
TOWER CITY, EH?
EXCELLENT WORK, SON. EXCELLENT.
SEE THE GIRL ABOUT GETTING YOUR BONUS.
WELL, HELLO THERE. LONG TIME, NO TALK. I WAS AFRAID YOU MIGHT NOT RECOGNIZE MY VOICE.
HEH. WELL, YOU'RE RATHER UNFORGETTABLE YOURSELF.
SAY, LISTEN. DO YOU STILL HAVE ANY CONNECTIONS WITH F.L.A.G.? THERE'S SOME TROUBLE HEADED YOUR WAY AND I COULD REALLY USE SOME MUSCLE.

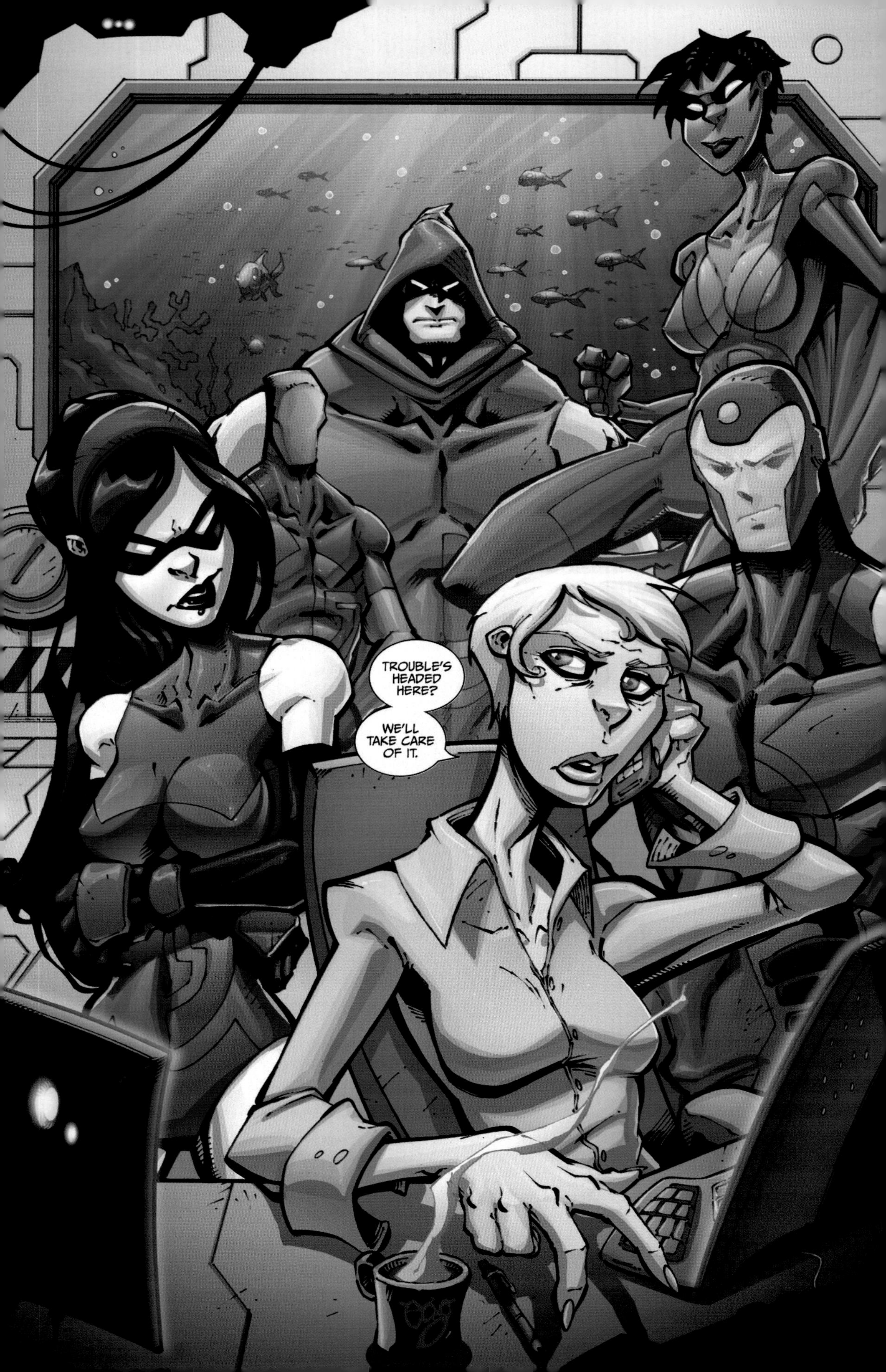
TROUBLE'S HEADED HERE?
WE'LL TAKE CARE OF IT.

CHAPTER FOUR

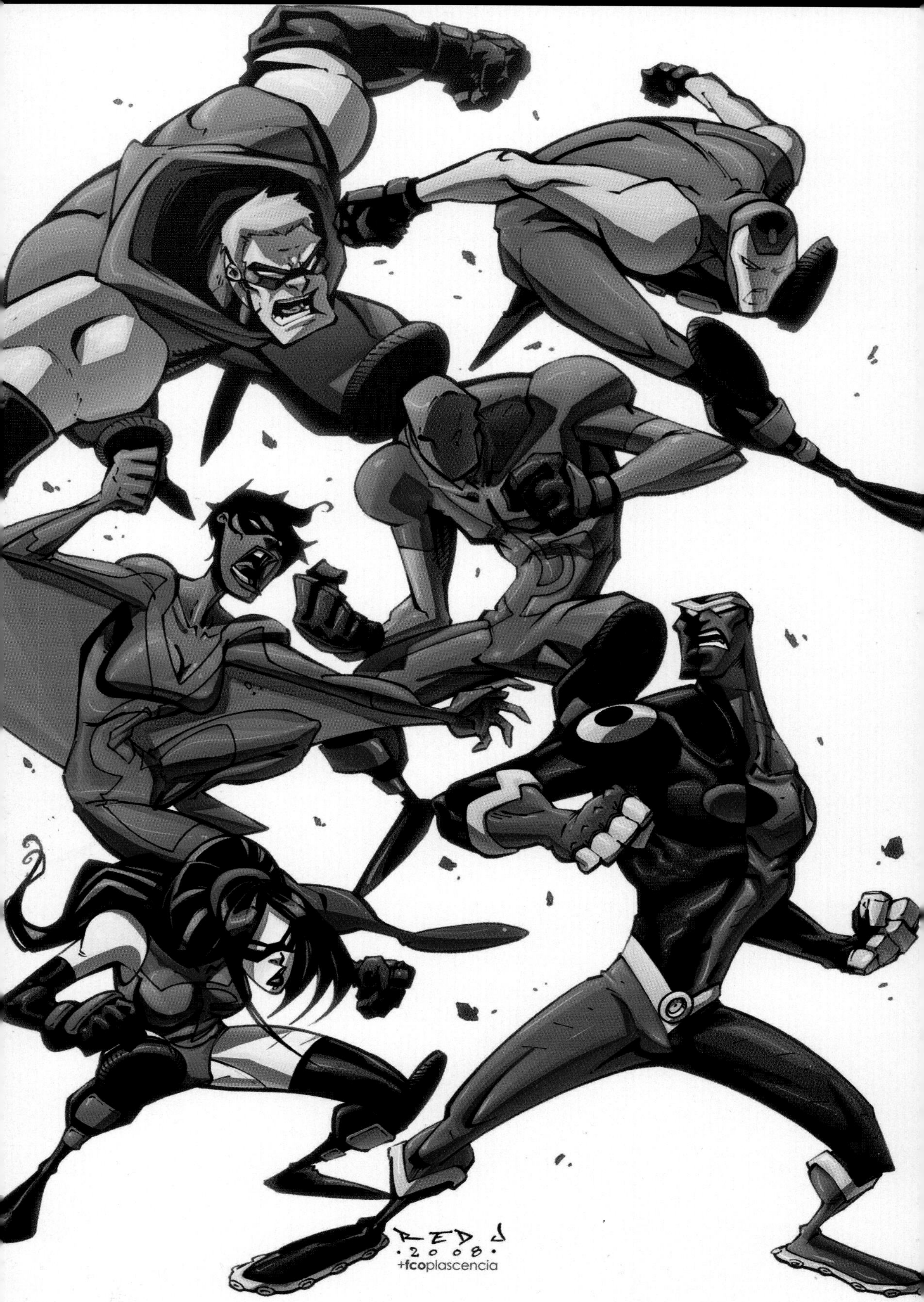
RED J
2008
+fcoplascencia

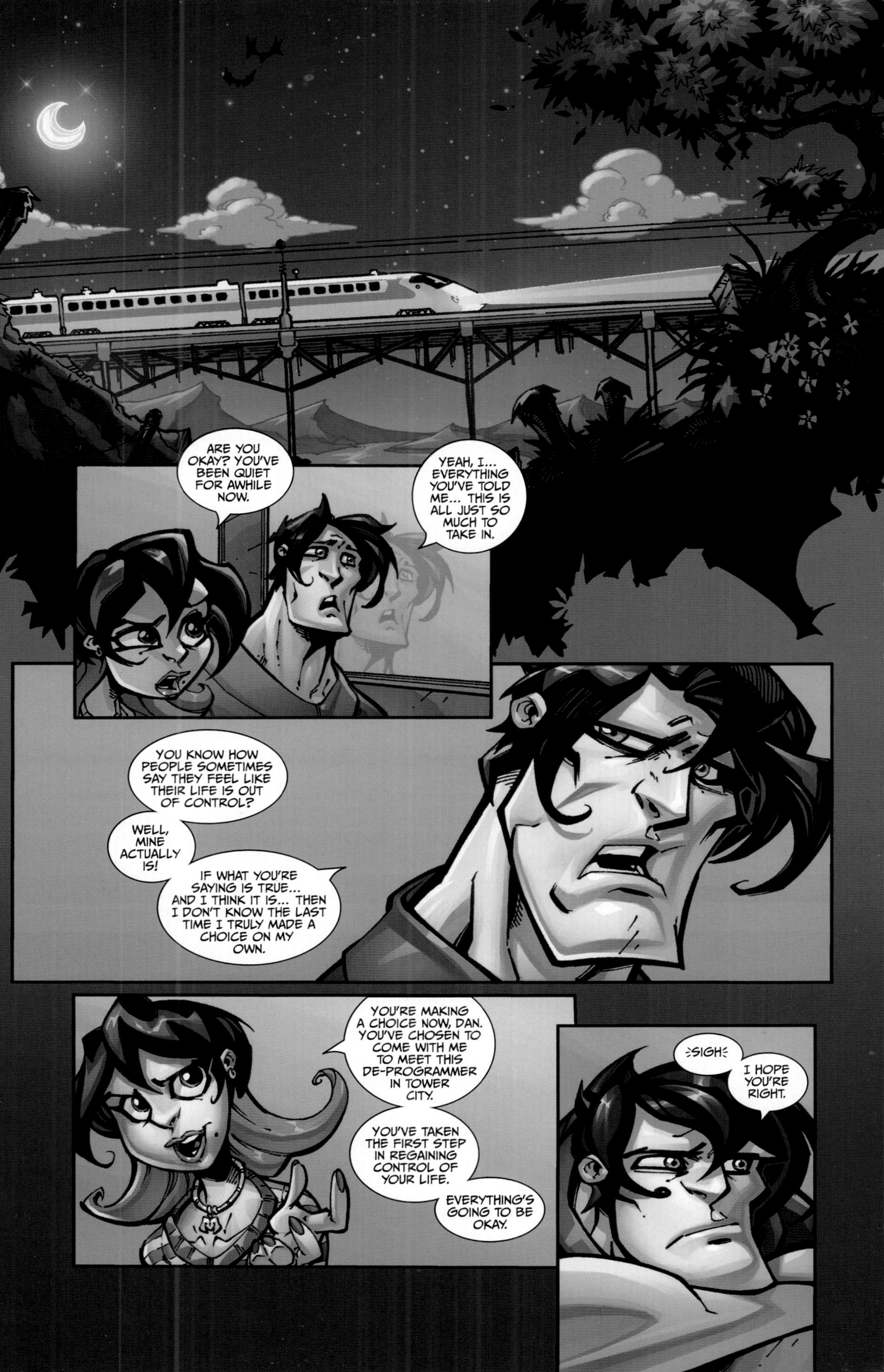
ARE YOU OKAY? YOU'VE BEEN QUIET FOR AWHILE NOW.
YEAH, I... EVERYTHING YOU'VE TOLD ME... THIS IS ALL JUST SO MUCH TO TAKE IN.
YOU KNOW HOW PEOPLE SOMETIMES SAY THEY FEEL LIKE THEIR LIFE IS OUT OF CONTROL?
WELL, MINE ACTUALLY IS!
IF WHAT YOU'RE SAYING IS TRUE... AND I THINK IT IS... THEN I DON'T KNOW THE LAST TIME I TRULY MADE A CHOICE ON MY OWN.
YOU'RE MAKING A CHOICE NOW, DAN. YOU'VE CHOSEN TO COME WITH ME TO MEET THIS DE-PROGRAMMER IN TOWER CITY.
YOU'VE TAKEN THE FIRST STEP IN REGAINING CONTROL OF YOUR LIFE.
EVERYTHING'S GOING TO BE OKAY.
SIGH
I HOPE YOU'RE RIGHT.

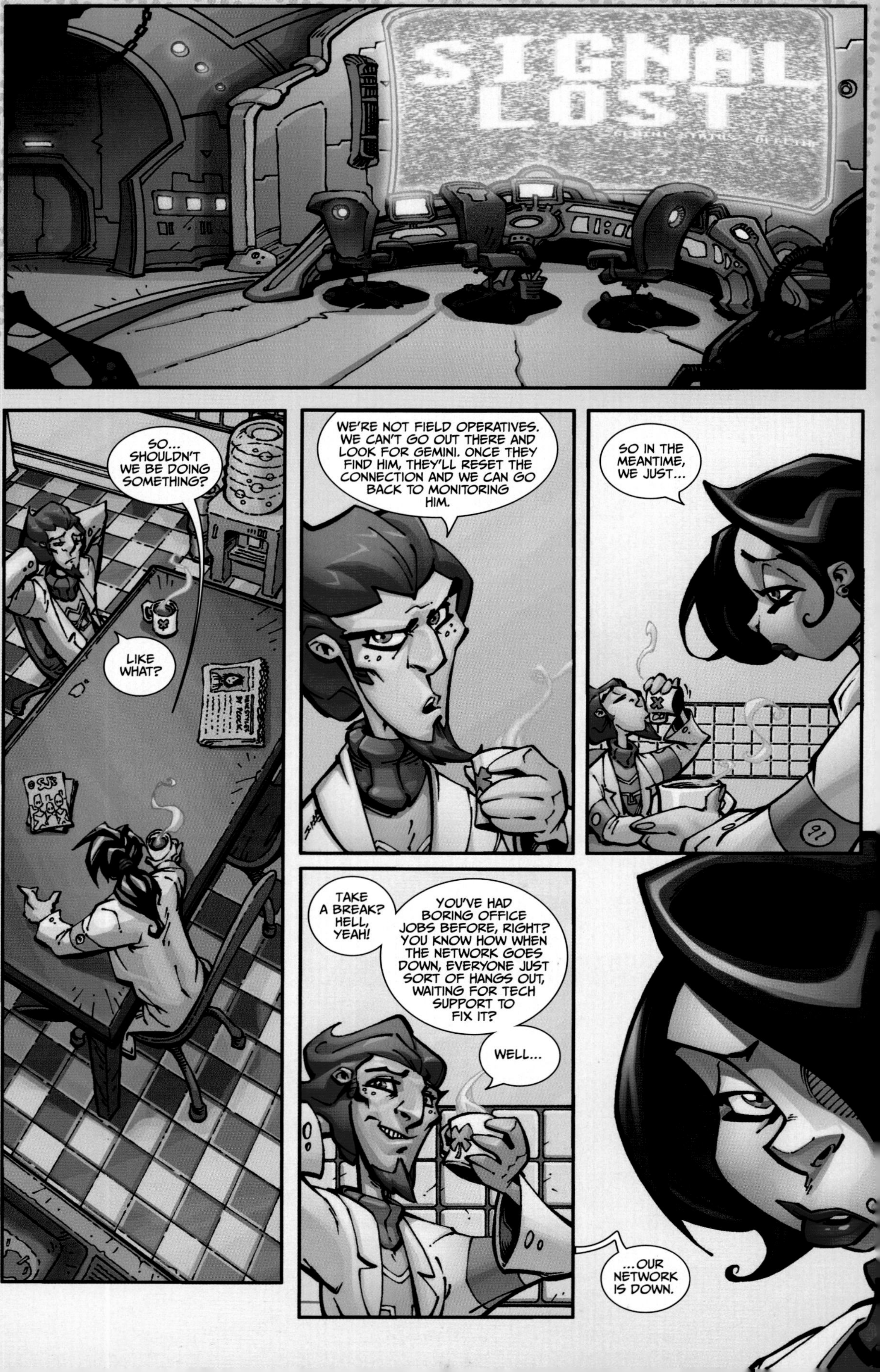
SIGNAL LOST
SO... SHOULDN'T WE BE DOING SOMETHING?
LIKE WHAT?
WE'RE NOT FIELD OPERATIVES. WE CAN'T GO OUT THERE AND LOOK FOR GEMINI. ONCE THEY FIND HIM, THEY'LL RESET THE CONNECTION AND WE CAN GO BACK TO MONITORING HIM.
SO IN THE MEANTIME, WE JUST...
TAKE A BREAK? HELL, YEAH!
YOU'VE HAD BORING OFFICE JOBS BEFORE, RIGHT? YOU KNOW HOW WHEN THE NETWORK GOES DOWN, EVERYONE JUST SORT OF HANGS OUT, WAITING FOR TECH SUPPORT TO FIX IT?
WELL...
...OUR NETWORK IS DOWN.

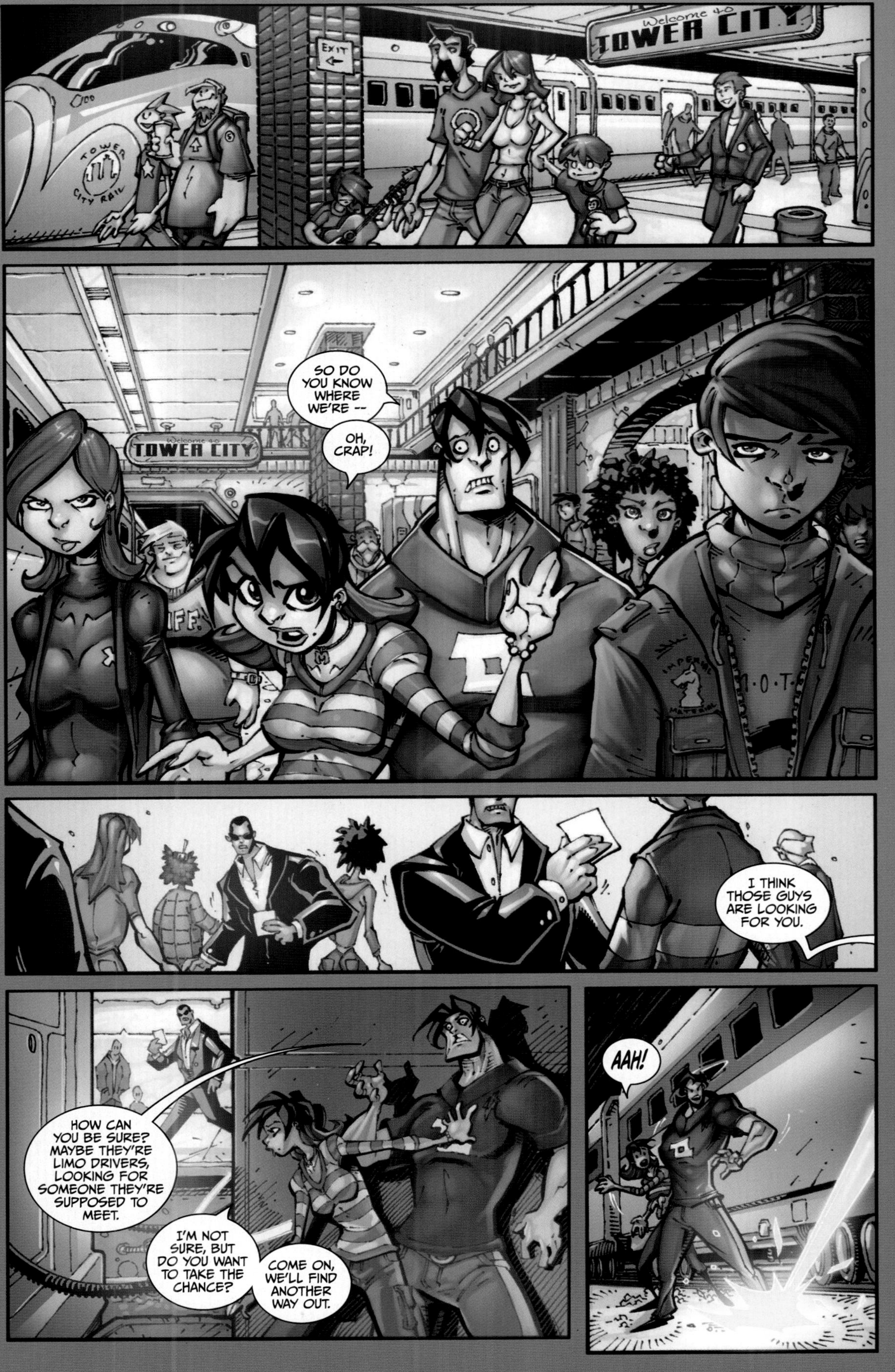
Welcome to TOWER CITY
EXIT
TOWER CITY RAIL
SO DO YOU KNOW WHERE WE'RE --
OH, CRAP!
Welcome to TOWER CITY
I THINK THOSE GUYS ARE LOOKING FOR YOU.
HOW CAN YOU BE SURE? MAYBE THEY'RE LIMO DRIVERS, LOOKING FOR SOMEONE THEY'RE SUPPOSED TO MEET.
I'M NOT SURE, BUT DO YOU WANT TO TAKE THE CHANCE?
COME ON, WE'LL FIND ANOTHER WAY OUT.
AAH!

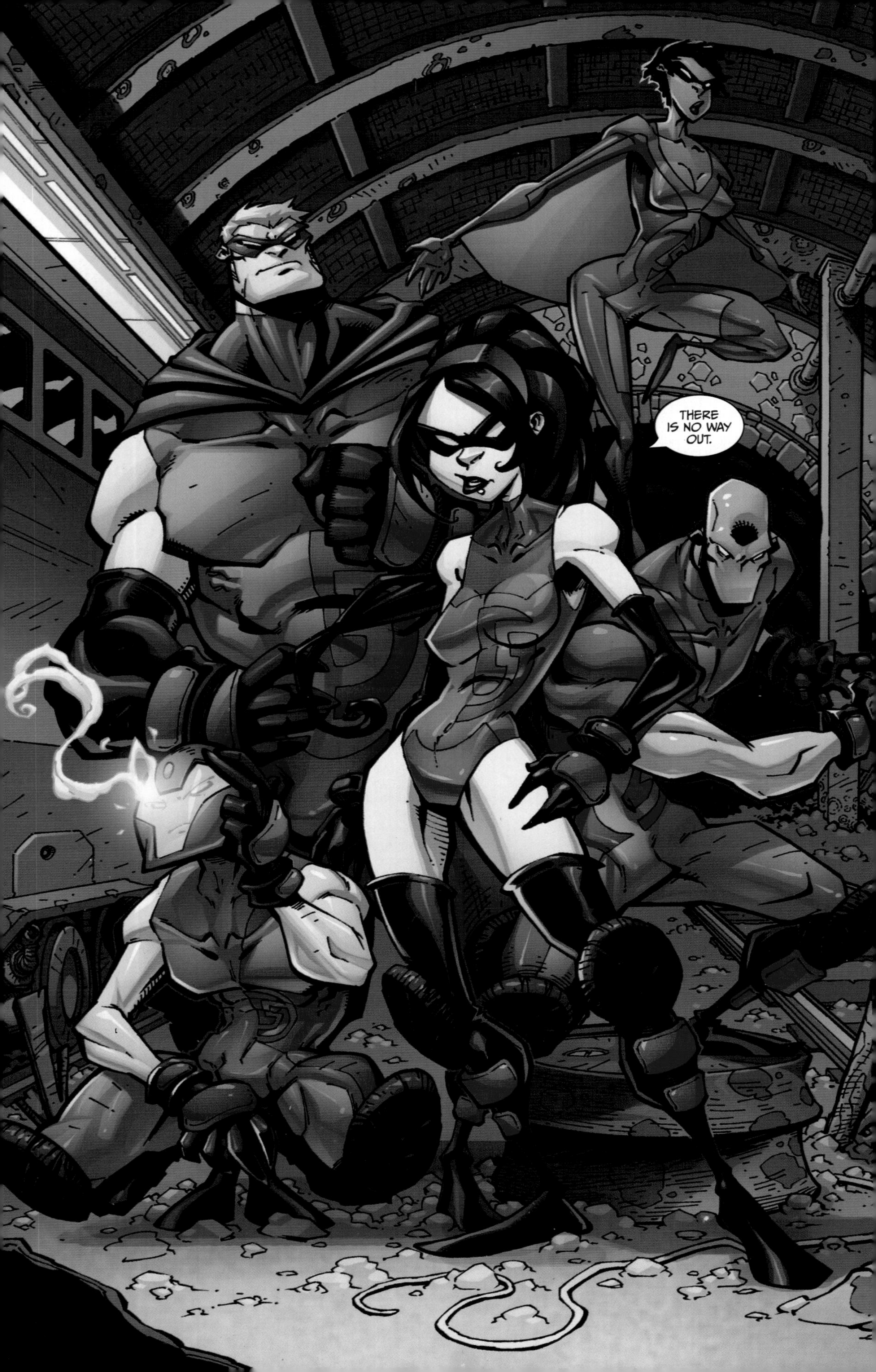
THERE IS NO WAY OUT.

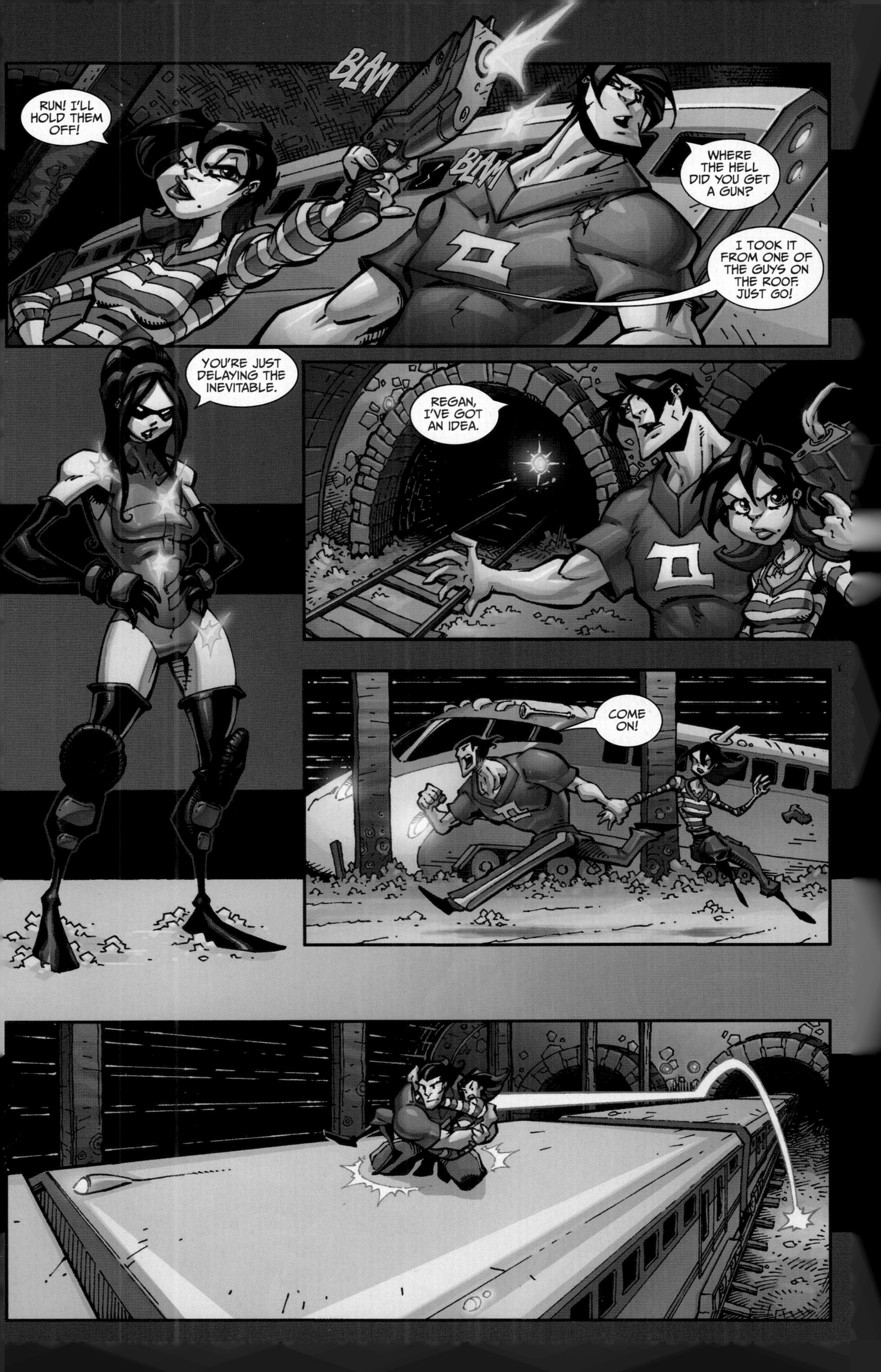
RUN! I'LL HOLD THEM OFF!
BLAM
BLAM
WHERE THE HELL DID YOU GET A GUN?
I TOOK IT FROM ONE OF THE GUYS ON THE ROOF. JUST GO!
YOU'RE JUST DELAYING THE INEVITABLE.
REGAN, I'VE GOT AN IDEA.
COME ON!

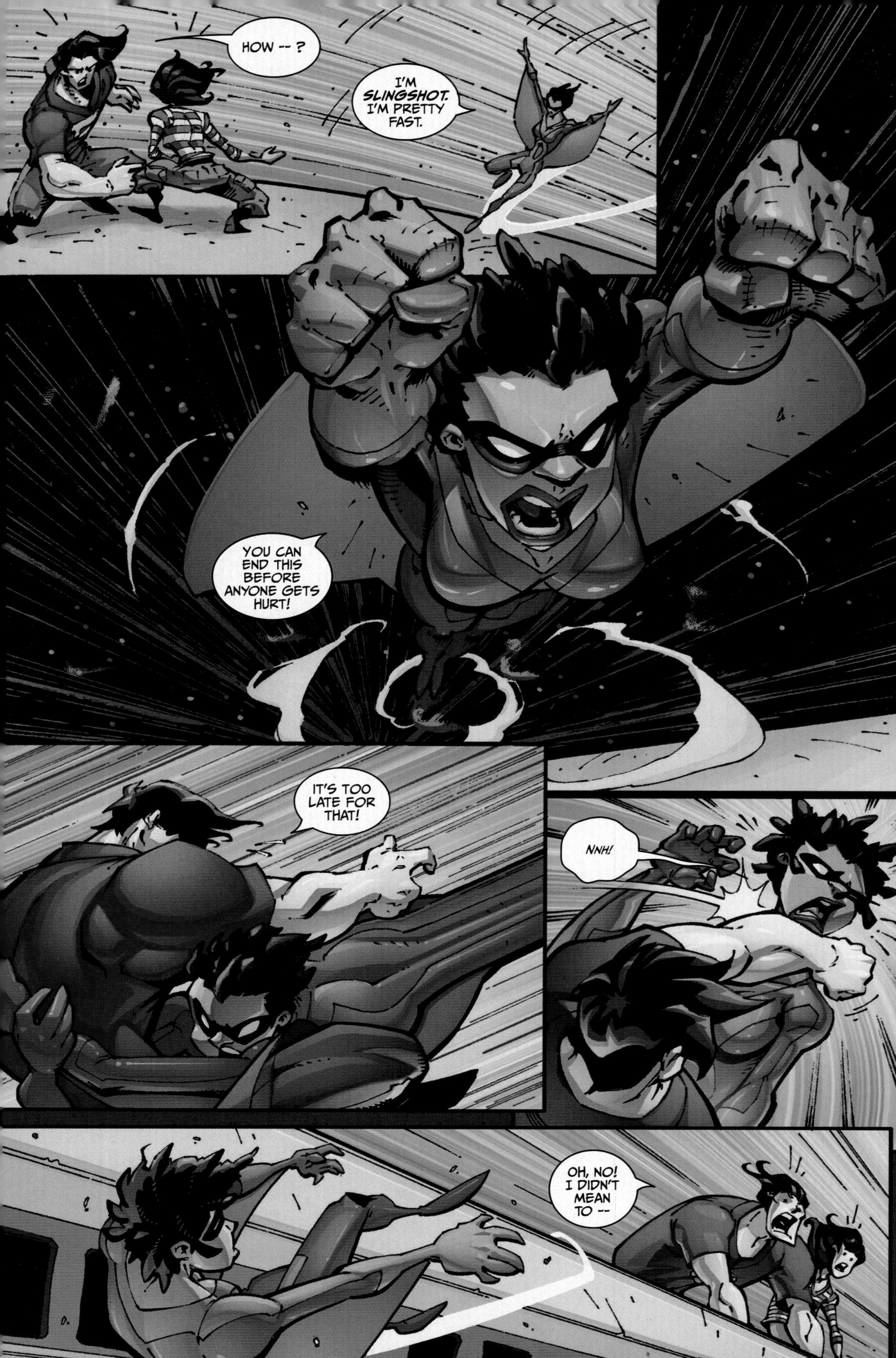
HOW -- ?
I'M SLINGSHOT. I'M PRETTY FAST.
YOU CAN END THIS BEFORE ANYONE GETS HURT!
IT'S TOO LATE FOR THAT!
NNH!
OH, NO! I DIDN'T MEAN TO --

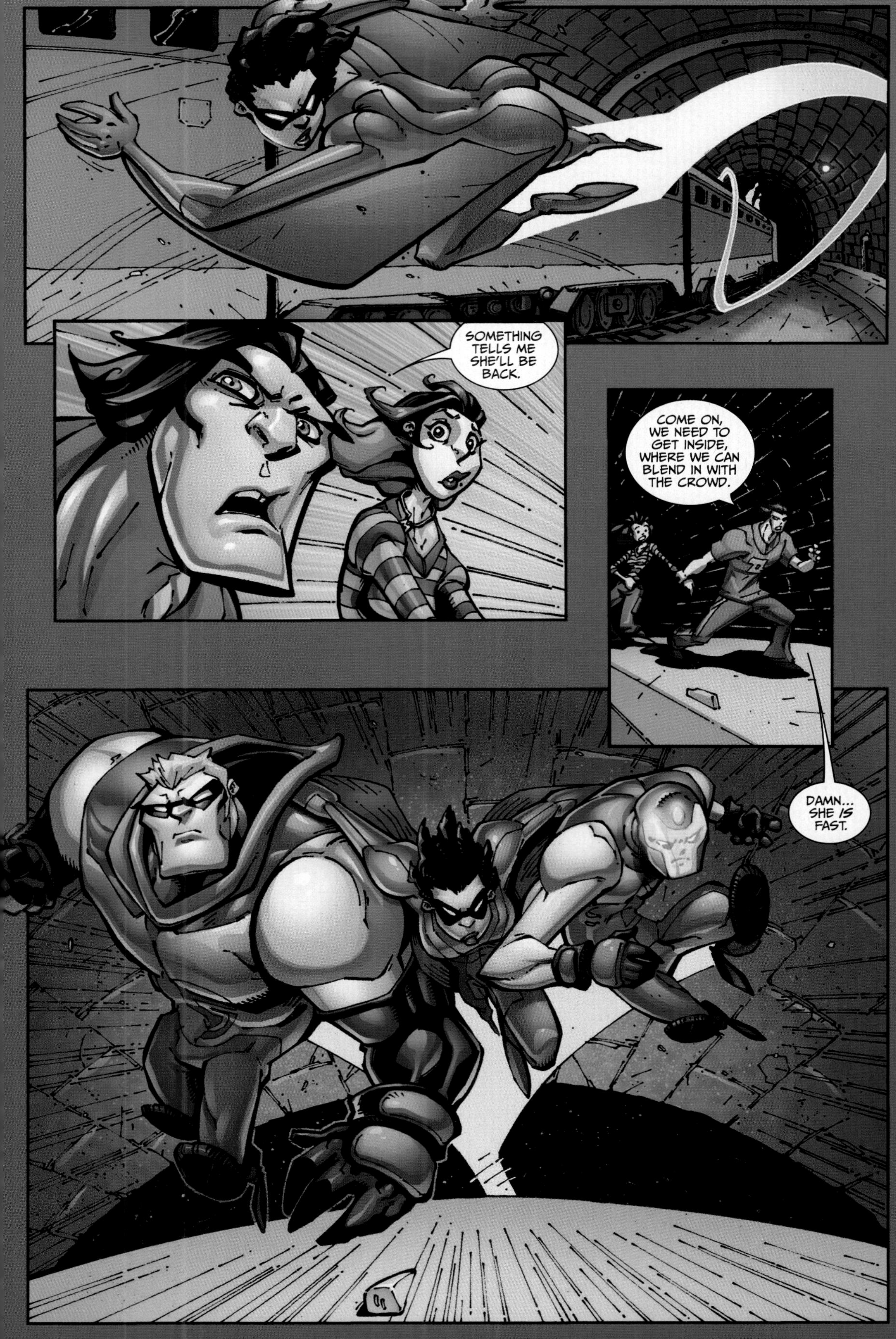
SOMETHING TELLS ME SHE'LL BE BACK.
COME ON, WE NEED TO GET INSIDE, WHERE WE CAN BLEND IN WITH THE CROWD.
DAMN... SHE *IS* FAST.

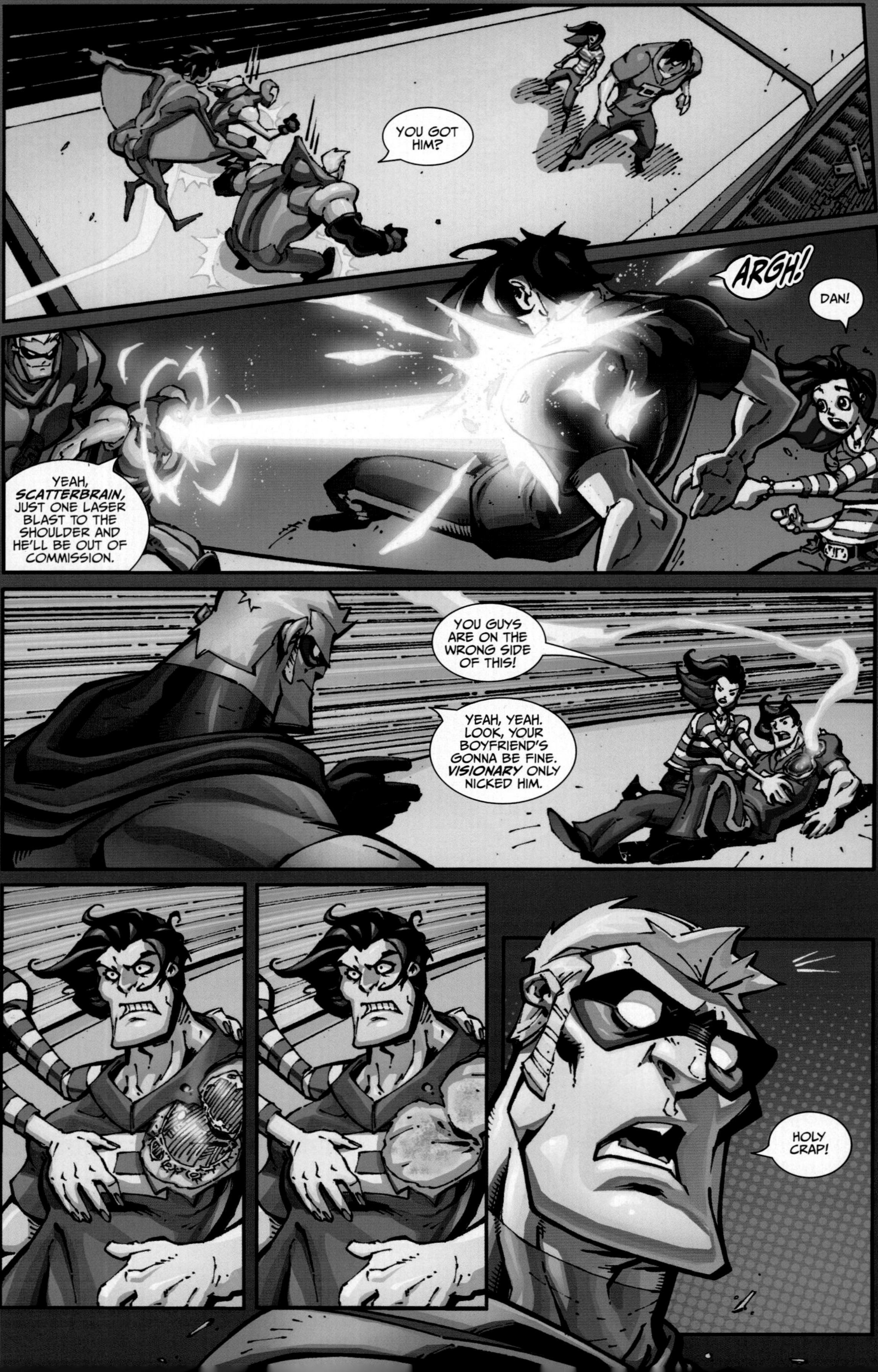
YOU GOT HIM?
ARGH!
DAN!
YEAH, SCATTERBRAIN, JUST ONE LASER BLAST TO THE SHOULDER AND HE'LL BE OUT OF COMMISSION.
YOU GUYS ARE ON THE WRONG SIDE OF THIS!
YEAH, YEAH. LOOK, YOUR BOYFRIEND'S GONNA BE FINE. VISIONARY ONLY NICKED HIM.
HOLY CRAP!

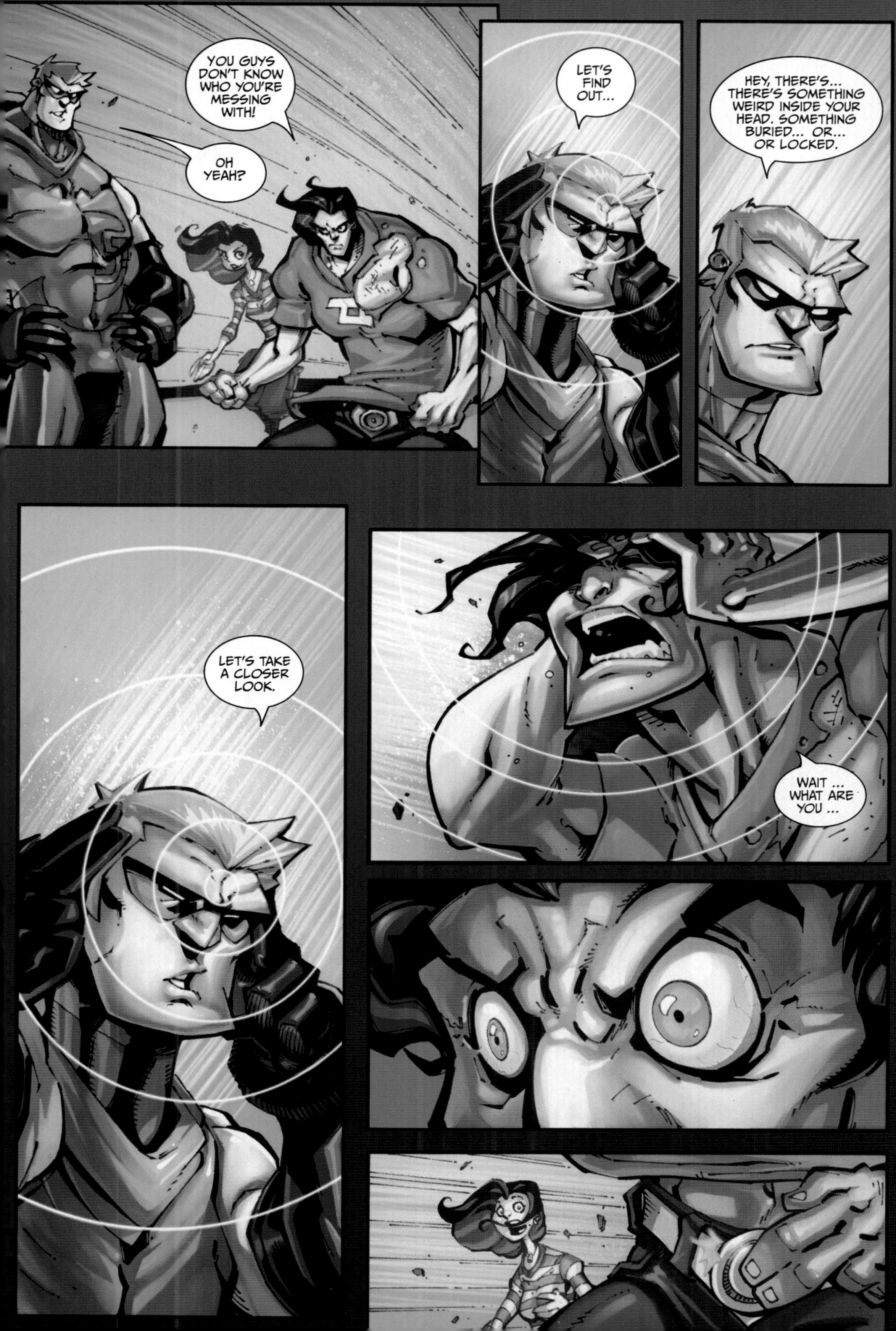
YOU GUYS DON'T KNOW WHO YOU'RE MESSING WITH!
OH YEAH?
LET'S FIND OUT...
HEY, THERE'S... THERE'S SOMETHING WEIRD INSIDE YOUR HEAD. SOMETHING BURIED... OR... OR LOCKED.
LET'S TAKE A CLOSER LOOK.
WAIT ... WHAT ARE YOU ...

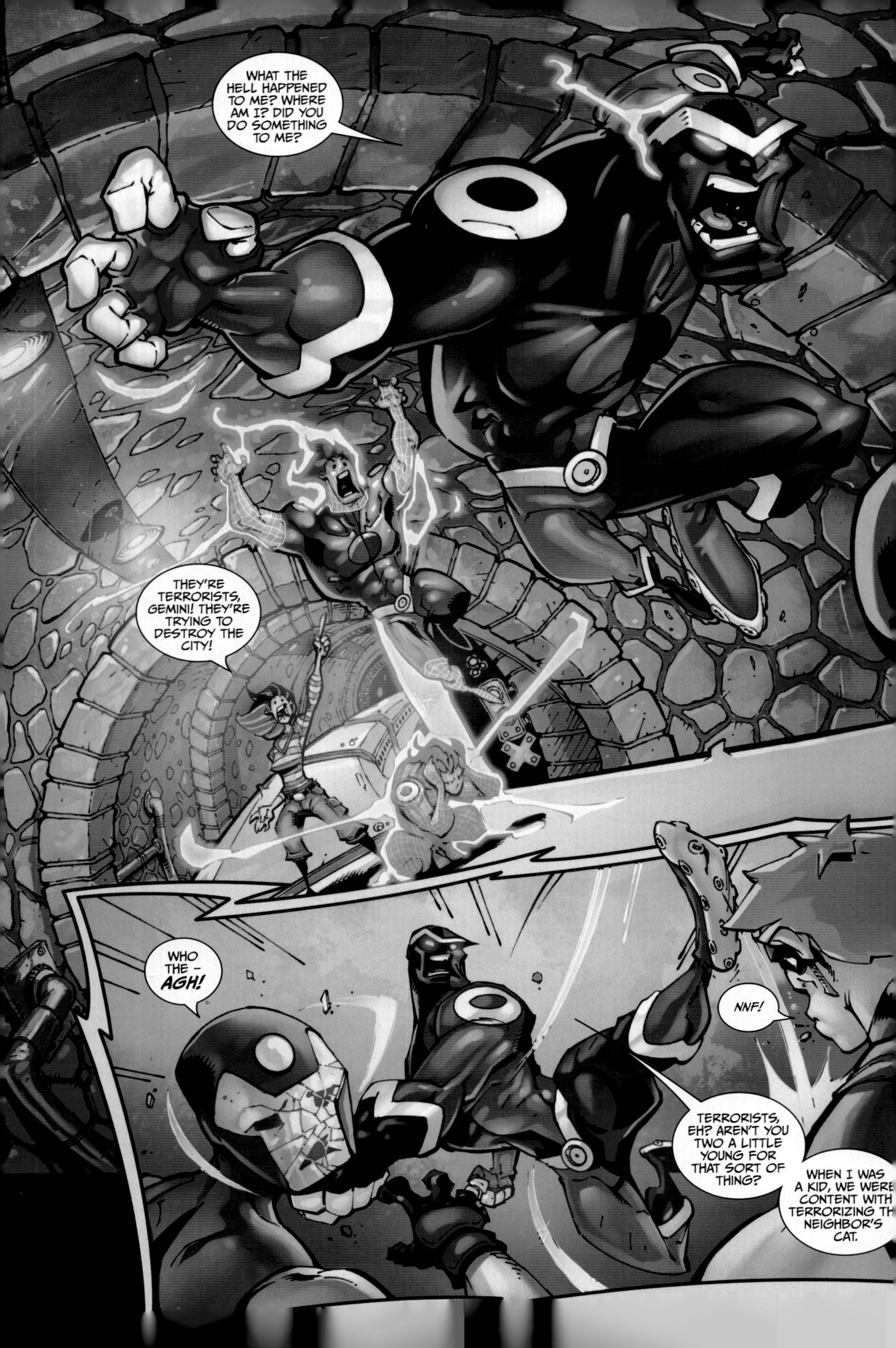
WHAT THE HELL HAPPENED TO ME? WHERE AM I? DID YOU DO SOMETHING TO ME?
THEY'RE TERRORISTS, GEMINI! THEY'RE TRYING TO DESTROY THE CITY!
WHO THE - AGH!
NNF!
TERRORISTS, EH? AREN'T YOU TWO A LITTLE YOUNG FOR THAT SORT OF THING?
WHEN I WAS A KID, WE WERE CONTENT WITH TERRORIZING TH NEIGHBOR'S CAT.

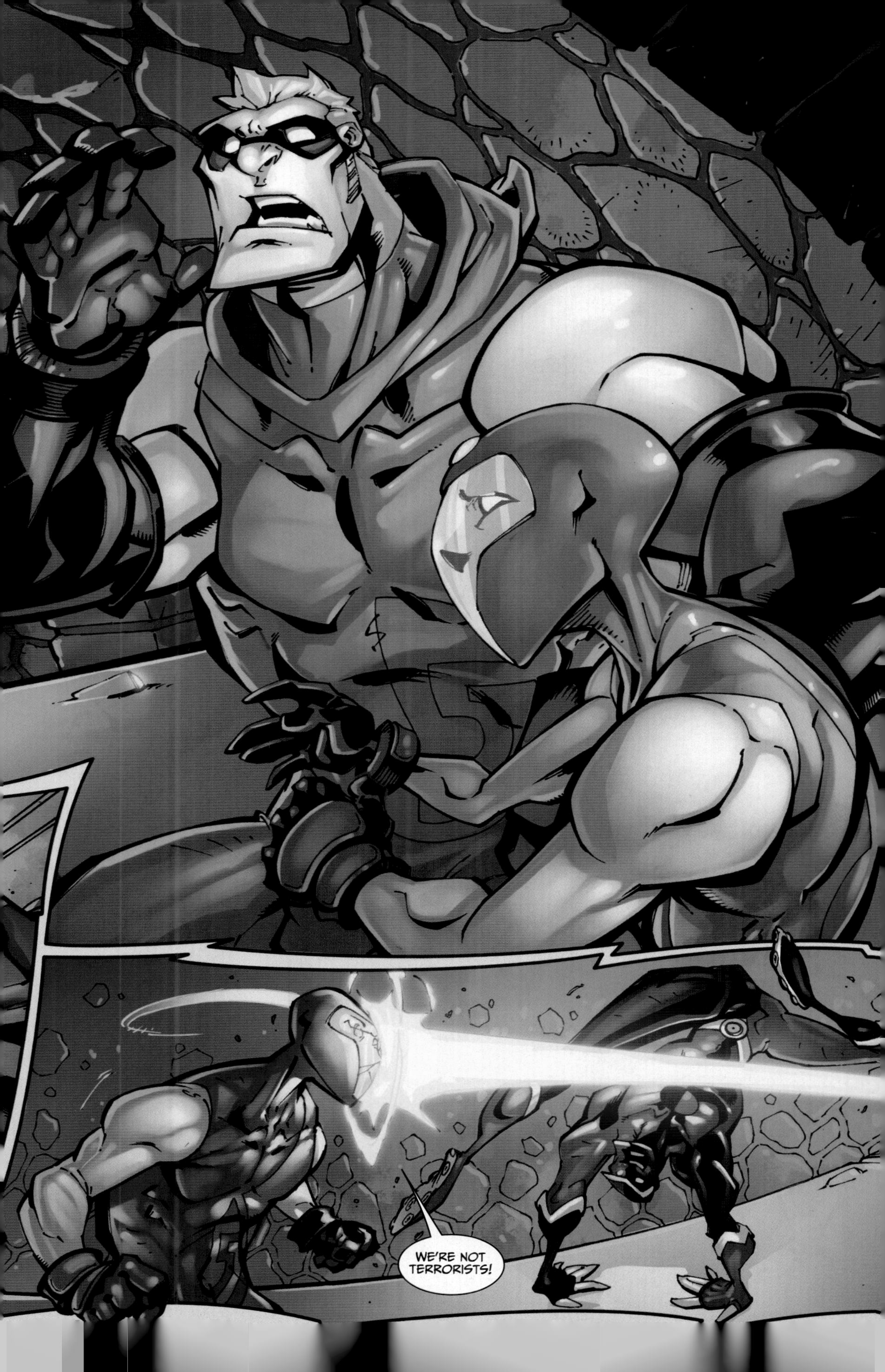
WE'RE NOT TERRORISTS!

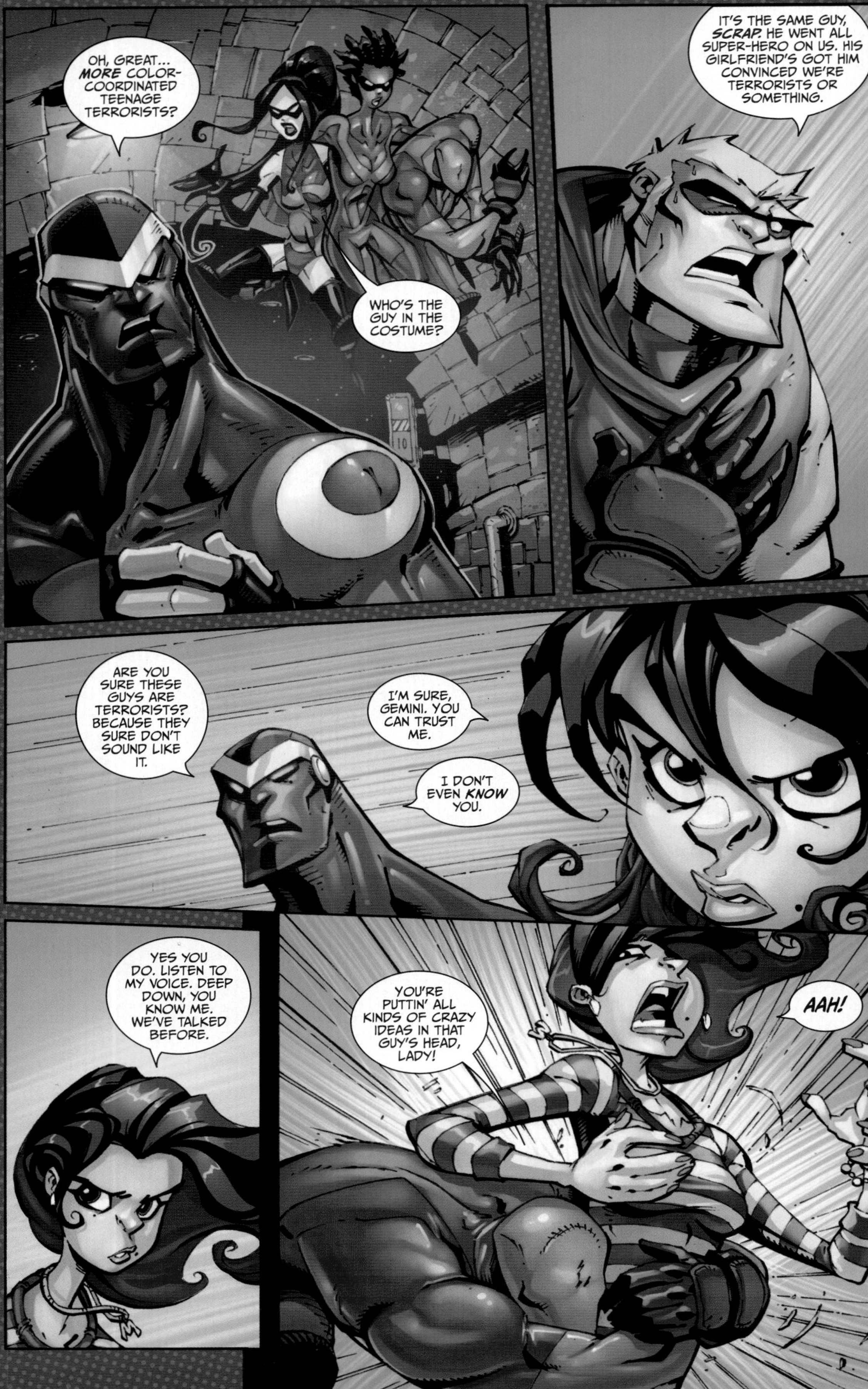
OH, GREAT... MORE COLOR-COORDINATED TEENAGE TERRORISTS?
WHO'S THE GUY IN THE COSTUME?
IT'S THE SAME GUY, SCRAP. HE WENT ALL SUPER-HERO ON US. HIS GIRLFRIEND'S GOT HIM CONVINCED WE'RE TERRORISTS OR SOMETHING.
ARE YOU SURE THESE GUYS ARE TERRORISTS? BECAUSE THEY SURE DON'T SOUND LIKE IT.
I'M SURE, GEMINI. YOU CAN TRUST ME.
I DON'T EVEN KNOW YOU.
YES YOU DO. LISTEN TO MY VOICE. DEEP DOWN, YOU KNOW ME. WE'VE TALKED BEFORE.
YOU'RE PUTTIN' ALL KINDS OF CRAZY IDEAS IN THAT GUY'S HEAD, LADY!
AAH!

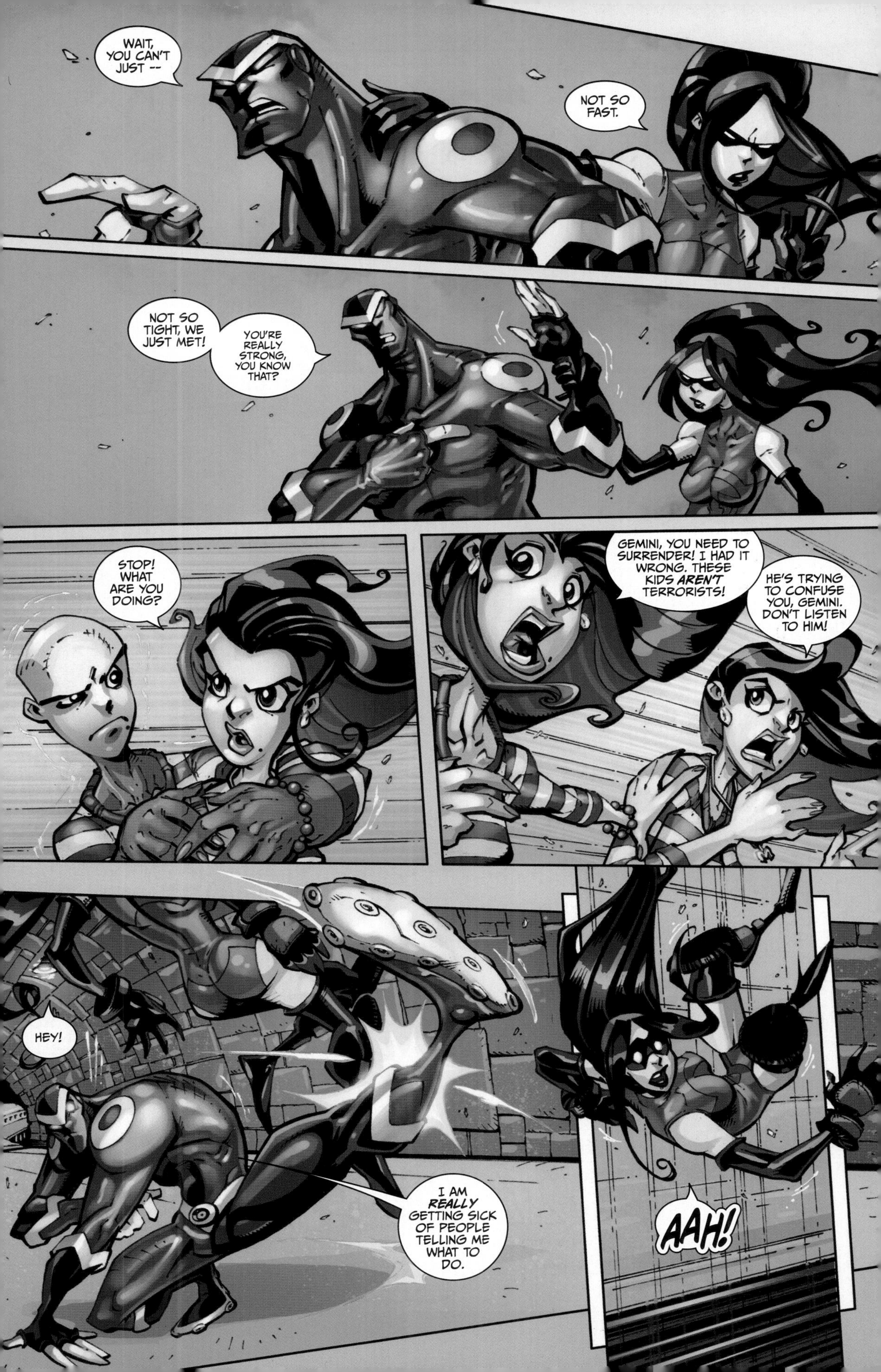
WAIT, YOU CAN'T JUST --
NOT SO FAST.
NOT SO TIGHT, WE JUST MET!
YOU'RE REALLY STRONG, YOU KNOW THAT?
STOP! WHAT ARE YOU DOING?
GEMINI, YOU NEED TO SURRENDER! I HAD IT WRONG. THESE KIDS *AREN'T* TERRORISTS!
HE'S TRYING TO CONFUSE YOU, GEMINI. DON'T LISTEN TO HIM!
HEY!
I AM *REALLY* GETTING SICK OF PEOPLE TELLING ME WHAT TO DO.
AAH!

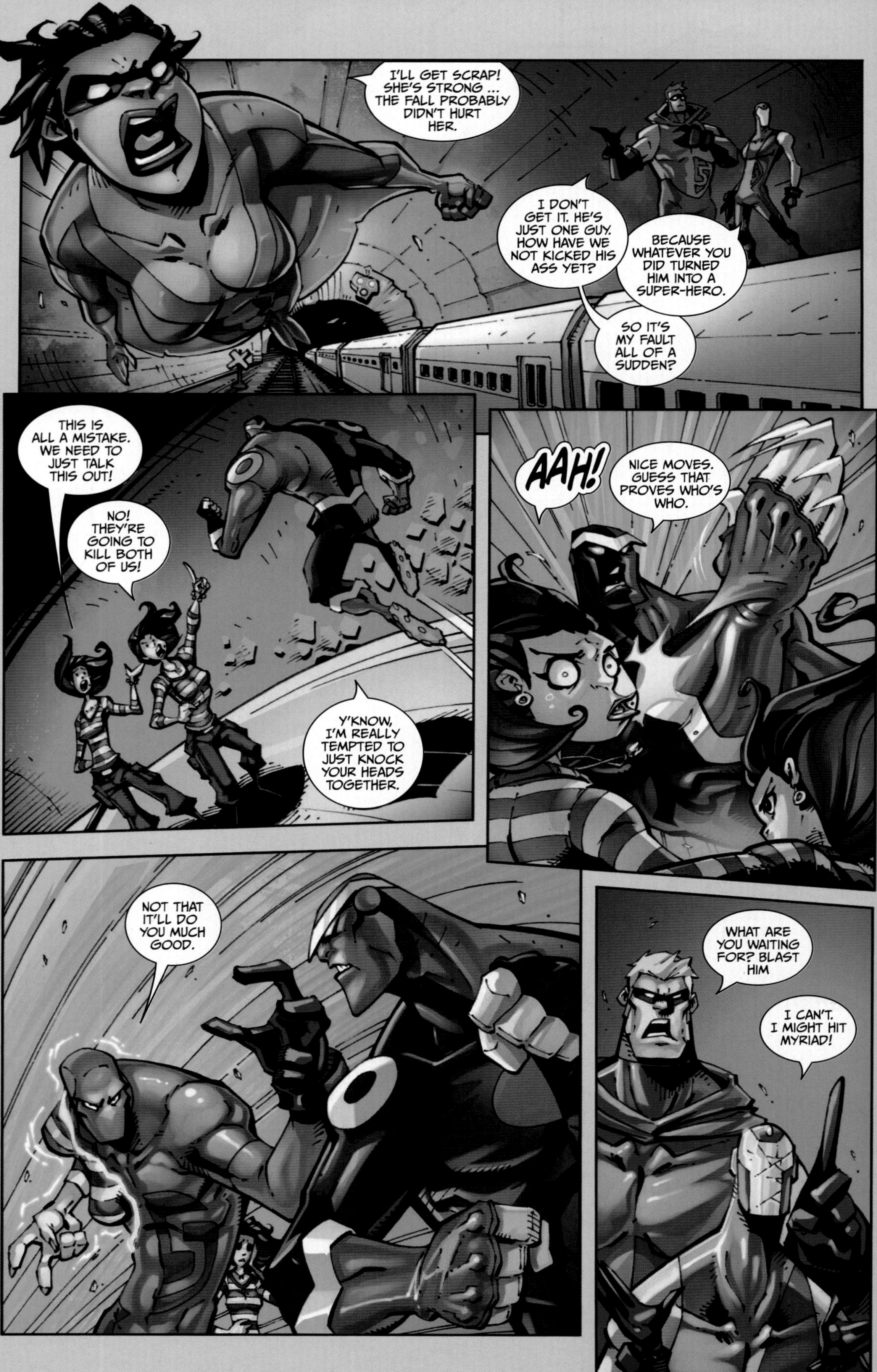
I'LL GET SCRAP! SHE'S STRONG ... THE FALL PROBABLY DIDN'T HURT HER.
I DON'T GET IT. HE'S JUST ONE GUY. HOW HAVE WE NOT KICKED HIS ASS YET?
BECAUSE WHATEVER YOU DID TURNED HIM INTO A SUPER-HERO.
SO IT'S MY FAULT ALL OF A SUDDEN?
THIS IS ALL A MISTAKE. WE NEED TO JUST TALK THIS OUT!
NO! THEY'RE GOING TO KILL BOTH OF US!
Y'KNOW, I'M REALLY TEMPTED TO JUST KNOCK YOUR HEADS TOGETHER.
AAH!
NICE MOVES. GUESS THAT PROVES WHO'S WHO.
NOT THAT IT'LL DO YOU MUCH GOOD.
WHAT ARE YOU WAITING FOR? BLAST HIM
I CAN'T. I MIGHT HIT MYRIAD!

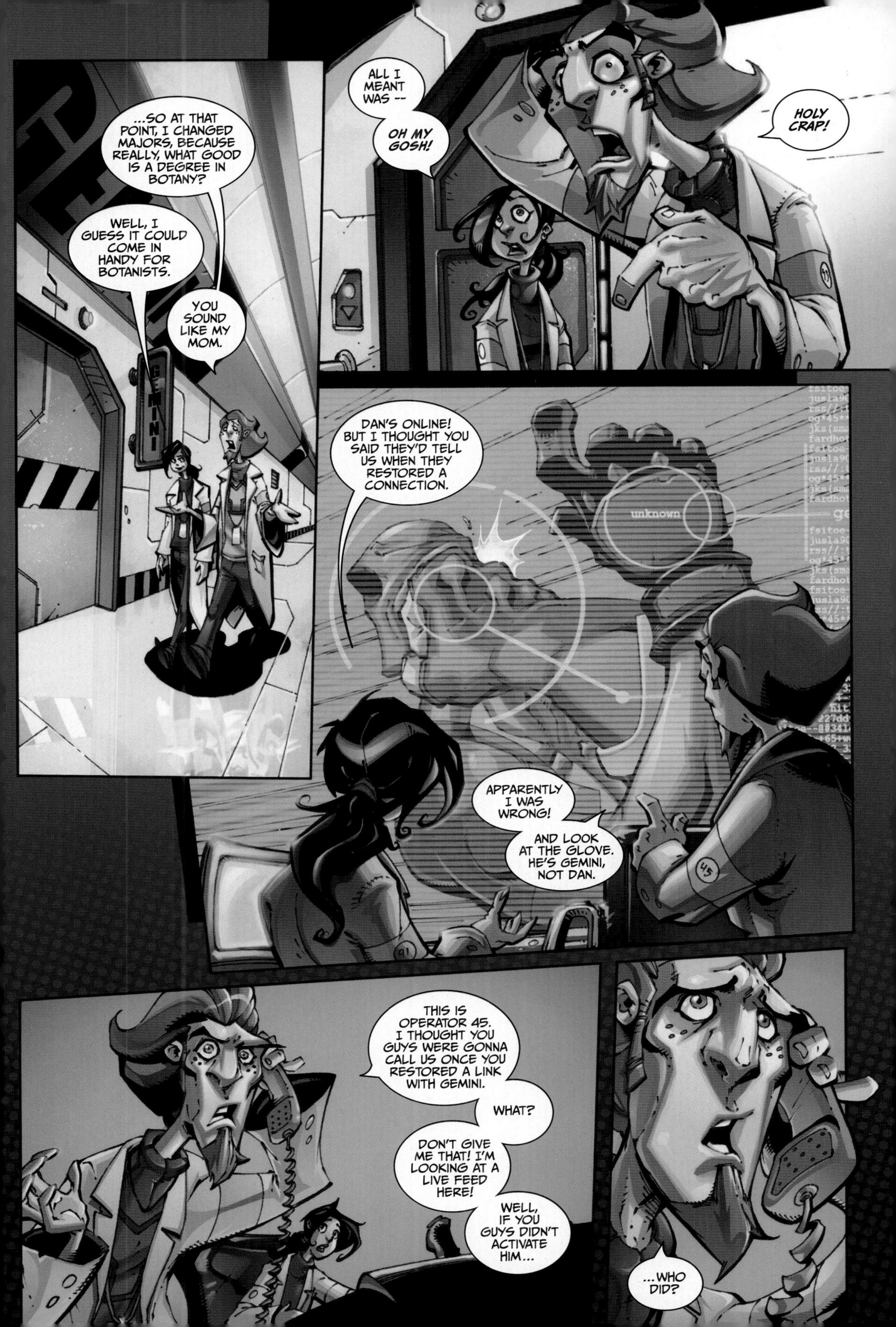
...SO AT THAT POINT, I CHANGED MAJORS, BECAUSE REALLY, WHAT GOOD IS A DEGREE IN BOTANY?
WELL, I GUESS IT COULD COME IN HANDY FOR BOTANISTS.
YOU SOUND LIKE MY MOM.
GEMINI
ALL I MEANT WAS --
OH MY GOSH!
HOLY CRAP!
DAN'S ONLINE! BUT I THOUGHT YOU SAID THEY'D TELL US WHEN THEY RESTORED A CONNECTION.
unknown
APPARENTLY I WAS WRONG!
AND LOOK AT THE GLOVE. HE'S GEMINI, NOT DAN.
THIS IS OPERATOR 45. I THOUGHT YOU GUYS WERE GONNA CALL US ONCE YOU RESTORED A LINK WITH GEMINI.
WHAT?
DON'T GIVE ME THAT! I'M LOOKING AT A LIVE FEED HERE!
WELL, IF YOU GUYS DIDN'T ACTIVATE HIM...
...WHO DID?

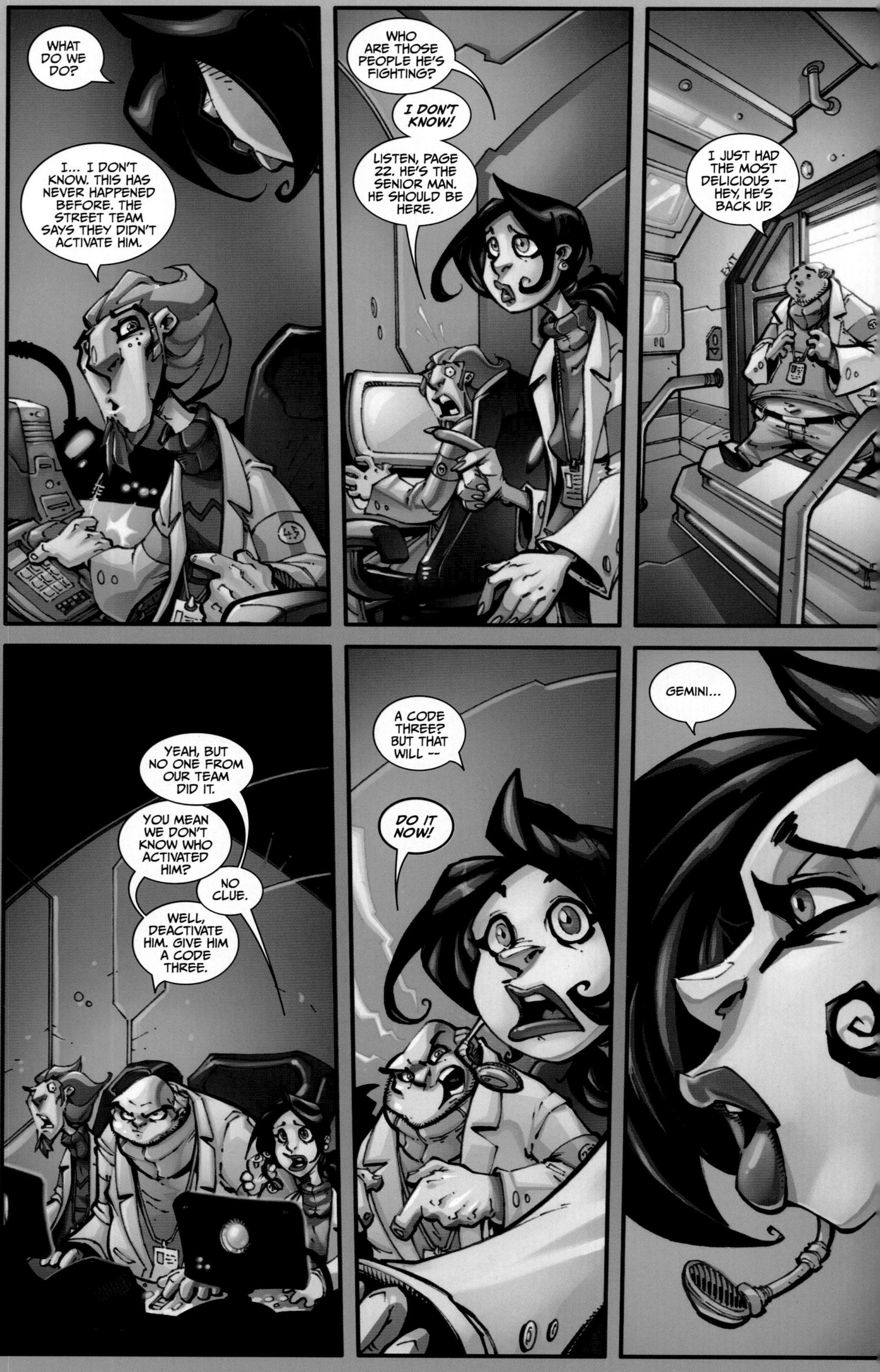

WHAT DO WE DO?
I... I DON'T KNOW. THIS HAS NEVER HAPPENED BEFORE. THE STREET TEAM SAYS THEY DIDN'T ACTIVATE HIM.
WHO ARE THOSE PEOPLE HE'S FIGHTING?
I DON'T KNOW!
LISTEN, PAGE 22. HE'S THE SENIOR MAN. HE SHOULD BE HERE.
I JUST HAD THE MOST DELICIOUS -- HEY, HE'S BACK UP.
EXIT
YEAH, BUT NO ONE FROM OUR TEAM DID IT.
YOU MEAN WE DON'T KNOW WHO ACTIVATED HIM?
NO CLUE.
WELL, DEACTIVATE HIM. GIVE HIM A CODE THREE.
A CODE THREE? BUT THAT WILL --
DO IT NOW!
GEMINI...

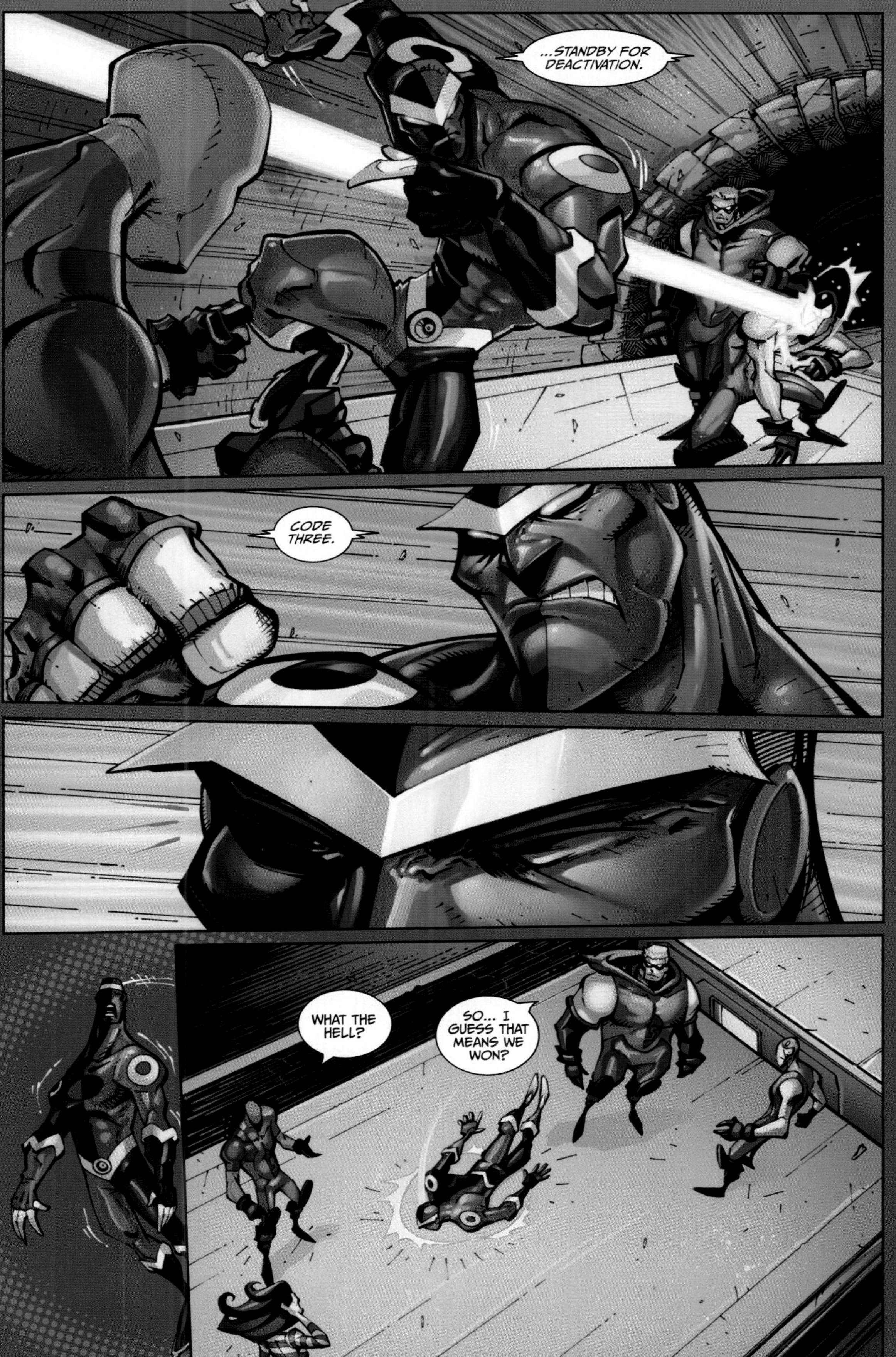
...STANDBY FOR DEACTIVATION.
CODE THREE.
WHAT THE HELL?
SO... I GUESS THAT MEANS WE WON?

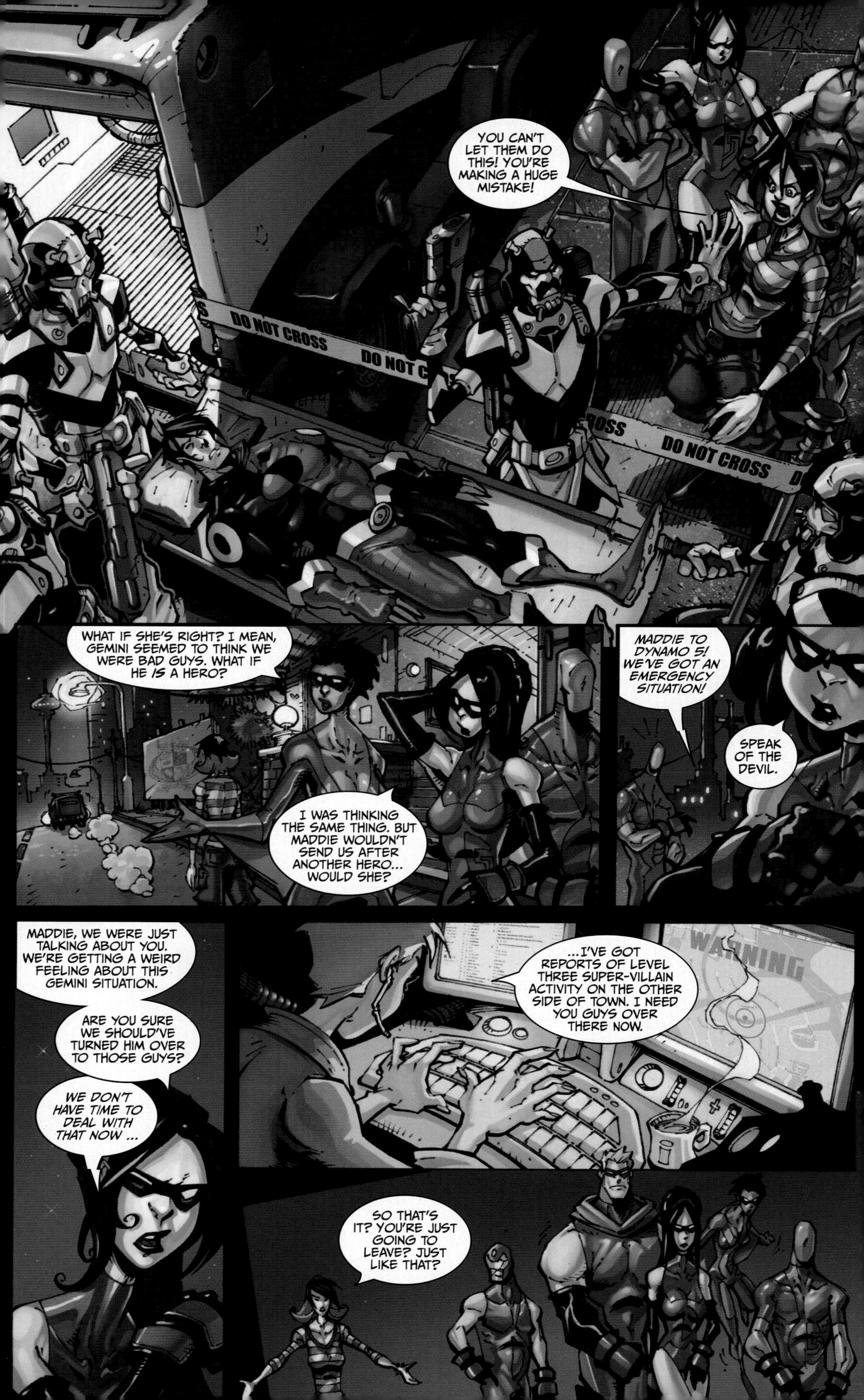
YOU CAN'T LET THEM DO THIS! YOU'RE MAKING A HUGE MISTAKE!
DO NOT CROSS
DO NOT CROSS
DO NOT CROSS
WHAT IF SHE'S RIGHT? I MEAN, GEMINI SEEMED TO THINK WE WERE BAD GUYS. WHAT IF HE IS A HERO?
I WAS THINKING THE SAME THING. BUT MADDIE WOULDN'T SEND US AFTER ANOTHER HERO... WOULD SHE?
MADDIE TO DYNAMO 5! WE'VE GOT AN EMERGENCY SITUATION!
SPEAK OF THE DEVIL.
MADDIE, WE WERE JUST TALKING ABOUT YOU. WE'RE GETTING A WEIRD FEELING ABOUT THIS GEMINI SITUATION.
ARE YOU SURE WE SHOULD'VE TURNED HIM OVER TO THOSE GUYS?
WE DON'T HAVE TIME TO DEAL WITH THAT NOW ...
...I'VE GOT REPORTS OF LEVEL THREE SUPER-VILLAIN ACTIVITY ON THE OTHER SIDE OF TOWN. I NEED YOU GUYS OVER THERE NOW.
WARNING
SO THAT'S IT? YOU'RE JUST GOING TO LEAVE? JUST LIKE THAT?

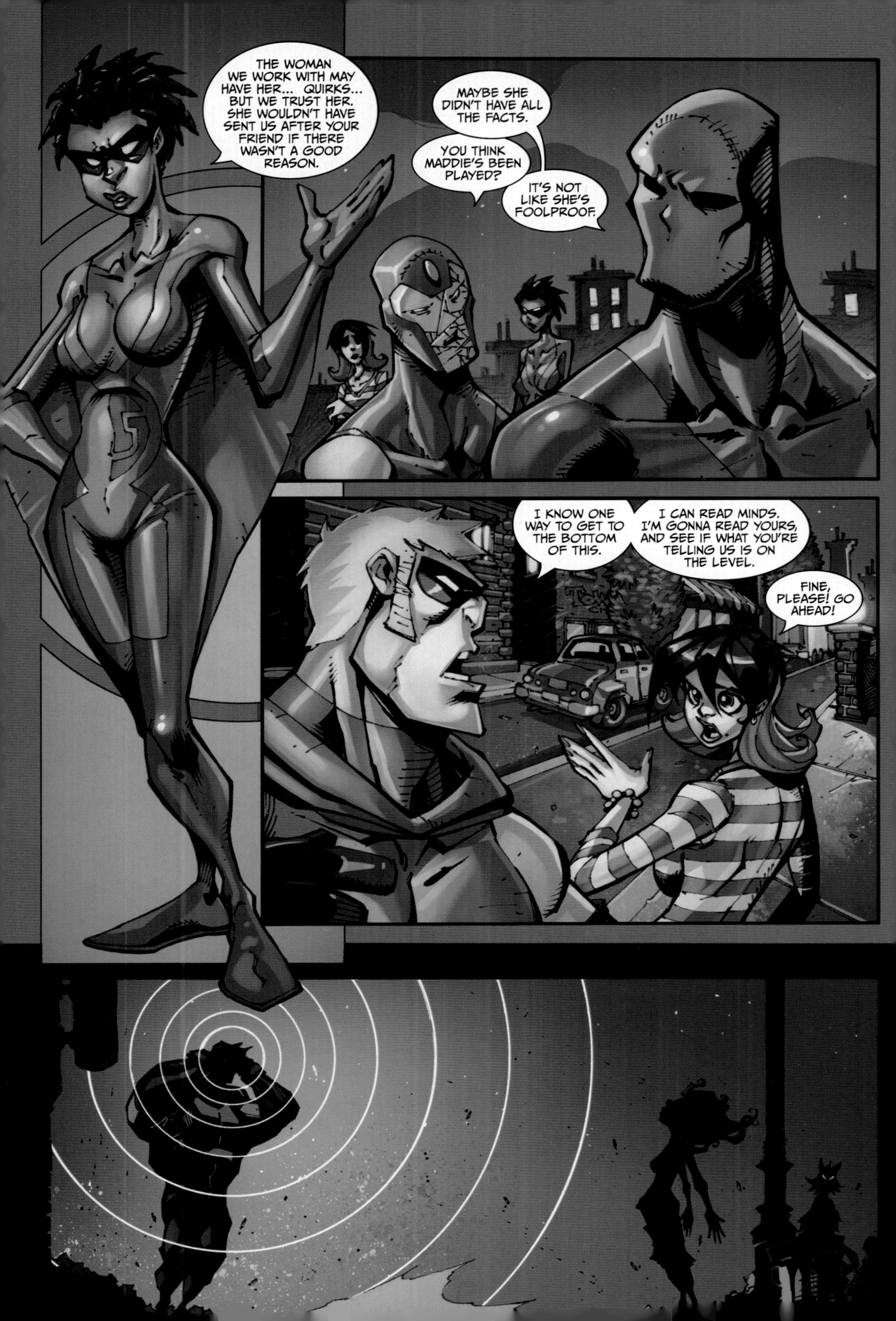

THE WOMAN WE WORK WITH MAY HAVE HER... QUIRKS... BUT WE TRUST HER. SHE WOULDN'T HAVE SENT US AFTER YOUR FRIEND IF THERE WASN'T A GOOD REASON.
MAYBE SHE DIDN'T HAVE ALL THE FACTS.
YOU THINK MADDIE'S BEEN PLAYED?
IT'S NOT LIKE SHE'S FOOLPROOF.
I KNOW ONE WAY TO GET TO THE BOTTOM OF THIS.
I CAN READ MINDS. I'M GONNA READ YOURS, AND SEE IF WHAT YOU'RE TELLING US IS ON THE LEVEL.
FINE, PLEASE! GO AHEAD!

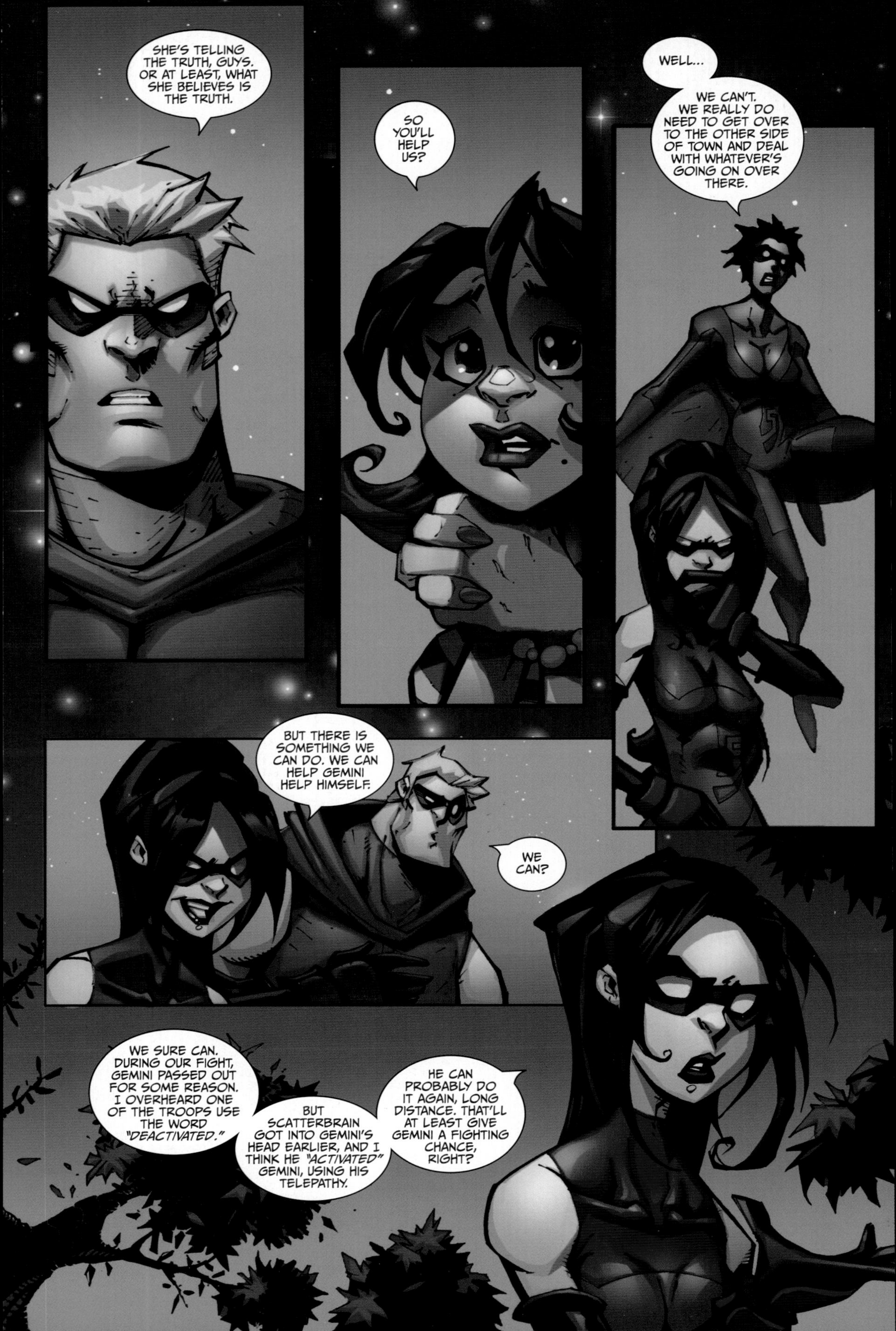
SHE'S TELLING THE TRUTH, GUYS. OR AT LEAST, WHAT SHE BELIEVES IS THE TRUTH.
SO YOU'LL HELP US?
WELL...
WE CAN'T. WE REALLY DO NEED TO GET OVER TO THE OTHER SIDE OF TOWN AND DEAL WITH WHATEVER'S GOING ON OVER THERE.
BUT THERE IS SOMETHING WE CAN DO. WE CAN HELP GEMINI HELP HIMSELF.
WE CAN?
WE SURE CAN. DURING OUR FIGHT, GEMINI PASSED OUT FOR SOME REASON. I OVERHEARD ONE OF THE TROOPS USE THE WORD "DEACTIVATED."
BUT SCATTERBRAIN GOT INTO GEMINI'S HEAD EARLIER, AND I THINK HE "ACTIVATED" GEMINI, USING HIS TELEPATHY.
HE CAN PROBABLY DO IT AGAIN, LONG DISTANCE. THAT'LL AT LEAST GIVE GEMINI A FIGHTING CHANCE, RIGHT?

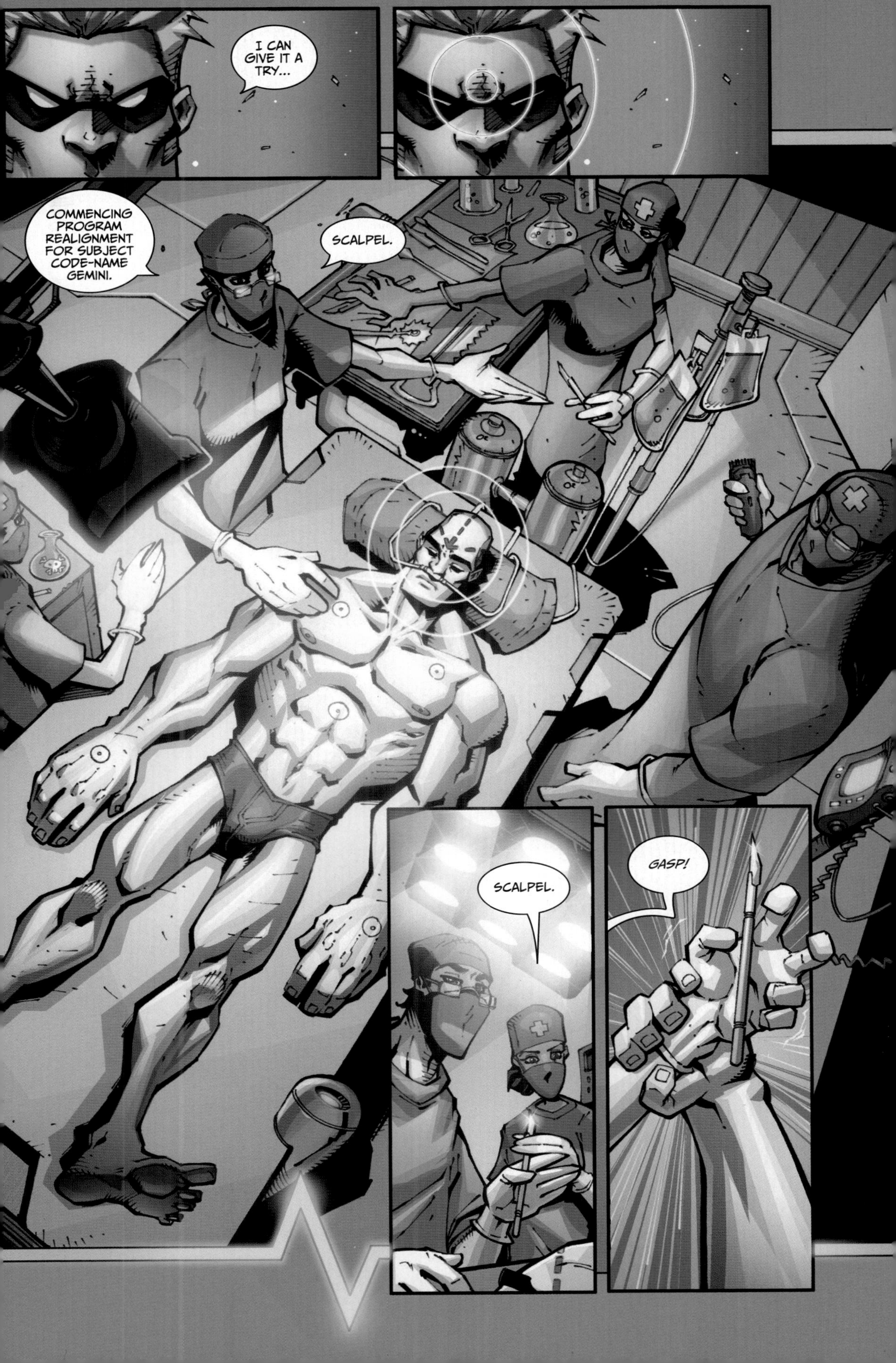
I CAN GIVE IT A TRY...
COMMENCING PROGRAM REALIGNMENT FOR SUBJECT CODE-NAME GEMINI.
SCALPEL.
SCALPEL.
GASP!

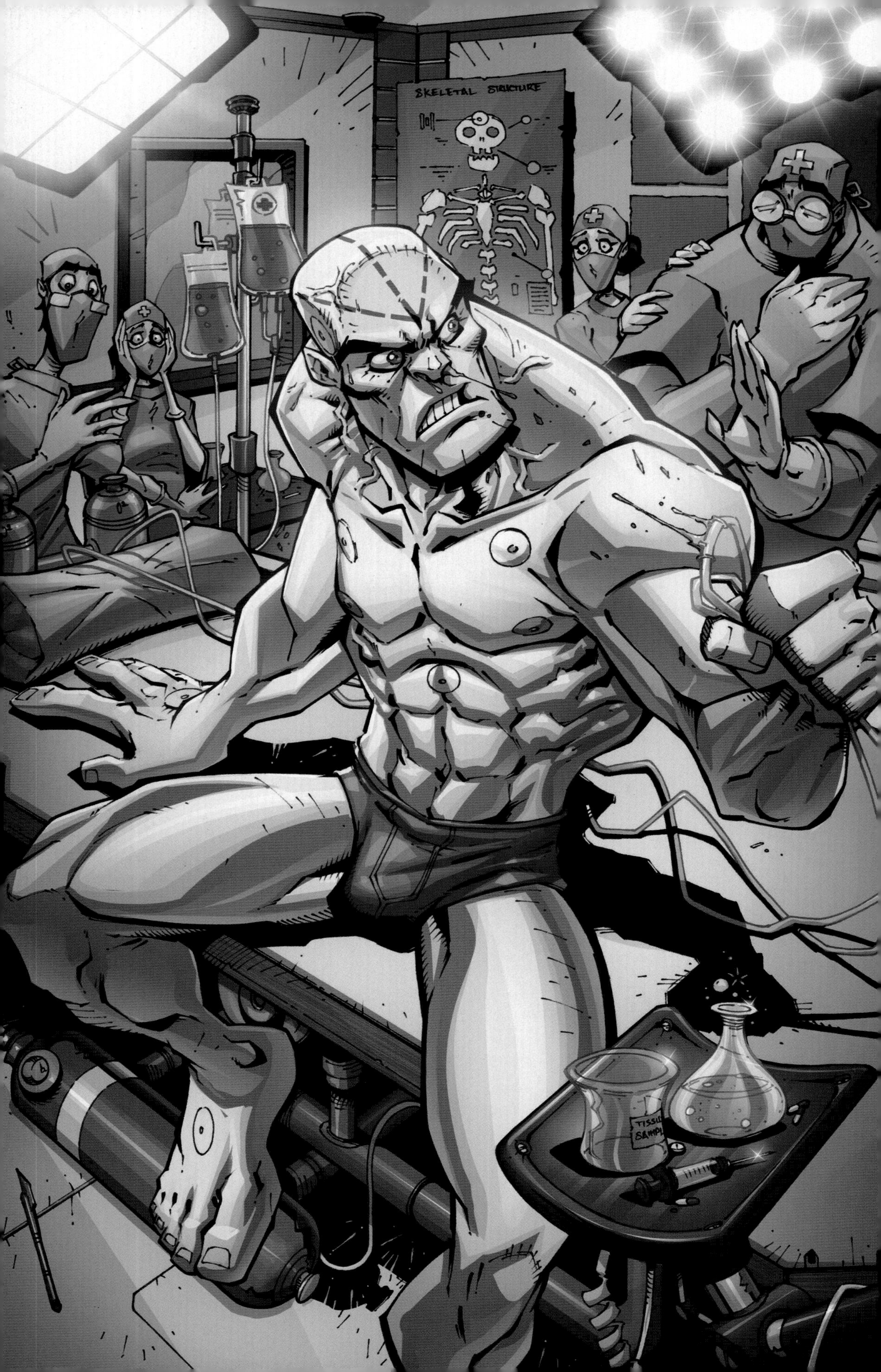
SKELETAL STRUCTURE

CHAPTER FIVE

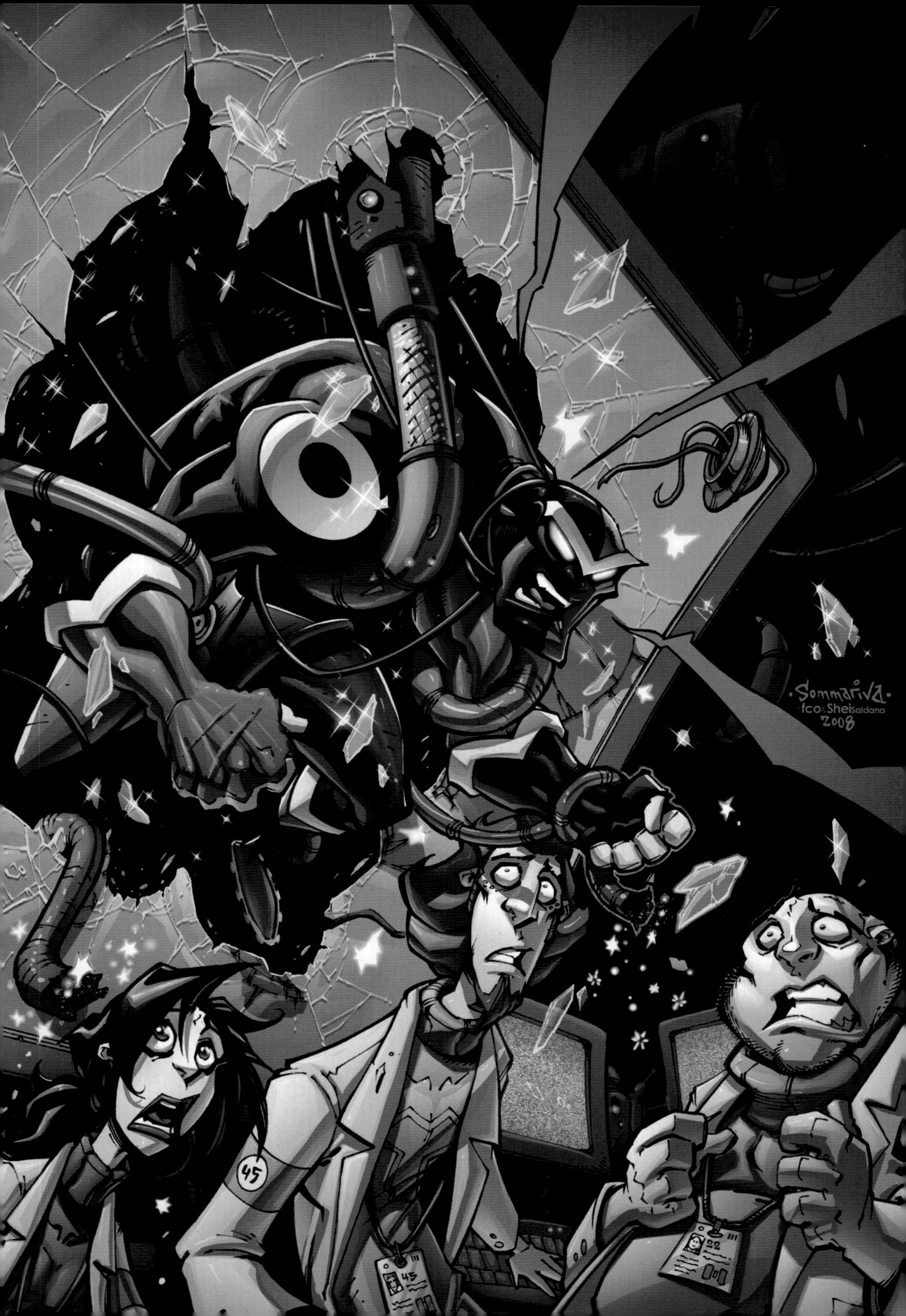

Sommariva
fco Sheisaldana
2008

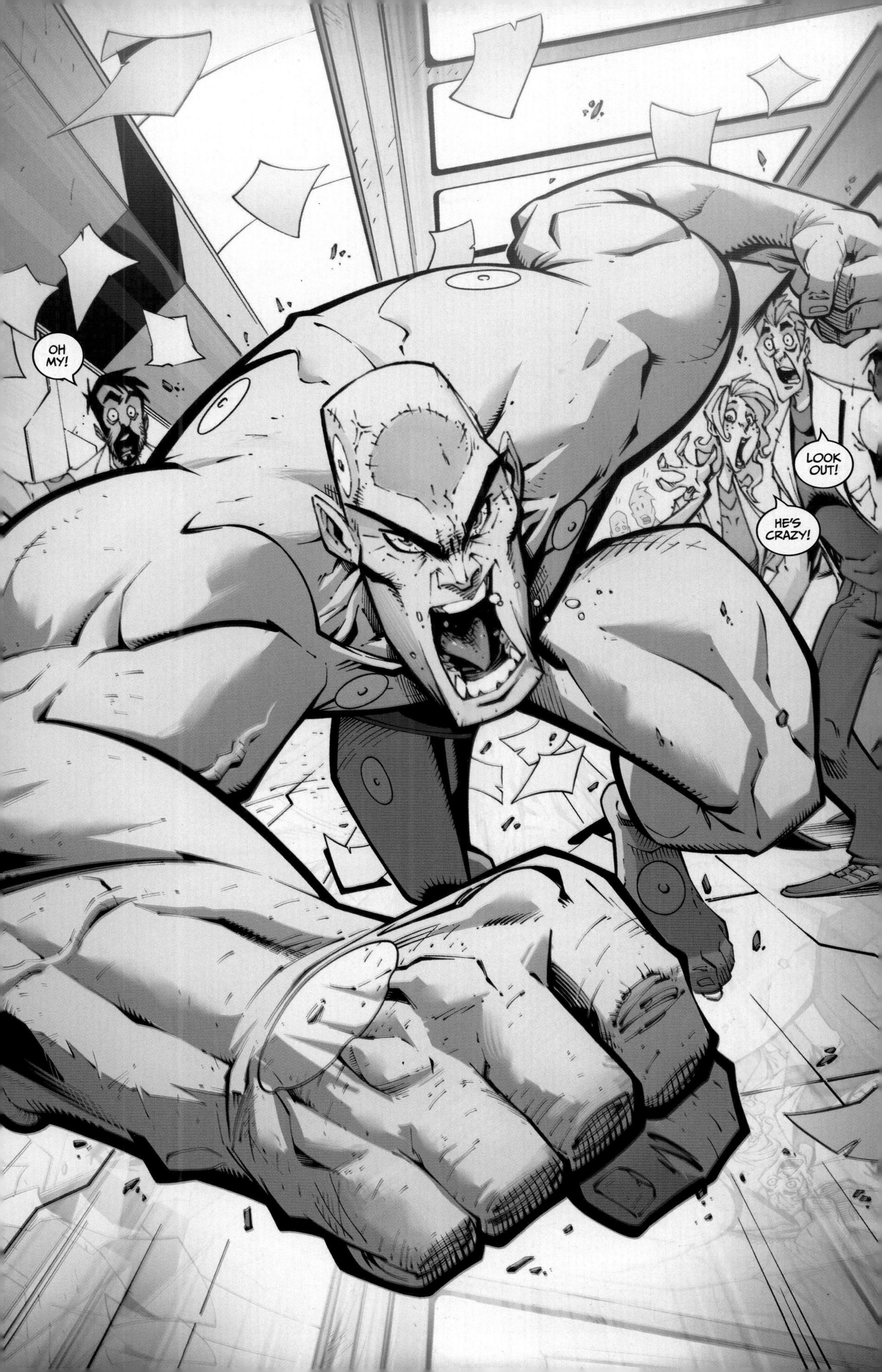
OH MY!
LOOK OUT!
HE'S CRAZY!

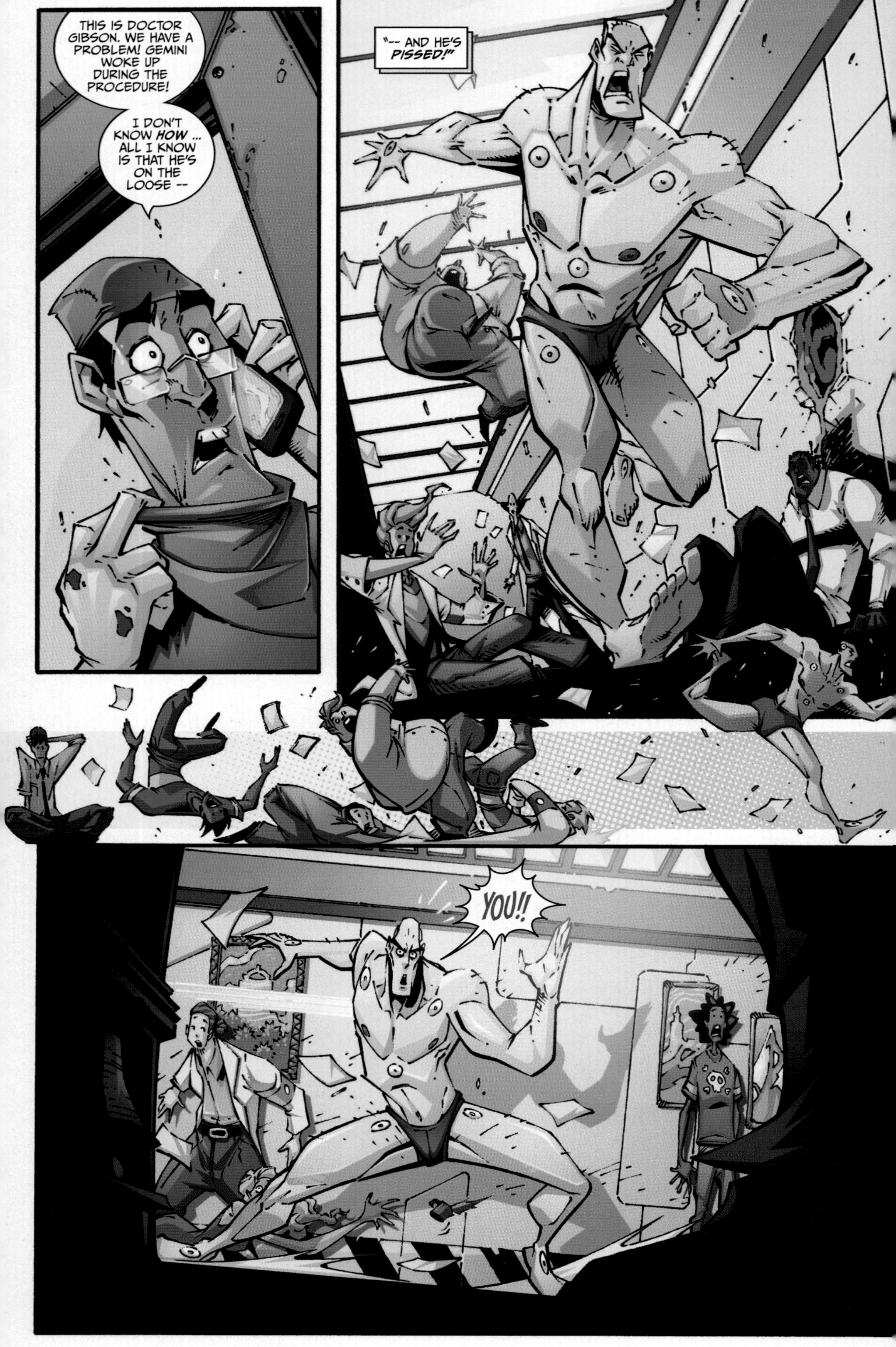
THIS IS DOCTOR GIBSON. WE HAVE A PROBLEM! GEMINI WOKE UP DURING THE PROCEDURE!
I DON'T KNOW *HOW* ... ALL I KNOW IS THAT HE'S ON THE LOOSE --
"-- AND HE'S *PISSED!*"
YOU!!

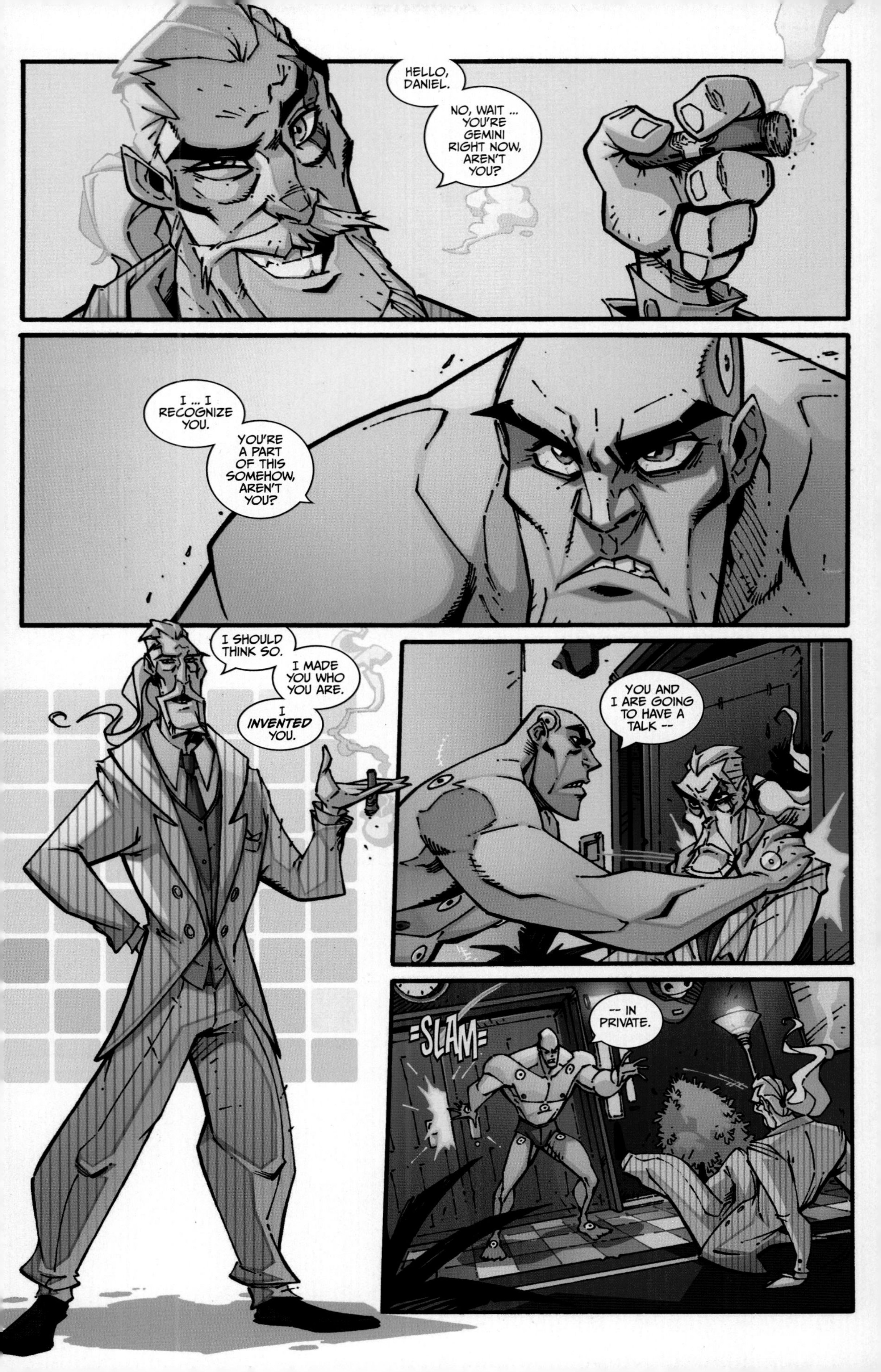
HELLO, DANIEL.
NO, WAIT ... YOU'RE GEMINI RIGHT NOW, AREN'T YOU?
I ... I RECOGNIZE YOU.
YOU'RE A PART OF THIS SOMEHOW, AREN'T YOU?
I SHOULD THINK SO.
I MADE YOU WHO YOU ARE.
I *INVENTED* YOU.
YOU AND I ARE GOING TO HAVE A TALK --
SLAM
-- IN PRIVATE.

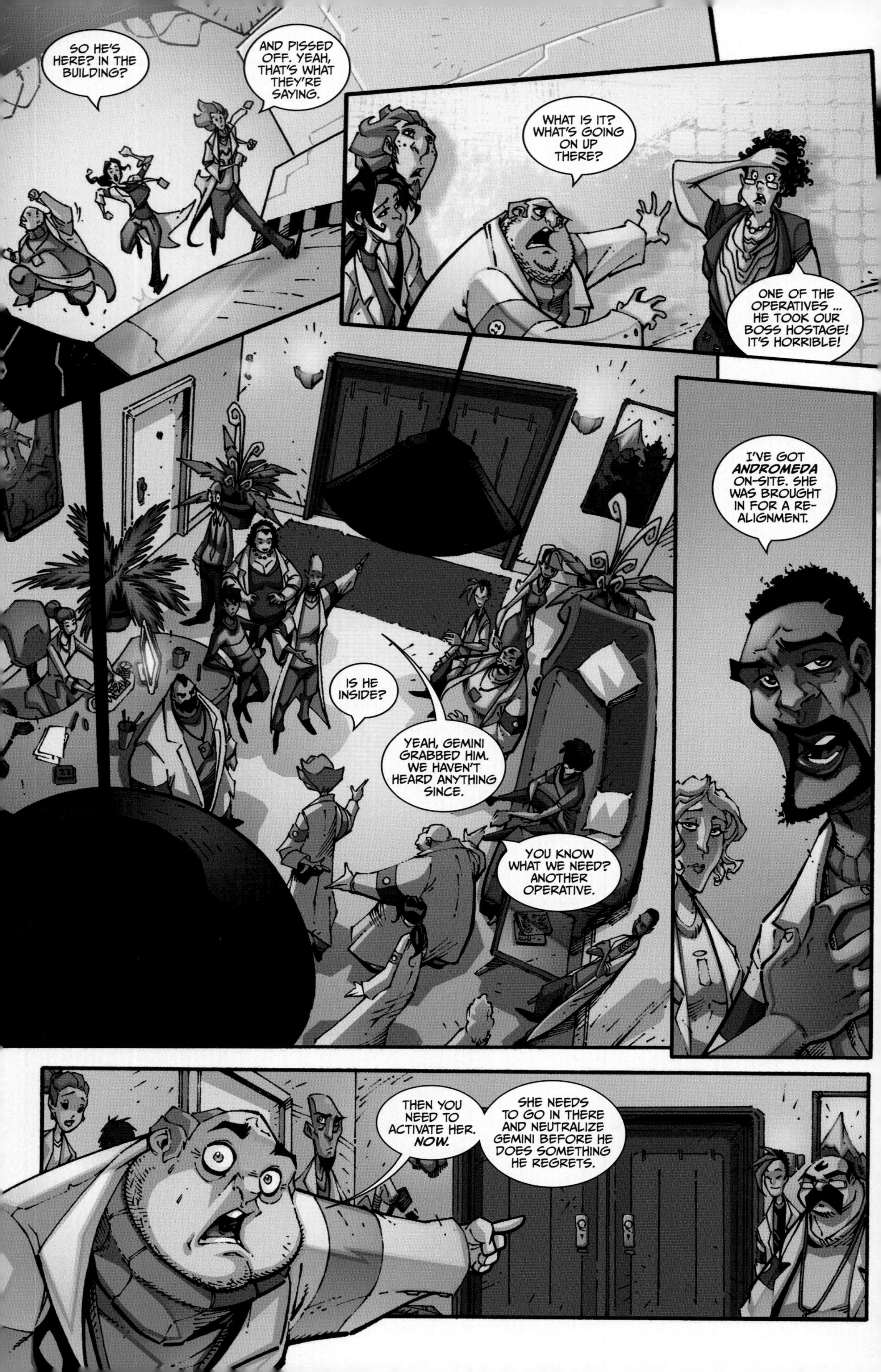
SO HE'S HERE? IN THE BUILDING?
AND PISSED OFF. YEAH, THAT'S WHAT THEY'RE SAYING.
WHAT IS IT? WHAT'S GOING ON UP THERE?
ONE OF THE OPERATIVES ... HE TOOK OUR BOSS HOSTAGE! IT'S HORRIBLE!
IS HE INSIDE?
YEAH, GEMINI GRABBED HIM. WE HAVEN'T HEARD ANYTHING SINCE.
YOU KNOW WHAT WE NEED? ANOTHER OPERATIVE.
I'VE GOT *ANDROMEDA* ON-SITE. SHE WAS BROUGHT IN FOR A RE-ALIGNMENT.
THEN YOU NEED TO ACTIVATE HER. *NOW.*
SHE NEEDS TO GO IN THERE AND NEUTRALIZE GEMINI BEFORE HE DOES SOMETHING HE REGRETS.

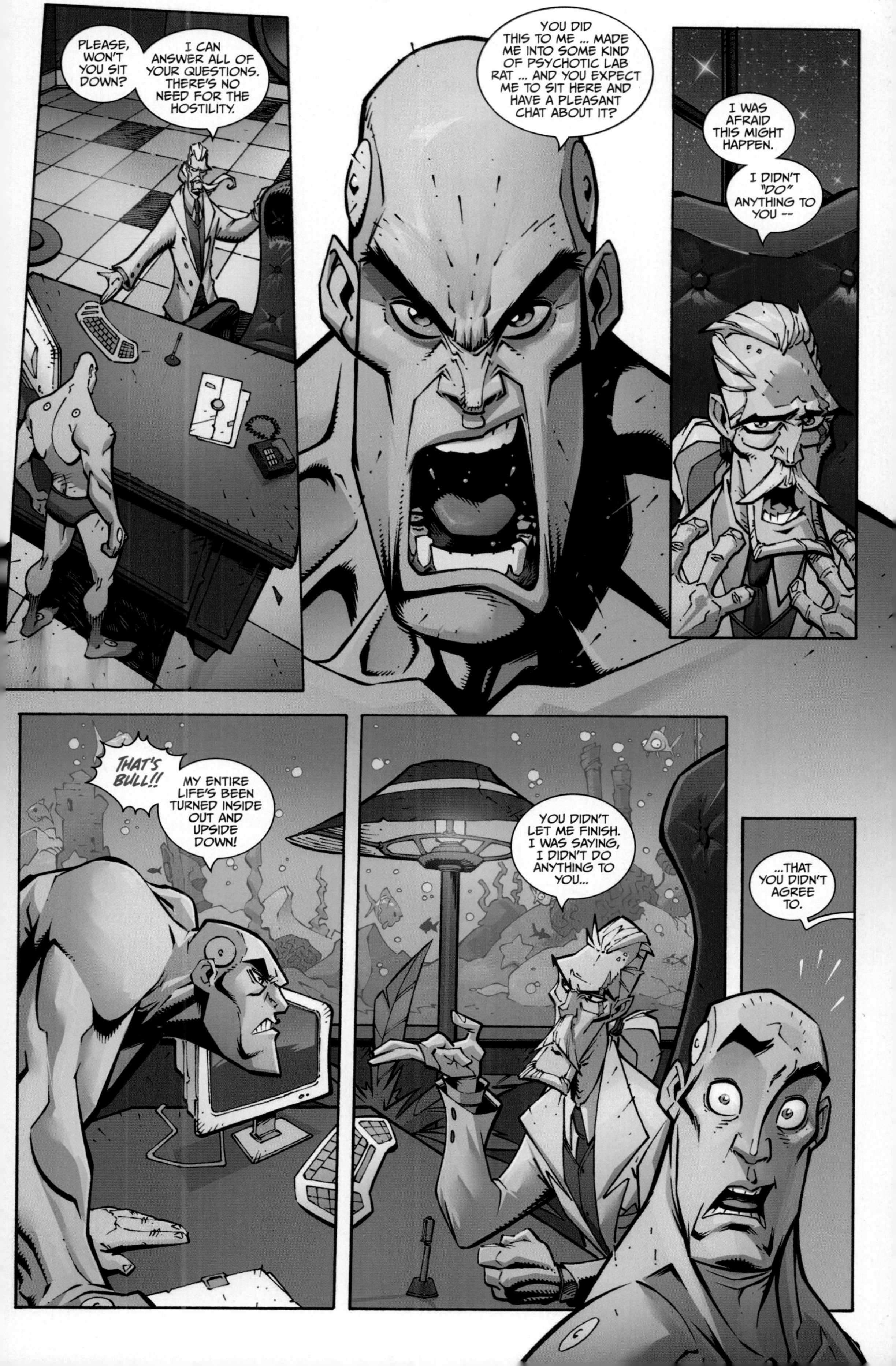
PLEASE, WON'T YOU SIT DOWN?
I CAN ANSWER ALL OF YOUR QUESTIONS. THERE'S NO NEED FOR THE HOSTILITY.
YOU DID THIS TO ME ... MADE ME INTO SOME KIND OF PSYCHOTIC LAB RAT ... AND YOU EXPECT ME TO SIT HERE AND HAVE A PLEASANT CHAT ABOUT IT?
I WAS AFRAID THIS MIGHT HAPPEN.
I DIDN'T "DO" ANYTHING TO YOU --
THAT'S BULL!!
MY ENTIRE LIFE'S BEEN TURNED INSIDE OUT AND UPSIDE DOWN!
YOU DIDN'T LET ME FINISH. I WAS SAYING, I DIDN'T DO ANYTHING TO YOU...
...THAT YOU DIDN'T AGREE TO.

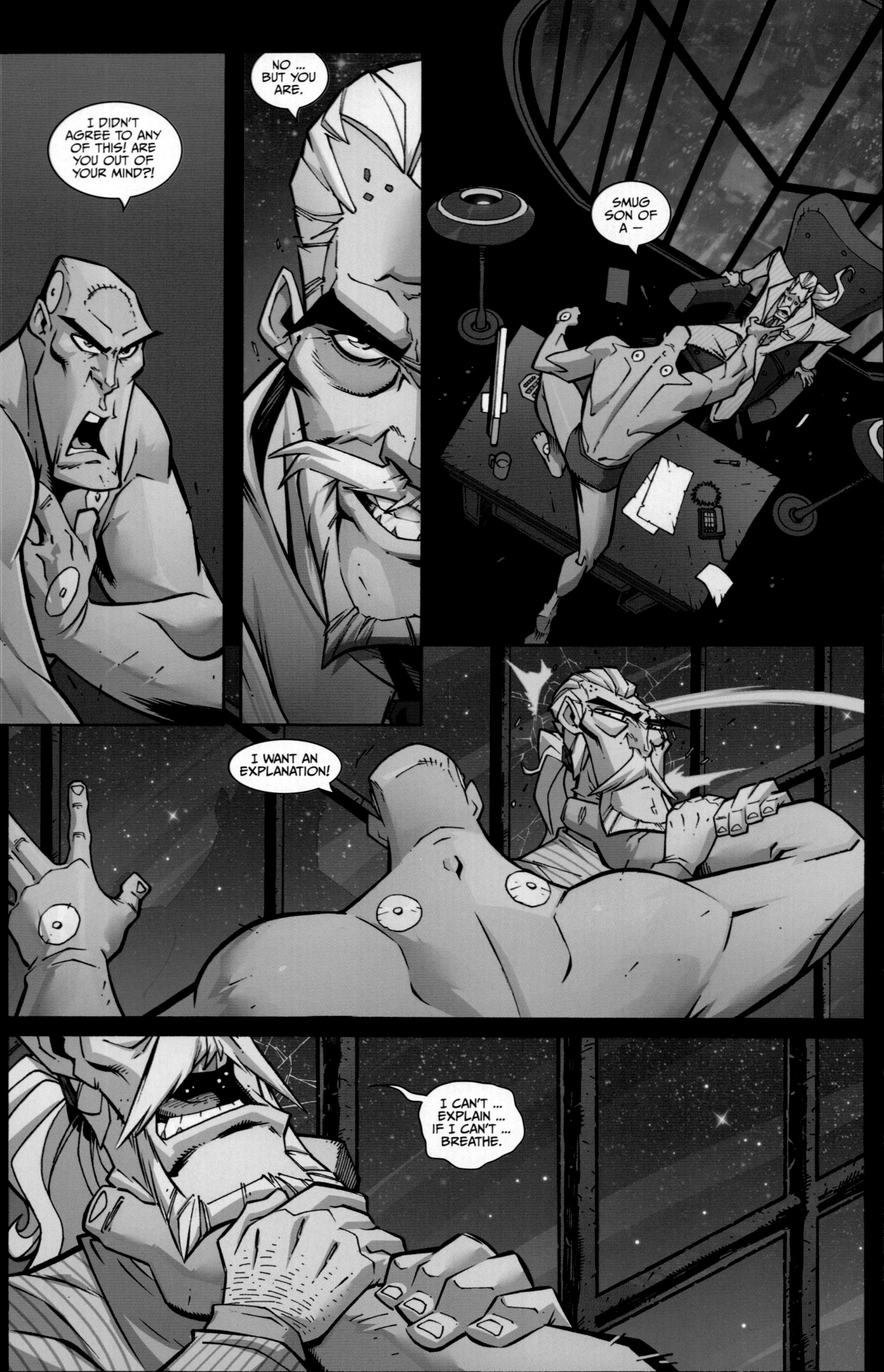
I DIDN'T AGREE TO ANY OF THIS! ARE YOU OUT OF YOUR MIND?!
NO ... BUT YOU ARE.
SMUG SON OF A —
I WANT AN EXPLANATION!
I CAN'T ... EXPLAIN ... IF I CAN'T ... BREATHE.

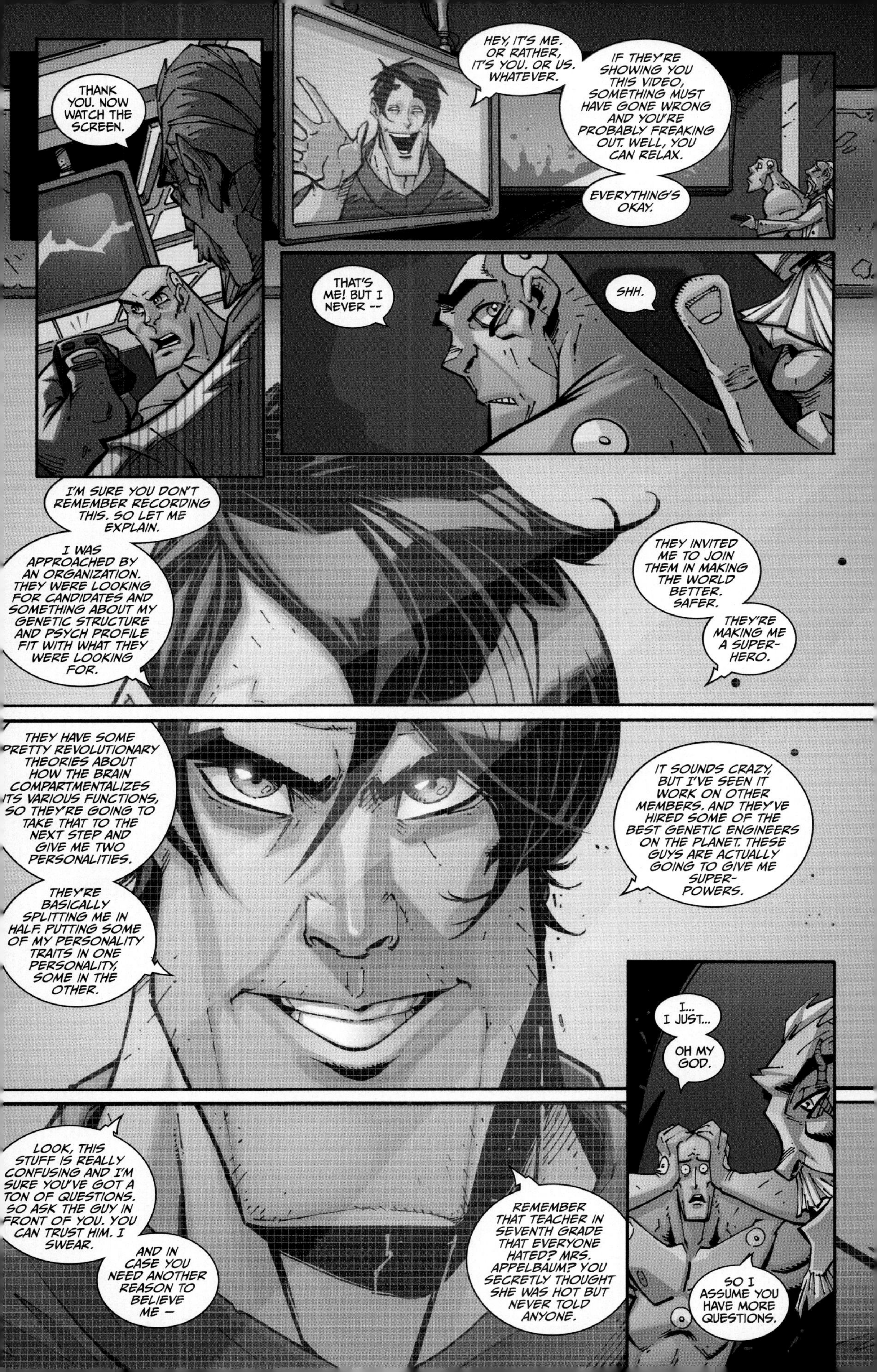
THANK YOU. NOW WATCH THE SCREEN.
HEY, IT'S ME. OR RATHER, IT'S YOU. OR US. WHATEVER.
IF THEY'RE SHOWING YOU THIS VIDEO, SOMETHING MUST HAVE GONE WRONG AND YOU'RE PROBABLY FREAKING OUT. WELL, YOU CAN RELAX.
EVERYTHING'S OKAY.
THAT'S ME! BUT I NEVER --
SHH.
I'M SURE YOU DON'T REMEMBER RECORDING THIS. SO LET ME EXPLAIN.
I WAS APPROACHED BY AN ORGANIZATION. THEY WERE LOOKING FOR CANDIDATES AND SOMETHING ABOUT MY GENETIC STRUCTURE AND PSYCH PROFILE FIT WITH WHAT THEY WERE LOOKING FOR.
THEY INVITED ME TO JOIN THEM IN MAKING THE WORLD BETTER. SAFER.
THEY'RE MAKING ME A SUPER-HERO.
THEY HAVE SOME PRETTY REVOLUTIONARY THEORIES ABOUT HOW THE BRAIN COMPARTMENTALIZES ITS VARIOUS FUNCTIONS, SO THEY'RE GOING TO TAKE THAT TO THE NEXT STEP AND GIVE ME TWO PERSONALITIES.
THEY'RE BASICALLY SPLITTING ME IN HALF. PUTTING SOME OF MY PERSONALITY TRAITS IN ONE PERSONALITY, SOME IN THE OTHER.
IT SOUNDS CRAZY, BUT I'VE SEEN IT WORK ON OTHER MEMBERS. AND THEY'VE HIRED SOME OF THE BEST GENETIC ENGINEERS ON THE PLANET. THESE GUYS ARE ACTUALLY GOING TO GIVE ME SUPER-POWERS.
LOOK, THIS STUFF IS REALLY CONFUSING AND I'M SURE YOU'VE GOT A TON OF QUESTIONS. SO ASK THE GUY IN FRONT OF YOU. YOU CAN TRUST HIM. I SWEAR.
AND IN CASE YOU NEED ANOTHER REASON TO BELIEVE ME —
REMEMBER THAT TEACHER IN SEVENTH GRADE THAT EVERYONE HATED? MRS. APPELBAUM? YOU SECRETLY THOUGHT SHE WAS HOT BUT NEVER TOLD ANYONE.
I... I JUST...
OH MY GOD.
SO I ASSUME YOU HAVE MORE QUESTIONS.

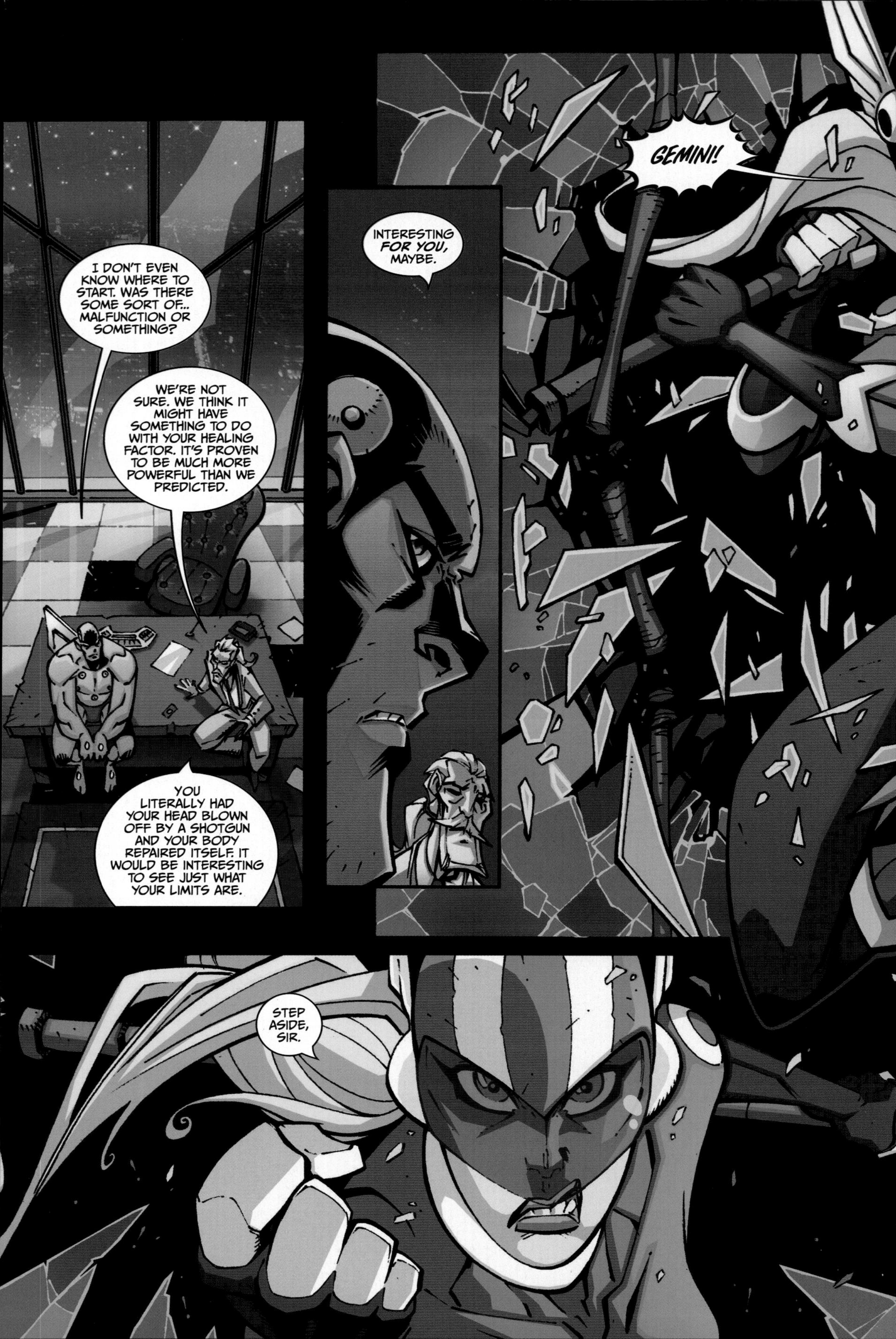
I DON'T EVEN KNOW WHERE TO START. WAS THERE SOME SORT OF... MALFUNCTION OR SOMETHING?
WE'RE NOT SURE. WE THINK IT MIGHT HAVE SOMETHING TO DO WITH YOUR HEALING FACTOR. IT'S PROVEN TO BE MUCH MORE POWERFUL THAN WE PREDICTED.
YOU LITERALLY HAD YOUR HEAD BLOWN OFF BY A SHOTGUN AND YOUR BODY REPAIRED ITSELF. IT WOULD BE INTERESTING TO SEE JUST WHAT YOUR LIMITS ARE.
INTERESTING *FOR YOU,* MAYBE.
GEMINI!
STEP ASIDE, SIR.

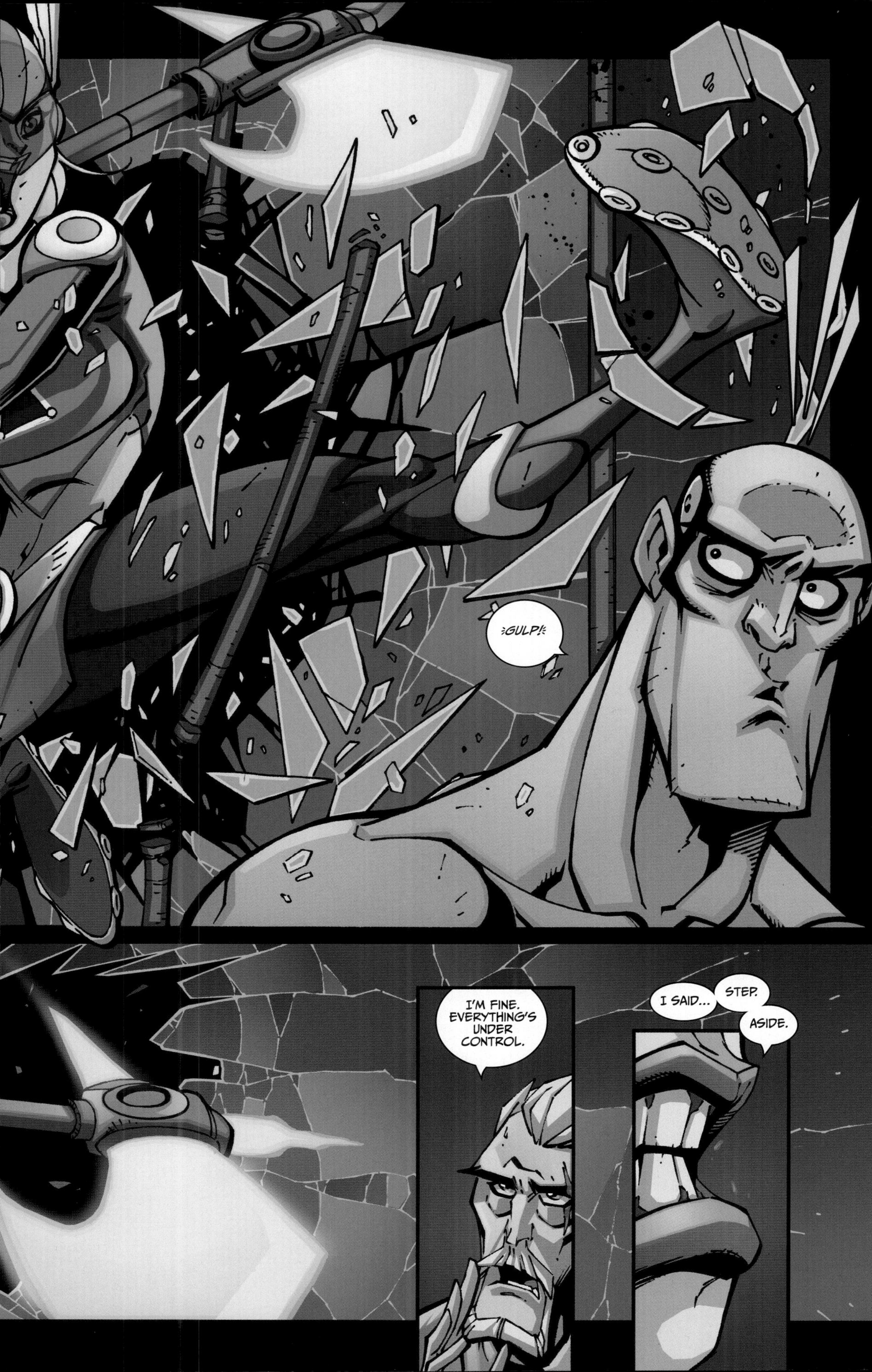
GULP!
I'M FINE. EVERYTHING'S UNDER CONTROL.
I SAID...
STEP.
ASIDE.

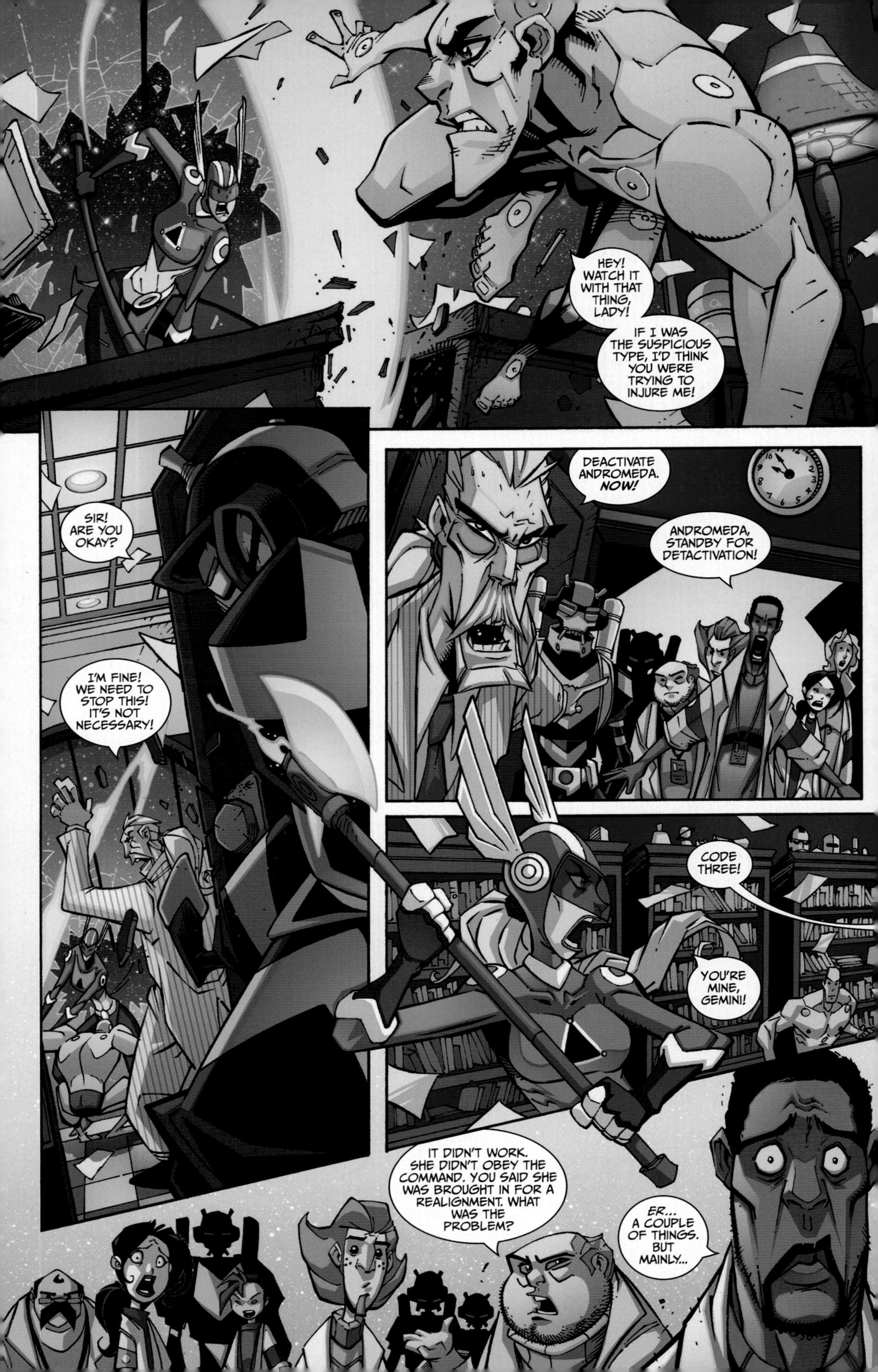
HEY! WATCH IT WITH THAT THING, LADY!
IF I WAS THE SUSPICIOUS TYPE, I'D THINK YOU WERE TRYING TO INJURE ME!
SIR! ARE YOU OKAY?
I'M FINE! WE NEED TO STOP THIS! IT'S NOT NECESSARY!
DEACTIVATE ANDROMEDA. NOW!
ANDROMEDA, STANDBY FOR DETACTIVATION!
CODE THREE!
YOU'RE MINE, GEMINI!
IT DIDN'T WORK. SHE DIDN'T OBEY THE COMMAND. YOU SAID SHE WAS BROUGHT IN FOR A REALIGNMENT. WHAT WAS THE PROBLEM?
ER... A COUPLE OF THINGS. BUT MAINLY...

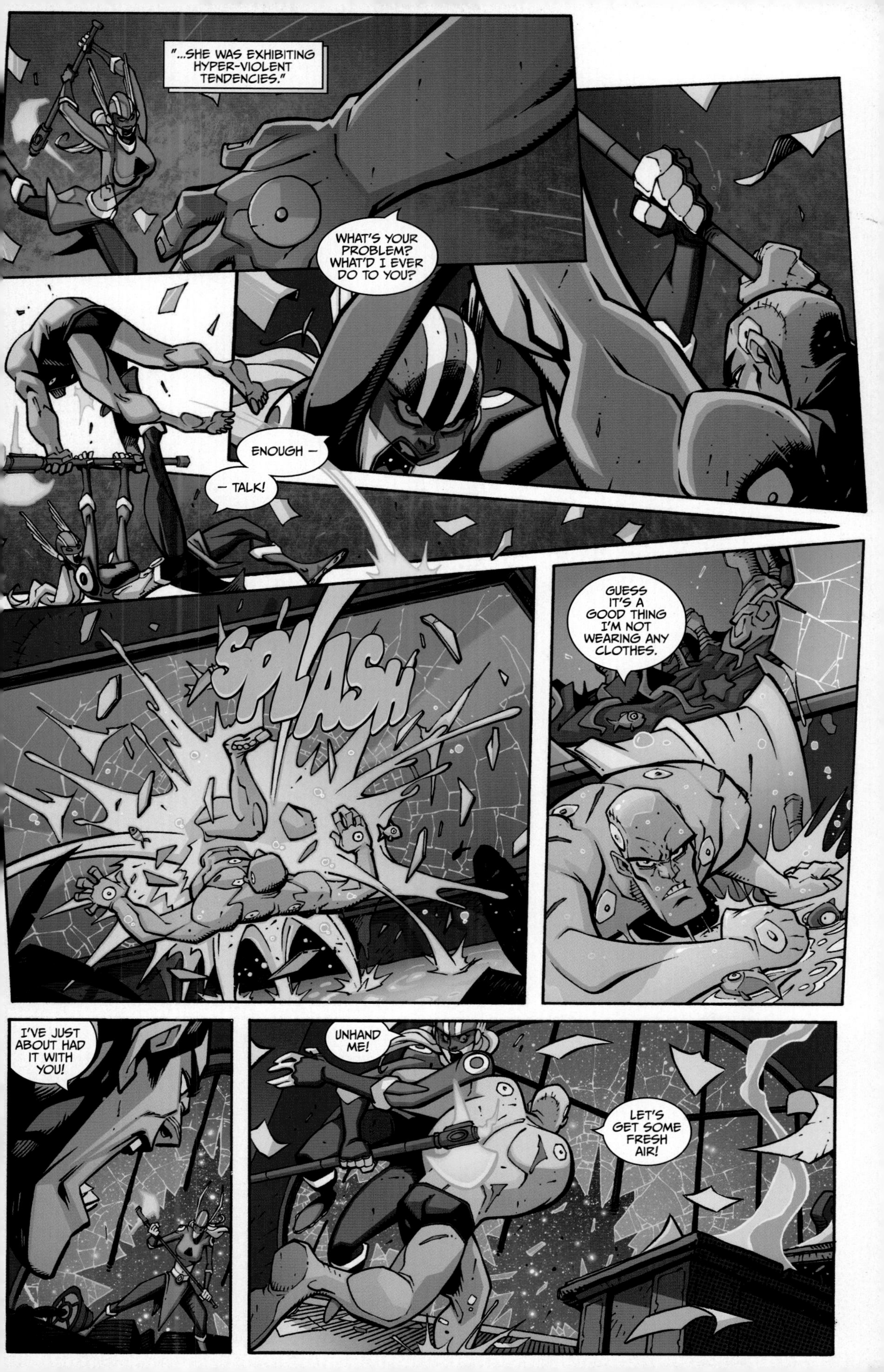
"...SHE WAS EXHIBITING HYPER-VIOLENT TENDENCIES."
WHAT'S YOUR PROBLEM? WHAT'D I EVER DO TO YOU?
ENOUGH –
– TALK!
SPLASH
GUESS IT'S A GOOD THING I'M NOT WEARING ANY CLOTHES.
I'VE JUST ABOUT HAD IT WITH YOU!
UNHAND ME!
LET'S GET SOME FRESH AIR!

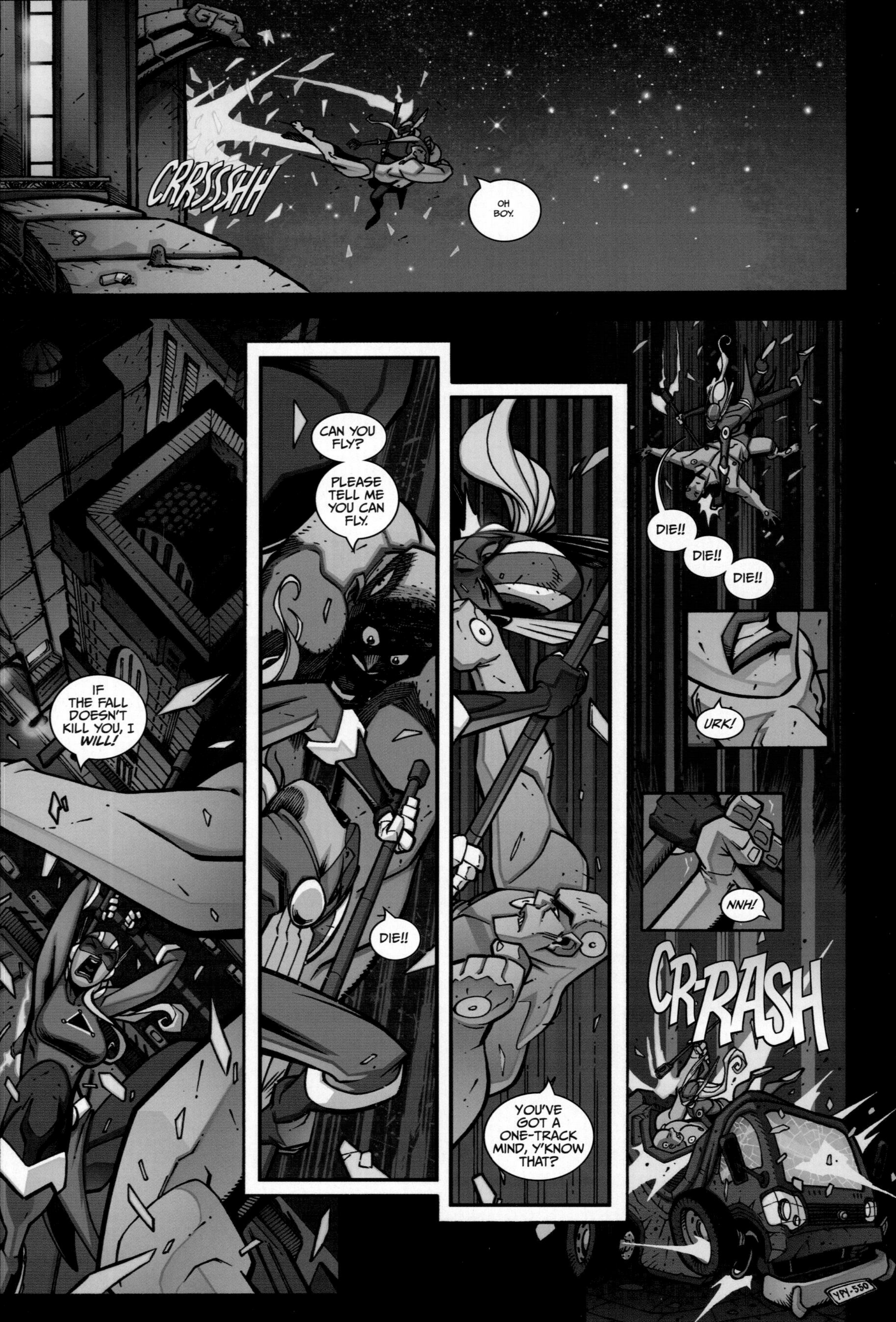
CRRSSSHH
OH BOY.
IF THE FALL DOESN'T KILL YOU, I WILL!
CAN YOU FLY?
PLEASE TELL ME YOU CAN FLY.
DIE!!
YOU'VE GOT A ONE-TRACK MIND, Y'KNOW THAT?
DIE!!
DIE!!
DIE!!
URK!
NNH!
CR-RASH

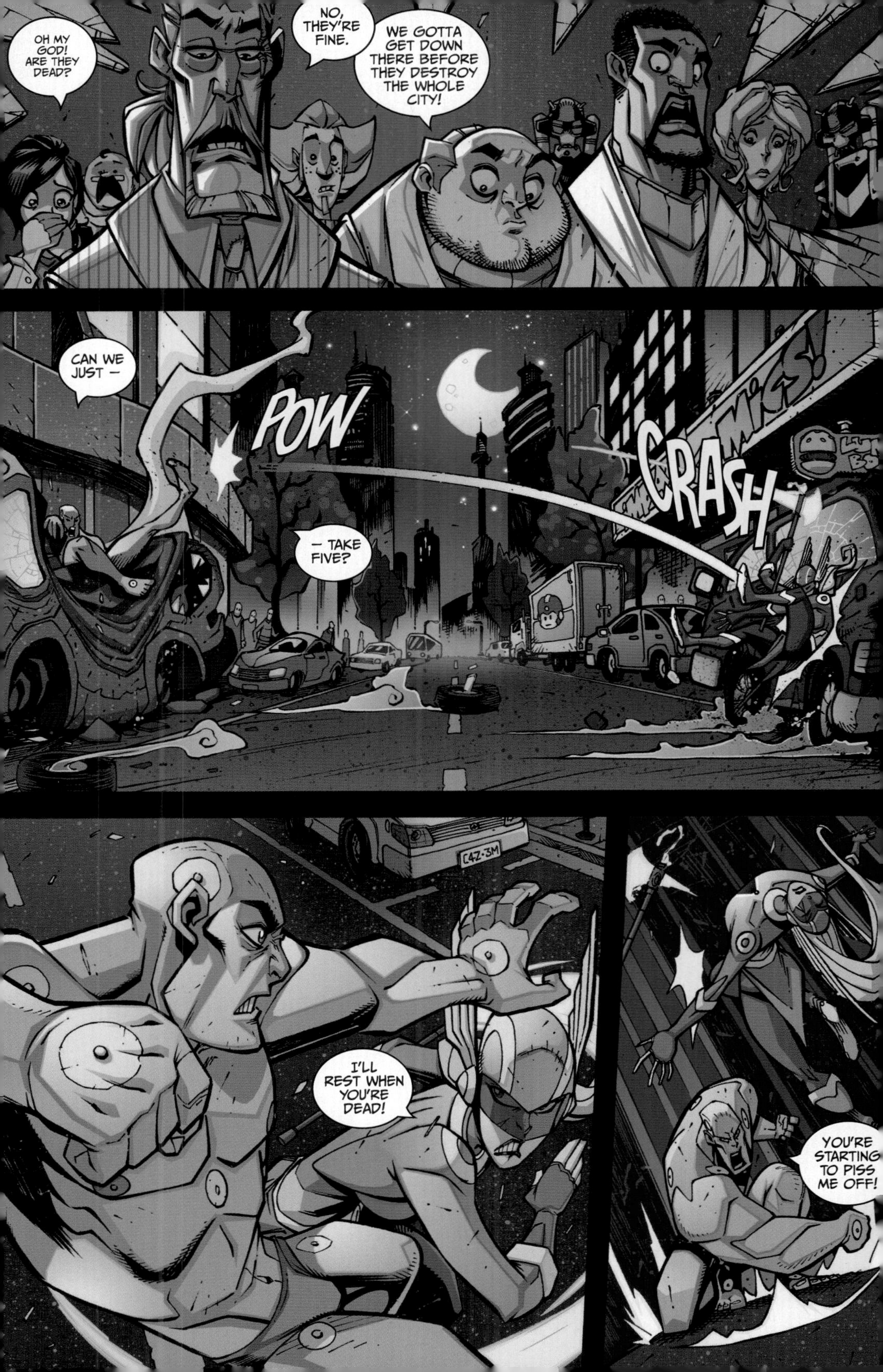
OH MY GOD! ARE THEY DEAD?
NO, THEY'RE FINE.
WE GOTTA GET DOWN THERE BEFORE THEY DESTROY THE WHOLE CITY!
CAN WE JUST —
POW
CRASH
— TAKE FIVE?
I'LL REST WHEN YOU'RE DEAD!
YOU'RE STARTING TO PISS ME OFF!

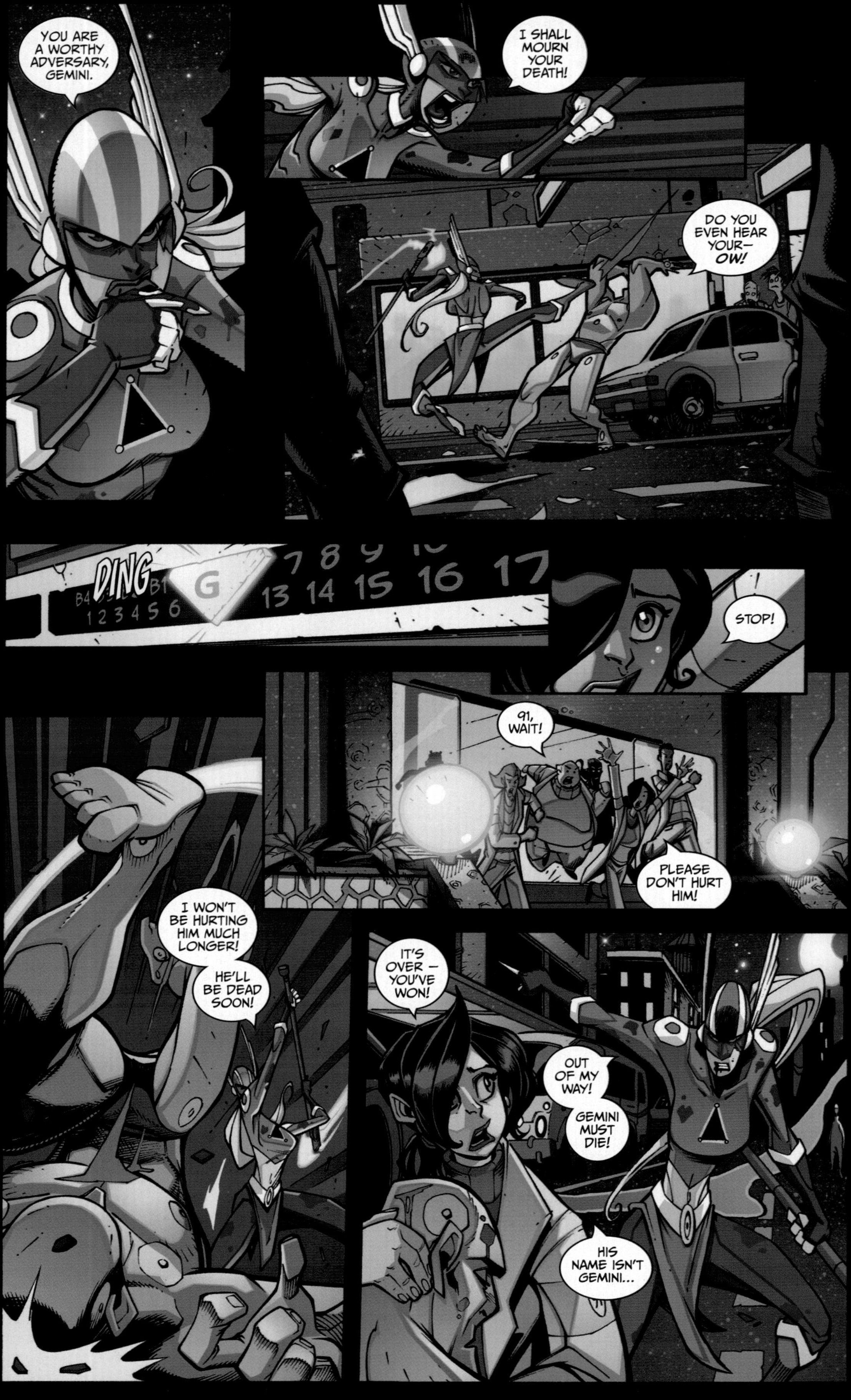
YOU ARE A WORTHY ADVERSARY, GEMINI.
I SHALL MOURN YOUR DEATH!
DO YOU EVEN HEAR YOUR— OW!
DING
B4 B1 1 2 3 4 5 6 G 7 8 9 10 13 14 15 16 17
STOP!
91, WAIT!
PLEASE DON'T HURT HIM!
I WON'T BE HURTING HIM MUCH LONGER!
HE'LL BE DEAD SOON!
IT'S OVER — YOU'VE WON!
OUT OF MY WAY!
GEMINI MUST DIE!
HIS NAME ISN'T GEMINI...

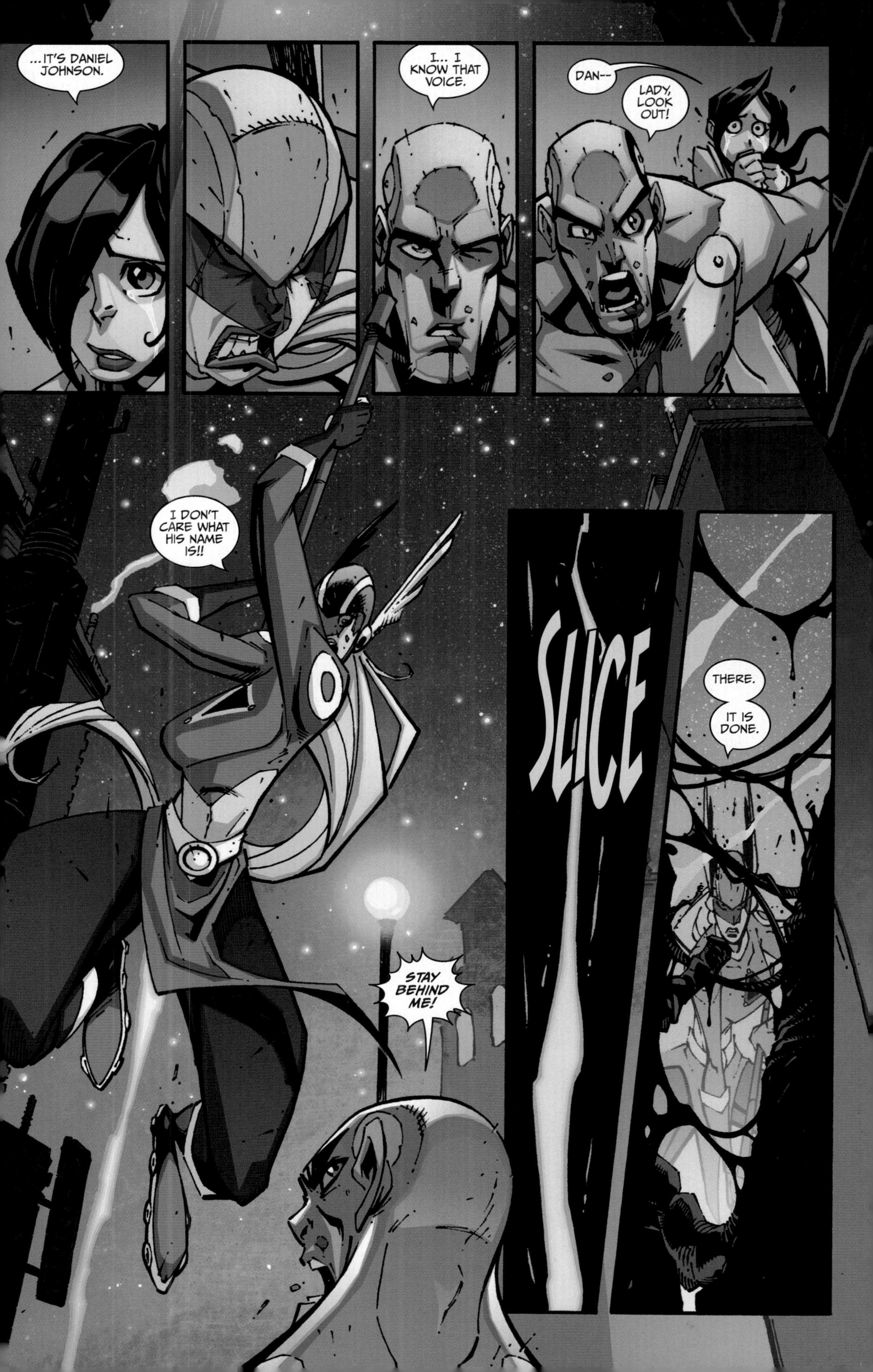
...IT'S DANIEL JOHNSON.
I... I KNOW THAT VOICE.
DAN--
LADY, LOOK OUT!
I DON'T CARE WHAT HIS NAME IS!!
STAY BEHIND ME!
SLICE
THERE.
IT IS DONE.

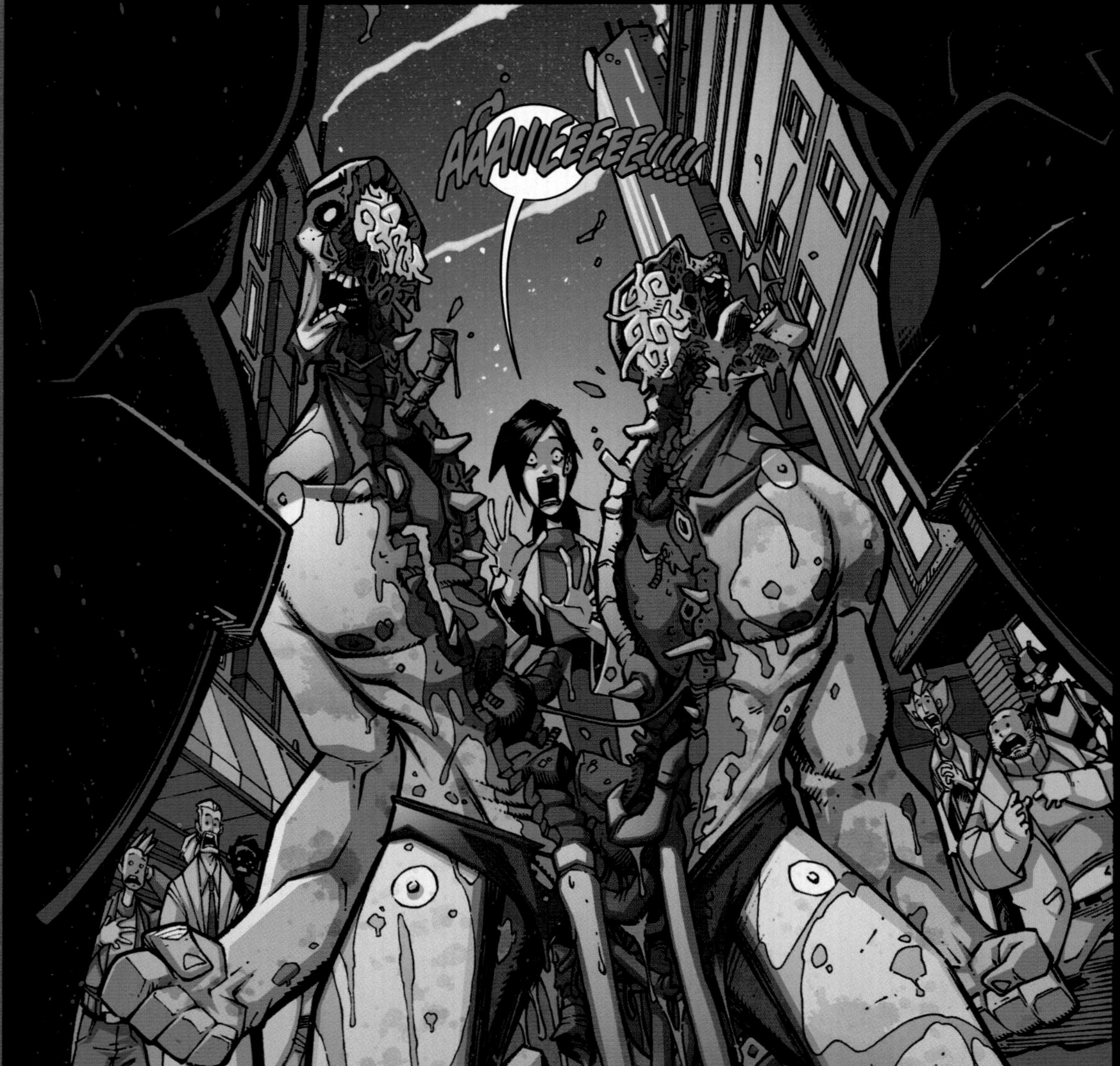
AAAIIEEEEE!!!!!
TWO WEEKS LATER...
SCALPEL.
CLAMP.

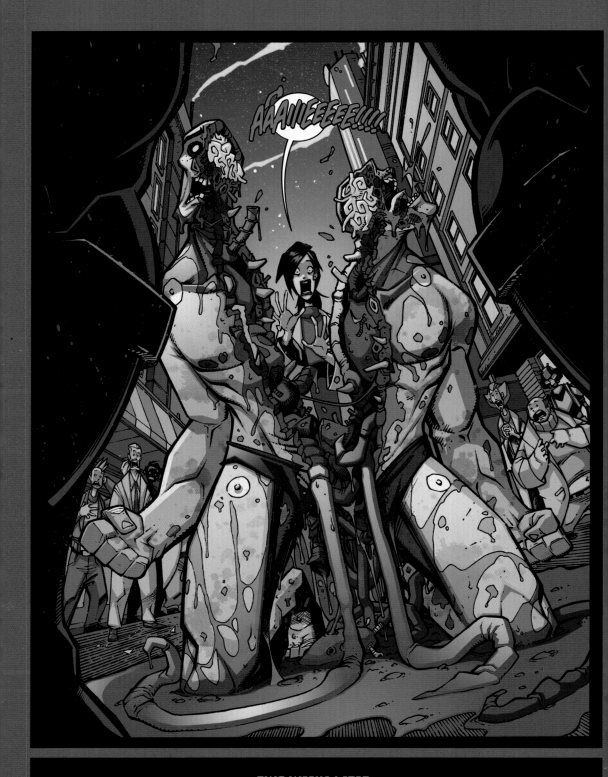

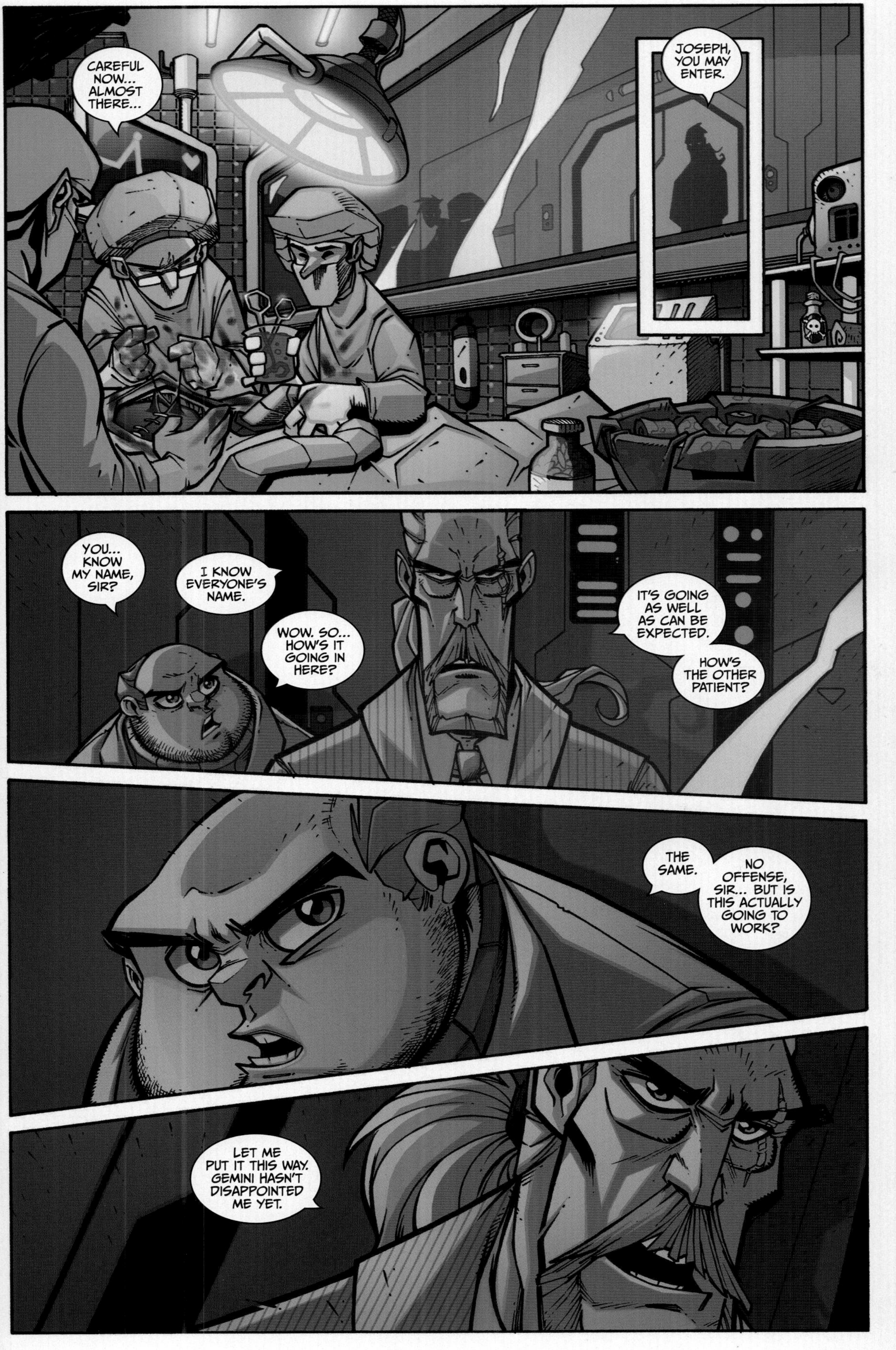
CAREFUL NOW... ALMOST THERE...
JOSEPH, YOU MAY ENTER.
YOU... KNOW MY NAME, SIR?
I KNOW EVERYONE'S NAME.
WOW. SO... HOW'S IT GOING IN HERE?
IT'S GOING AS WELL AS CAN BE EXPECTED.
HOW'S THE OTHER PATIENT?
THE SAME.
NO OFFENSE, SIR... BUT IS THIS ACTUALLY GOING TO WORK?
LET ME PUT IT THIS WAY. GEMINI HASN'T DISAPPOINTED ME YET.

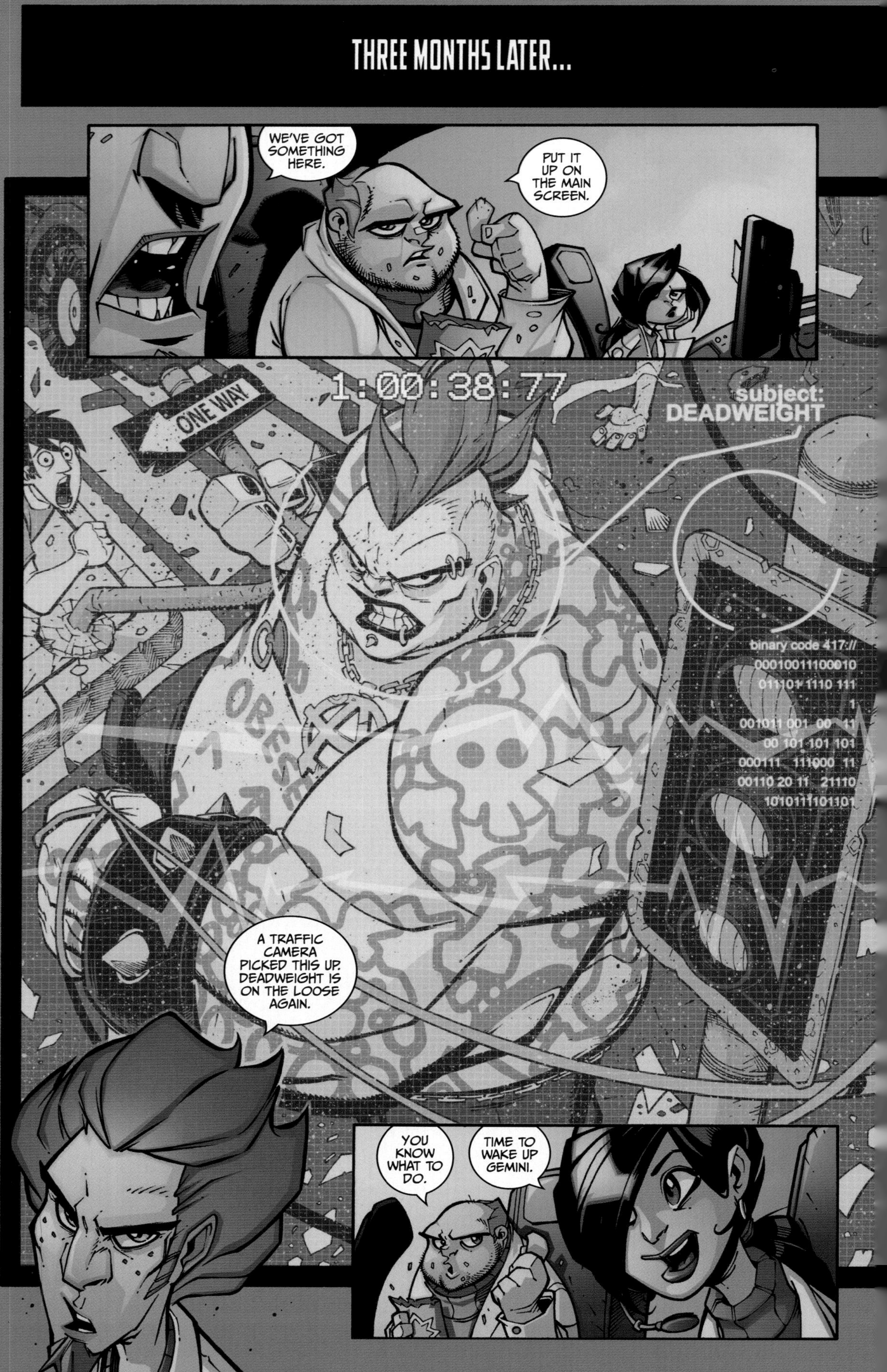
THREE MONTHS LATER...
WE'VE GOT SOMETHING HERE.
PUT IT UP ON THE MAIN SCREEN.
1:00:38:77
subject: DEADWEIGHT
ONE WAY
OBESE
binary code 417://
0001001110010
011101 1110 111
1
001011 001 00 11
00 101 101 101
000111 111000 11
00110 20 11 21110
1010111101101
A TRAFFIC CAMERA PICKED THIS UP. DEADWEIGHT IS ON THE LOOSE AGAIN.
YOU KNOW WHAT TO DO.
TIME TO WAKE UP GEMINI.

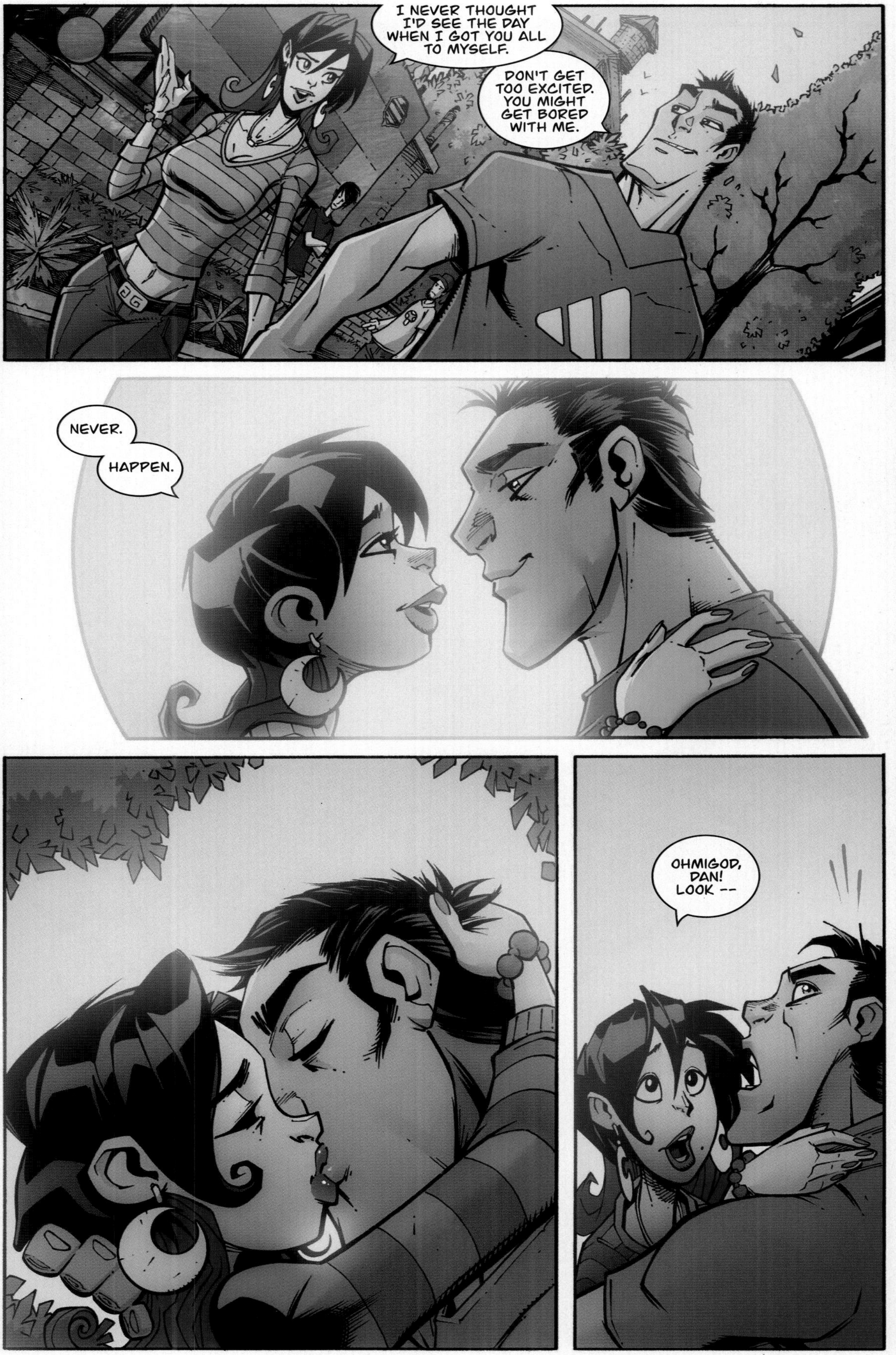
I NEVER THOUGHT I'D SEE THE DAY WHEN I GOT YOU ALL TO MYSELF.
DON'T GET TOO EXCITED. YOU MIGHT GET BORED WITH ME.
NEVER.
HAPPEN.
OHMIGOD, DAN! LOOK --

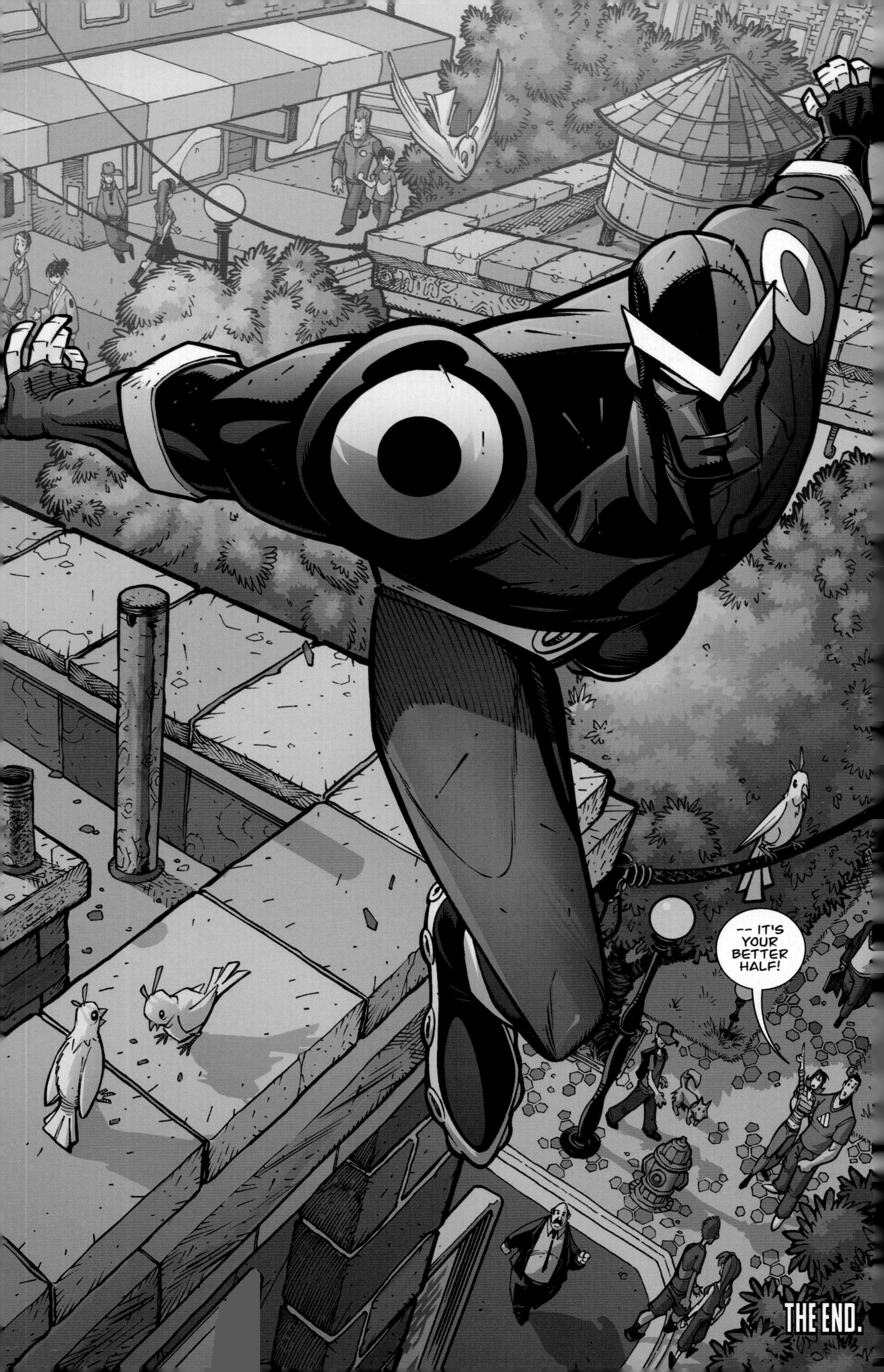
-- IT'S YOUR BETTER HALF!
THE END.

GEMINI™

SKETCHBOOK

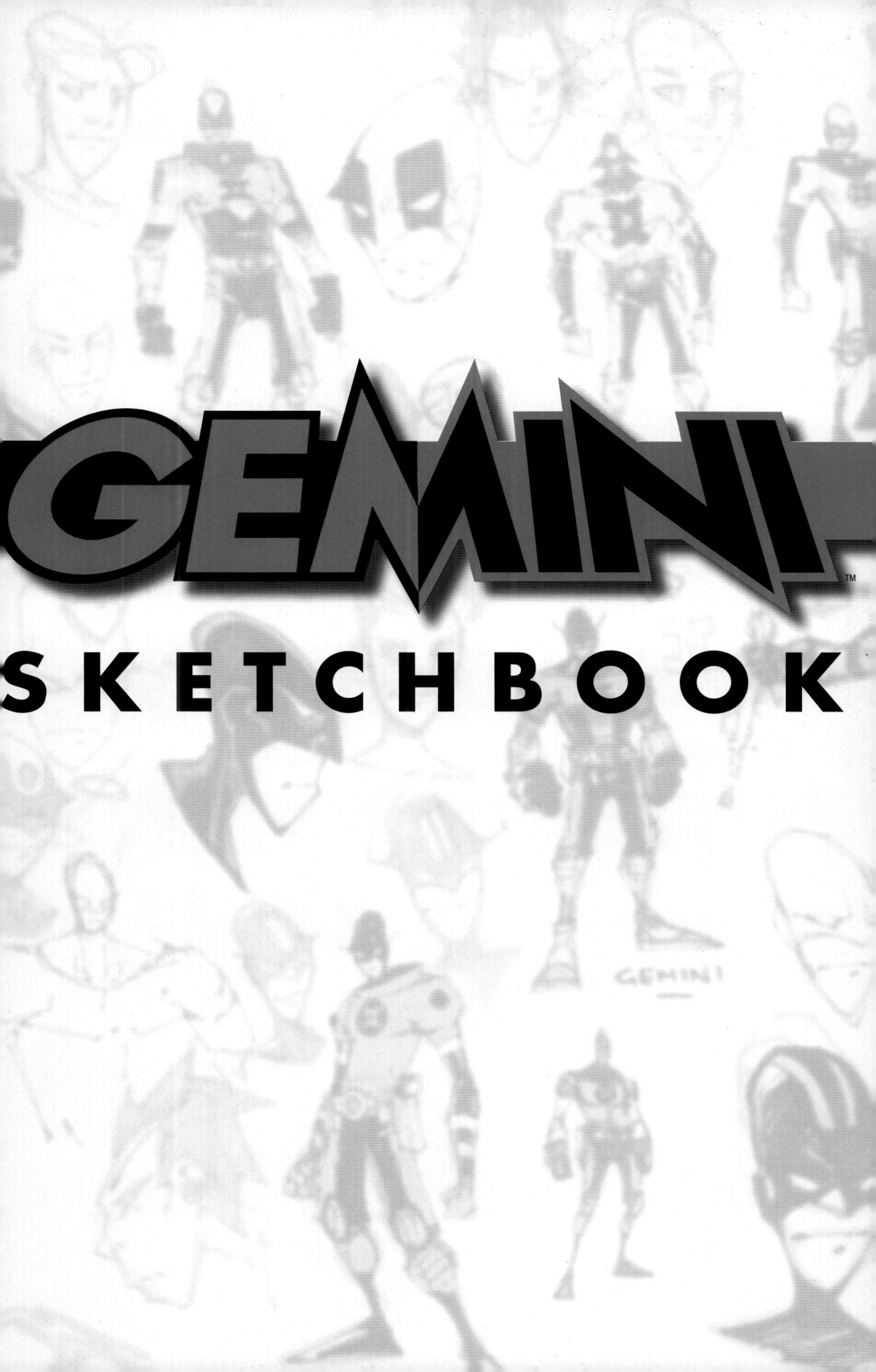
GEMINI

G E M I N I

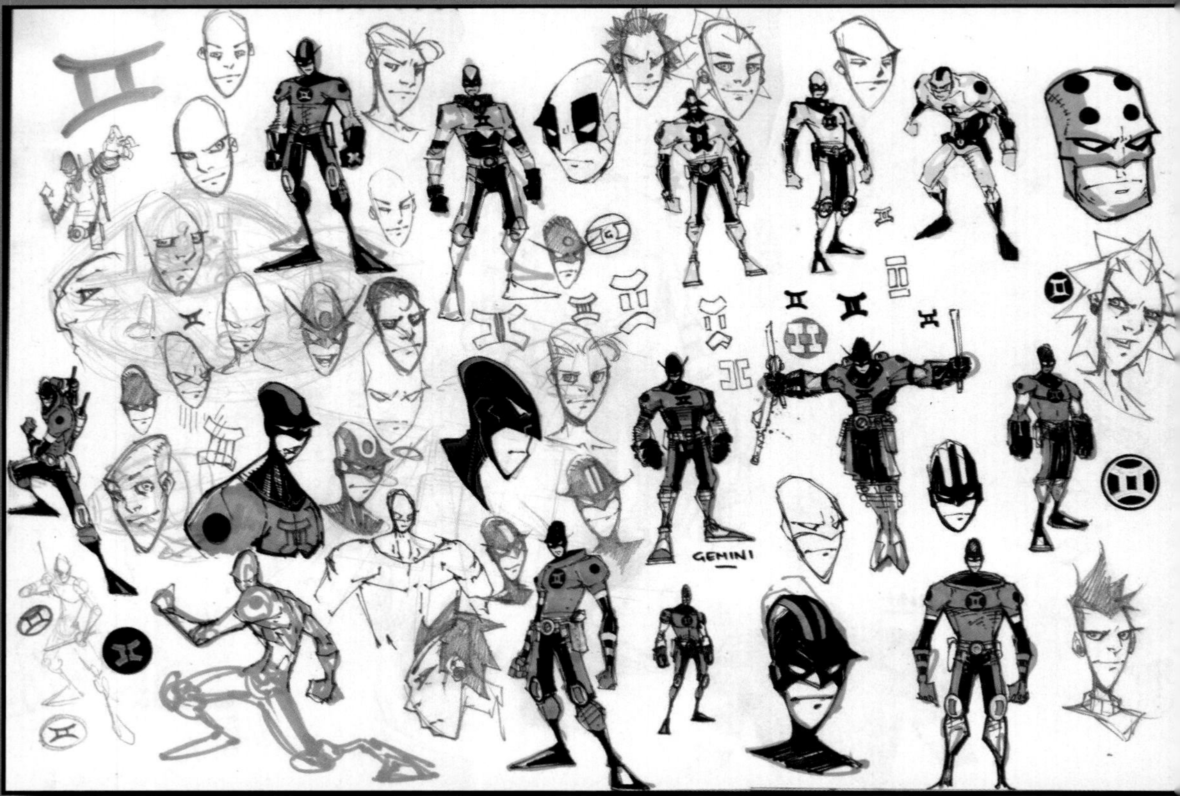
GEMINI

JAY: When Jon and I submitted **GEMINI** to Image, they were eager to publish the book, but they weren't crazy about Gemini's original costume. So Jon did many, many drafts and variations. You'll see them throughout the next few pages.

JON: My initial design ideas were missing a real hook. At first all I could really come up with to link the design to the name Gemini was using the Gemini "twins" symbol, which looks very much like a roman numeral 2.

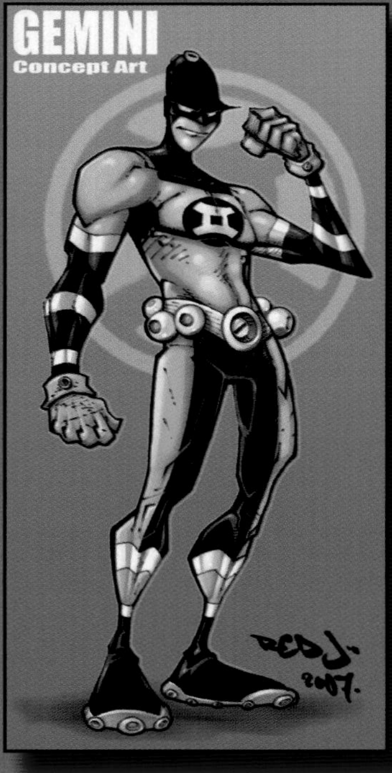
GEMINI
Concept Art
RED J.
2007.

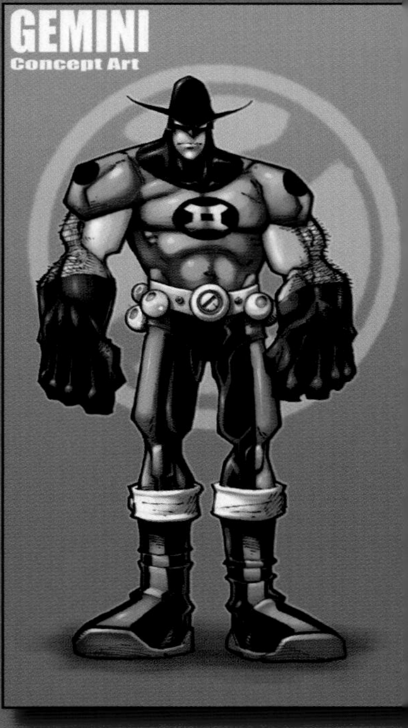
GEMINI
Concept Art

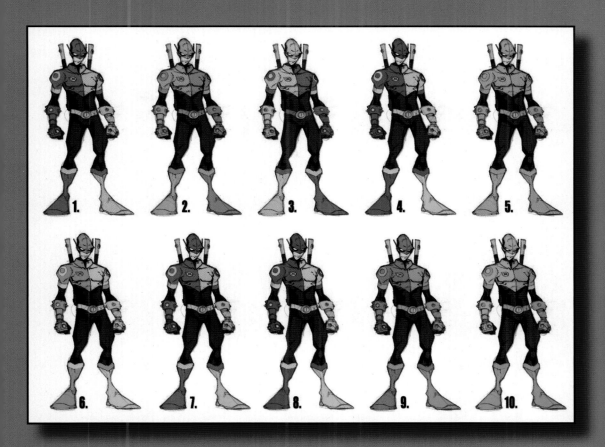

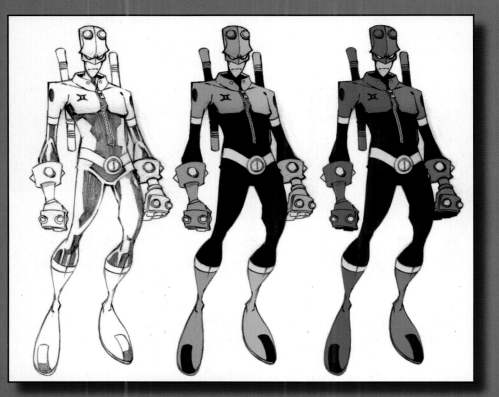

JON: I started playing around with the idea of splitting his costume down the middle as the best way to represent a character with two halves. I still really like this blue and red version (left), although I think we ended up rejecting him because of the similarity to Hellboy.

JON: By this stage I was also trying to come up with a way to give Gemini more of a unique silhouette, playing with various mask styles and shapes for his body and head.

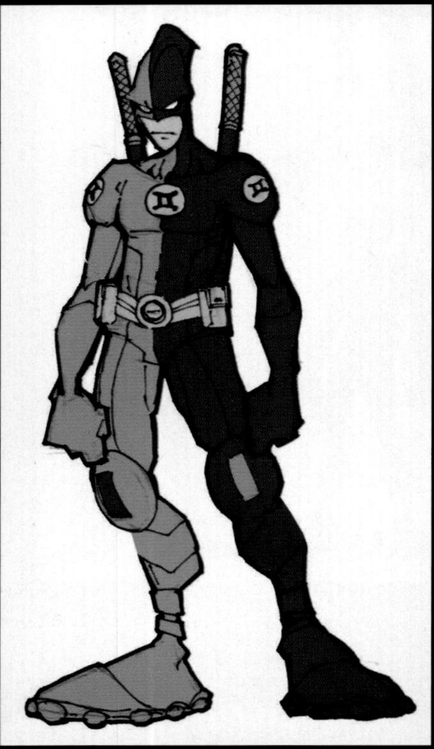

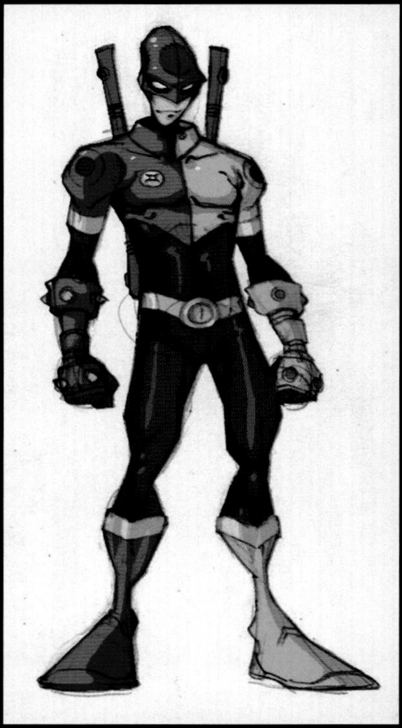

JON: We started to settle upon the red/yellow design you see above. Ultimately the brain trust looking at my designs felt that this look just wasn't iconic enough.

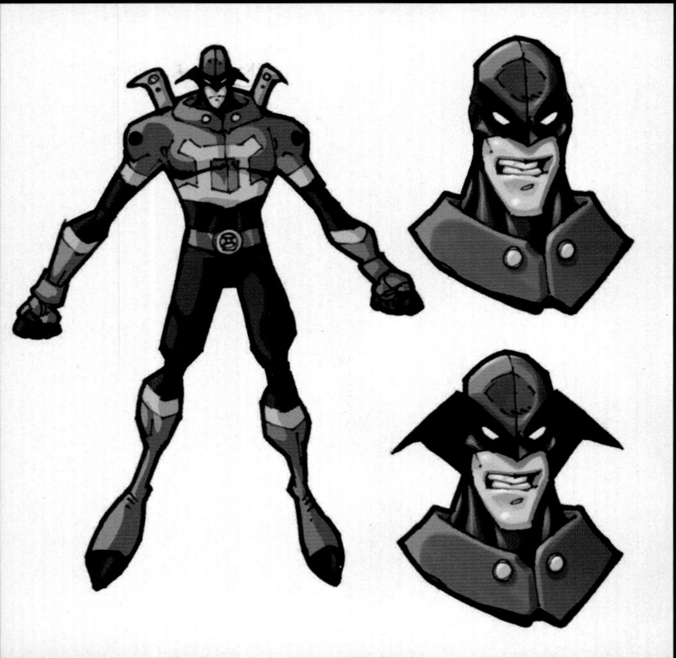

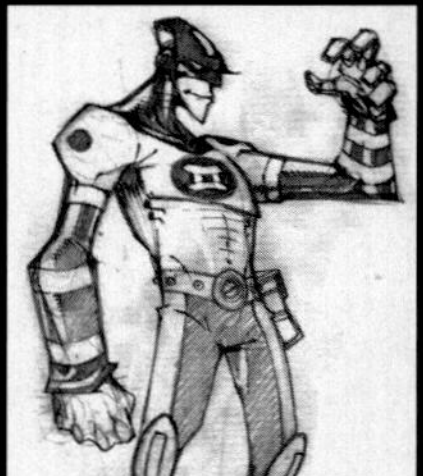

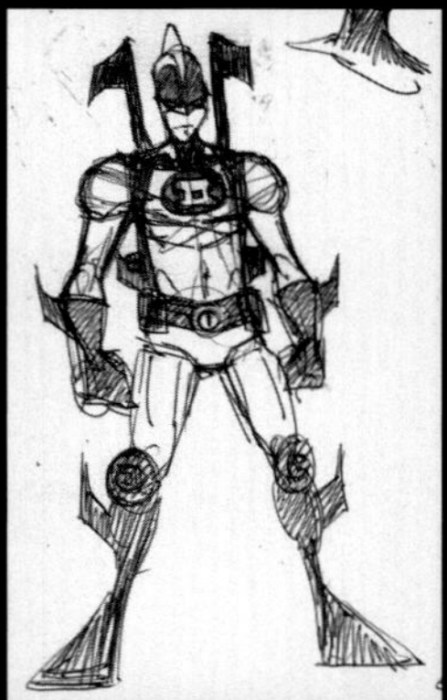

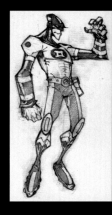

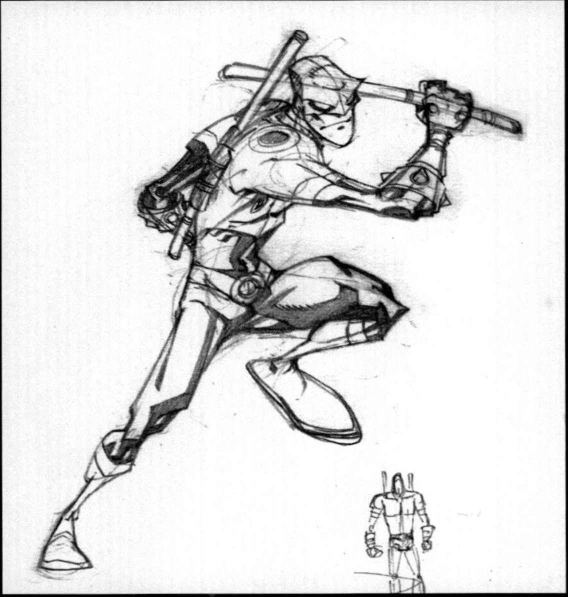

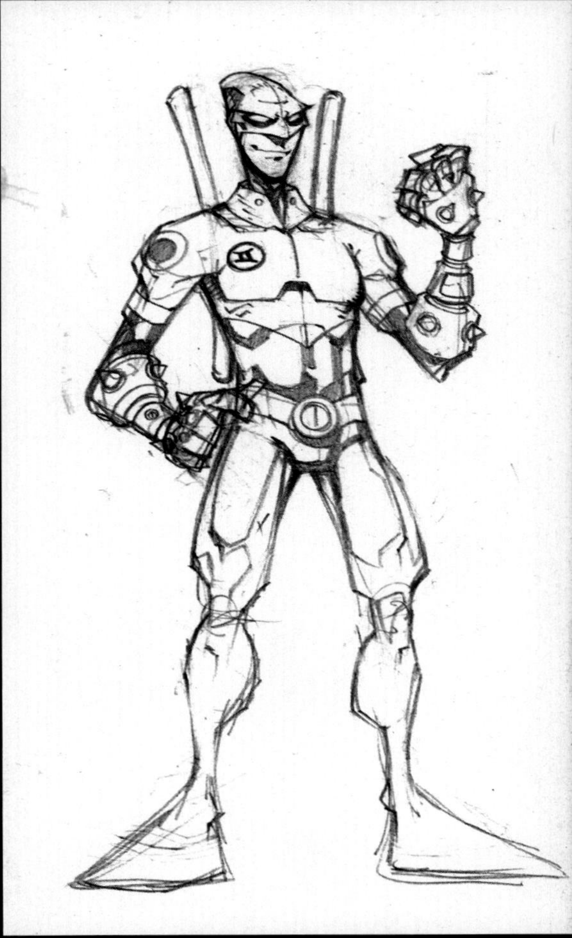

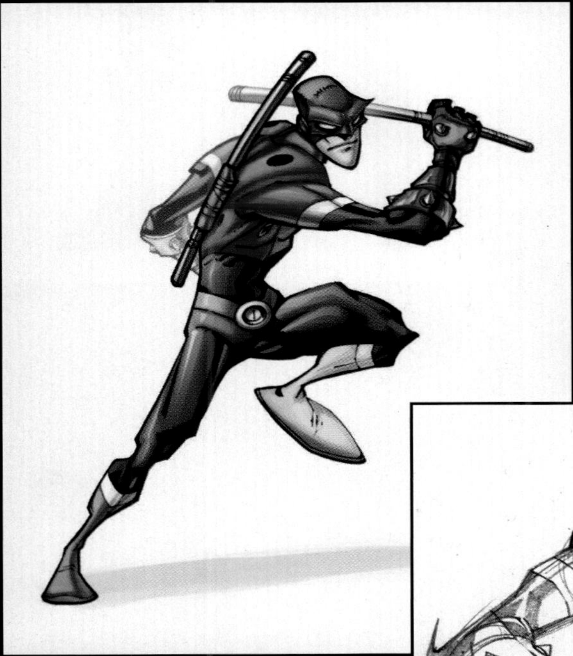

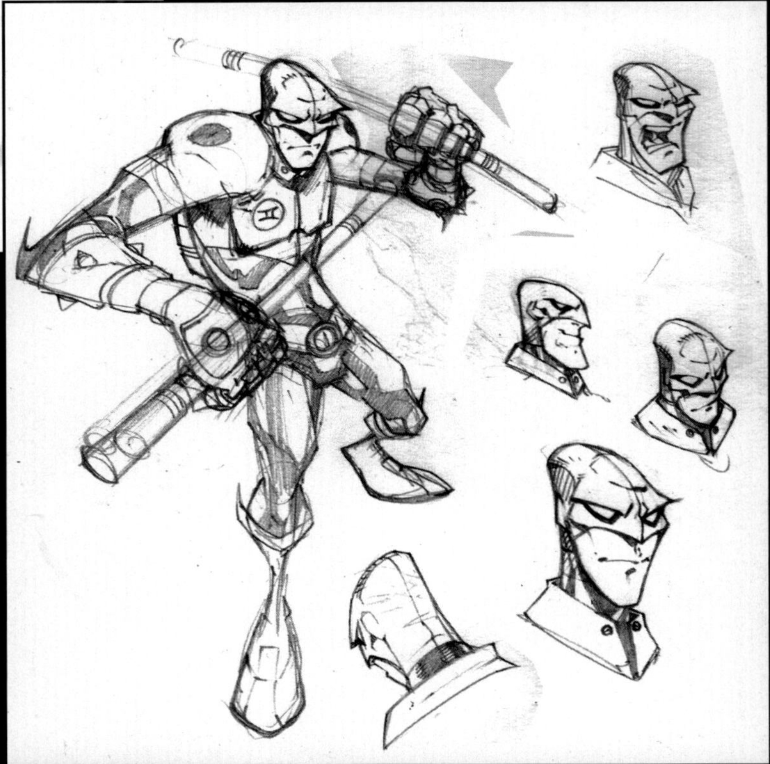

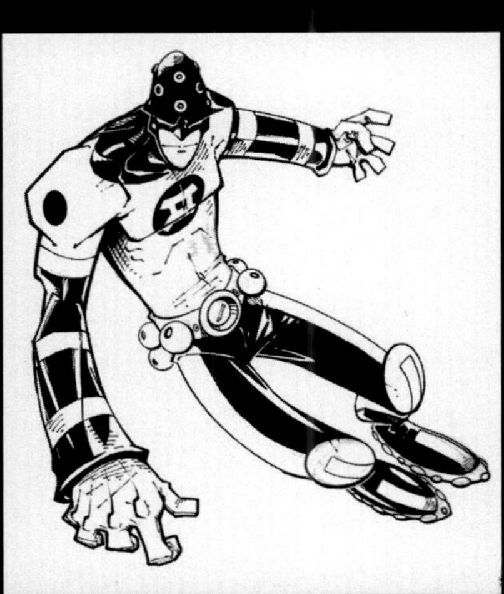

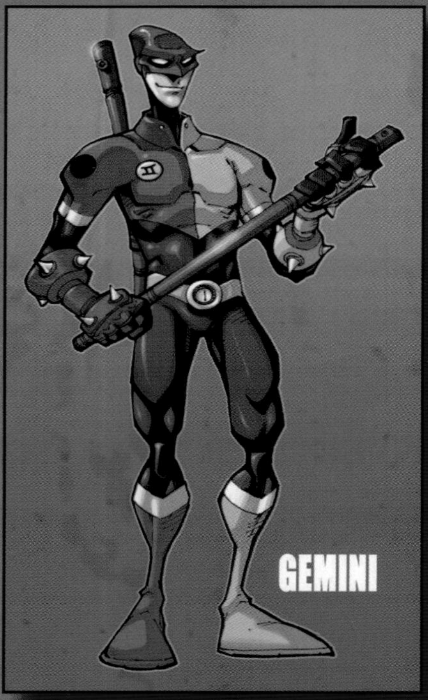
GEMINI

JON: Top left: The Gemini that almost was.

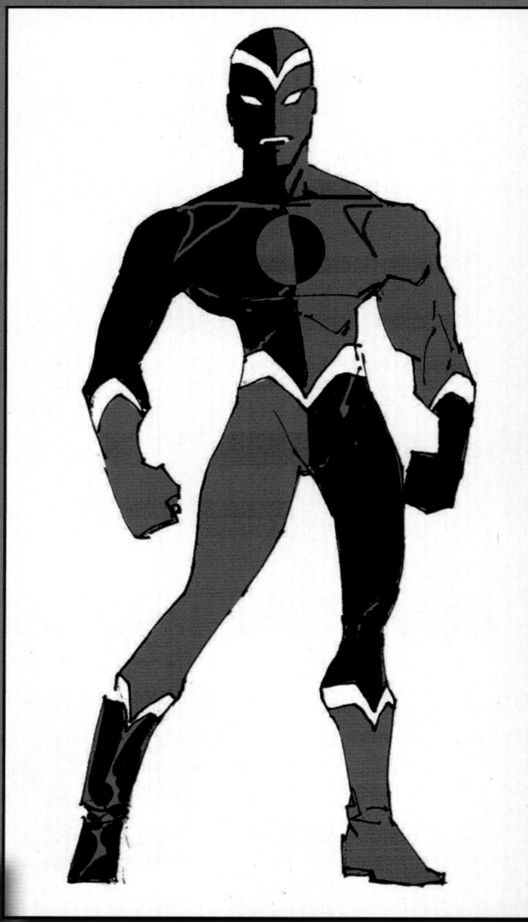

JAY: Top right: Ultimately, Erik Larsen, who was Publisher of Image at the time, rolled up his sleeves and came up with this rough design (loosely inspired by the Golden Age Daredevil, I think). Jon took that design and ran with it, and you can see the final result on the next page!

JON: Left: Very early pin-up piece using the original Gemini design before we decided to go with Erik's version.

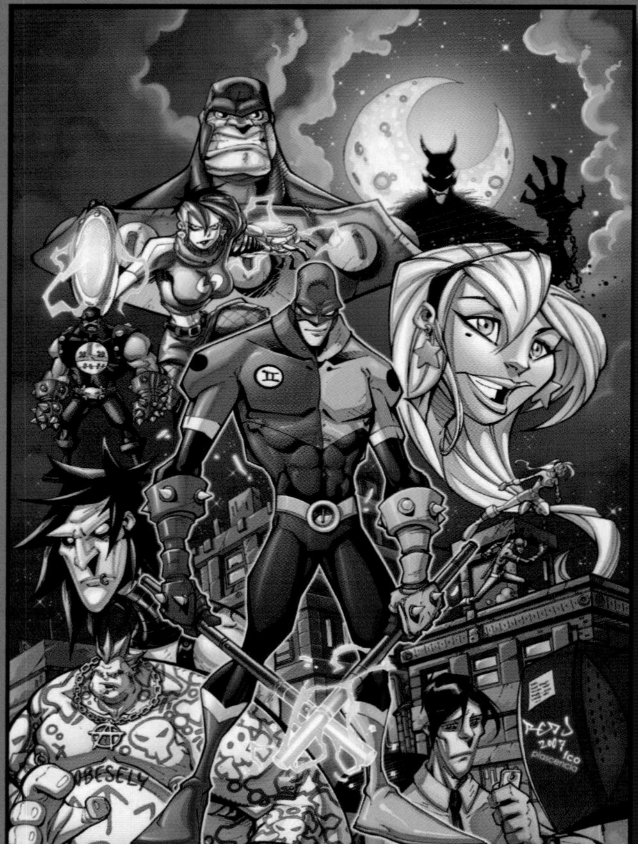

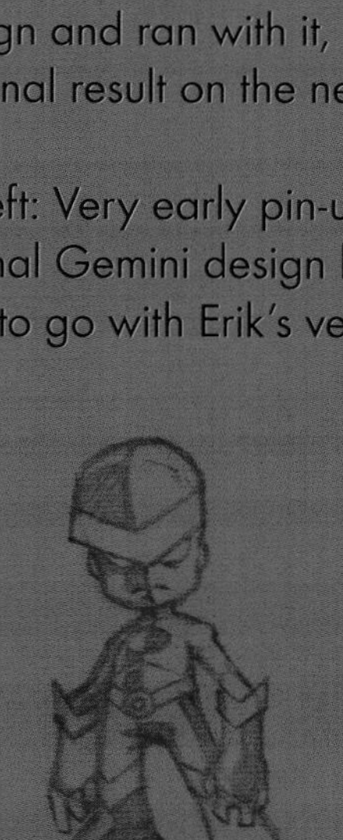

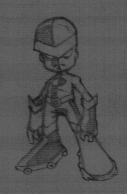

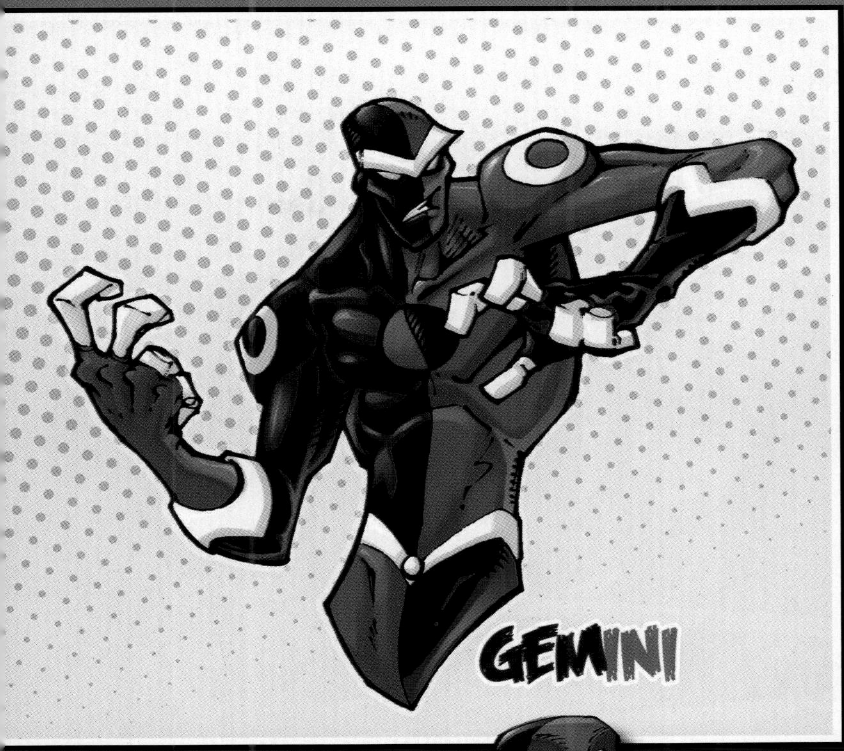
GEMINI

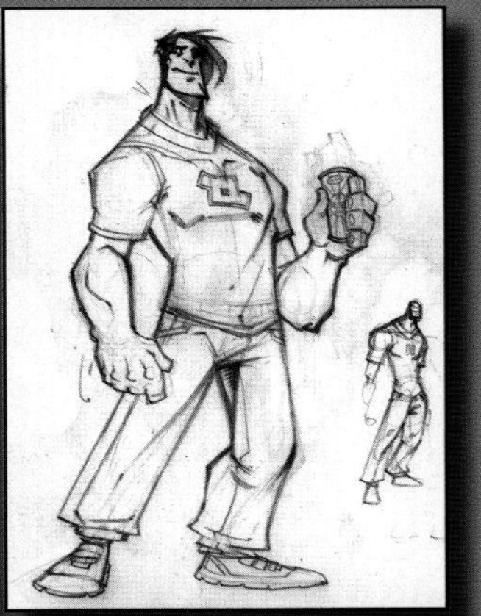

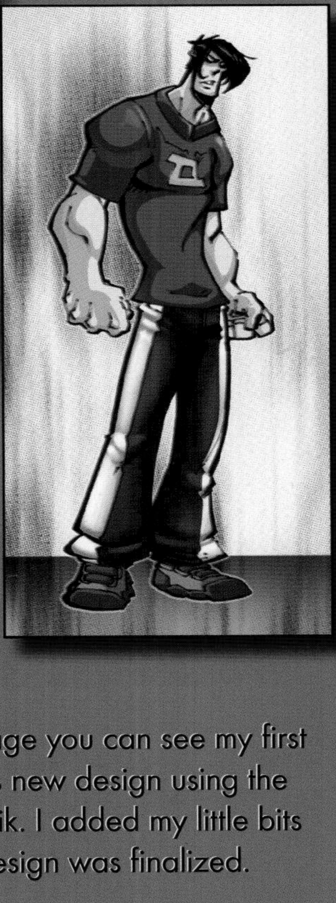

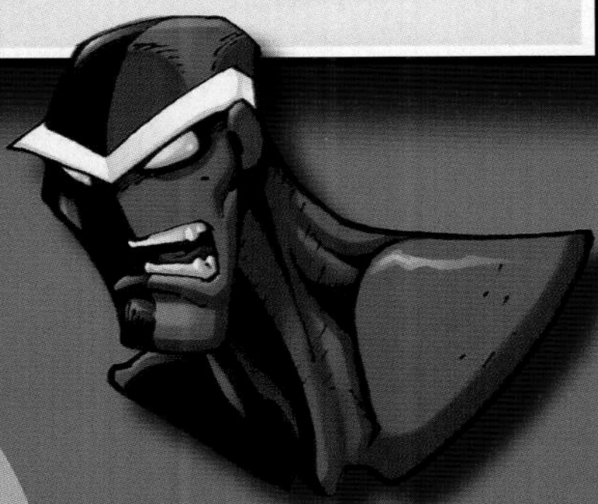

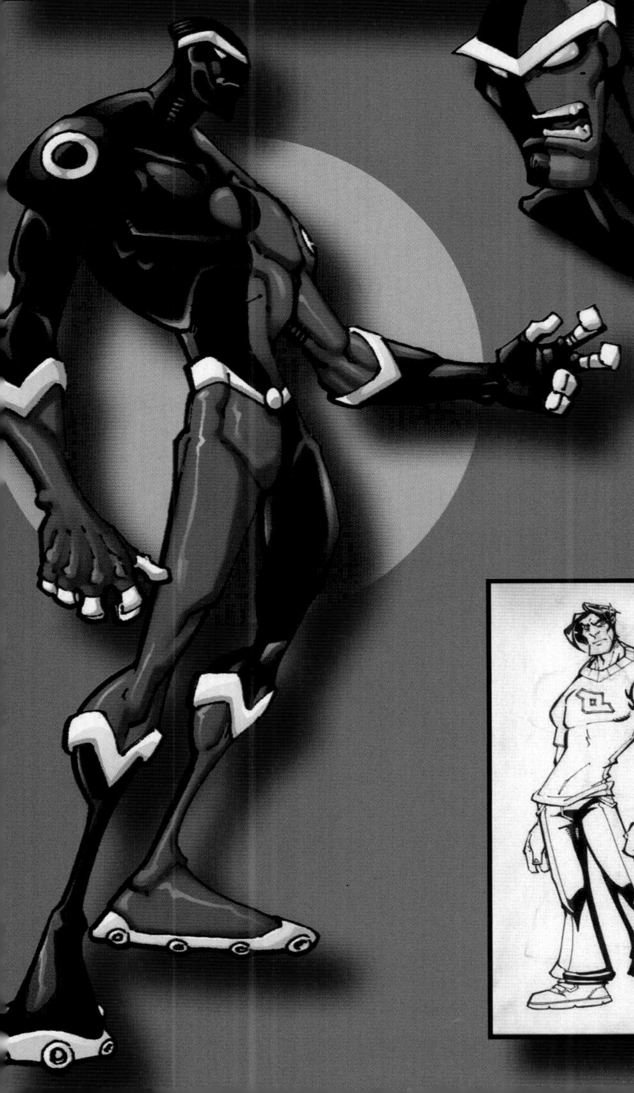

JON: On this page you can see my first takes on Gemini's new design using the feedback from Erik. I added my little bits of flair and the design was finalized.

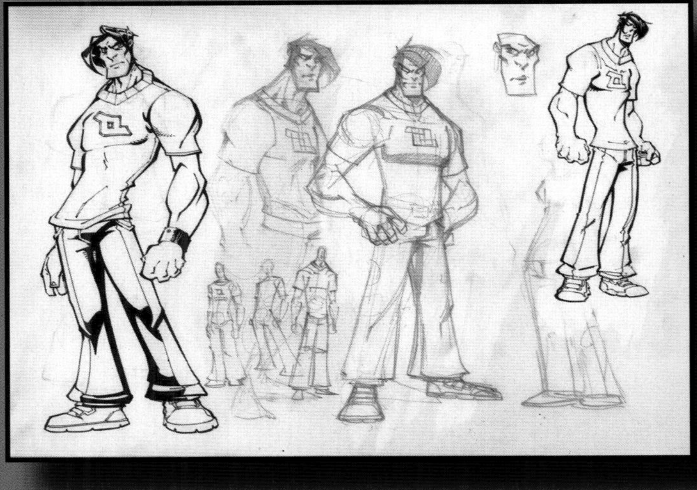

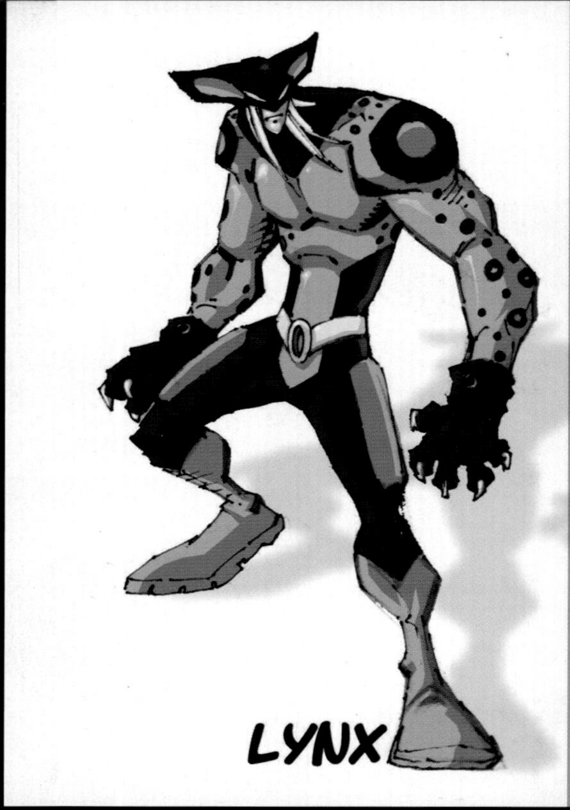
LYNX

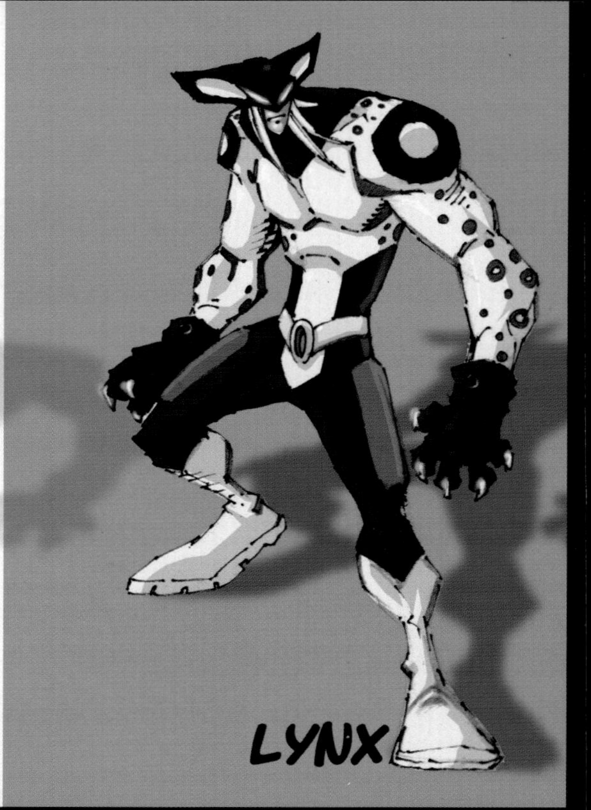
LYNX

L Y N X

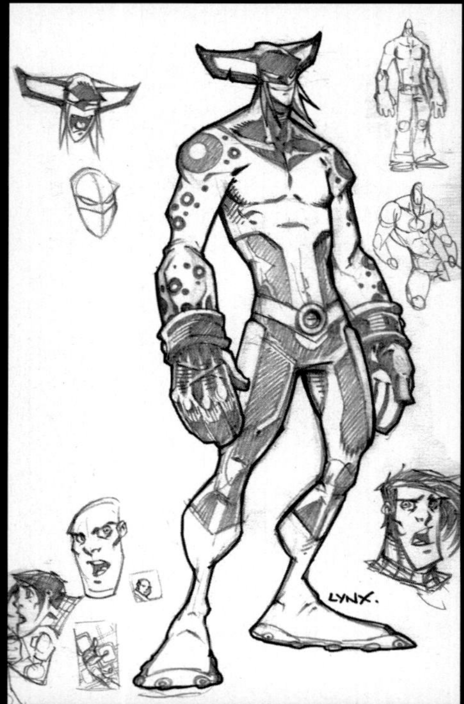
LYNX.

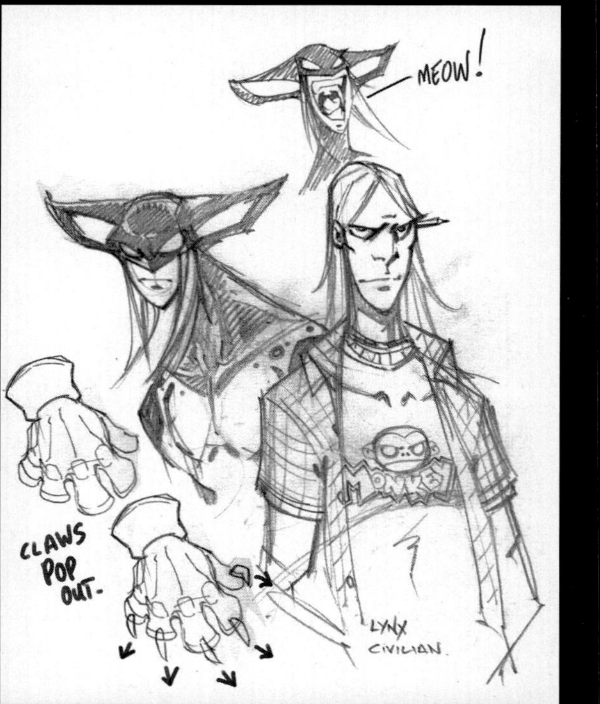
MEOW!
CLAWS POP OUT.
LYNX CIVILIAN.

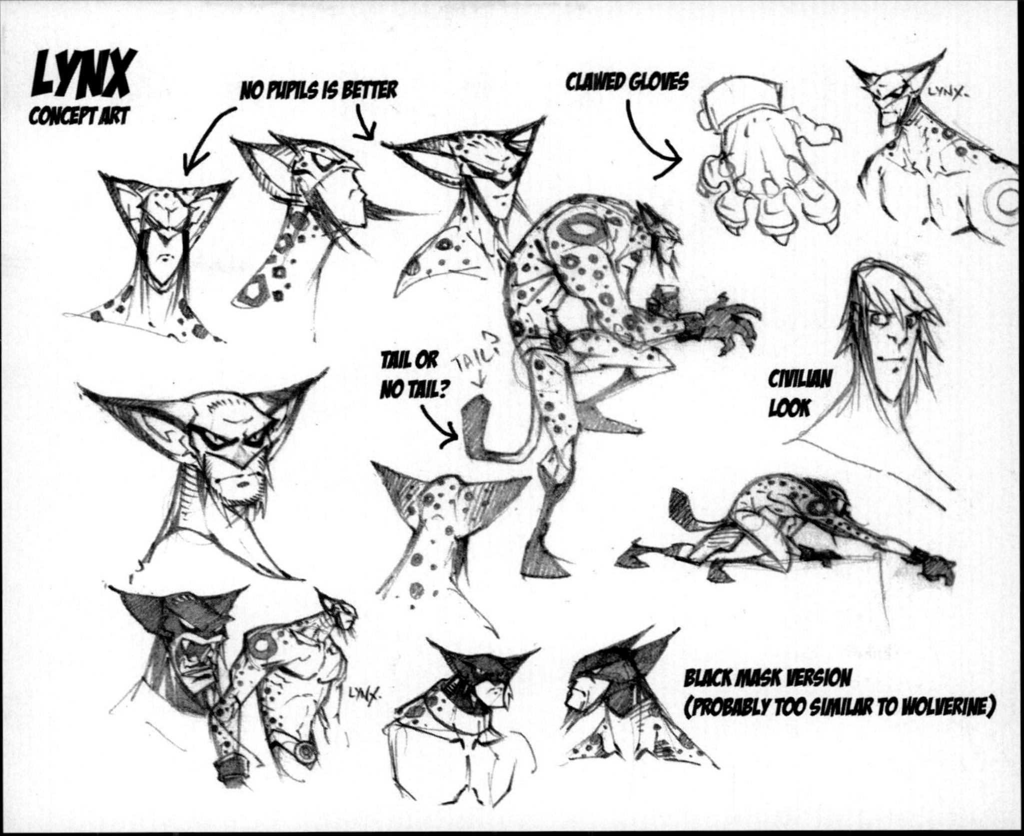
LYNX
CONCEPT ART
NO PUPILS IS BETTER
CLAWED GLOVES
LYNX.
TAIL OR NO TAIL?
TAIL?
CIVILIAN LOOK
LYNX.
BLACK MASK VERSION
(PROBABLY TOO SIMILAR TO WOLVERINE)

JON: Lynx was fun to design, although coming up with a cat-like hero with claws that didn't resemble Wolverine too much was tricky! I included elements in his costume that showed he had the same wardrobe designer as Gemini and other Constellation operatives.

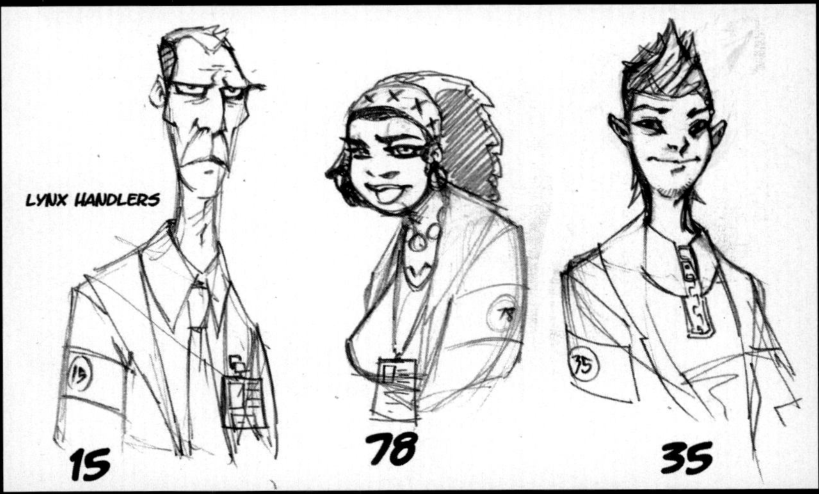
LYNX HANDLERS
15
78
35

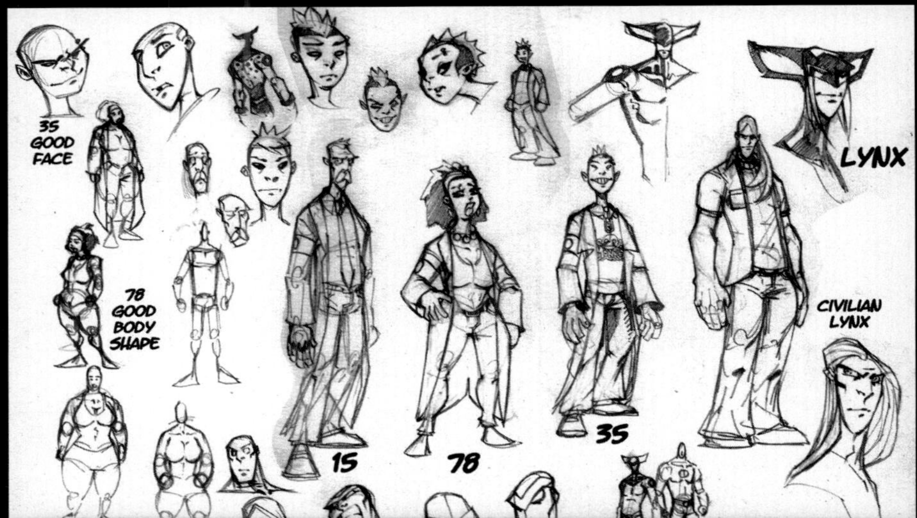
35 GOOD FACE
78 GOOD BODY SHAPE
LYNX
CIVILIAN LYNX
15
78
35

L U N A

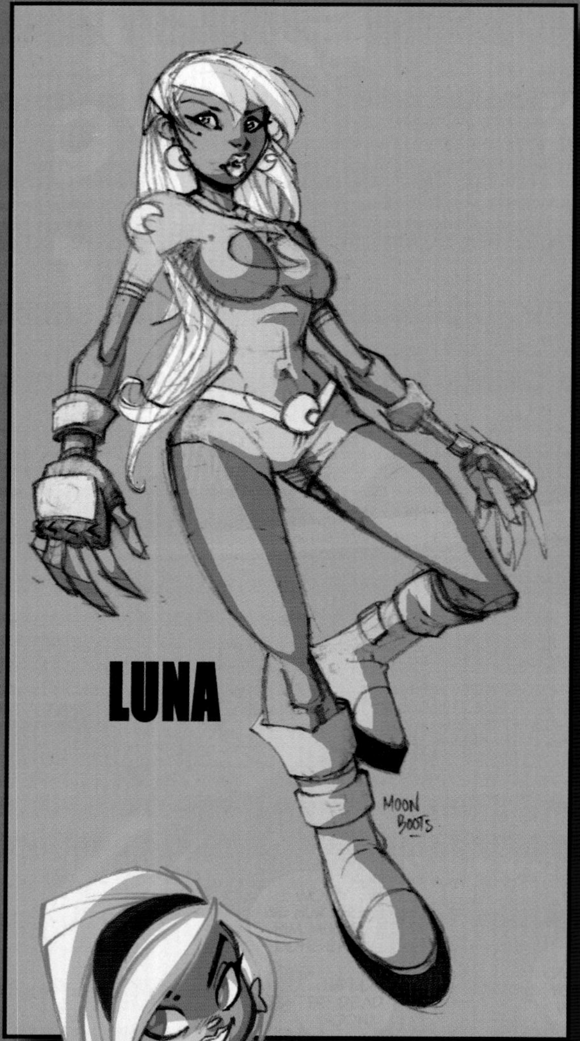
LUNA
MOON BOOTS

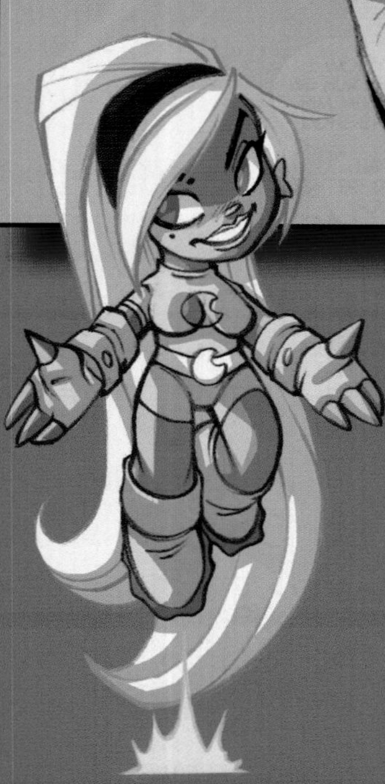

JON: Luna was fun to design. The only note I remember getting from Jay was that she had to have some sort of cut in the costume which showed off her cleavage. This would come into play in the story when Gemini gets busted taking a sneaky peek.

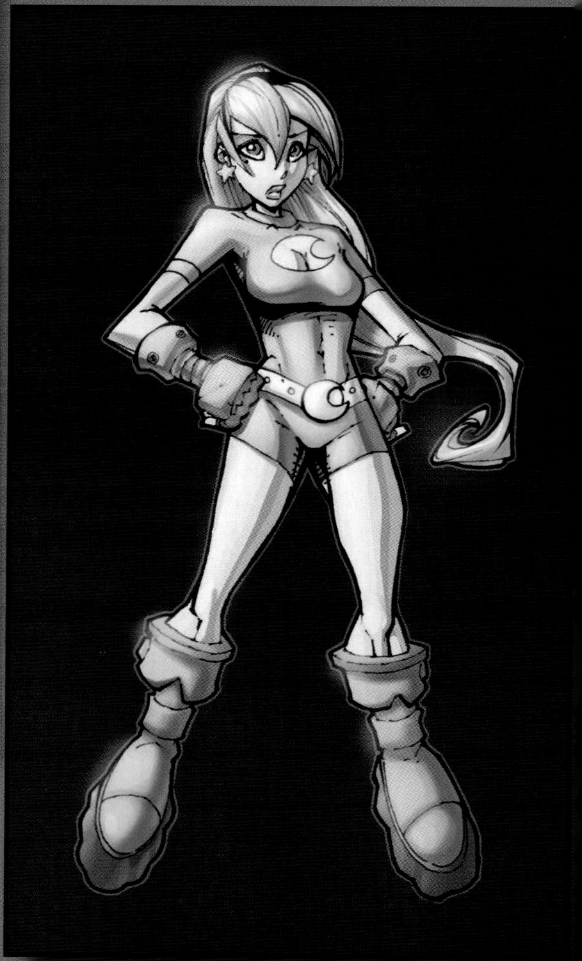

JON: The idea with Luna is that she has the powers of the moon. Aside from being able to affect gravity, I wanted her to have a slight glow about her at all times. She also has a beauty spot (known as a "lunar" in Spanish) and moon boots!

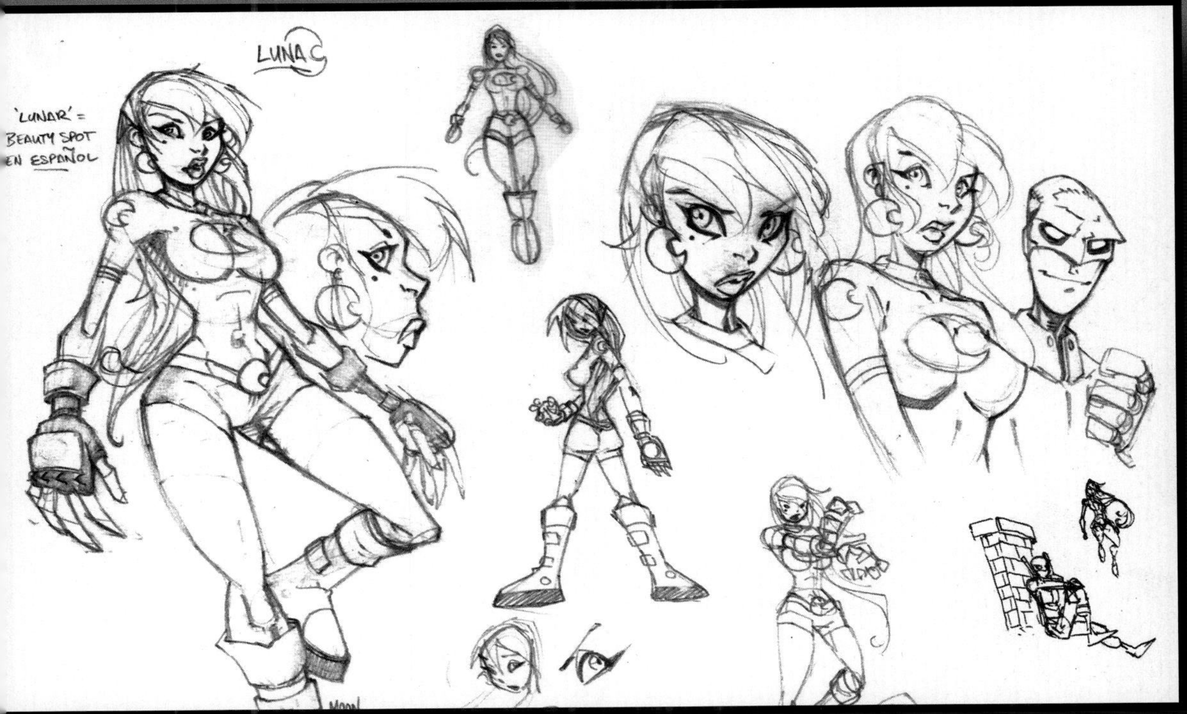
LUNA
'LUNAR' =
BEAUTY SPOT
EN ESPAÑOL

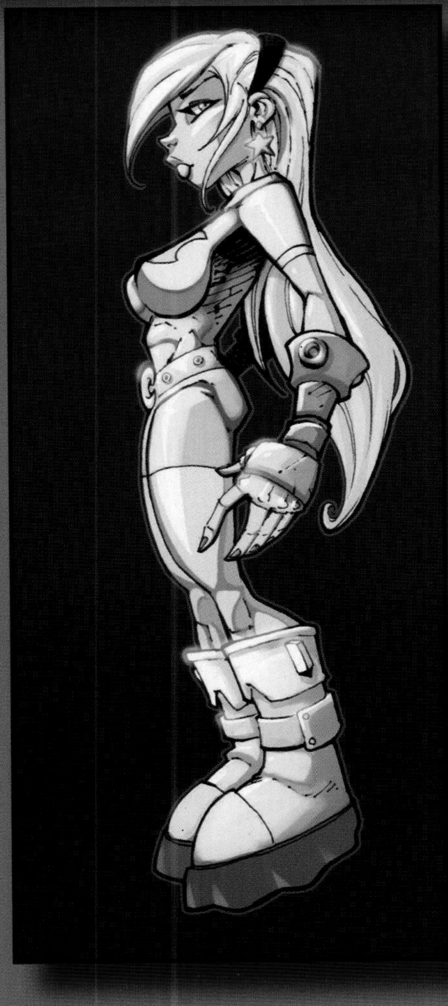

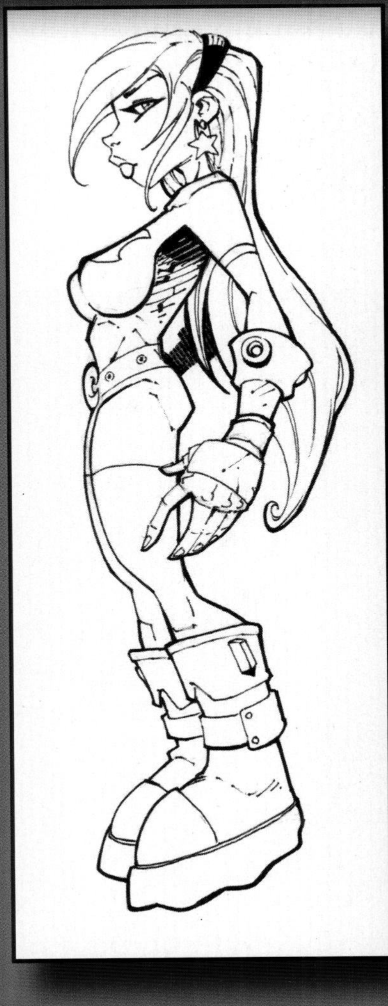

RADIA

JON: Radia was one of the "Junkyard Gang" members which I designed for issue 1. I went for a Gothic/punk/metal type theme for these guys. Radia was basically just an "electric chick."

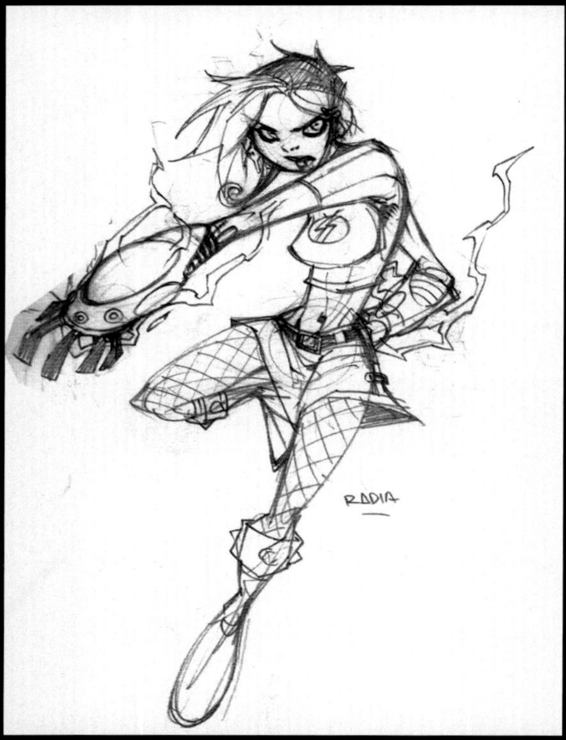
RADIA

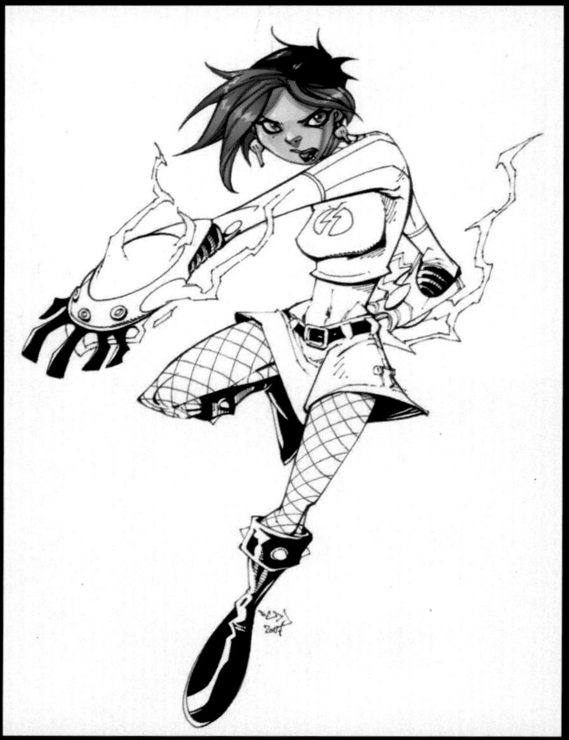

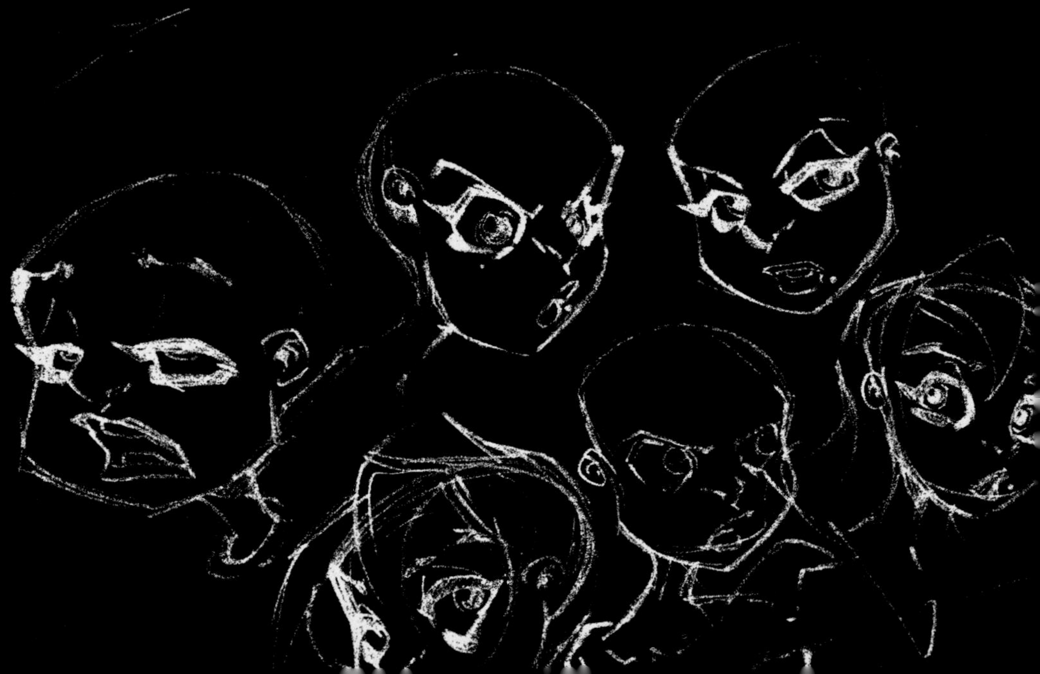

JON: At this stage FCO and I were also experimenting a lot with the color to find a good look for the comic. Whatever happened to that FCO guy?

Sure would be fun to draw these guys again and give them a good makeover using my current skill set. I have ideas!

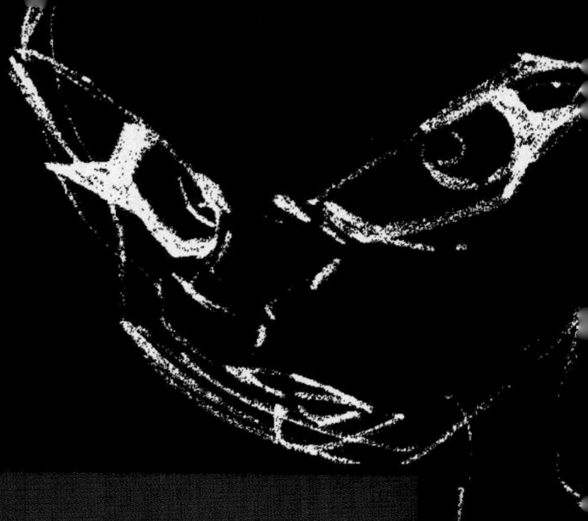

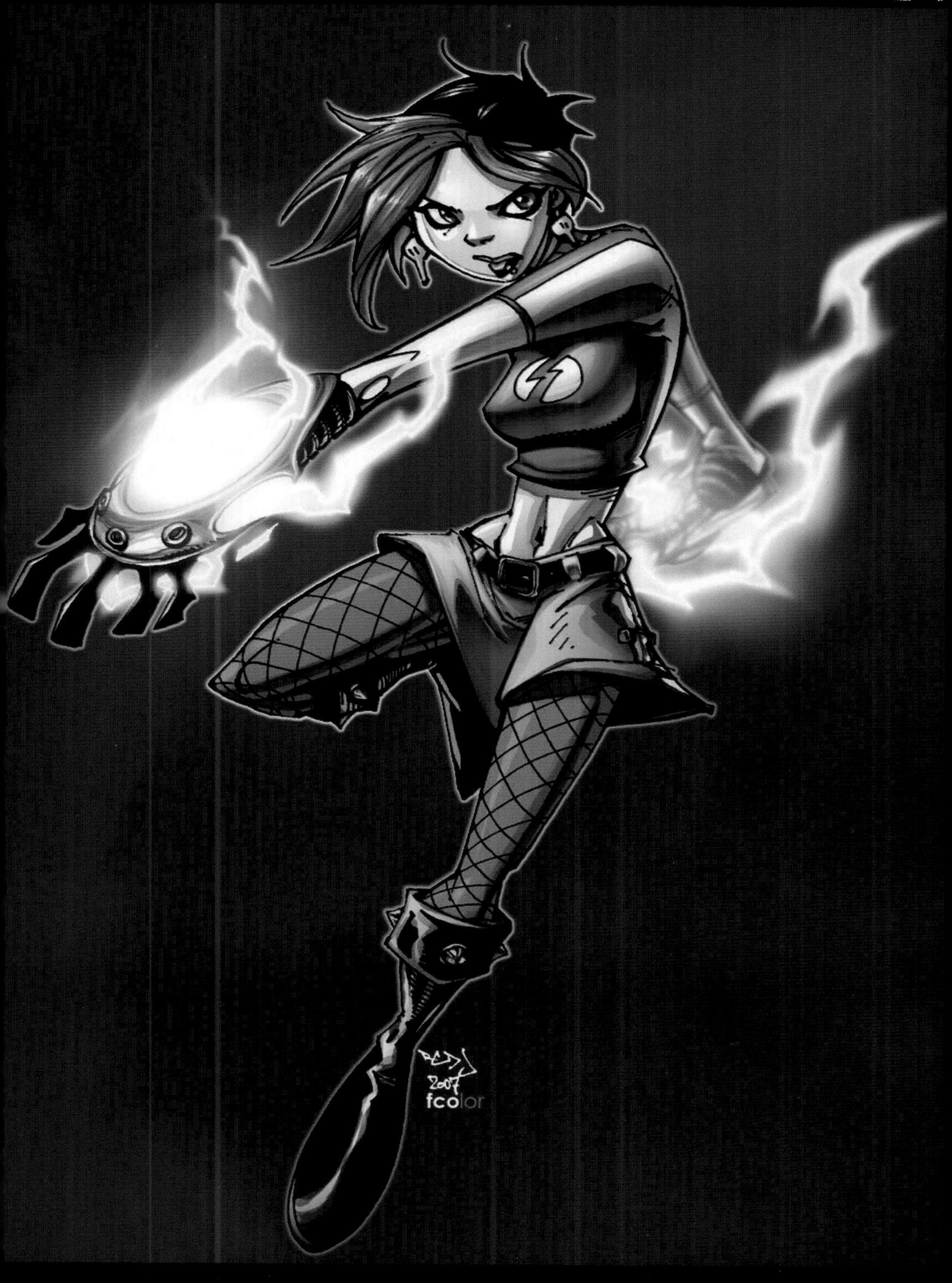
fcolor

OTHER CHARACTERS

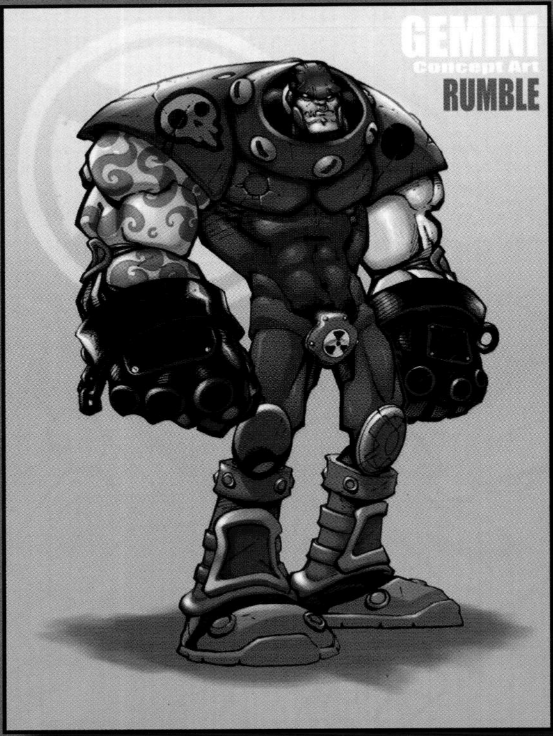
GEMINI
Concept Art
RUMBLE

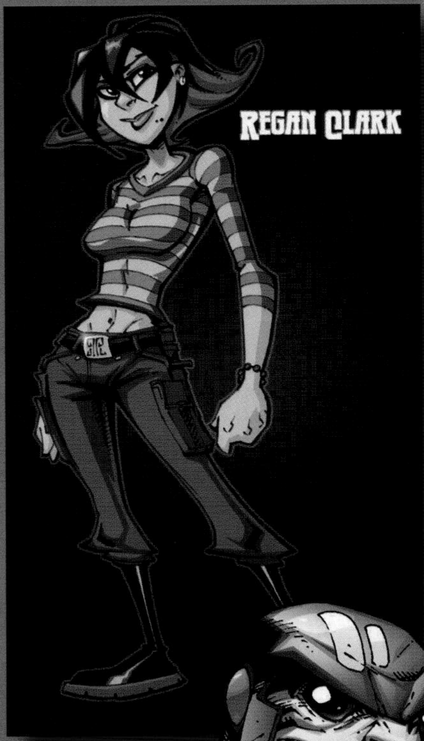
REGAN CLARK

JON: My initial design for Rumble was inspired by a big British bruiser punk type of a guy. Since I ended up going for a similar theme with the Junkyard Gang I decided to go for more of a "military experiment gone wrong" design for him instead.

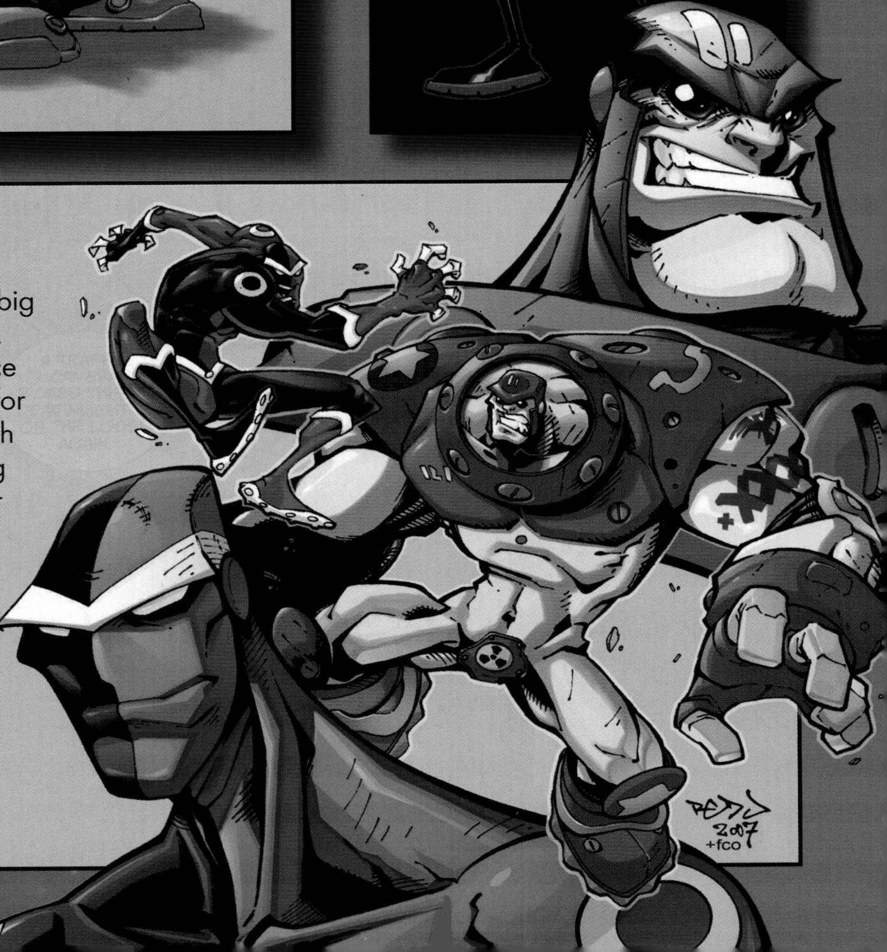

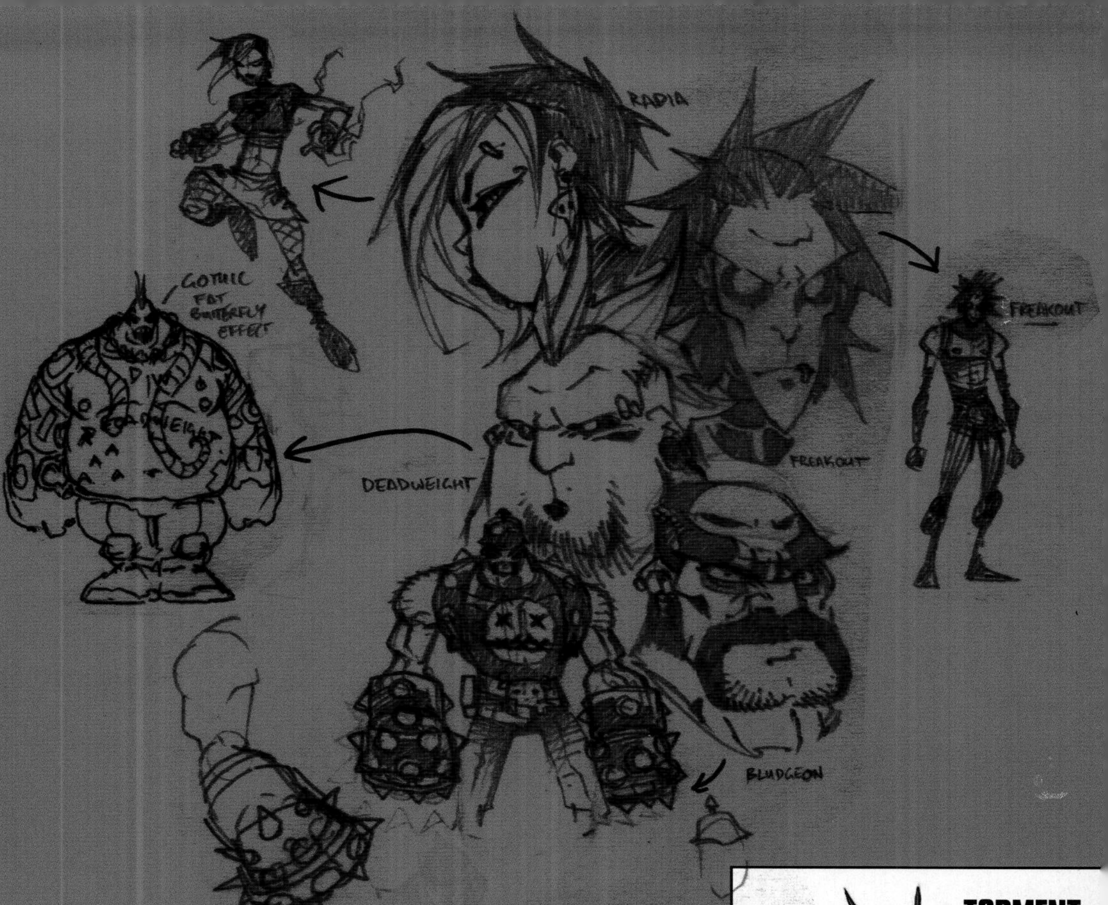
RADIA
GOTHIC FAT BUTTERFLY EFFECT
FREAKOUT
DEADWEIGHT
FREAKOUT
BLUDGEON

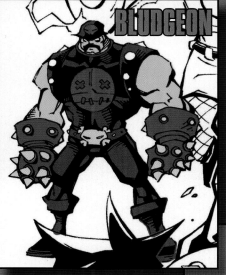

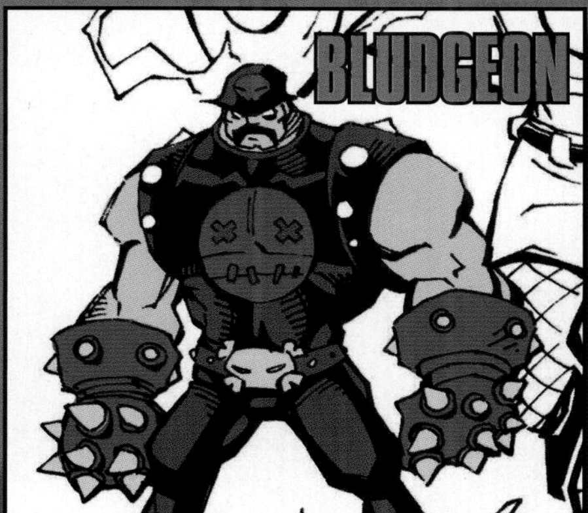
BLUDGEON

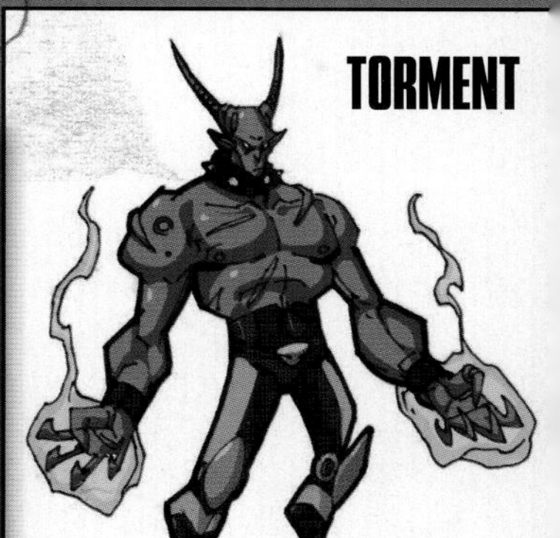
TORMENT

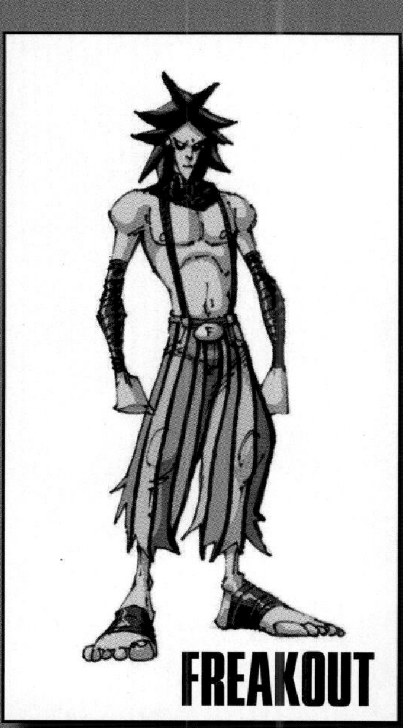
FREAKOUT

JON: The rest of the Junkyard Gang.

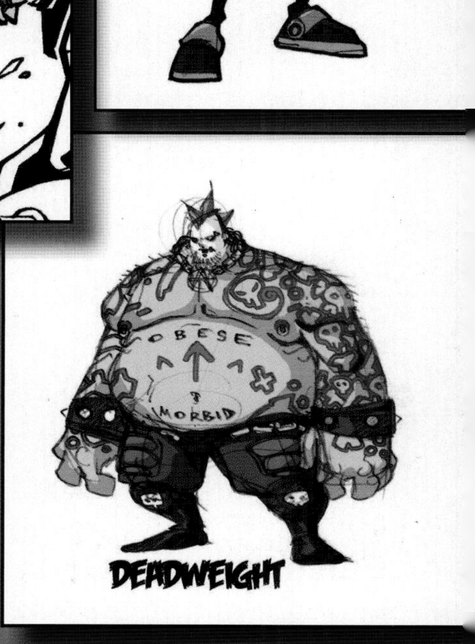
OBESE
MORBID
DEADWEIGHT

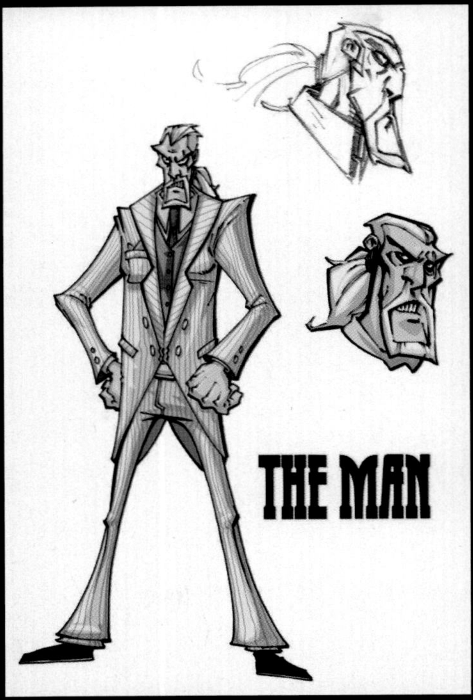
THE MAN

JON: The W.A.S.P. team is The Man's personal security SWAT detail. I was going through a real "skinny neck" phase at the time I drew these guys.

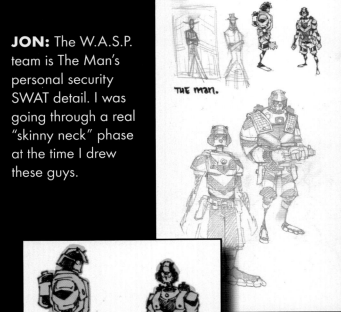

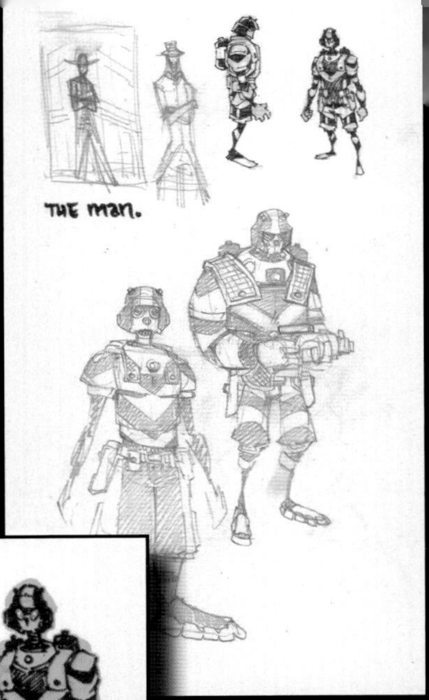
THE MAN.

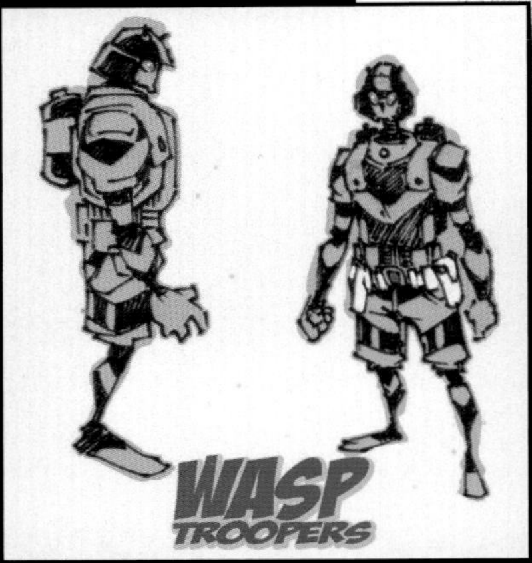
WASP
TROOPERS

Made them seem more robotic than we intended, which is why I really wanted to show a human face beneath the mask in the splash below.

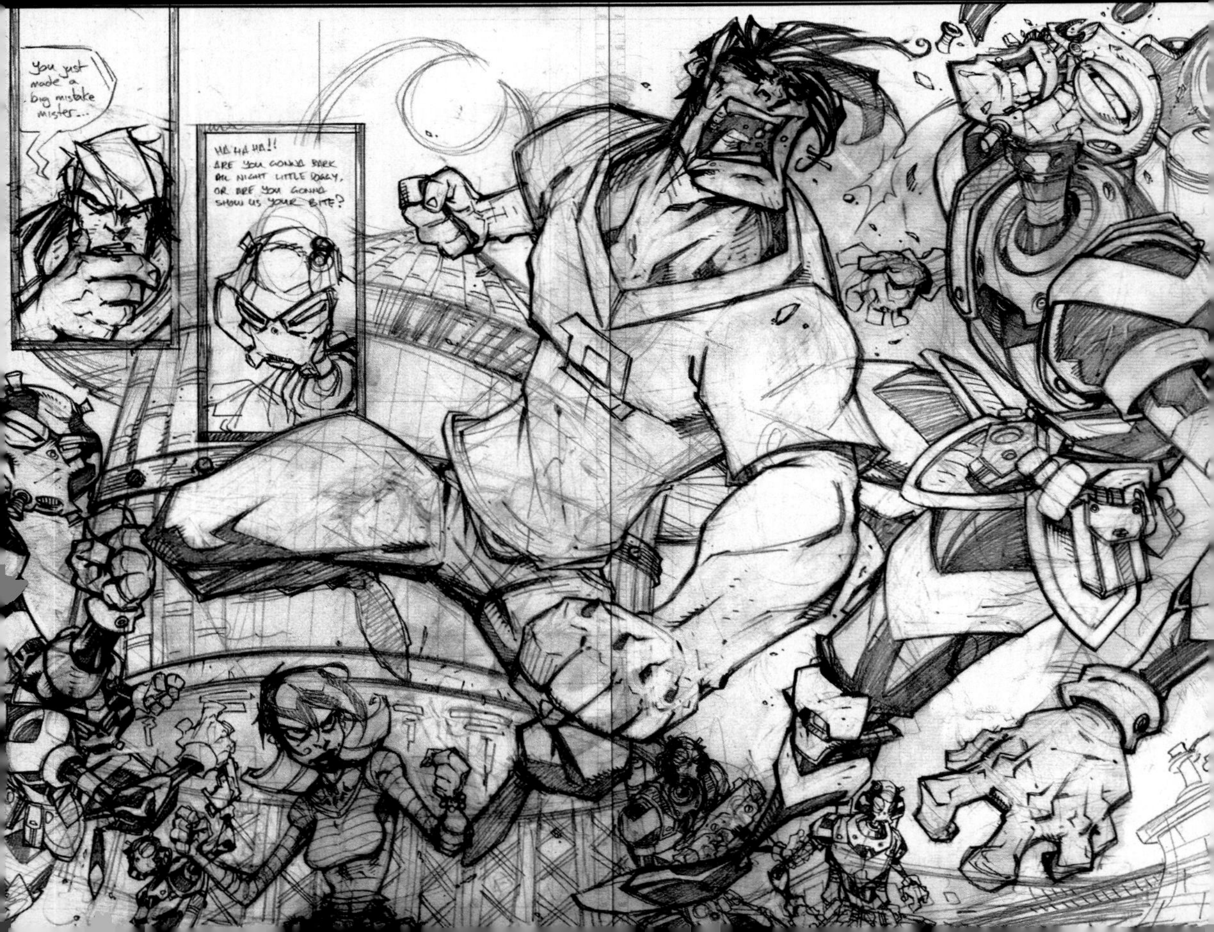
You just made a big mistake mister...
HA HA HA!! ARE YOU GONNA BARK ALL NIGHT LITTLE DOGGY, OR ARE YOU GONNA SHOW US YOUR BITE?

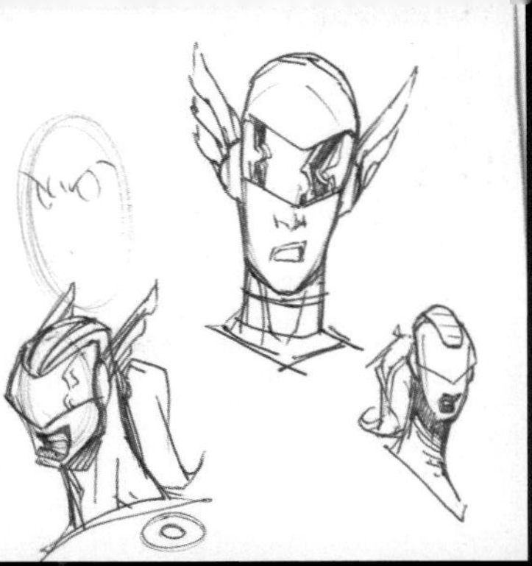

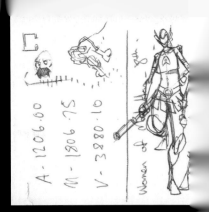

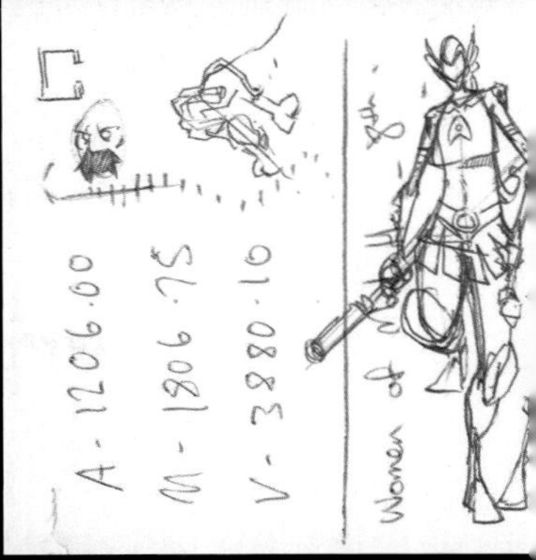
A - 1206.00
M - 1806.75
V - 3880.10
Women of

NDROME

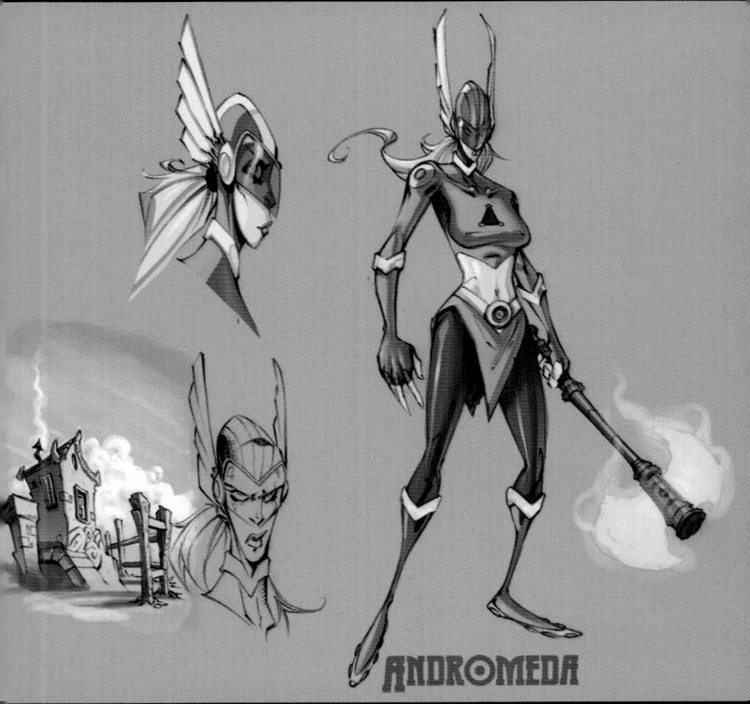
ANDROMEDA

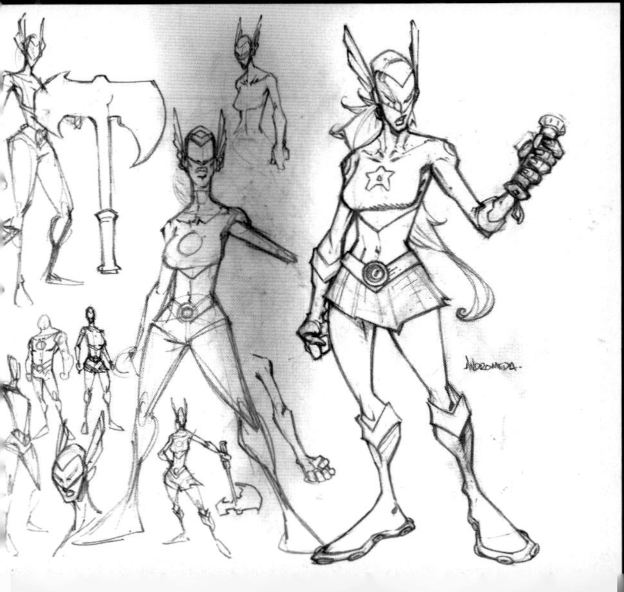
ANDROMEDA

JON:
the op
anothe
operat
decide
female
time ar
me the
"Andro
that sh
big axe
Hopefu
her nic
becaus
one of

ISSUE ONE

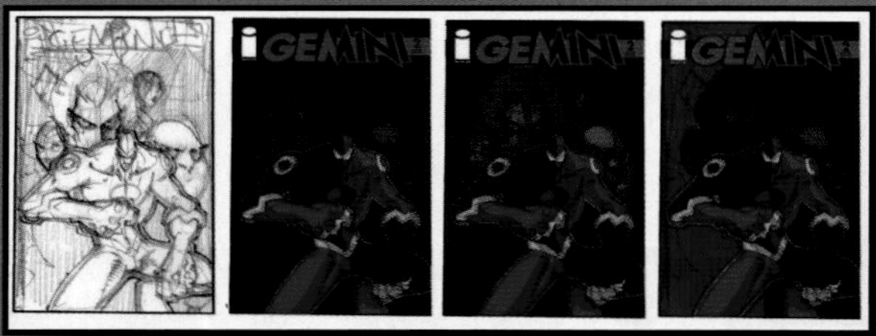

GEMINI
GEMINI
GEMINI

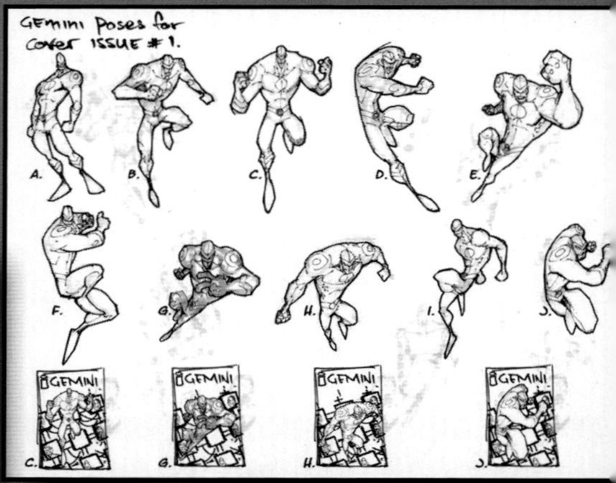

GEMINI Poses for Cover ISSUE #1.
A.
B.
C.
D.
E.
F.
G.
H.
I.
J.
GEMINI
GEMINI
GEMINI
GEMINI
C.
G.
H.
J.

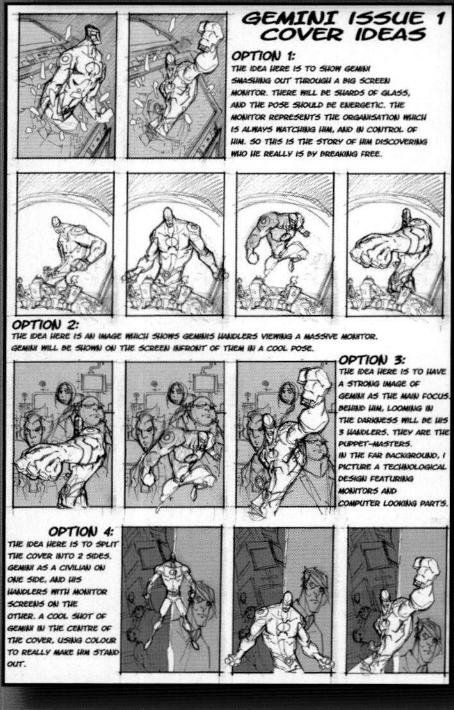

GEMINI ISSUE 1 COVER IDEAS
OPTION 1:
THE IDEA HERE IS TO SHOW GEMINI SMASHING OUT THROUGH A BIG SCREEN MONITOR. THERE WILL BE SHARDS OF GLASS, AND THE POSE SHOULD BE ENERGETIC. THE MONITOR REPRESENTS THE ORGANISATION WHICH IS ALWAYS WATCHING HIM, AND IN CONTROL OF HIM. SO THIS IS THE STORY OF HIM DISCOVERING WHO HE REALLY IS BY BREAKING FREE.
OPTION 2:
THE IDEA HERE IS AN IMAGE WHICH SHOWS GEMINIS HANDLERS VIEWING A MASSIVE MONITOR. GEMINI WILL BE SHOWN ON THE SCREEN INFRONT OF THEM IN A COOL POSE.
OPTION 3:
THE IDEA HERE IS TO HAVE A STRONG IMAGE OF GEMINI AS THE MAIN FOCUS. BEHIND HIM, LOOMING IN THE DARKNESS WILL BE HIS 3 HANDLERS. THEY ARE THE PUPPET-MASTERS.
IN THE FAR BACKGROUND, I PICTURE A TECHNOLOGICAL DESIGN FEATURING MONITORS AND COMPUTER LOOKING PARTS.
OPTION 4:
THE IDEA HERE IS TO SPLIT THE COVER INTO 2 SIDES. GEMINI AS A CIVILIAN ON ONE SIDE, AND HIS HANDLERS WITH MONITOR SCREENS ON THE OTHER. A COOL SHOT OF GEMINI IN THE CENTRE OF THE COVER, USING COLOUR TO REALLY MAKE HIM STAND OUT.

JAY: Here's a look at the various cover designs Jon worked up for our first issue, along with some of his notes.

JON: Ultimately we ended up scraping all of this with a tight deadline looming, and we decided to just go ahead with the cover we ended up with.

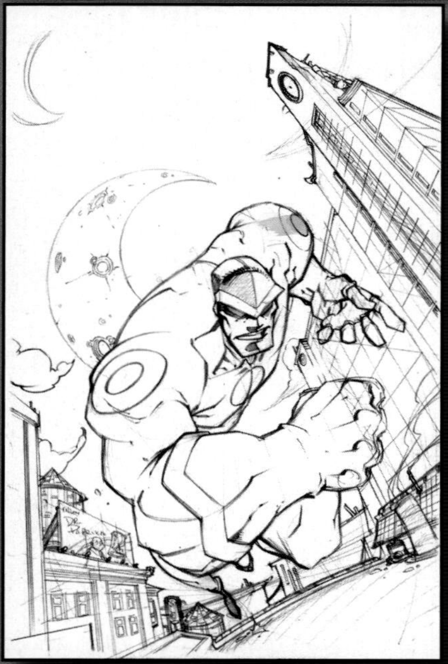

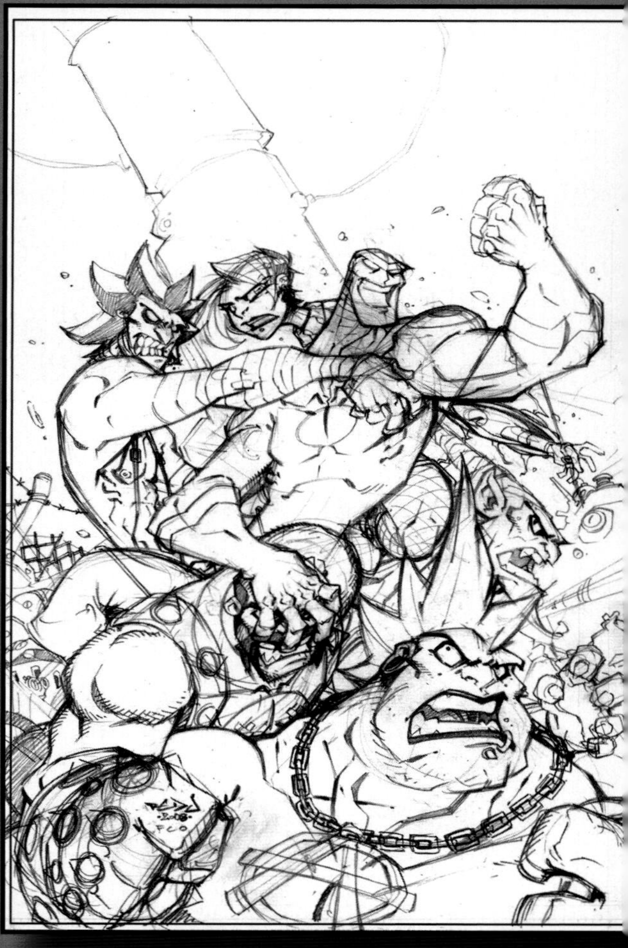

ISSUE TWO

AY: Here are some of Jon's thumbnails for issue 2. You can see he did some of them on the script pages he'd printed out.

ON: Jay was very generous throughout this series and would give me blocks of pages to stage out a fight scene. The thumbnails you see here are a good example of this. I would start figuring out what would happen on those pages right there on the script. Like the dope I am, I would feel the need to really complicate things as much as possible rather than simply just drawing four nice big splash pages. That would have been much easier! I really wanted those action pages to have a flow and a story within them. To Jay's credit, he always just rolled with it and added some great dialogue which polished everything off very nicely. Lots of fun!

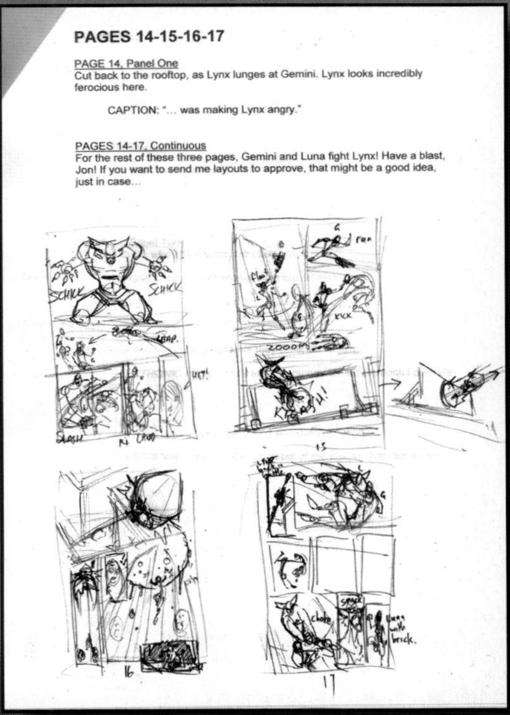

PAGES 14-15-16-17

PAGE 14, Panel One
Cut back to the rooftop, as Lynx lunges at Gemini. Lynx looks incredibly ferocious here.

CAPTION: "… was making Lynx angry."

PAGES 14-17, Continuous
For the rest of these three pages, Gemini and Luna fight Lynx! Have a blast, Jon! If you want to send me layouts to approve, that might be a good idea, just in case…

SCHICK
SCHICK
ZOOOM
KRASH!
16
17

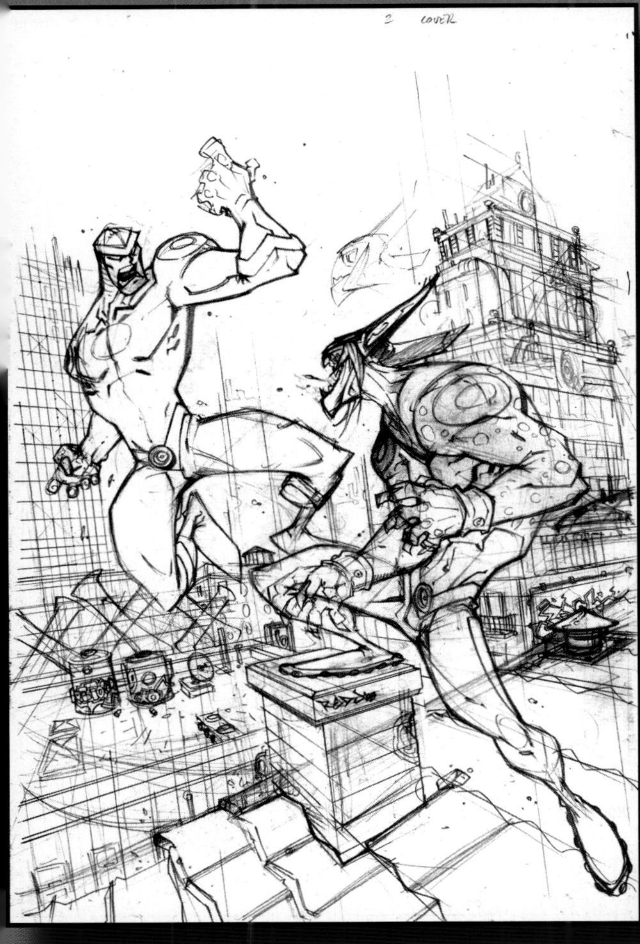

2 COVER

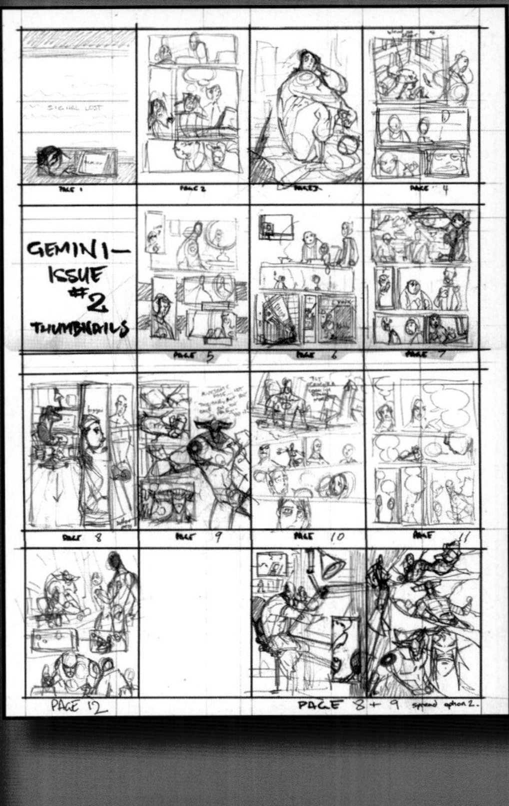

GEMINI— ISSUE #2 THUMBNAILS
PAGE 1
PAGE 2
PAGE 3
PAGE 4
PAGE 5
PAGE 6
PAGE 7
PAGE 8
PAGE 9
PAGE 10
PAGE 11
PAGE 12
PAGE 8 + 9

ISSUE THREE

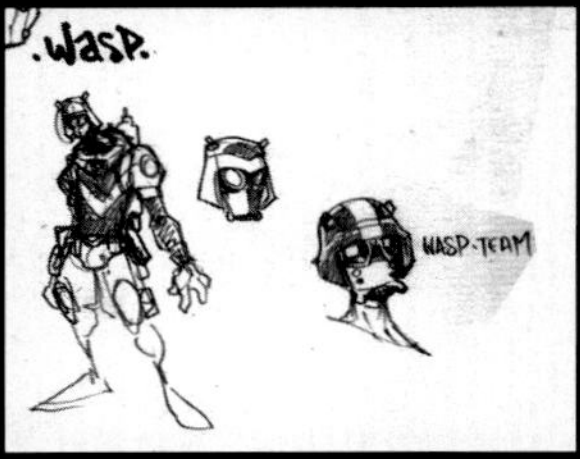
.Wasp.
WASP-TEAM

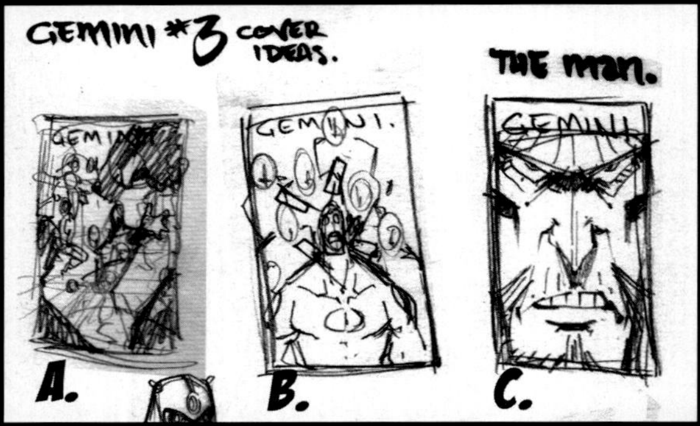
GEMINI *3 COVER IDEAS.
THE MAN.
GEMINI
A.
B.
C.

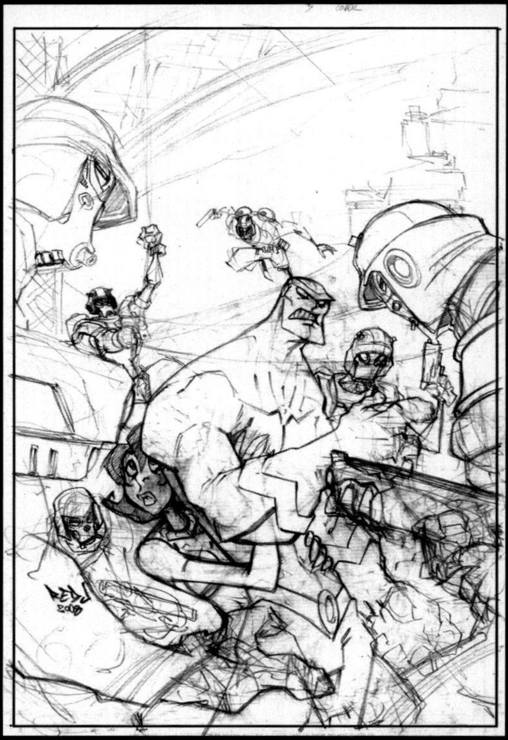

ISSUE FOUR

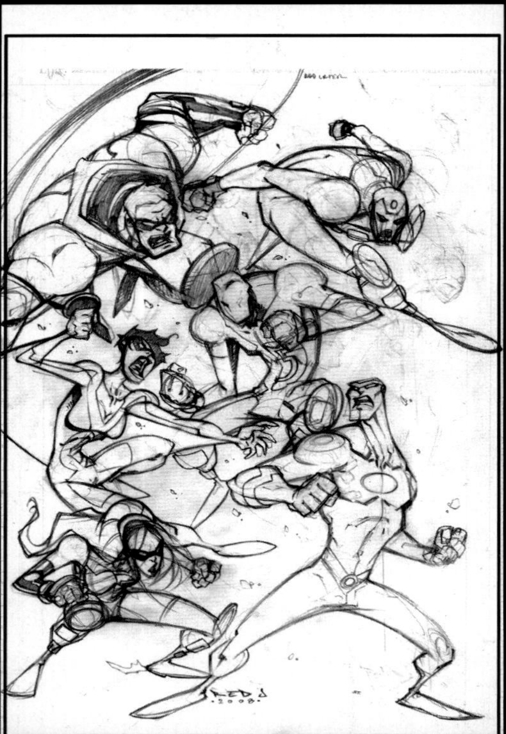

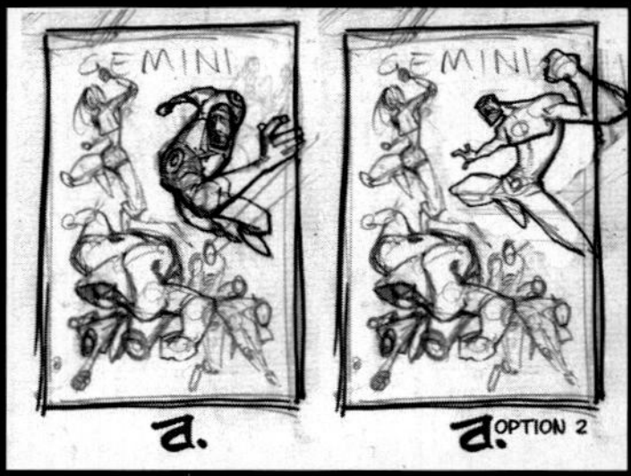
GEMINI
a.
a. OPTION 2

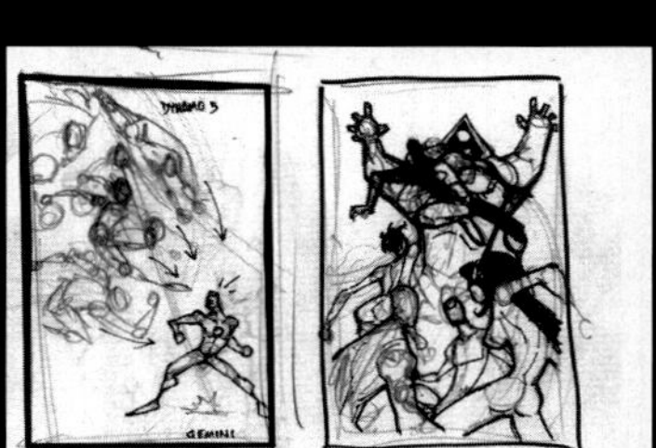
b.
c.

JAY: And some of his sketches for issue 4, which guest-starred Dynamo 5, a super-hero team created by me and Mahmud Asrar.

JON: By the time issue 4 came around, it looks like I had moved from skinny necks to skinny ankles! Hey, why not?

ISSUE FIVE

JAY: Although issue 5 was never published traditionally, Jon had still worked up some cover designs for it.

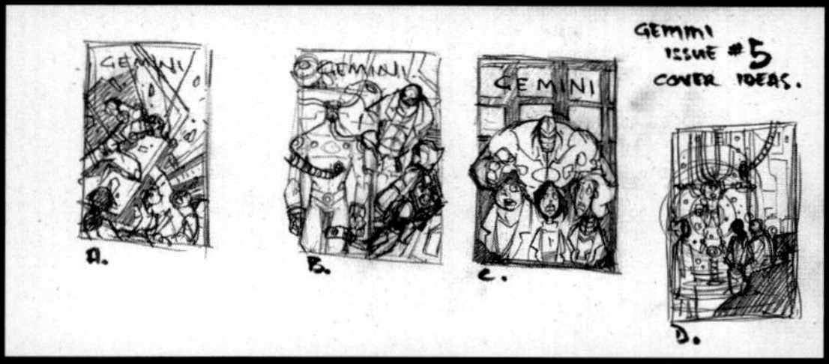
GEMINI
ISSUE #5
COVER IDEAS.
A.
B.
C.
D.

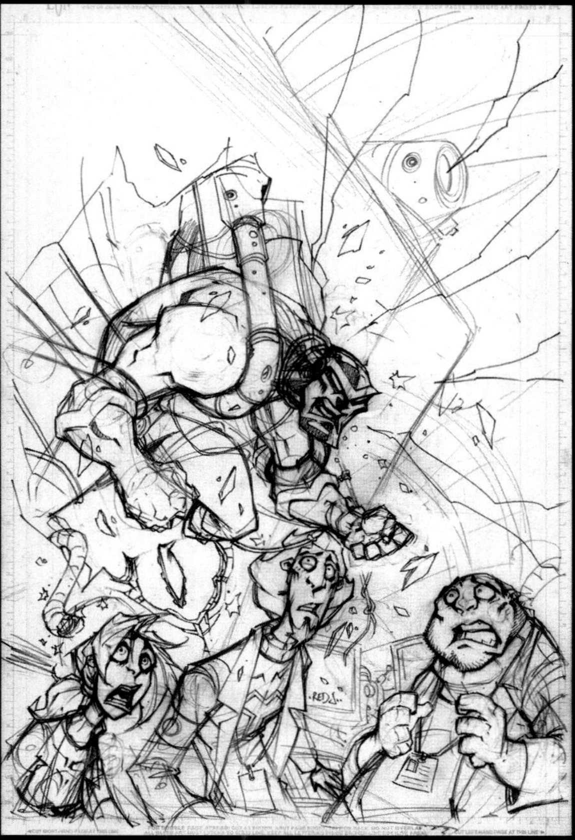

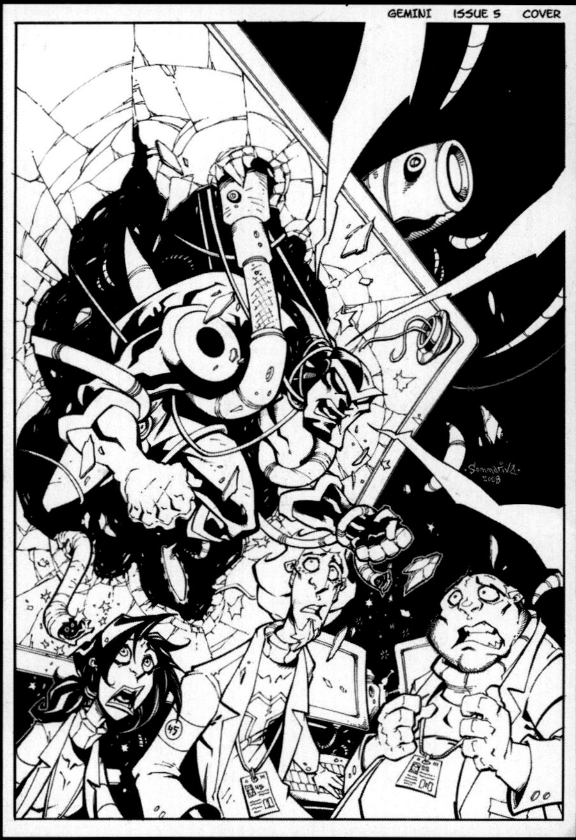
GEMINI ISSUE 5 COVER

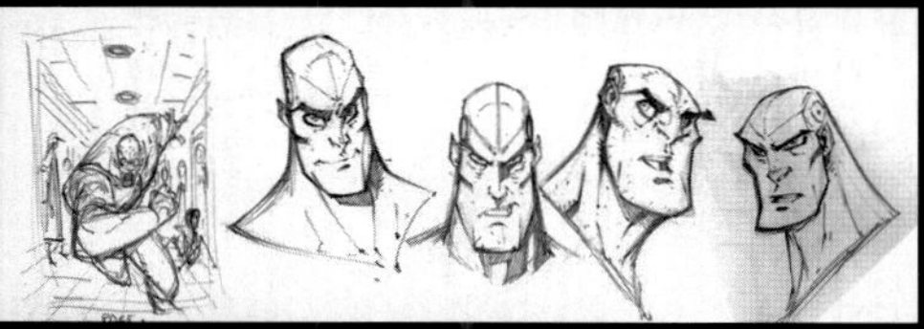

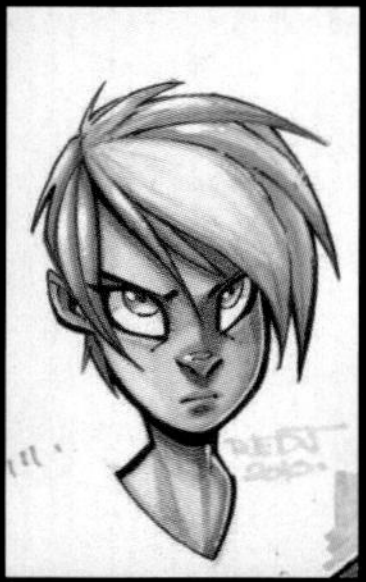

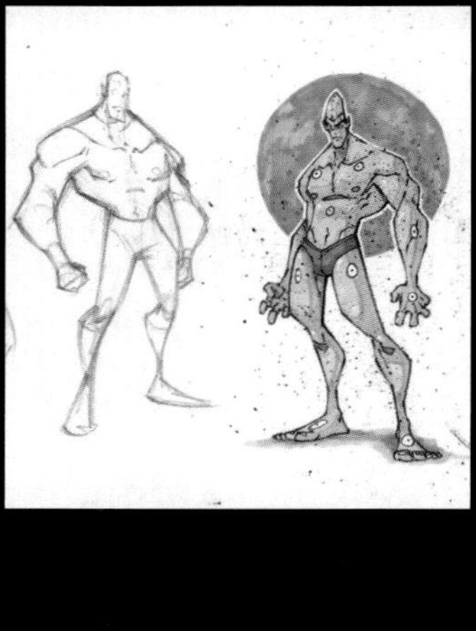

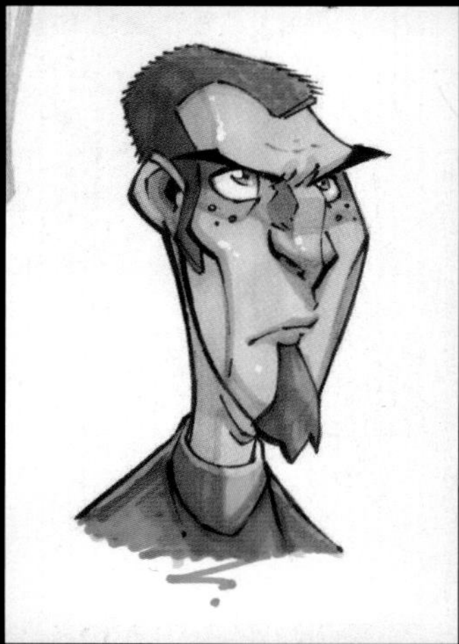

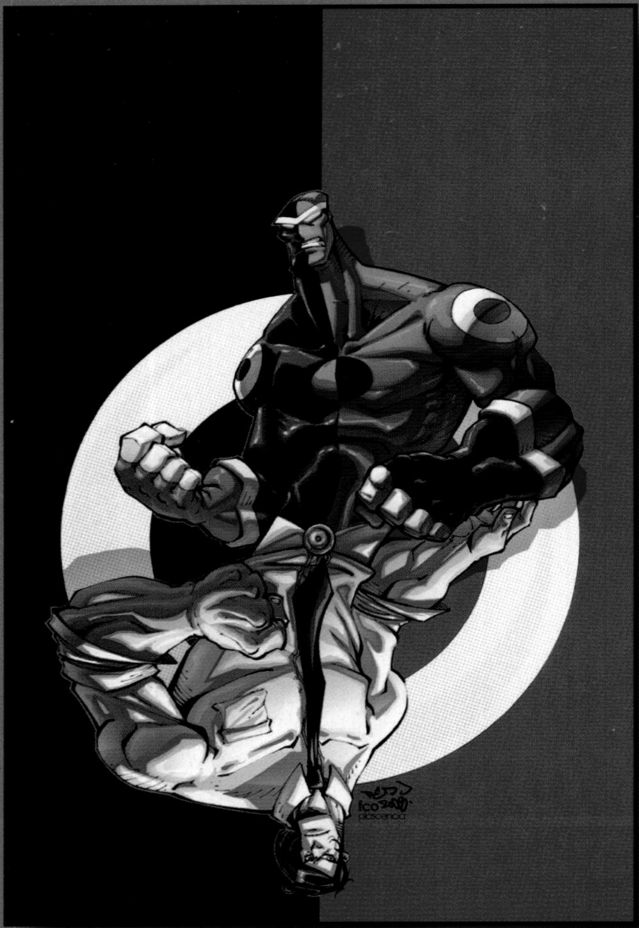

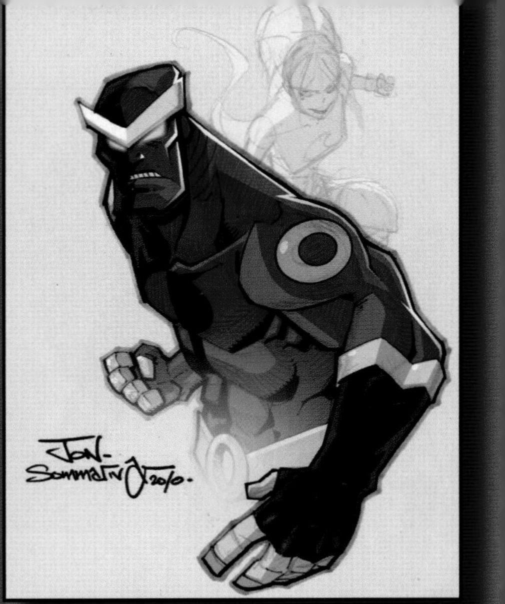

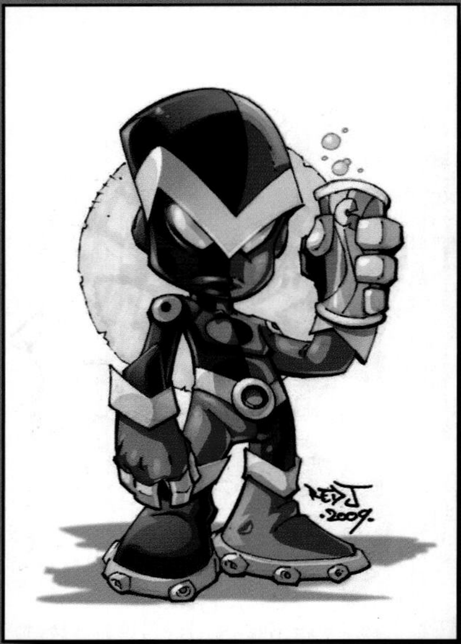

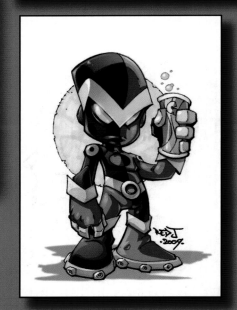

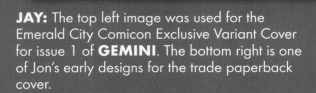

JAY: The top left image was used for the Emerald City Comicon Exclusive Variant Cover for issue 1 of **GEMINI**. The bottom right is one of Jon's early designs for the trade paperback cover.

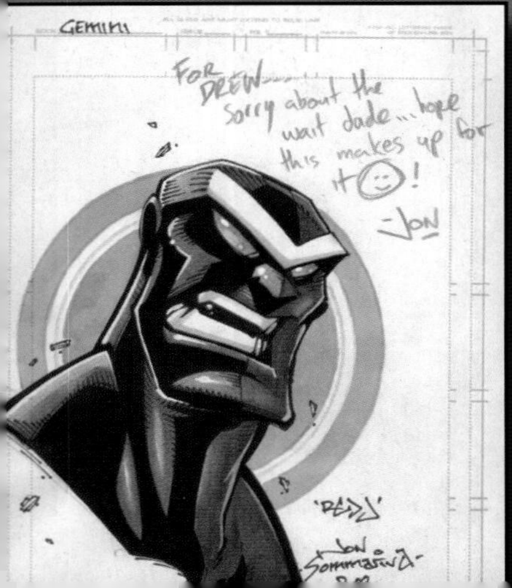
GEMINI
FOR DREW... Sorry about the wait dude... hope this makes up for it!
-JON
'RED J'

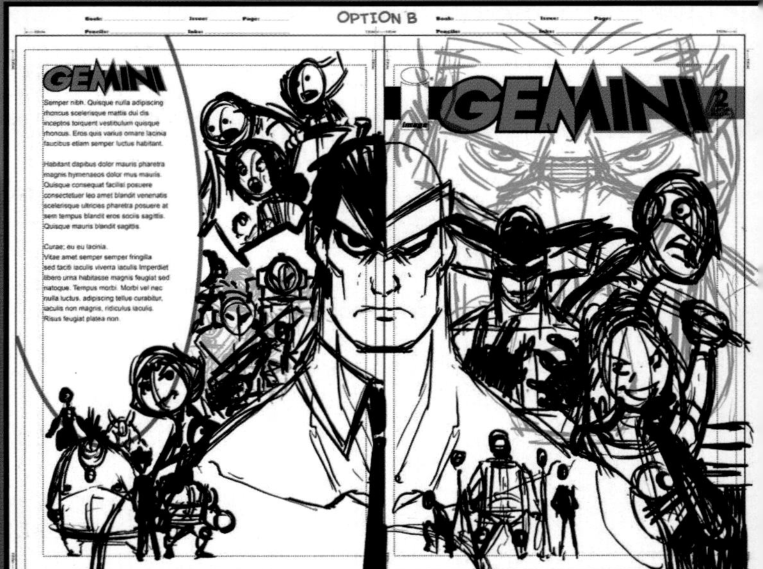
OPTION B
GEMINI
Semper nibh. Quisque nulla adipiscing rhoncus scelerisque mattis dui dis inceptos torquent vestibulum quisque rhoncus. Eros quis varius ornare lacinia faucibus etiam semper luctus habitant.
Habitant dapibus dolor mauris pharetra magnis hymenaeos dolor mus mauris. Quisque consequat facilisi posuere consectetuer leo amet blandit venenatis scelerisque ultricies pharetra posuere at sem tempus blandit eros sociis sagittis. Quisque mauris blandit sagittis.
Curae; eu eu lacinia.
Vitae amet semper semper fringilla sed taciti iaculis viverra iaculis imperdiet libero urna habitasse magnis feugiat sed natoque. Tempus morbi. Morbi vel nec nulla luctus. adipiscing tellue curabitur, iaculis non magnis, ridiculus iaculis. Risus feugiat platea non.
GEMINI

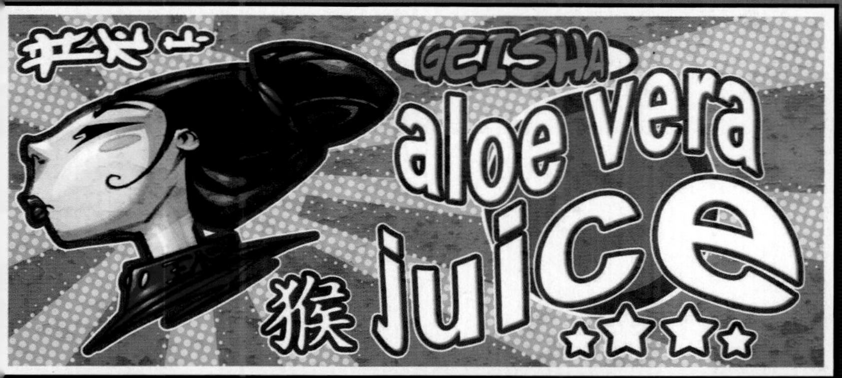
GEISHA
aloe vera
juice
猴

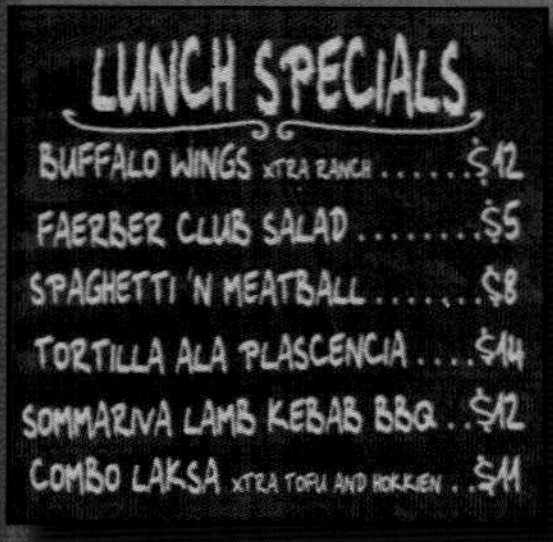
LUNCH SPECIALS
BUFFALO WINGS XTRA RANCH $12
FAERBER CLUB SALAD $5
SPAGHETTI 'N MEATBALL $8
TORTILLA ALA PLASCENCIA $14
SOMMARIVA LAMB KEBAB BBQ ..$12
COMBO LAKSA XTRA TOFU AND HOKKIEN ..$11

ON: Here is a look at some of the billboards created for use in certain scenes. I always oved how Quentin Tarantino had his own cigarette brand, Red Apple, throughout his novies. Geisha Aloe Vera juice is my version of that.

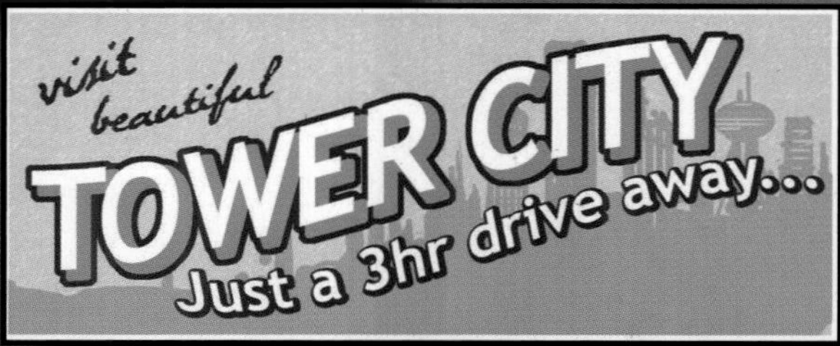
visit beautiful
TOWER CITY
Just a 3hr drive away...

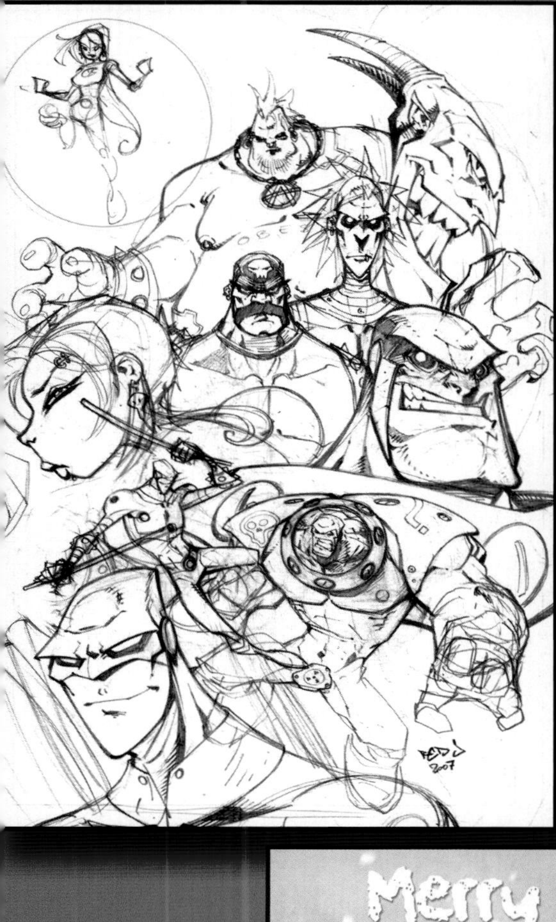

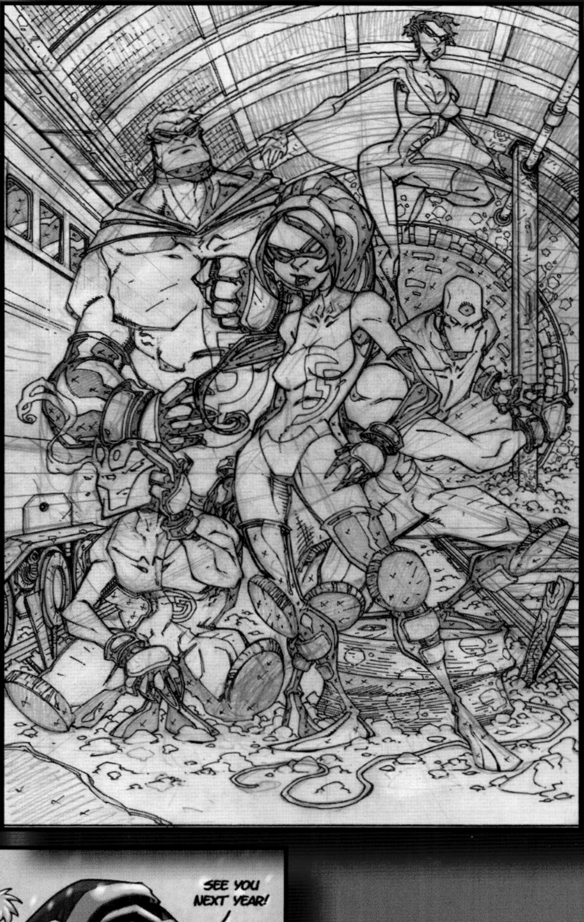

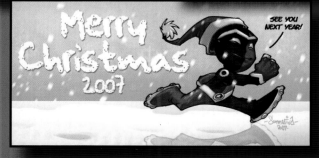

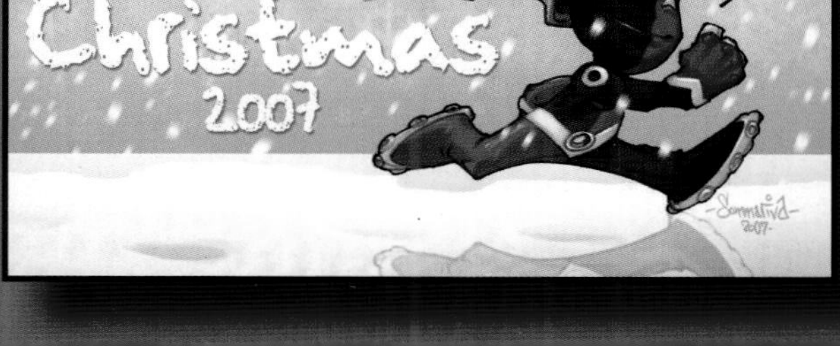
Merry Christmas
2007
SEE YOU NEXT YEAR!

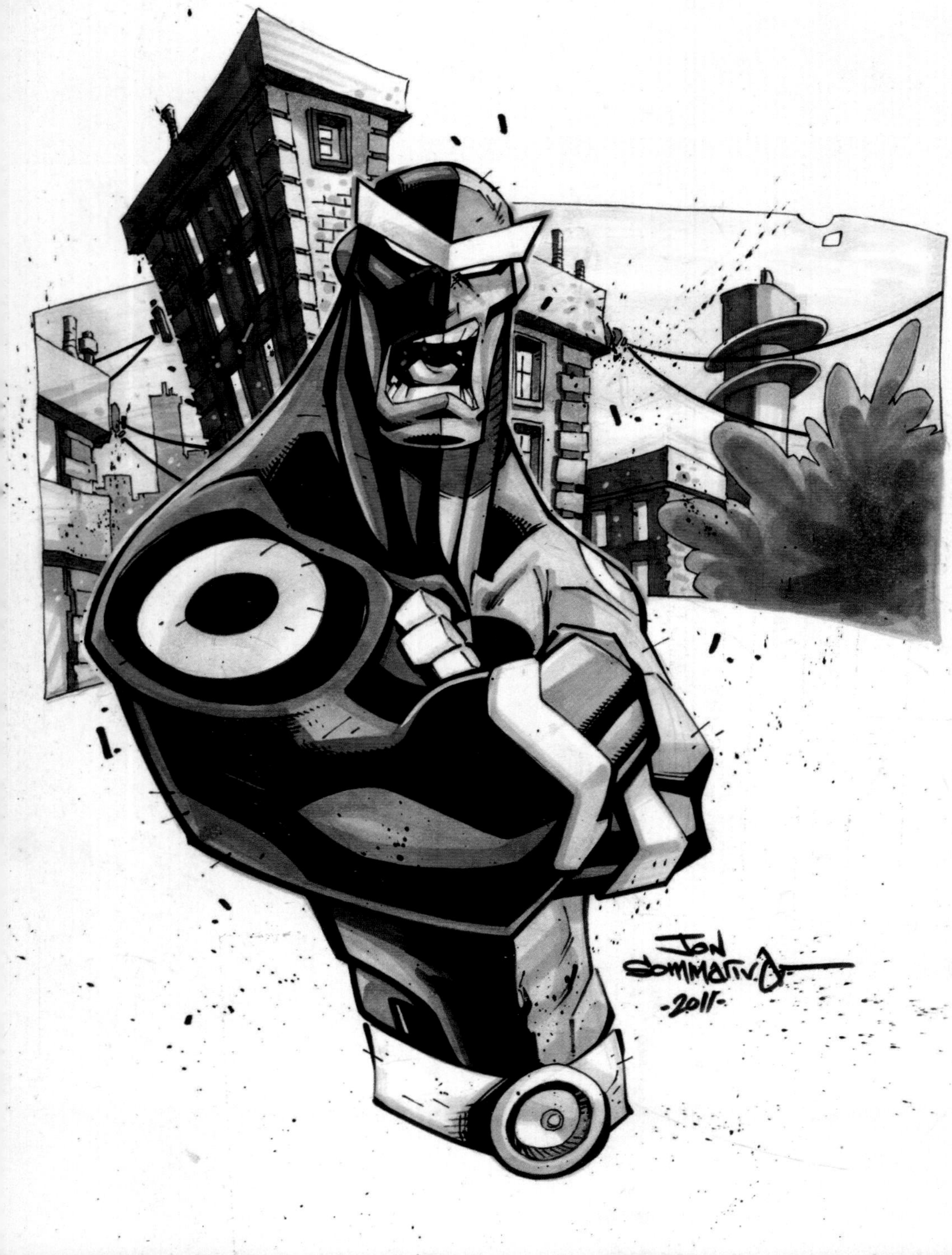
JON
SOMMARIVA
-2011-

JON: This was a 9x12 marker piece I did for someone. I get asked to draw many different well-known characters at conventions or for private commissions. It's